Voices From the Middle

Narrative Inquiry By, For, and About the Middle Level Community

a volume in
The Handbook of Research in Middle Level Education

Series Editor:
Vincent A. Anfara, Jr.
The University of Tennessee, Knoxville

The Handbook of Research in Middle Level Education

Vincent A. Anfara, Jr., Series Editor

The Handbook of Research in Middle Level Education (2001)
edited by Vincent A. Anfara, Jr.

Middle School Curriculum, Instruction, and Assessment (2002)
edited by Vincent A. Anfara, Jr. and Sandra L. Stacki

*Leaders for a Movement: Professional Preparation and Development of
Middle Level Teachers and Administrators* (2003)
edited by P. Gayle Andrews and Vincent A. Anfara, Jr.

Reforming Middle Level Education: Considerations for Policymakers (2004)
edited by Sue C. Thompson

Making a Difference: Action Research in Middle Level Education (2005)
edited by Micki M. Caskey

The Young Adolescent and the Middle School (2007)
edited by Steven B. Mertens, Vincent A. Anfara, Jr.,
and Micki M. Caskey

An International Look at Educating Young Adolescents (2009)
edited by Steven B. Mertens, Vincent A. Anfara, Jr.,
and Kathleen Roney

*Voices From the Middle: Narrative Inquiry By, For, and About
the Middle Level Community* (2010)
edited by Kathleen F. Malu

Voices From the Middle

Narrative Inquiry By, For, and About the Middle Level Community

edited by

Kathleen F. Malu
William Paterson University of New Jersey

Information Age Publishing, Inc.
Charlotte, North Carolina • www.infoagepub.com

Library of Congress Cataloging-in-Publication Data

Voices from the middle : narrative inquiry by, for, and about the middle
level community / edited by Kathleen F. Malu.
     p. cm. — (The handbook of research in middle level education)
  Includes bibliographical references.
  ISBN 978-1-61735-177-8 (paperback) — ISBN 978-1-61735-178-5 (hardcover) —
ISBN 978-1-61735-179-2 (e-book)
  1. Middle school education—Research—United States. 2. Narrative inquiry
(Research method)—United States. I. Malu, Kathleen F. II. Title. III.
Series.

  LB1623.5.V66 2010
  373.23'6072—dc22

                                                    2010038059

The Handbook of Research in Middle Level Education is endorsed by the Middle Level Education Research Special Interest Group, an affiliate of the American Educational Research Association.

As stated in the organization's Constitution, the purpose of MLER is to improve, promote, and disseminate educational research reflecting early adolescence and middle-level education.

The Handbook of Research in Middle Level Education

EDITORIAL REVIEW BOARD

Dedication

In the lovely quiet and coolness of an August evening, I download the page proofs for this volume. I am in Kigali, Rwanda in the final months of my Fulbright Scholarship. I returned to this country, a place that holds deep personal and professional ties. The serendipity of this moment captures me—I am finishing work on this, an edited volume of rich narratives about teachers, parents, and children, and I am in a nation that has a long and deep tradition of storytelling.

I dedicate this volume to my students at Kigali Institute of Education, studying to become teachers, and to all of Rwanda's children. These two groups hold tomorrow's hope of *amahoro*, peace, for this nation. I dedicate this volume to teachers, teacher educators, parents, and children worldwide who seek peace and understanding.

Kathleen F. Malu
Kigali, Rwanda 2010

CONTENTS

PREFACE

Stefinee Pinnegar and Cheryl Craig

Across our lives, we negotiate and renegotiate our experiences lived in context and thus differentiate our conceptions of our self in relationship with others. The impetus for renegotiations comes from changes in our own development and cultural or social transitions. Adolescence is the time in life of greatest change, other than infancy, and thus provides daunting challenges but also richest opportunities for growth. By then, students are involved in new school organizations and social contexts removed from their home and the direct control of the home and family. They often have friends their parents have never met. As a result of physical development, they increasingly look more like adults than children. They have more endurance. They are given more freedom. At school, there is no longer a single teacher with whom they spend most of the day and they have more control over how they organize and spend their time. They make intellectual gains because completion of brain myleinzation means their thinking and motor control are more fluid. Not only can they solve problems in systematic ways but they can also attend to multiple dimensions, assume other perspectives, think about how and what they are thinking and they can do this with few or no physical props. In short, they can use their lives as sources of learning. They are positioned to live and tell, and relive and retell, their experiences and to take on the challenges of storying an identity.

Voices From the Middle: Narrative Inquiry By, For, and About the Middle Level Community
pp. xi–xii

In their lived experiences, teachers and students enact together new and contradictory plotlines as they negotiate the constantly shifting terrain of the school landscape of adolescents. When moment to moment romance blossoms and dies, friendships are betrayed then healed and renegotiated. As their teachers live alongside them, adolescents are busy positioning, enacting and repositioning themselves on the new and old plotlines. Adolescents constantly live, tell, relive, and retell old and new contradictory and complementary stories of self in order to discover their identity, to learn to take up intimate relationships, and develop their autonomy as increasingly independent agents and self-determining human beings.

The researchers in this volume use the three-dimensional narrative space of temporality, sociality, and place to mine luminal spaces where change is the norm. They pause at a particular moment of living alongside in order to support learners in reimagining their pasts, which alters their tenuous present and opens new vistas for their futures. In engaging us by placing ourselves in roles as adult actors living alongside and supporting students we either come to know or they catch us off guard and we find ourselves as adolescent actors in the same story. As we move forward and backward in these plotlines, connect to the research narratives about adolescents and their identity, or simply immerse ourselves in particular stories of particular adolescents in particular places and times, we reexperience adolescence, our experiences as teachers or adults in supporting their development, and we reconsider our own pasts. Thus, this collection of narrative inquiries opens for us the possibility of new plotlines for living alongside adolescent learners in more sensitive, caring, and supportive ways. The chapters additionally cause us to think how middle schools could become more educative and humane places. And they heal us from the experiences of adolescence and school that remain painful to us.

The merging of narrative with middle years is a wise inquiry decision. We commend editor, Kathleen F. Malu, this volume's authors, the Middle Level Research SIG, and the series editor, Vincent Anfara, on this timely book project. Finally, we hope that readers will find this collaboration between the Middle Level Research SIG and the Narrative Research SIG not only illuminative, but also instructive as they continue to refine the plotlines of the stories they live by.

ACKNOWLEDGMENTS

This volume would not have been possible without the support of many individuals. First is series editor, Vincent Anfara. He encouraged me from the start and helped me successfully navigate the entire process from "Call for chapters" to Internet challenges from a distance, to final edits. I gratefully acknowledge all the contributors to this volume. Their dedication to excellence, their patience, prompt replies to emails, and words of encouragement and support were invaluable to me! I am grateful to George Johnson, Sarah Williams, and other individuals unknown to me at Information Age Publishing, who helped me over the "page proof hurtle." I thank the technical and support staff at William Paterson University of New Jersey, including Caresse Morse, Tom Norton, and Judi Norton and to WPUNJ administrator, Steve Hahn, who facilitated a laptop exchange for me while in Rwanda. Finally, I send special thank yous to Helen Churko, Kate Shackford, and Richard.

INTRODUCTION

Narratives in the Middle

Kathleen F. Malu

Storytelling and the role that stories play in teaching and learning trace back to the dawn of humankind. Throughout history and across the continents, time and geography mark the movement of stories. Storytellers are the vehicles for this movement. Revered and celebrated, storytellers seek to preserve, share, and pass down a community's narratives, from one generation to the next. As stories are handed down, each generation hopes the next will learn what the story might reveal. This volume speaks to this long tradition. In addition to the impact that stories have from one generation to the next, they also have horizontal influence. This influence lies in their resonance and the interpretations the teller and listener place on them. Stories that travel within and across communities create this horizontal influence. It is my intent for this volume to preserve stories to be passed down through the years and concurrently to share them across the breadth and depth of the middle level education community and beyond.

The need for continued research at the middle level is clear and urgent. The previous volumes of this handbook series are a testament to

Voices From the Middle: Narrative Inquiry By, For, and About the Middle Level Community
pp. xv–xix

this. While quantitative studies continue to be essential, it is important that we explore the complexities of life in the middle. One way to capture the rich, diverse mosaic of voices and experiences of the middle level community is by telling their stories using narrative inquiry methodology. This volume, a collection of narrative research studies, reveals the stories of young adolescent students, teachers, coaches, teacher educators, parents, researchers, and community members who work in the middle. Through these narratives, the authors in this volume weave intricate webs of connections, conflicts, reflections, and questions, framing them within current research theory and practice. These narratives highlight the nuances, diversity, and future directions that research needs to explore.

A note on the terms, narrative inquiry and narrative research. Because Clandinin (2007) reports that these terms are used "interchangeably," I make no distinction between their use in this handbook. See Pinnegar and Daynes (2007) and Clandinin and Rosiek (2007) for further explanations regarding these terms.

The volume begins with an overview of the elements of narrative research. Kim (chapter 1) outlines the current status of and highlights why it is important for the middle level community to engage in narrative inquiry research. She presents a detailed explanation of the essential elements that narratives should include and helps us understand why we need this research at the middle level.

In the following five chapters we hear stories that feature young adolescents. Yoon (chapter 2) reveals the shifting identities that her young English language learner immigrant participants use to navigate between the mainstream and English as a second language classrooms. Her participants express their conflicting emotions as they share their experiences with Yoon. Coulter (chapter 3) explores the nuances and complexities of bullying by narrating stories of three immigrant girls and their experiences with bullying. Coulter uses these stories to examine the inherent conflicts in the school's bullying prevention program. Piazza (chapter 4) uses traditional literacy assessments to challenge the "struggling reader" label given to the young adolescent African American males she evaluates. Piazza reflects on biases she identifies within herself as she revisits her research over time. Rhodes (chapter 5) tells the stories of six adolescent readers as they ponder Izzy's (Voigt, 2005) story and the meanings it holds for them. Depending on the discussion setting, these adolescents shift their interpretations, highlighting different aspects of Izzy's story in the various contexts Rhodes creates for them. Sandy's reading journey (Schaefer, chapter 6) is as emotional for Sandy as it is for Schaefer. Schaefer narrates Sandy's literacy development by revealing journal entries, reflections, and discussions that take readers from Sandy's initial hatred for reading to her fall, into love.

The next five chapters present the voices of middle level educators, including preservice, novice, experienced, and veteran teachers, and a literacy coach. Turner (chapter 7) narrates the experiences and reflections of pre-service teachers who must integrate instruction and simultaneously focus on high stakes test preparation. These preservice teachers share their frustrations and dilemmas as they learn to teach and test. Dana, Delane, and George (chapter 8) present the narratives and reflections of veteran middle school teachers and their perceptions and adjustments to the era of high stakes tests. These exemplary teachers express their struggles trying to balance their wish to return to the "Camelot" days of middle level education and the pressures of high stakes testing. Bahr and Pendergast (chapter 9) present the stories of Australian middle school teachers who entered teaching through different pathways. Noting the importance of having a national teacher education program for middle level educators, this study highlights the key role that middle level teachers and leaders can play in reform efforts. Matteson, Fletcher, Tidwell, and Garrett (chapter 10) narrate their own stories about why and how they entered doctoral programs. Through their friendships and supportive team work in one middle school, they decide to pursue doctorates, in part, because of these influential experiences.

This collection of middle level educators' narratives ends with Smith's (chapter 11) research about a middle school literacy coach and a typical day in her life at the school. Smith reveals the successes and struggles this coach experiences as she tries to be effective in a position that is inherently difficult and complex.

Chapters 12, 13, and 14 are narrated by researchers who work in middle schools. Brause (chapter 12) returns to a middle school as a writers' workshop teacher and narratives her experiences. These experiences prompt her to reflect deeply and raise to a conscious level issues regarding how instruction is implicitly organized and what is really taught at the middle level. Ruppert (chapter 13) reenters the middle level as a mathematics teacher for 1 year to explore the issues and reflect on the possibilities of using middle level practices in a K-8 setting. Vinz (chapter 14) presents narratives about four teachers she visits in a middle school and the narratives they write about her visit. After sharing their narratives with each other, Vinz reflects on middle level teaching practices, professional development, and research opportunities for narrative inquiry.

The next two chapters report the experiences of two middle level researchers who are mothers with middle level children. Malu (chapter 15) tells the story of her experiences as a White mother with a Black son, during the time that he attends a public middle school. Her story of parental involvement reveals the complex ways in which she worked and her son learned in this middle school setting. Reyes (chapter 16) narrates her struggles to fulfill the multiple roles she plays including parent, community member, former classroom teacher, and university professor when her school district tries to reconfigure the middle school. Her insider status gives her challenges and opportunities depending on the circumstances.

McLurkin (chapter 17) reports the narrative of a retired teacher with more than 40 years of experience. McLurkin (chapter 17) tells Doris's story about the after-school literacy program she established and continues to run for middle level children. McLurkin's narrative captures Doris's passion and dedication to this program and the children she serves.

This volume ends with information to encourage the use of narrative inquiry by, for, and about the middle level community. After reporting the conclusions of the authors in this volume, Malu (chapter 18) suggests how teachers and researchers can engage in narrative inquiry and offers ideas for future research. Lists of resources including books and journals, and electronic media to help novice and experienced researchers engage in narrative inquiry conclude this chapter.

As editor I sequenced these chapters using the following criteria. I selected the beginning chapters with their focus on middle level children because I try to always "put children first." The next logical step for me was to place the teachers' narratives after those of the children. I followed this group with the narratives of university researchers who worked with children, and then researchers who worked with teachers, and finally researchers who assumed multiple roles in the middle level community.

This is not the only sequence in which these narratives can be read. Reading these chapters thematically is an alternate way to explore this volume. Here are a few suggestions. Note that chapters in each theme are listed alphabetically. If readers want to explore themes of identify, race, ethnicity, and gender, I suggest examining the chapters of Coulter, Malu, Piazza, Reyes, Rhodes, Schaefer, and Yoon. The themes of high stakes tests, assessment, and No Child Left Behind are considered by Bahr and Pendergast, Dana, Delane, and George, Kim, McLurkin, Piazza, Schaefer, and Turner. For narratives of professional development and research, examine Kim, Matteson, et al., Smith, and Vinz. For university faculty looking for new experiences, consider Brause, McLurkin, Ruppert, Schaefer, and Vinz. To explore themes of adolescent literacy development, turn to Piazza, Rhodes, Schaefer, and Yoon. Threads, large and small, of parent voices are revealed in chapters by Coulter, Malu, McLurkin, Piazza, Reyes, Rhodes, Ruppert, and Schaefer. Bahr and Pendergast, Brause, Coulter, McLurkin, Ruppert, and Smith present a variety of different middle level program models. For an overview of narrative inquiry and/or the possibilities of using it in the middle examine Kim and Vinz.

Narratives that identify the setting as urban include Bahr and Pendergast, Brause, Dana, Delane, and George, Malu, McLurkin, Piazza, Rhodes, Ruppert, Schaefer, Smith, Vinz. Narratives with settings identified as rural or suburban include Coulter, Reyes, and Turner.

It is my intention that this volume, by for and about the middle level community, give readers new insights into this community and inspire them to pursue narrative inquires in their own settings.

REFERENCES

Clandinin, D. J. (Ed.). (2007). Preface. In D. J. Clandinin (Ed.), *Handbook of narrative inquiry: Mapping a methodology* (pp. ix-xvii). Thousand Oaks, CA: Sage Publications.

Clandinin, D. J., & Rosiek, J. (2007). Mapping a landscape of narrative inquiry: Borderland spaces and tensions. In D. J. Clandinin (Ed.), *Handbook of narrative inquiry: Mapping a methodology* (pp. 35-75). Thousand Oaks, CA: Sage Publications.

Pinnegar, S., & Daynes, J. G. (2007). Locating narrative inquiry historically: Thematics in the turn to narrative. In D. J. Clandinin (Ed.), *Handbook of narrative inquiry: Mapping a methodology* (pp. 3-34). Thousand Oaks, CA: Sage Publications.

Voigt, C. (2005). *Izzy, Willy-Nilly.* New York, NY: Simon & Schuster.

CHAPTER 1

WALKING IN THE "SWAMPY LOWLANDS"

What It Means to be a Middle Level Narrative Inquirer

Jeong-Hee Kim

Research on middle level education has burgeoned over the last decade. However, with the No Child Left Behind Act of 2001, there has been a stronger push toward evidence-based, positivistic scientific research. In this chapter, I define narrative inquiry and interrogate what it means to be a middle level narrative inquirer in the midst of this prevailing positivistic research arena. Then, I explore how narrative inquiry can contribute to promoting more genuine dialogue among stakeholders and narrowing the gap between research and practice to better serve the middle level community.

INTRODUCTION

Almost half a century ago, middle schools were created, in part, because of the failure of the implementation of the junior high school concept. Middle schools broadly include Grades 5 through 8 (Alt, Choy, & Ham-

Voices From the Middle: Narrative Inquiry By, For, and About the Middle Level Community
pp. 1–17

mer, 2000); but the most common configuration includes Grades 6 through 8. Since the landmark report, *Turning Points: Preparing American Youth for the 21st Century* (Carnegie Council on Adolescent Development, 1989), the trend toward establishing middle schools has grown. According to the most recent report, there are currently 16,227 middle schools in the United States (National Center for Education Statistics, 2008). This is a huge increase from 11,712 in 1993-94 (Alt et al., 2000). In response to this growth of middle schools, research on middle level education burgeoned in the last decade and awareness about educating young adolescents increased significantly, resulting in a more favorable policy environment toward middle school education (Kasak, 2004). Kasak attributes such optimistic trends to three broad factors: (1) several high profile foundations such as the Carnegie Corporation and the Kellogg Foundation joined to work to improve middle grades education; (2) the National Middle School Association, created in 1973, provided influential guidelines for teacher preparation programs to the National Council for Accreditation of Teacher Education (NCATE), thus increasing its presence, visibility, and membership; and (3) the National Forum to Accelerate Middle-Grades Reform, an affiliation of the country's top associations, foundations, researchers, and practitioners, was created to improve middle grades education in 1997 (Kasak, 2004, p. 232).

Despite many positive reports on the implementation of middle schools, successful reports from this recent middle school reform movement seem to be sporadic and criticisms abound. Alt et al. (2000), for example, argue that there is no single, fixed definition of middle school and further point out how some extreme critics of middle schools disparage middle schools as "the wasteland of our primary and secondary landscape" (Tucker & Coding, 1998, cited in Alt et al., 2000, p. 2). Although some middle schools have undergone structural innovations such as interdisciplinary teaming, small learning communities, flexible scheduling, empowering middle school staff, among others (Anfara, Mertens, & Caskey, 2007), many middle schools remain the same as the junior high schools that they were supposed to reform (Cuban, 1992). Dickinson (2001) supports this criticism by contending that the majority of middle schools are in a state of "arrested development" (p. 4), which refers to a structural problem such as little implementation of the middle school concept and disposition problems such as the lack of belief in or attention to the concept. He further details the causes that brought about the current state of "arrested development" in many middle schools, calling for the gap between research and practice to be narrowed.

It seems, then, what is urgently needed to ameliorate this state of arrested development of middle schools is a call for research that promotes more meaningful dialogue between researchers and practitioners that will contribute to sustaining and implementing the middle school concept. Hence, this volume, *Voices From the Middle: Narrative Inquiry By, For and About the Middle Level Community*, in the *Handbook of Research in Middle Level Education* series is timely and relevant, focusing on the voices of the individuals who are the essential part of the middle level community: teachers, young adolescents, parents, researchers, and teacher educators.

Narrative inquiry methodology that embodies voices or stories of research participants has made a significant contribution to education research (Elbaz-Luwisch, 2007). However, the current political context with the passage of the No Child Left Behind (NCLB) Act of 2001 does not favor qualitative research and, in particular, narrative inquiry. The NCLB used the phrase, *scientifically based research*, 111 times (Barone, 2007), calling explicitly and exclusively for the use of scientific research that involves hard, measurable and quantifiable data. Further, the National Research Council (2002) published the report, *Scientific Research in Education*, calling for evidence-based education research that uses "rigorous, systematic and objective procedures to obtain valid knowledge" (Maxwell, 2004, p. 3), referring to experimental or quasi-experimental designs. In this positivistic epistemology of practice (Schön, 1983), it is believed that problems of American public education can be addressed with prescribed solutions derived from so-called "scientifically based research." Education and its various components are viewed as value-neutral, stable, fixed, predictable, and generic enough that those prescribed solutions can be applied universally to every classroom. Such adherence to this positivistic thinking demonstrates that we are back to the "good, ole' boy" thinking, or "Déjà vu all over again," as Lather (2008, p. 362) calls it, in spite of the paradigm shift we experienced, staying away from the positivism that underpins the use of objectivism and measurement. In this current political climate, qualitative education research that goes against the "mighty push" (Viadero, 2008, cited in Lather, 2008, p. 362) toward objective scientism is disciplined and punished as "embarrassing" (Lather, 2008, p. 362). As the hegemonic metanarrative of positivism sways the sword of power and authority, qualitative researchers, and narrative researchers in particular, are once again under the influence of a political tornado.

What then are the implications of this political research arena for this volume that gives voice to the middle level community? Why do we insist on researching stories of the middle level community against the "mighty push" toward "scientifically based" research? Why do we desperately need stories and narratives by, for, and about the middle level community? How can narrative research methodology contribute to promoting dialogues among stakeholders that include teachers, students, parents, teacher educators, researchers, and community groups? The purpose of this chapter is to address these questions and explore what it means to be a narrative inquirer for the middle level community. Further, my focus is to interrogate how narrative inquiry can inform the middle level community while narrowing the gap between research, theory, and practice in middle schools.

In the remainder of this chapter, I first describe the current status of narrative inquiry situated within the qualitative research paradigm, and then I engage in narrative theorizing to explore the meaning of doing narrative research focusing on the questions raised above. I argue that narrative inquiry is not about just telling stories, but it should be practiced as: (1) an aesthetic inquiry, providing moments of epiphany for the reader; (2) Bakhtinian novelness, embracing different voices that have been typically marginalized; and (3) lived theory, making connections to the larger educational community. I conclude that as we need research that goes beyond providing quick fixes and further promotes dialogue and discussion between researchers and practitioners, the work of narrative inquiry can fulfill such a mission to better serve the population of the middle level community.

CHARACTERIZING NARRATIVE INQUIRY
WITHIN QUALITATIVE RESEARCH

For more than half a century, educational researchers have challenged the positivist view of social reality as predictable and potentially controllable by the tools designed to quantitatively measure and test the social phenomena. These challenges resulted in the paradigm shift (Kuhn, 1962) from quantitative to qualitative research that focuses on the understanding of human action through interpretation rather than prediction and control. Denzin and Lincoln (1994) define qualitative research as:

> multimethod in focus, involving an interpretive naturalistic approach to its subject matter ... qualitative researchers study things in their natural settings attempting to make sense of, or interpret, phenomena in terms of the meanings people bring to them. (p. 2)

Qualitative researchers informed by postmodern and poststructural theories use words rather than numbers in their analysis and they often collect and analyze stories of their research participants. Similarly, narrative inquiry, placed under the label of qualitative research methodology (Pinnegar & Daynes, 2007), attempts to access participants' life experiences and engage in a process of storytelling and retelling to understand multidimensional meanings (Leavy, 2009).

Building on the tenets of qualitative research including research methods, approaches, and strategies, narrative inquiry has become a field of its own with its distinctive nature and significance (Bruner, 2002; Clandinin, 2007).

It is Connelly and Clandinin (1990) who first established the importance of narrative inquiry as a research methodology in the field of education research. Since then, the use of narrative inquiry has gained acceptance among educational researchers and become an influential research methodology in studying the lived experiences of teachers and students (Casey, 1993; Clandinin & Connelly, 2000; Clandinin, Pushor, & Orr, 2007; Goodson, 1995). In addition, there has been a series of narrative turns (Pinnegar & Daynes, 2007) that reaffirms narrative research as a legitimate way of knowing that shapes our conceptions and understandings about the world around us (Bruner, 1986, 1994).

Narrative inquiry, a "theory/practice/reflection cycle of inquiry" (Smith, 2008, p. 65), is now cross-disciplinary and enjoys a "renaissance" across the social sciences, including the field of education (Josselson, 2003) and its applications extend beyond research methodology (Denzin & Lincoln, 2005; Fludernik, 2005; Riessman & Speedy, 2007). Narrative inquiry is used, for instance, as curricula and pedagogical strategies in the field of teacher education (Conle, 2003; Coulter, Michael, & Poynor, 2007); as an intentional reflexive process of teachers interrogating their own teaching and learning (Lyons & LaBoskey, 2002); as a medium for professional development for pre-service and in-service teachers (Conle, 2000a); and as an inquiry into the interrelationships between literacy, pedagogy, and multiculturalism (Clark & Medina, 2000; Grinberg, 2002; Phillion, He, & Connelly, 2005). Through this burgeoning of publications in recent years, narrative inquiry has made a transformative impact in education and contributed to the advancement of education research on research methods and methodology, curriculum, teaching and learning, and teacher education.

However, we should also note that narrative inquiry is still a "field in the making" (Chase, 2000, p. 651) and it has been criticized by positivist researchers for its potential drawbacks, such as, lack of narratology (narrative theory), romanticizing the protagonist, and focusing on art rather than research. Narrative inquiry also confronts challenges due to the difficulty of presenting a complex, layered, and dynamic reality (Elbaz-Luwisch, 2007) and there is no single accepted narrative research method at present (Webster & Mertova, 2007). These concerns require our continuous efforts toward narrative theorizing, which is an intentional process of questioning and interrogating the nature of narrative research to improve its role in education (Kim, 2008). In the next section, therefore, I engage in narrative theorizing explaining why stories are important and how narrative inquiry can better help to serve our research community in middle level education.

WHY STORIES?

Narrative inquiry uses stories that teachers and students live by as "the phenomenon studied in inquiry" (Connelly & Clandinin, 2006, p. 477). The contemporary educational philosopher, Dunne (2005), emphasizes the importance of stories in education research, drawing upon Aristotle who long ago suggested that stories can instruct and move us precisely because they reveal universal themes in their depiction of particular cases and characters. Dunne (2005) argues that education research needs to be complemented by stories that can bring out:

> the complex weaving of plot and characters, the dense meshing of insights and oversights, of convergent or contrary motivations and interests, or anticipated or unanticipated responses from the internal environment—or irruptions from the external one—all conspiring to bring relative success or failure (p. 386).

From Dunne's perspective, a variety of narrative modes are critical in education research because the epiphany power of exemplary stories in particular settings may prove capable of illuminating other settings. Dunne (2003) claims that research into teaching is best served by narrative modes of inquiry since "to understand a teacher's practice (on her own part or on the part of an observer) is to find an illuminating story (or stories) to tell of what she has been involved in with her students" (p. 367).

Stories give shape to things in the real world and even give a title to reality (Bruner, 2002). Stories are what we use to make sense of the world. Story making, then, is our medium for coming to terms with the surprises, oddities, or certain themes of the research phenomenon we study (Bruner, 2002). We need to be good storytellers and listeners making sense of what goes on in middle schools and engaging in dialogues among adolescents, parents, practitioners, researchers, and policy makers. In so doing, we can see the lives of others and their own lives as a whole into which the fragmented parts of narratives can be integrated and embodied (MacIntyre & Dunne, 2002).

It is critical, then, for us to develop ethical relationships with our participants in order to become good storytellers and good listeners. The essence of narrative inquiry lies in this ethical relationship between the researcher and the participant. The researcher endeavors to obtain data from "a deeply human, genuine, empathic, and respectful relationship to the participant about significant and meaningful aspects of the participant's life" (Josselson, 2007, p. 539). If we want to inform the middle level community through narrative inquiry, we need to be able to elicit meaningful stories from our participants that can enlighten our research field. This means that we need to be transparent about our research interests so as to make an alliance and trustworthy relationship with the participant. Good narrative practice, according to Josselson (2007), requires researchers to engage in ethical practices that respect the dignity and welfare of our participants. Researchers must collaborate with participants in the area of the participants' experiences and stories that are of interest to us. In other words, we should honor the "sacredness of our participants' humanity" (Hendry, 2007, p. 496). In so doing, the process of doing narrative inquiry becomes a sacred space where:

> 1) people feel "safe" within it, safe to be and experiment with who they are and who they are becoming; 2) people feel "connected"—perhaps to each other, or a community, or nature, or the world they are constructing on their word processors; 3) people feel passionate about what they are doing, believing that their activity "makes a difference"; and 4) people recognize, honor, and are grateful for the safe communion (Richardson, 1997, cited in Hendry, 2007, p. 496).

This kind of sacred place is created through the ethical practice of respecting the dignity of our participants and honoring the sacredness of their humanity as we develop trustworthy relationships with them. Hence, narrative inquiry becomes a site of communion where the researcher and the researched are interconnected in an inquiry, meaningfully informing each other (Hendry, 2007).

"WALKING ON THE SWAMPY LOWLANDS" THROUGH NARRATIVE INQUIRY

Being a narrative inquirer to live by, for and about stories and voices from the middle means to develop an ethical relationship that honors the sacredness of the humanness of our participants in the middle level community. This urges us to maintain the ambiguity or complexity of our participants' lived experiences in the research text. Schön (1983) uses a road metaphor to point out how positivistic professionals walk on the "high, hard ground" where rigor or relevance is equivalent to scientifically based research seeking technical solutions. These positivists, according to Schön, tend to be inattentive to uncertain, unique, and unstable phenomena, discarding them as "messy" and trivial data. On the other hand, there are those who choose the swampy lowlands and carefully engage themselves in messy but crucially important problems, focusing on "experience, trial and error, intuition, and muddling through" (Schön, 1983, p. 43). They resist confining their research to a narrowly defined, scientific experiment that provides quick fixes. Understanding and investigating the complex meaning of stories through research is their primary goal and they do not reduce research to certainty and measurable objectivity.

This metaphor of "walking on the swampy lowlands" is further supported by Dewey (1934) who posits that human beings excel in complexity and minuteness of differentiations because:

> There are more opportunities for resistance and tension, more drafts upon experimentation and invention, and therefore more novelty in action, greater range and depth of insight and increase of poignancy in feeling. As an organism increases in complexity, the rhythms of struggle and consummation in its relation to its environment are varied and prolonged. (p. 23)

As such, we narrative inquirers who choose to walk on the swampy lowlands expose ourselves to the complexity of the stories that reveal tension and conflicts. Rather than finding quick fixes that can be applied uniformly to other situations, we pay attention to the complex weaving of particular stories and voices that tend to be discarded by positivists as "messy" and trivial data. In doing so, we pursue open-endedness, and various alternatives and possibilities that welcome continuous dialogue among different stakeholders.

When narrative inquirers "muddle through" complex stories in order to provide a sacred space where the dignity of our participants is honored, we understand that narrative inquiry is not about just "telling stories". Hence, I argue that narrative inquiry should be engaged as: (1) an aesthetic inquiry that offers epiphanies; (2) Bakhtinian novelness that embraces multiple voices; and (3) lived theory that sheds light on the larger educational community.

Narrative Inquiry as Aesthetic Inquiry

I suggest that we practice narrative inquiry as an aesthetic inquiry. This means that we understand narrative inquiry in relation to experience as aesthetics and aesthetic experience as a way of knowing. Narrative inquiry is the study of lived experience, and narrative is the best way of representing and understanding lived experience (Connelly & Clandinin, 2006). The purpose of narrative inquiry, then, is to capture the meaning of the lived experience of participants through their stories in order to inform the reader of the meaning as a mode of knowledge. However, we should note that not all lived experiences are aesthetic experiences. Dewey (1938) comments that there are enemies of the aesthetic experience:

> They are the humdrum; slackness of loose ends; submission to convention in practice and intellectual procedure. Rigid abstinence, coerced submission, tightness on one side and dissipation, incoherence and aimless indulgence on the other, are deviations in opposite directions from the unity of an experience. (Dewey, 1938, p. 40)

If our practice of narrative inquiry is subject to rigid attachment to convention, coerced submission to such practice, inflexibility, and incoherence, we will end up dissolving the wholeness of an experience, thus preventing the aesthetic experience from taking place. Aesthetic experience is indeed the fulfillment of human beings in their struggles and achievements (Dewey, 1934). It is a mode of knowledge in which "tangled scenes of life are made more intelligible in esthetic experience" (Dewey, 1938, p. 290). Gadamer (1988) contends that artistic or aesthetic experience can produce a certain kind of knowledge that is different from scientific knowledge. Gadamer (1988) writes:

> Artistic experience is a mode of knowledge ... certainly different from that sensory knowledge which provides science with the data from which it constructs the knowledge of nature, and certainly different from all moral rational knowledge and indeed from all conceptual knowledge, but still knowledge, i.e. the transmission of truth. (p. 87)

Aesthetic experience is experience par excellence as it reflects the nature of experience in general (Iser, 2006). Hence, when we generate artistic or aesthetic experiences as a mode of knowledge through our participants' stories that we study, we engage in an aesthetic inquiry in which the aesthetic is integral to the research. In doing so, we help our readers with their cognitive, perceptual, emotional, and imaginative understanding of the world (Greene, 2001). That is, through stories, we provide an aesthetic experience for the reader to gain empathic understandings, knowledge, and perceptions of the world in which lived experience takes place. Indeed, the nature of narrative inquiry lies in its power of epiphany that the reader experiences (Dunne, 2005). Story that is capable of illuminating other settings becomes a metaphor that provides the reader with an "aha" moment leading to a sudden leap of understanding. This kind of story used in narrative inquiry provides an aesthetic experience while being so particular, so local, so unique, yet it has "such reach that gives story its loft beyond the particular, its metaphoric loft" (Bruner, 2002, p. 25). This metaphoric loft beyond the particular is what makes well-constructed narrative inquiry so powerful and so essential. In doing so, we transcend not only the limits of doing research that applies to only a particular situation but also the limits of being a researcher that is bound to authority as the knower. This transcendence is what makes us become humble, empathetic coparticipants who think together with those whom we research. In brief, when we practice narrative inquiry as an aesthetic inquiry, we produce an aesthetic understanding of the meaning of our participants' lived experiences as a mode of knowledge, which transcends the particular context.

Narrative Inquiry as Bakhtinian Novelness

Second, I suggest that narrative inquirers involve themselves with Bakhtinian novelness. Bakhtin, a Russian literary theorist, refers to novelness as the particular features that all stories share. Bakhtin made a distinction between "novels" and "novelness," the former referring to actual examples of the literary genre we recognize as the novel, and the latter referring to major features that all novels share, but which are not confined to novels as such (Holquist, 1994).

Bakhtin posits that there are three major features of novelness that are necessary in sharing the event of existence that is bound to one another through dialogue: *polyphony, chronotope*, and *carnival. Polyphony* refers to "a plurality of independent, unmerged voices and consciousness" (Bakhtin, 1963/1984, p. 6). In the polyphonic novel, different voices are heard without having one voice privileged over the others. The polyphonic narrative produces no final, complete truth, but unfinalizable truths that are open to potentiality, freedom, creativity, and surprise, evolving from the interaction among participants. Polyphony goes against the domination of the metanarrative, which is frequently advocated by scientifically based research that provides a clean-cut solution to educational problems.

Chronotope means time and space. Time and space are dependent on each other as "time, as it were, thickens, takes on flesh, becomes artistically visible; likewise, space becomes charged and responsive to the movement of time, plot and history" (Bakhtin, 1963/1984, cited in Morson & Emerson, 1990, p. 371). While time is always historical and biographical, space is always social (Morson & Emerson, 1990); thus, chronotope denotes historical, biographical, and social relations that determine the parameters of events and lived experiences to be studied. Chronotope contributes to our understanding of stories as it is "the intrinsic connectedness of temporal and spatial relationships" (Holquist, 1994, p. 109). In that sense, chronotope allows the lived experiences of our research participants to be illuminated from historical and social perspectives while providing a vicarious experience for the reader.

Finally, *carnival*, according to Bakhtin (1963/1984), is associated with popular carnivals in which everyone is an active participant, openness and different cultures are celebrated, hierarchy is invisible, and norms are reversed. It is a means for displaying a self in relation to others, making familiar relations strange and strange relations familiar (Holquist, 1994). When we consider the concept of carnival in our narrative work we draw attention to a variety of relations and we focus on the fact that social relations are culturally produced rather than naturally given and mandated. Further, different social relations and views among participants are equally valued while one formal and privileged way of thinking is discarded.

These three features of novelness have profound implications for narrative inquiry. Incorporating them into stories helps awaken our consciousness of otherness and forces us to dig deeper into the complex layers of meaning that may be hidden in the undercurrents of the educational phenomena. Narrative inquirers who engage in Bakhtinian novelness can not possibly walk on the "high, hard ground" where all the different voices are supposed to be convergent, rather than divergent, producing controllable quick fixes. Narrative inquiry is ineluctably perplexing, complex, complicated, and ambiguous as its goal is not to create one "pretty and neat" solution. Rather, the purpose of narrative research is "to stimulate critical thinking by opening up possibilities for critique and to provoke multiple interpretations, rather than lead the reader to a solitary conclusion" (Rosiek & Atkinson, 2007, p. 508). More specifically, the purpose is to invite the readers to the sphere of possible contact with the developing, incomplete, and evolving situation, allowing them to rethink and reevaluate their own views and experiences. Bakhtin says "the novel's roots must ultimately be sought in folklore" (1975/1981, p. 38). This implies that novelness is for, of, and by lay people who traditionally did not have power and privilege. Hence, engaging in Bakhtin's novelness means paying attention to particularities, especially voices of the disenfranchised that may go unnoticed in evidence-based, scientific research.

Narrative Inquiry as Lived Theory

Finally, I suggest that we practice narrative inquiry as lived theory that sheds light on the broader social and educational context. Narrative inquiry is known as a storytelling methodology that brings out theoretical ideas about the nature of human experiences as lived experiences (Clandinin & Connelly, 2000). Eisner (1991) contends that storytelling without explicit interpretation or theory is insufficient. According to Eisner, although a descriptive dimension of a story would provide readers with vicarious experiences of events, the educational significance of the story should be provided along with explicit interpretation employing social science theory in order to raise meaningful questions that deepen the conversation. Hence, a theory can be used as an intellectual tool to understand, analyze, and evaluate stories (Bal, 1997).

Interweaving theory into a story helps us justify why our study is important. This is a central element in narrative inquiry. Clandinin et al. (2007) argue that narrative inquirers should pay attention to three kinds of justification: the personal, the practical, and the social. They contend that narrative inquirers sometimes write only a personal justification, which seems to cause their research to fail to make a connection to the larger society. We need to justify how our research will make a difference in our and others' particular practices, and further, we need to address the larger social and educational issues by being able to answer the "So what?" and "Who cares?" questions (Clandinin et al., 2007).

In a similar vein, Goodson (1992) argues that stories should be used only as a starting point for a process of coming to know and they should be extended by a theory that connects stories to the larger society. In this way, stories can help us understand the meaning of the individual lives interrogated from the historical, social, and political perspectives. Conle (2000b) explains that a narrative research text should have two voices speaking simultaneously: the narrator's voice that presents the case and the theoretical voice that conceptualizes what is presented. These two voices may not be compatible, but can be beneficial because "narrative inquirers will benefit from a theoretical understanding of the process they are engaged in; and those who are used to theoretical discourse may benefit from lending an ear to experiential testimony" (Conle, 2000b, p. 194).

When we theorize the lived experience of our participants, the lived experience becomes *lived theory* in which the meaning we make of experience can become part of our narrative (Conle, 1999). Thus, lived theory, grounded in participants' lived experiences, promotes dialogical relations between reality and theoretical concepts expanding the reader's horizon. One of the main roles of narrative inquiry is to challenge the reader's taken-for-granted ideas and to raise disturbing questions about educational issues, asking all involved to reconsider and reorient their thinking (Barone, 2007). Gadamer (1988) calls this process a fusion of horizons where the horizons of readers are continuously under adjustment through empathic understanding while simultaneously upholding differences. Hence, narrative inquiry serves as a medium to connect the lives and stories of individuals to the understanding of larger human and social phenomena (Hatch & Wisniewski, 1995), broadening the reader's horizons. Furthermore, it can create social change not as an imposition of a totalizing view, but as a bridge connecting the complexity of the daily life of the participant and larger educational, societal issues. Narrative inquiry, then, is more than a descriptive kind of inquiry; it becomes interventionist in the sense that it involves questions of social justice and change (Clandinin, 2007).

EPILOGUE

In this chapter, I argued that narrative inquirers intentionally choose to walk on the swampy lowland through complex stories to inform the education community in general, and the middle level education community in particular. Narrative inquiry can be used as a way to bridge the gap between research and practice by paying attention to the voices of individuals who live in this community. More specifically, I argued that the field of narrative inquiry can be advanced when we practice it, first, as an aesthetic mode of knowledge that holds the complexity and ambiguity of lived experiences as a whole; second, as Bakhtinian novleness of polyphony, chronotope, and carnival where voices of stakeholders who traditionally did not have power and privilege are raised and heard; and finally as lived theory that informs the larger educational society while broadening our horizons through empathic understanding.

The importance of research on the education of young adolescents is increasingly recognized through the ongoing middle school movement that emerged in response to the acknowledgement that young adolescents have unique developmental needs (Mertens, Anfara, & Caskey, 2007). Many middle level researchers and teachers, for example, have exerted their efforts to make a difference in their research and practice through action research (see Caskey, 2005). However, the increasing number of students in the "forgotten middle" (see ACT, 2008, p. 9) is alarming. Many young adolescents are not ready to succeed in high school after they graduate from middle school. This huge gap between research and practice calls for more engaging dialogue among researchers, practitioners, and policymakers. Narrative inquiry can truly fill this gap by providing compelling stories of our stakeholders.

Lather (2008) posits that it is time to break out of the surveillance of education research that focuses on standardization and regulation. I concur. Even though scientifically based research contributes to informing the middle level community, there is an urgent need to go beyond such positivistic understandings of our community that tend to overlook the complexity and subtle nuances of the needs and interests of our stakeholders. Narrative inquiry that pays attention to the voices and lived experiences of the wide variety of middle level participants and stakeholders provides a vivid portraiture of what goes on in classrooms, which we desperately need to know, so we can better serve our young adolescents. Further, narrative inquiry, although not a panacea for solving educational problems (Kim, 2008), provides a mode of knowledge that is grounded in compassion, empathy, and ethics, helping us directly or vicariously to access the lived experiences of our young adolescents.

In closing, I want us to carefully ponder what it means to be a middle level narrative inquirer. It means "walking on the swampy lowland" and it takes into account "the complexity and messiness of practice-in-context" (Lather, 2008, p. 362). This perspective requires a more philosophical stance and a less instrumental consideration of doing research. In other words, narrative inquiry engages a philosophy of speculation on the meanings of the world around us as lived experiences. Thus doing narrative inquiry is more about human responsibility than about epistemology. We all agree that there is much work to do for the improvement of middle level education. One step toward this effort is to listen to the voices and stories of our young adolescents and the community that surrounds them. The voices and stories that are presented in this volume will fulfill our human responsibility to listen carefully so that we can make a difference. Then, as Bruner (2002) puts it, narrative is indeed serious business.

REFERENCES

ACT. (2008). *The forgotten middle: Ensuring that all students are on target for college and career readiness before high school*. Iowa City, IA: Author.

Alt, M. N., Choy, S. P., & Hammer, C. H. (2000). *In the middle: Characteristics of public schools with a focus on middle schools* (No. NCES 2000-312). Washington, DC: U.S. Department of Education, National Center for Education Statistics.

Anfara, V. A., Jr., Mertens, S. B., & Caskey, M. M. (2007). Introduction: The young adolescent and the middle school. In S. B. Mertens, V. A. Jr. Anfara, Jr., & M. M. Caskey (Eds.), *The young adolescent and the middle school* (pp. ix-xxxiii). Charlotte, NC: Information Age.

Bakhtin, M. M. (1984). *Problem of Dostoevsky's poetics*. Minneapolis, MN: University of Minnesota Press. (Original work published 1963)

Bakhtin, M. M. (1981). *The dialogic imagination: Four essays by M.M. Bakhtin*. Austin, TX: University of Texas Press. (Original work published 1975)

Bal, M. (1997). *Narratology: Introduction to the theory of narrative* (2nd ed.). Toronto, Ontario, Canada: University of Toronto Press.

Barone, T. (2007). A return to the gold standard?: Questioning the future of narrative construction as educational research. *Qualitative Inquiry, 13*(4), 454-470.

Bruner, J. (1986). *Actual minds, possible worlds*. Cambridge, MA: Harvard University Press.

Bruner, J. (1994). Life as narrative. In A. H. Dyson & C. Genishi (Eds.), *The need for story: Cultural diversity in classroom and community* (pp. 28-37). Urbana, IL: National Council of Teachers of English.

Bruner, J. (2002). *Making stories: Law, literature, life*. New York, NY: Farrar, Straus and Giroux.

Carnegie Council on Adolescent Development. (1989). *Turning points: Preparing American youth for the 21st century*. New York, NY: Carnegie Corporation.

Casey, K. (1993). *I answer with my life: Life histories of women teachers working for social change*. New York, NY: Routledge.

Caskey, M. M. (Ed.). (2005). *Making a difference: Action research in middle level education*. Greenwich, CT: Information Age.

Chase, S. (2000). Narrative inquiry. In N. K. Denzin & Y. S. Lincoln (Eds.), *Handbook of qualitative research* (pp. 651-679). Thousand Oaks, CA: Sage.

Clandinin, D. J. (Ed.). (2007). *Handbook of narrative inquiry*. Thousand Oaks, CA: Sage.

Clandinin, D. J., & Connelly, M. (2000). *Narrative inquiry: Experience and story in qualitative research*. San Francisco, CA: Jossey-Bass.

Clandinin, D. J., Pushor, D., & Orr, A. M. (2007). Navigating sites for narrative inquiry. *Journal of Teacher Education, 58*(1), 21-35.

Clark, C., & Medina, C. (2000). How reading and writing literacy narratives affect preservice teachers' understandings of literacy, pedagogy, and multiculturalism. *Journal of Teacher Education, 51*(1), 63-76.

Conle, C. (1999). Why narrative? Which narrative? Struggling with time and place in life and research. *Curriculum Inquiry, 29*(1), 7-32.

Conle, C. (2000a). Narrative inquiry: Research tool and medium for professional development. *European Journal of Teacher Education, 23*(1), 49-63.

Conle, C. (2000b). Thesis as narrative or "What is the inquiry in narrative inquiry?" *Curriculum Inquiry, 30*(2), 190-214.

Conle, C. (2003). An anatomy of narrative curricula. *Educational Researcher, 32*(3), 3-15.

Connelly, F. M., & Clandinin, D. J. (1990). Stories of experience and narrative inquiry. *Educational Researcher, 19*(4), 2-14.

Connelly, F. M., & Clandinin, D. J. (2006). Narrative inquiry. In J. L. Green, G. Camilli, & P. Elmore (Eds.), *Handbook of complementary methods in education research* (3rd ed., pp. 477-487). Mahwah, NJ: Erlbaum.

Coulter, C., Michael, C., & Poynor, L. (2007). Storytelling as pedagogy: An unexpected outcome of narrative inquiry. *Curriculum Inquiry, 37*(2), 103-122.

Cuban, L. (1992). What happens to reforms that last? The case of the junior high school. *American Educational Research Journal, 29*(2), 227-251.

Denzin, N., & Lincoln, Y. (Eds.). (2005). Introduction. In *The Sage handbook of qualitative research* (pp. 1-29). Thousand Oaks, CA: Sage.

Denzin, N. K., & Lincoln, Y. L. (Eds.). (1994). *Handbook of qualitative research*. Thousand Oaks, CA: Sage.

Dewey, J. (1934). *Art as experience*. New York, NY: Capricorn Books.

Dewey, J. (1938). *Experience and education*. New York, NY: Macmillan.

Dickinson, T. S. (Ed.). (2001). Reinventing the middle school: A proposal to counter arrested development. In *Reinventing the middle school* (pp. 3-20). New York, NY: RoutledgeFalmer.

Dunne, J. (2003). Arguing for teaching as a practice: A reply to Alasdair MacIntyre. *Journal of Philosophy of Education, 37*(2), 353-369.

Dunne, J. (2005). An intricate fabric: Understanding the rationality of practice. *Pedagogy, Culture and Society, 13*(3), 367-389.

Eisner, E. (1991). *The enlightened eye: Qualitative inquiry and the enhancement of educational practice.* New York, NY: Macmillan.

Elbaz-Luwisch, F. (2007). Studying teachers' lives and experience: Narrative inquiry into K-12 teaching. In D. J. Clandinin (Ed.), *Handbook of narrative inquiry: Mapping a methodology* (pp. 357-382). Thousand Oaks, CA: Sage.

Fludernik, M. (2005). Histories of narrative theory (II): From structuralism to the present. In J. Phelan & P. Rabinowitz (Eds.), *A companion to narrative theory* (pp. 36-59). Malden, MA: Blackwell.

Gadamer, H. G. (1988). *Truth and method* (G. Barden & J. Cumming, Trans.). New York, NY: Crossroad.

Goodson, I. (1995). The story so far: Personal knowledge and the political. In J. A. Hatch & R. Wisniewski (Eds.), *Life history and narrative* (pp. 86-97). London, England: Falmer Press.

Goodson, I. (Ed.). (1992). *Studying teachers' lives.* New York, NY: Teachers College Press.

Greene, M. (2001). *Variations on a blue guitar: The Lincoln Center Institute lectures on aesthetic education.* New York, NY: Teachers College Press.

Grinberg, J. G. A. (2002). "I had never been exposed to teaching like that": Progressive teacher education at Bank Street during the 1930's. *Teachers College Record, 104*(7), 1422-1460.

Hatch, J. A., & Wisniewski, R. (Eds.). (1995). Life history and narrative: Questions, issues, and exemplary works. In *Life history and narrative* (pp. 113-136). London, England: The Falmer Press.

Hendry, P. (2007). The future of narrative. *Qualitative Inquiry, 13*(4), 487-498.

Holquist, M. (1994). *Dialogism: Bakhtin and his world.* New York, NY: Routledge.

Iser, W. (2006). *How to do theory.* Malden, MA: Blackwell.

Josselson, R. (2003). Introduction. In R. Josselson, A. Lieblich, & D. McAdams (Eds.), *Up close and personal: The teaching and learning of narrative research* (pp. 3-12). Washington, DC: American Psychological Association.

Josselson, R. (2007). The ethical attitude in narrative research: Principles and practicalities. In D. J. Clandinin (Ed.), *Handbook of narrative inquiry: Mapping a methodology* (pp. 537-566). Thousand Oaks, CA: Sage.

Kasak, D. (2004). What of the future? In S. C. Thompson (Ed.), *Reforming middle level education: Considerations for policymakers* (pp. 231-250). Greenwich, CT: Information Age.

Kim, J. H. (2008). A romance with narrative inquiry: Toward an act of narrative theorizing. *Curriculum and Teaching Dialogue, 10*(1 & 2), 251-267.

Kuhn, T. S. (1962). *The structure of scientific revolutions* (2nd ed.). Chicago, IL: University of Chicago Press.

Lather, P. (2008). New wave utilization research: (Re)Imagining the research/policy nexus. *Educational Researcher, 37*(6), 361-364.

Leavy, P. (2009). *Method meets art: Arts-based research practice*. New York, NY: The Guilford Press.

Lyons, N., & LaBoskey, V. K. (Eds.). (2002). Why narrative inquiry or exemplars for a scholarship of teaching? In *Narrative inquiry in practice: Advancing the knowledge of teaching* (pp. 11-30). New York, NY: Teachers College Press.

MacIntyre, A., & Dunne, J. (2002). Alasdair MacIntyre on education: In dialogue with Joseph Dunne. *Journal of Philosophy of Education, 36*(1), 1-19.

Maxwell, J. (2004). Causal explanation, qualitative research, and scientific inquiry in education. *Educational Researcher, 33*(2), 3-11.

Mertens, S. B., Anfara, Jr., V. A., & Caskey, M. M. (Eds.). (2007). *The young adolescent and the middle school*. Charlotte, NC: Information Age.

Morson, G. S., & Emerson, C. (1990). *Mikhail Bakhtin: Creation of a prosaics*. Stanford, CA: Stanford University Press.

National Center for Education Statistics. (2008). *Numbers and types of public elementary and secondary schools from the common core of data: School year 2006-07-First look*. Washington, DC: U.S. Department of Education.

National Research Council. (2002). *Scientific research in education*. Washington, DC: National Academy Press.

No Child Left Behind Act of 2001 Pub. L. No. 107-110 (2001).

Phillion, J., He, M. F., & Connelly, F. M. (Eds.). (2005). *Narrative & experience in multicultural education*. Thousand Oaks, CA: Sage.

Pinnegar, S., & Daynes, J. G. (2007). Locating narrative inquiry historically. In D. J. Clandinin (Ed.), *Handbook of narrative inquiry: Mapping a methodology* (pp. 3-34). Thousand Oaks, CA: Sage.

Riessman, C. K., & Speedy, J. (2007). Narrative inquiry in the psychotherapy professions. In D. J. Clandinin (Ed.), *Handbook of narrative inquiry: Mapping a methodology* (pp. 426-456). Thousand Oaks, CA: Sage.

Rosiek, J., & Atkinson, B. (2007). The inevitability and importance of genres in narrative research on teaching practice. *Qualitative Inquiry, 13*(4), 499-521.

Schön, D. A. (1983). *The reflective practitioner: How professionals think in action*. New York, NY: Basic Books.

Smith, T. (2008). Fostering a praxis stance in pre-service teacher education. In S. Kemmis & T. Smith (Eds.), *Enabling praxis: Challenges for education* (pp. 65-84). Rotterdam, Netherlands: Sense.

Webster, L., & Mertova, P. (2007). *Using narrative inquiry as a research method: An introduction to using critical event narrative analysis in research on learning and teaching*. New York, NY: Routledge.

CHAPTER 2

THE LIVED EXPERIENCES OF MIDDLE SCHOOL ENGLISH LANGUAGE LEARNERS

Shifting Identities Between Classrooms

Bogum Yoon

Grounded in identity and positioning theories, this study explored the experiences and identity shifts of English language learners (ELLs) who attended a middle school in the United States. Using the method of narrative inquiry, this chapter reports how the students viewed and portrayed themselves differently in the mainstream classroom and the English as a second language (ESL) classroom. Although the ELLs participated actively in the ESL classroom, they positioned themselves as passive and invisible in the mainstream classroom. It appears that the ELLs' different sense of identities in these 2 classrooms was related to their teachers' and classmates' approaches that positioned them as powerful students or as powerless students. These findings suggest the significance of teachers' and classmates' roles on the ELLs' identity development for their success in language and literacy learning.

Voices From the Middle: Narrative Inquiry By, For, and About the Middle Level Community
pp. 19–36

"I feel more comfortable in the ESL classroom. I can talk there."

"I like being in the ESL class. There are people who don't speak English very well. Everybody is the same. My friends are there. But in other classes, everybody looks at me. I don't like it."

"I feel comfortable in the ESL class. All of the people in the ESL class are from other countries. So I feel comfortable because we have a common thing. But in the other classes, they are all American people."

"I feel freedom here."

When I interviewed four (1 Bolivian, 2 Koreans, 1 Russian) middle school English language learners (ELLs) about their schooling experiences in their new country, the United States, the students were eager to share their feelings about the English as a second language (ESL) class and their regular classes. The student descriptions about their ESL class interested me because I wondered if the descriptions related to the way they positioned themselves in the classroom. The ELLs, who viewed the ESL class as their comfort zone, participated actively in the ESL classroom, although they positioned themselves as passive and invisible in the mainstream classroom.

This observation made me wonder how the students' positioning as active or passive was possible given that the ELLs' English ability level did not change from the mainstream classroom to the ESL classroom. This question led me to a more focused analysis of their different participatory behaviors and positioning between the classrooms.

The central purpose of this chapter is to report the ELLs' shifting identities, that I observed through their participatory actions and positioning between the mainstream classroom and the ESL classroom. Although many middle school ELL studies focus on the students' language learning in the ESL classroom setting, few studies discuss the issues of student identity in the regular classroom and the ESL classroom context. Given that student identity is related to their language and literacy learning (Gee, 1996; Miller, 1999, 2000; Norton, 2000; Yoon, 2008), it is important to examine how ELLs portray themselves in classrooms when they interact with their teachers and peers. This study aims to help teachers better understand the needs of middle school ELLs for their success in language and literacy learning.

THEORETICAL PERSPECTIVES
ON IDENTITY, POSITIONING, AND ELLS

In this study, I use "identity" to refer to the multiple and shifting presentations of self that are demonstrated through actions and emotions. The ELLs' participation and emotional patterns in the classroom are major indicators for interpreting their identities. The choice of the indicators is guided by Harré and van Langenhove (1991) who note that individuals' identities are disclosed in their speech and actions, and their attitudes or emotions are evident in relevant discursive activities. Psychological and emotional perspectives of identities are included in the indicators. The participating students' ethnic identities, including Bolivian, Korean, and Russian, are not the major focus, but their psychological and emotional identities, such as a sense of feeling powerful or powerless, is the main focus of this study. In short, in this chapter, I adopt the concept of identity constituted by the emotions that the students disclose through their speech, attitudes, and participation in classroom activities. Positioning theory guided me to define this notion of identity.

Positioning theory is defined as "the study of local moral orders as ever-shifting patterns of mutual and contestable rights and obligations of speaking and acting" (Harré & van Langenhove, 1999, p. 1). This theory focuses on individuals' discourse and intentional acts. "Positioning" is a metaphorical term originally introduced to analyze interpersonal encounters from a discursive viewpoint (Hollway, 1984). It has a specific meaning in the analysis of interactions between people and, in the technical sense, it has an effect on the possibilities for interpersonal and intergroup action.

Positioning is relational and reciprocal; it is an active and discursive practice. People position others (positioning) and the others position them back (repositioning). While positioning and repositioning each other, power relations are always embedded in action. In short, positioning focuses on the characteristics of dynamic power relationships. People can reposition themselves by challenging the positioning given by others. It is, however, often difficult to enact the agency to reposition oneself in an unequal society where hidden power relations are continuously at work (Walsh, 1991).

People not only position others, they also position themselves. This is what Davies and Harré (1990) call "reflexive positioning in which one positions oneself" (p. 48). Individuals view the world from a certain position (Davies & Harré, 1990) and self-positioning that individuals take up guides the way in which they act and think about their roles, assignments, and duties in a given context. This notion is relevant to this study regarding ELLs' views of themselves. The students' views of themselves help to explain how they position themselves in the classroom.

Reflexive positioning serves to lead our attention to individual agency, the desire/motivation of being in action (Johnston, 2004). Individuals might act and position themselves differently in various contexts. They might position themselves as powerful in a given situation and as powerless in another situation. These multiple representations of self suggest that an individual agency is enacted in the process of constructing identity. Agency involves deciding which positions individuals take up.

Although reflexive positioning affords the insights that individuals' identity creation and re-creation is their own work and that individuals are active in achieving their own identities, it does not offer details as to how and why the same person positions herself differently in different contexts. Interactive positioning "in which what one person says positions another" (Davies & Harré, 1990, p. 48) fills the gap of reflexive positioning by providing the idea that the phenomena occur in relation to others. How people construct a positive identity can be dependent on how they are positioned by others. In this view, positioning someone in certain ways limits or extends what that person can say and do (Adams & Harré, 2001) and inhibits or provides the options of choice of speaking forms, actions, and thoughts, limiting or extending his/her rights (Harré & van Langenhove, 1999). Positioning individuals as deficient may deny their rights to correct their cognitive performance (Harré & Moghaddam, 2003) and positioning them as intelligent may allow them the possibility to improve performance.

How do these characteristics of positioning relate to individual identities? According to Taylor, Bougie, and Caouette (2003), the identity process operates from a perspective of positioning. Any positioning including interpersonal and intergroup positioning involves issues surrounding individuals' identity (Tan & Moghaddam, 1995). Individual identity is dynamically created and recreated through positioning, and it changes through positioning in social interactions. As people position each other, assignments such as rights, duties, and obligations are involved. How people construct a positive identity is largely dependent on how they are positioned by others. If people are positioned as powerful, the positioning helps people form their identity as powerful. If people are positioned as powerless, the positioning does not assist in constructing their positive identity. Individuals' identity development can be closely related to how they are positioned.

Due to the dynamic characteristics of positioning, the concept of positioning is often used when researchers deal with identity as a fluid notion. The notion of identity has been represented in many different ways such as voice, the self, self-identity, social identity, and cultural identity (Miller, 1999). Many scholars (e.g., Miller, 1999; Norton, 2000) agree that identity is a complicated concept which cannot be defined in one simple phrase. Two relevant perspectives on identity are important here: essentialist and anti-essentialist (Hall, 1996). Essentialist perspectives focus on *who I am*, treating identity as a fixed concept. Antiessentialist viewpoints focus on *who I become*, dealing with identity as a shifting notion. Anti-essentialist views follow the postmodern concept of identity, which avoids static notions and keeps the options for change open. Identity is a noun, but it acts like a verb (Bauman, 1996). It is a constant becoming (Wenger, 1998).

This study takes the antiessentialist stance because the stance provides a lens for viewing the four ELLs' identity development. The participants in the study shifted their identities as powerful or powerless according to the contexts they were in, demonstrating that their identities were multiple and changing. Identity is not the presentation of *who I am* but *who I become* in a social matrix, which is continuously in the process of transformation through relationship to others (Greene, 1991). An example, showing that an individual's identity can be detected through speech acts, illustrates this process. One of my participants, Natasha, introduced herself with "I am Russian" before she presented her writing project to her mainstream peers and parents. However, none of the American students began introductions with "I am American." Natasha mentioned that she did not present herself in the same way when she was in her country, Russia. In other words, she adjusted her presented identity according to whom she was with. The student *became* Russian in the U.S. context. In short, identity can be explained only in a situated context. When Natasha was with Russians, she did not have to represent herself as Russian, just as her peers did not present themselves as American in the U.S. context. Natasha's identity was shaped through her awareness that she was different from others. This example demonstrates how identity might be constructed through differences in situated contexts (Hall, 1996).

Interactive positioning offers the insight that others play an important part as individuals achieve their identity. Natasha's identity development as a powerful or powerless student was dependent, in part, upon her perception of how the others positioned her. This concept is relevant to this study regarding mainstream teachers' and peers' positioning of ELLs. Teachers and peers can intentionally or unintentionally position ELLs in more positive or more negative ways through their interactions. They might position ELLs without realizing that they may be expanding or limiting the students' opportunities to develop a positive sense of themselves as learners. Theoretically, it seems evident that if teachers and classmates positioned ELLs as powerful and provided them with many opportunities to develop their positive identity, then the students would be able to participate in learning more actively.

THE PROCESS OF DATA COLLECTION AND ANALYSIS

Data Collection

I collected data over a semester at a middle school, which is located in New York State. A "collective case study" (Stake, 1995) method was employed to study four ELLs: Jun, Natasha, Sandra, and Ha (all names are pseudonyms). See Table 2.1 for the students' profiles.

Table 2.1.   Student Profiles

Name	*Sex/Grade/Age*	*Ethnicity*	*Length of Stay (Years)*	*ESL Placement*	*SES*
Jun	M/6/11	Korean	Two	Advanced	Middle
Natasha	F/6/11	Russian	One	Beginner/ Intermediate	Middle
Sandra	F/7/12	Bolivian	Two	Advanced	Middle
Ha	M/7/12	Korean (U.S. citizen)	Two	Advanced	Middle

Note: ESL = English as a second language, SES = socioeconomic status.

The primary form of data was in-depth interviews with these students and extensive observations in their regular classroom and their ESL classroom. Two formal interviews and several informal interviews were completed with the students. All formal interviews with the students were audiotaped and transcribed verbatim.

For classroom observations, I visited the school almost every day over one semester. After I observed Jun and Natasha in Mr. Brown's English language arts/reading/social studies class (2 hour block schedule) in the morning, I observed Sandra and Ha in Mrs. Taylor's English language arts class in the afternoon right after their lunch break. I observed all of them again in the ESL class in the afternoon. Because I was attempting to capture the students' behaviors in the classroom, I took field notes. I also audiotaped classroom observations and cross-checked them with the field notes.

Since identity can be detected through people's speech and acts (Harré & Moghaddam, 2003), I listened closely to the students' dialogues and observed their behaviors. I observed the students' numerous behaviors and interactions in each classroom. These behaviors and interactions could be interpreted as expressions of their identity. In order to confirm the trustworthiness of my observations, in interviews, I asked them several questions and used a stimulated recall method in the informal and formal interviews. I did not ask them questions such as "What was your identity?" or "What was your positioning?" Rather, I asked about their emotions during specific events, such as "How did you feel at that time?" or "Tell me about what happened at that time" to identify their perceived positioning and identity. Overall, my focus was on eliciting dialogues, listening to the students during interviews, and observing their behaviors across classroom contexts while they interacted with their teachers and peers.

Data Analysis

Interview transcripts, field notes, and audiotaped transcripts of classroom observations, research logs, interview memos, and documents such as "student work" were used for data analysis. Student work was useful in identifying the students' perceived positioning and identity. Connelly and Clandinin's (1990) and Clandinin and Connelly's (2000) narrative inquiry method was used to understand the complexities of ELLs' positioning and identities. The lived experiences of the students were treated individually focusing on their views of themselves in the classroom. After the analysis of each student narrative, I started a cross-case analysis in order to build general pattern explanations that helped to account for the four student narratives. During that process, I focused on differences or similarities in the students' sense of themselves and positioning between the mainstream classroom and the ESL classroom.

Since thick, rich descriptions are the key components of the genre of narrative (Geertz, 1973), in this chapter, I include the findings when the interview data and my observation data support each other. That is, the observation data of the students' identities were constantly analyzed by comparing the interview data to investigate their emotions.

In the following sections, I present the findings of the study. First, the story of the ELLs' experiences in the mainstream classroom will be addressed, followed by their experiences in the ESL classroom. In the introduction of each section, brief classroom environments, structures, and teachers' pedagogical approaches will be provided to help readers better understand the middle school ELLs' positioning in the classroom.

THE STORY OF THE ELLS' EXPERIENCES
IN THEIR MAINSTREAM CLASSROOM

Positioning of Jun and Natasha: Isolated and Powerless

I observed Jun (Korean) and Natasha (Russian) in Mr. Brown's classroom for one semester. Jun and Natasha were the only ELLs in his class of 26 students. Mr. Brown led his class in a student-centered, "democratic" way. He provided students with choice. His students could choose their partners to work with and express their opinions when they wanted to. This teacher rarely "forced" his students to answer questions that he posed. To talk or not to talk was the student's choice, and Mr. Brown respected it. Most of the students interacted well with each other.

In this classroom, however, Jun and Natasha looked nervous and uneasy throughout the semester. They rarely presented their ideas in the whole class discussions. Even when they did, they spoke with very soft voices. For example, when Mr. Brown asked the whole class, "How many pages do you usually read before you abandon a book you begin to read?" Jun answered with a soft voice, "15 pages." This was one of a very few times that he raised his hand and answered the teacher's question throughout the semester.

Jun's lack of participation and silence did not seem to relate to his English proficiency. In an interview with me, he mentioned that his English was good enough to understand what his teacher and classmates talked about:

> I understand what they are talking about. I mostly understand them. About 90 %. But I don't want to talk in this class.... Why? I don't know. I just don't feel like it. In ESL, I talk a lot, as you know. I feel more comfortable there, but not in this class.

Jun did not state clearly the reason behind his silence but, based on the statements above, his lack of participation in Mr. Brown's classroom was related to his discomfort. Jun was not the only one who shared his uneasiness. Natasha also stated that she did not "feel comfortable" in Mr. Brown's classroom.

Jun and Natasha's discomfort was shown through their positioning in the mainstream classroom. They positioned themselves as quiet, isolated, and powerless in the mainstream classroom. While many of their American peers sitting on a rug exchanged their ideas, I observed that the two ELLs usually listened at their desks without coming onto the rug in Mr. Brown's classroom. Sometimes there were two or three other students, but Jun and Natasha were the only two who did not come to the rug on a regular basis. When Mr. Brown and his American students engaged in lively discussions about topics such as television shows (e.g., *Survivor*) and football games, Jun and Natasha simply listened. My observation data did not show that Mr. Brown or his students encouraged the two ELLs to join the discussions.

It appears that Jun and Natasha portrayed themselves as quiet and isolated in the classroom and their portrayals were connected to how Mr. Brown and his American students positioned them. In the classroom, Mr. Brown rarely played an active role to help the ELLs. He stated, in an interview with me, "I don't teach specifically for them [ELLs]. I think the ESL teacher's job is to make their time beneficial." Viewing himself as a teacher for general education students, Mr. Brown seldom called on Jun and Natasha to share their experiences or ideas in class.

Some of their classmates also positioned the ELLs as unwelcome members by resisting to work with them. While most of their American classmates easily found partners to work with, the two ELLs did not. For instance, one day in September, every student including Jun, was supposed to find a partner who had the same interest in reading. After Jun looked at his list, which had all of the students' reading preferences, including favorite authors and genres, he found two peers whose favorite author was *Roald Dahl*. Realizing one of the girls was absent that day, he slowly approached the other girl before he realized she was already working with a partner. Showing disappointment, he strolled to his desk. Finally, after looking around the whole classroom, he went to a boy who was working alone. Mr. Brown often chastised the boy because he did not turn in his homework. Later in the interview, Jun expressed his frustration:

> I cannot find a partner. Everybody has a partner. They already have friends who they work with. Here is a pair, and there is a pair. It is hard for me to cut in. I don't have a friend to work with.

Jun said that he was fascinated by Roald Dahl's writing style and had read 22 of the author's works. Jun wanted to share his enthusiasm with someone who had the same interest, but he had to partner with the boy who had a different interest. By talking about an author that he had outgrown, Jun did not have an opportunity to be involved in a more meaningful learning activity.

Another example also illustrated how Jun's positioning of himself as isolated and powerless was related to his classmates' positioning. There were a few times when Jun attempted to position himself as knowledgeable in the classroom, but his classmates refused to accept Jun's positioning. For instance, during one of the English language arts classes, students were revising their writing about the topics that they chose. I looked at each group to see what they were writing. When I approached Jun's group, one boy asked me how to spell "deserves." As soon as Jun heard it, he spelled it clearly and with confidence, "d-e-s-e-r-v-e-s." The first boy looked at me with a doubtful expression on his face and asked whether it was right. I said, "Yes, it is correct." Referring to this incident, Jun later stated, "They don't trust me. They don't think I know a lot of words." In that context with the boy, however, Jun remained quiet without repositioning himself as knowledgeable by telling him that he spelled the word correctly.

Natasha also had difficulties in positioning herself as confident and powerful when she worked with her classmates in Mr. Brown's room. Her classmates often positioned her as an unacceptable partner. For instance, she was sitting with two boys and two girls for small group work. After the group read about famous Egyptian leaders, they were busy writing the important characteristics of the leaders. Natasha could not write a sentence, but nobody offered help. When Natasha showed her frustration by saying, "I could not follow you," one of the American girls said bluntly, "You didn't say you didn't understand" as if blaming Natasha for not being able to follow the conversation. Natasha did not challenge her positioning as an incapable person. She remained quiet. She looked powerless. Repositioning did not occur under the mainstream student's power. During the break while most of the students went out to the restrooms and Mr. Brown was in the hall to monitor them, Natasha approached me in the corner and disclosed her resentment by saying, "I don't like this group." She did not reveal her anger to the group but rather suppressed it. This incident shows that Natasha sensed the mainstream students' hidden power.

Another example also demonstrated how Natasha's classmates positioned her as an unwelcome partner. Academically strong and characteristically nice according to Mr. Brown, the student sitting next to Natasha usually went to work with other friends. Unable to find a partner, Natasha usually worked with special education students or students who did not associate with other mainstream students.

As shown in Natasha and Jun's examples, some of the mainstream students' attitudes towards these students were not welcoming. Although Mr. Brown's class appeared to be highly interactive and student-centered, the two ELLs were isolated during whole group discussions and small group work, even when working with partners. No examples were found in the observation data that Mr. Brown supported the ELLs by offering help when they had difficulties in working with their mainstream students.

Positioning of Sandra and Ha: Passive and Invisible

Sandra (Bolivian) and Ha (Korean) were in Mrs. Taylor's English language arts (ELA) classroom. In her classroom, Mrs. Taylor emphasized students' individual work. Most of the time, each of her students sat alone, completing worksheets, taking quizzes, listening, or following along while she read a textbook to them. In Mrs. Taylor's class, all of the students' desks were arranged in vertical rows with five or six desks in each row. The students sat alphabetically by their last name.

It appeared that the classroom structure did not allow active interactions between the teacher and the students and the students among themselves. In this classroom, Sandra and Ha rarely participated in classroom activities and usually stayed quiet. Although many students looked attentive to Mrs. Taylor's lecture by sitting straight, I observed that Sandra usually bent her head down or scribbled something in her notebook, leaning against the back of her chair. Throughout the semester, few classmates approached Sandra to talk. Sandra also rarely approached any of her classmates in Mrs. Taylor's classroom.

Ha also did not seem to be engaged in the English class. When Mrs. Taylor read aloud from a textbook, *Reading Literature* (Welch & Bennett, 1981), he sometimes yawned and closed his eyes. Sometimes he read a Korean book, which he borrowed from another Korean boy, while others followed along in the book the teacher read. The Korean boy was the only one that Ha sometimes approached and talked with during breaks.

The classroom teacher's positioning of Sandra and Ha might also have affected their positioning of themselves as passive. Throughout the semester, Mrs. Taylor positioned Ha and Sandra as academically poor students and paid little attention to them. Mrs. Taylor attributed Sandra and Ha's academic struggles to their lack of work ethic. She talked seriously about Sandra's problem first:

> Sandra is the biggest problem. Most of my ESL students work very hard.... They have a really great work ethic, which is something that I wish my American students had. They really want to work hard. But I think Sandra is just not as focused in ELA or really anything.

Although Mrs. Taylor did not view Ha's work as problematic as that of Sandra's, she also viewed Ha in a negative way:

> Ha tends to be goofy. There are some problems here and there. Sometimes, he does good work. But sometimes, he gets a little off track. But maybe because he is getting silly or something like that.

In Mrs. Taylor's classroom, there were only a few times that Sandra and Ha raised their hands and answered questions throughout the semester. Sandra mentioned, "I don't have anything to say in ELA class. But it's ok. She [Mrs. Taylor] doesn't care." Sandra also added, "I just keep everything to myself. I don't think she likes me."

Sandra disclosed her feelings that Mrs. Taylor was not concerned about her and shared a story: "When I asked for a pass to go to the bathroom after a student went out, Mrs. Taylor refused to give it to me and had me wait until the student came back." Sandra interpreted the teacher's refusal as the sign that the teacher did not like her. Sandra complained, "It is hard for me to get a pass from her [Mrs. Taylor] although other students do not have any difficulties in getting it." Sandra's perception towards Mrs. Taylor might influence her positioning of herself as silent and invisible in the classroom.

As with Sandra, Ha also positioned himself as silent and passive most of the time in Mrs. Taylor's classroom. His participatory behaviors were completely different in the ESL classroom. I observed that he was very active in the ESL classroom. When I asked about the distinctive differences in his attitudes, he elaborated the reasons: "I don't have a chance to talk. I mean I don't have time to talk in the ELA class. In ESL class, I talk because there are Korean students." His remarks indicate that his different participation in those two classes was due to a lack of chances to talk in the ELA classroom and his consciousness of others.

Interview data showed that the way Ha and Sandra positioned themselves as passive and invisible was related to Mrs. Taylor's approach in English language arts. The ELLs expressed their difficulties in Mrs. Taylor's class when the teacher focused on English grammar and sentence structure. Sandra said, "It is difficult to write essays. I can write story-type writing, but I don't know how to write essays well. Grammar is too hard."

Ha explained his difficulties in the English class in depth:

> In ELA class, the teacher emphasizes writing. Writing is so hard to [sic] me because you have to be careful about capitalization, paragraphs, and punctuation. You have to make sentences. In Korea, I did not learn anything except basic words. I did not learn how to write paragraphs in English with an introduction, body, and conclusion. But here, the teacher focuses on writing in that way. ELA is one of the most difficult subjects for me.

Sandra (58.5%) and Ha (58.6%) received failing grades for the second grading period. Although the students expressed their difficulties, their needs were not met because the teacher was unaware of their difficulties. In Mrs. Taylor's class, Sandra and Ha positioned themselves as disengaged, silent, and secluded in their own world.

THE STORY OF THE ELLS' EXPERIENCES IN THEIR ESL CLASS

Positioning as Active Participants

Jun, Natasha, Sandra, and Ha positioned themselves as active participants in their ESL classroom. In this classroom, Mrs. Kidman, the ESL teacher, attempted to create a comfortable classroom atmosphere so that the students could talk about their cultures and languages freely and without pressure. Her efforts were shown through her talk and action. She often said to her class, "Our class is a safe place. You can make mistakes and somebody should not laugh and tease."

Mrs. Kidman not only characterized the ESL classroom as a safe place through her remarks, but she also attempted to have her students feel comfortable through her actions. She often greeted her students with a big, warm smile, standing in front of the door and saying, "Welcome to the ESL class." Typically, most of the ELLs ran into the classroom and responded to her by saying cheerfully, "Hi, Mrs. Kidman." In my observation, Jun, who seldom smiled in Mr. Brown's classroom, always smiled when he entered the ESL classroom.

In the ESL classroom where Mrs. Kidman often shared American culture and norms with the students, the ELLs seemed to be engaged in dialogues by listening carefully and responding promptly to the teacher. Following is a typical dialogue between Mrs. Kidman and the students:

Mrs. Kidman:	In this country, when someone is talking to you, you are expected to look at them. And you never ask, "How old are you?" In America, the biggest thing is I am always 39 [laugh]. Don't ask old people how old they are. Don't ask "Are you married?"
Natasha:	How about "What's your name?"
Mrs. Kidman:	That's ok. But if it is a personal question, you might not ask them when you first meet them. What about "How much do you weigh?"
Students:	[no answer]
Mrs. Kidman:	Don't do it. Don't do it.
Students:	[All laugh]

Mrs. Kidman also valued her students' cultures. She wanted her students to feel proud of their countries and languages. To this end, the teacher planned many activities such as the "Real Me Project" and "Thanksgiving" that allowed the students to write about themselves and their countries. Many activities were connected with the students' cultures. Mrs. Kidman mentioned that she did these activities purposefully, "I try to give them opportunities to share things about their language, their culture, and their countries so that they are more included."

In this classroom, Jun, Natasha, Sandra, and Ha did not seem to hesitate to talk about their problems or secrets. They positioned themselves as active and powerful students. For instance, in the "Real Me Project," Natasha, who was usually silent in Mr. Brown's mainstream classroom, shared with her peers that she and her sister were adopted by a Russian who was a radiologist. Her peers became excited about her adoption and asked questions such as, "Why didn't your grandmother adopt you?" "You said you are Russian, but how were you adopted in Ukraine?" Natasha explained in detail how her mother divorced her father and how she and her sister were abandoned and raised in an orphanage in Ukraine.

Natasha's active participation in the ESL classroom was also evidenced by her frequent talks with her peers. For instance, she shared her experience on the school bus with the whole class: "When I get on the bus, an American girl, who is a seventh grader, always say [sic] to me, 'Hey, Russian, sit down quickly.'" Natasha showed her anger on her face and raised her voice when she talked about the incident. She shared how terrible her feelings were when the girl called her "Russian," rather than her name. After she shared the story in the ESL classroom, I asked her whether she shared the same story with other mainstream classmates. Natasha mentioned that she did not share it with any of her mainstream classmates. Her remarks showed that she felt more comfortable with her ESL classmates.

Ha also demonstrated his active participation in the ESL classroom. He was not hesitant to write about his identity for the ESL project. He said:

> Although I was born here, I am not American. My father and mother are Korean, so I've never thought that I am American. Some American friends told me I am "half and half" because I have American citizenship but my parents are Korean. But most American people might not think I am American because they tend to judge me based on my color but not my citizenship. But I don't want to be American, or I don't want to be European. I feel comfortable with myself as Asian with my look and accent.... I feel comfortable in the ESL class because they [his peers] are all from other countries, just like me. I feel free in the ESL class.

Ha presented his writing to his peers and also added, "I hate when we don't have the ESL class. This is the class I can talk." When his peers were evaluating his presentation based on the "peer-review" rubric that Mrs. Kidman provided, Ha prompted his peers to give him an excellent grade. He said, "I did good" by giving the "thumbs up" sign.

Sandra also positioned herself as an active participant in the ESL classroom. For example, in a writing project, she wrote about how she felt comfortable in the ESL classroom compared to the other classrooms:

> I am really nervous in the real class [regular classes]. I will be really embarrassed if I make a mistake because there are American friends. They already know English. But in the ESL class, if I make a mistake, it is going to be ok because it is especially for ESL students, like me, who learn English.

Sandra, who usually leaned against the back of her chair and was not engaged in Mrs. Taylor's class, presented her project with a clear voice and confident attitude. When I asked Sandra about the differences in her participation between Mrs. Taylor's ELA class and the ESL class, she said, "My ESL teacher is just like my mom. I can talk anything to her. I can make mistakes here and I'm not afraid." Sandra actively attempted to interact with Mrs. Kidman. I observed that Sandra made an appointment with Mrs. Kidman to share her personal concerns about her family including her grandmother in Bolivia where the political situation was in turmoil.

As shown in these examples, the ESL classroom was a comfortable place where the ELLs found peace and freedom. The students who positioned themselves as isolated and invisible participated actively in their learning activities in Mrs. Kidman's classroom. In the ESL classroom where Mrs. Kidman attempted to exert a conscious effort to meet her students' cultural and social needs, the ELLs appeared to feel a sense of belonging and found peace.

REFLECTIONS AND DISCUSSIONS

The narrative analysis of this study breaks important ground in our understanding of the ELLs' multiple, complex, and shifting identities between classrooms. The theoretical framework of identity and interactive positioning (Harré & van Langenhove, 1991) provides insights into how the ELLs' self-positioning may be influenced by the way the classroom teachers and the mainstream students position them. This study suggests that, when the ELLs are positioned as unaccepted members in the mainstream classroom, they may position themselves as quiet, isolated, and passive.

As Walsh (1991) notes, participation and dialogue do not occur as freely among language learners when power relations are continuously at work. As shown in Mr. Brown's classroom where mainstream peers' hidden power operated, Jun and Natasha did not reposition their identity as powerful and active students. They tended to be quiet without challenging the hidden power. In Mrs. Taylor's classroom, where her mainstream students did not show any interest in interacting with Sandra and Ha, Mrs. Taylor rarely supported the ELLs by meeting their needs in a more active way. The students were not engaged in literacy learning. However, in the ESL classroom where Mrs. Kidman attempted to meet the ELLs' cultural and social needs by creating a comfortable classroom mood and by employing activities connected with the students' cultures, they felt a sense of belonging and actively participated in learning activities.

Although ELL identity shifts from passive to active are very complicated and cannot be explained with one single factor, this study suggests that shifts are possible when ELLs are accepted as cultural, social beings, as seen in Mrs. Kidman's classroom. According to Greenwood (1994), individuals actively negotiate and achieve their multiple identities as they are positioned and position themselves in different contexts. In the ESL classroom, where the ELLs are positioned as accepted cultural, social members, they position themselves as powerful and active participants.

These cultural and social aspects shed light on middle school ELL language teaching and learning. According to Brown (1994), "culture and language are intricately intertwined" (p. 25). Whenever teachers are involved in a complex system of cultural values and ways of thinking and acting in the classroom, they are in a position to help ELLs learn a language. Thus, in order to facilitate middle school ELLs' active participation in learning, the findings of this study suggest that teachers pay more careful attention to the ELLs' acceptance by viewing them as cultural, social beings.

Given that the self-question of "*Who am I*" can be understood from the question "*What am I allowed to do*" (Norton, 2000), mainstream teachers' and peers' continuous positioning of ELLs as important members is vital for their learning. If ELLs continue to be positioned as important or unimportant through social interactions, that positioning may influence the way the students see positive or negative reflections of themselves (Howie, 1999). Although a single positioning of ELLs may not critically influence the way they see themselves, a continuous positioning of ELLs in certain ways may affect their views of themselves accordingly.

This research gives us an understanding of more effective ways to help middle school ELLs' identity development. Given that middle school ELLs are more aware of peer pressure, self-esteem, and identity than very young children (Brown, 1987), mainstream teachers need to consider ELLs' cultural and social needs by providing a safe, comfortable, and collaborative environment in which they can work. As shown in the findings, when hidden power operates in the mainstream classroom, it is hard for ELLs to position and reposition themselves as powerful and visible participants. Teachers' awareness of hidden power agendas and their active support by learning about the middle school ELLs' cultural and social needs are crucial for ELLs to be able to actively engage in language and literacy learning.

REFERENCES

Adams, J. L., & Harré, R. (2001). Gender positioning: A sixteenth/seventeenth century example. *Journal for the Theory of Social Behaviour, 31*(3), 331-338.

Bauman, Z. (1996). From pilgrim to tourist—Or a short history of identity. In S. Hall & P. du Gay (Eds.), *Questions of cultural identity* (pp. 18-36). London, England: Sage.

Brown, H. D. (1987). *Principles of language learning and teaching.* Englewood Cliffs, NJ: Prentice-Hall.

Brown, H. D. (1994). *Teaching by principles: An interactive approach to language pedagogy*. Englewood Cliffs, NJ: Prentice Hall.

Clandinin, D.J., & Connelly, F. M. (2000). *Narrative inquiry: Experience and story in qualitative research*. San Francisco, CA: Jossey-Bass.

Connelly, F. M., & Clandinin, D. J. (1990). Stories of experience and narrative inquiry, *Educational Researcher, 19*(5), 2-14.

Davies, B., & Harré, R. (1990). Positioning: The discursive production of selves. *Journal for the Theory of Social Behaviour, 20*, 43-63.

Gee, J. P. (1996). *Social linguistics and literacies: Ideology in discourses* (2nd ed.). Bristol, PA: Taylor & Francis.

Geertz, C. (1973). *The interpretation of cultures*. New York, NY: Basic Books.

Greene, M. (1991). Forward. In C. Witherell & N. Noddings (Eds.), *Stories lives tell: Narrative and dialogue in education* (pp. ix-xi). New York, NY: Teachers College.

Greenwood, J. D. (1994). *Realism, identity, and emotion*. Thousand Oaks, CA: Sage.

Hall, S. (1996). Introduction: Who needs identity? In S. Hall & P. du Gay (Eds.), *Questions of cultural identity* (pp. 1-17). London, England: Sage.

Harré, R., & Moghaddam, F. (2003). *The self and others: Positioning individuals and groups in personal, political, and cultural contexts*. Westport, CT: Praeger.

Harré, R., & van Langenhove, L. (1991). Varieties of positioning. *Journal for the Theory of Social Behaviour, 21*, 393-408.

Harré, R., & van Langenhove, L. (Eds.). (1999). *Positioning theory*. Malden, MA: Blackwell.

Hollway, W. (1984). Gender difference and the production of subjectivity. In J. Henriques, W. Hollway, C. Urwin, C. Venn, & V. Walkerdine, *Changing the subject: Psychology, social regulation and subjectivity* (pp. 227-263). London, England: Methuen.

Howie, D. (1999). Preparing for positive positioning. In R. Harré, & L. van Langenhove (Eds.), *Positioning theory* (pp. 53-59). Malden, MA: Blackwell.

Johnston, P. (2004). *Choice words*. Portland, ME: Stenhouse Publishers.

Miller, J. (1999). Becoming audible: Social identity and second language use. *Journal of Intercultural Studies, 20*(2), 149-165.

Miller, J. M. (2000). Language use, identity, and social interaction: Migrant students in Australia. *Research on Language and Social Interaction, 33*(1), 69-100.

Norton, B. (2000). *Identity and language learning: Gender, ethnicity and educational change*. New York, NY: Longman.

Stake, R. (1995). *The art of case study research*. Thousand Oaks, CA: Sage.

Tan, S. L., & Moghaddam, F. M. (1995). Reflexive positioning and culture. *Journal for the Theory of Social Behaviour, 25*(4), 388-400.

Taylor, D. M., Bougie, E., & Caouette, J. (2003). Applying positioning principles to a theory of collective identity. In R. Harré & F. Moghaddam (Eds.), *The self and others: Positioning individuals and groups in personal, political, and cultural contexts* (pp. 197-215). Westport, CT: Praeger.

Walsh, C. A. (1991). *Pedagogy and the struggle for voice: Issues of language, power, and schooling for Puerto Ricans*. Toronto, Ontario, Canada: OISE Press.

Welch, B. Y., & Bennett, R. A. (1981). *Reading literature: Ginn literature series*. Lexington, MA: Ginn and Company.

Wenger, E. (1998). *Communities of practice*. New York, NY: Cambridge University Press.

Yoon, B. (2008). Uninvited guests: The influence of teachers' roles and pedagogies on the positioning of English language learners in regular classrooms. *American Educational Research Journal, 45*(2), 495-522.

CHAPTER 3

XAVIER AND THE BULLY BOX

Immigrant Adolescent Girls in a Bully-Free World

Cathy Coulter

Narrative research is used to explore issues of bullying for adolescent girls who are representative of diverse ethnic identities in a middle school where there is a schoolwide bullying prevention program. Using Polkinghorne's (1995) narrative analysis and Ecker's (1966) qualitative problem-solving process, data analysis yielded narrative constructions that embody the analysis. In addition, Erickson's (1986) modified analytic induction supported 4 assertions: (1) Valley Middle School is socially stratified; (2) The bullying prevention program has been coopted into the culture of bullying; (3) There are instances of severe bullying at Valley Middle School; (4) There is a culture of silence surrounding bullying at Valley Middle School.

Valley Middle School (all names of institution and persons are pseudonyms) is located in the north-central area of a sprawling city in the southwest. Nestled in the suburbs, it is surrounded by stucco houses and palm trees. It is strongly middle to upper middle class, pulling from households of working families with two car garages, a few apartment

Voices From the Middle: Narrative Inquiry By, For, and About the Middle Level Community
pp. 37–54

complexes, and a scattering of jumbo-loan homes. The surrounding neighborhood is mostly new development. Though a public seventh/ eighth grade school, it is a magnet school of technology. Classrooms are equipped with smart boards and computers are used throughout the school. Students are expected to be able to access school websites through the internet from home. The population is mostly White, with small percentages of Asian, Hispanic, and Indian populations.

Valley Middle School prides itself on its community-building efforts. The student body is broken into four teams, and content-area teachers plan and meet regularly as teams in order to support students. Seventh grade teachers begin the year with games and team-building activities. One of Valley Middle School's signature programs is the Olweus antibullying program, a schoolwide program designed to promote awareness and prevention of bullying.

From the outside, it seems Valley Middle School is taking important steps to promote a healthy, developmentally appropriate environment for its student body.

BULLYING AND CULTURAL IDENTITY

Research on bullying has grown in the last few decades. In 1973 Dan Olweus, the namesake of Valley Middle School's bullying prevention program, published a book on aggression in schools in Scandinavia. In 1993 he published his book, *Bullying in School: What We Know and What we Can Do* (1996b) in the United States. In the meantime, large-scale studies conducted by organizations such as the American Association of University Women (1993, 2001) on sexual harassment and bullying revealed staggering numbers. The 2001 study found that 81% of students in Grades 8 through 11 experienced some form of sexual harassment at least once in school. Issues of bullying made it into mainstream media as school districts were brought to court for not responding adequately to episodes of bullying and sexual harassment. Tragedies such as Columbine captured national attention and brought the implications of bullying to the public eye. Studies on bullying indicate that bullying damages victims and bullies, and that it can have long-lasting detrimental psychological and emotional effects (Duncan, 1999; Kampulainen et al., 1998; Olweus, 1993a; Sharp, 1995; Whitney & Smith, 1999).

Research by Olweus (1993b) and others (Atlas & Pepler, 1998; Jeffrey, Miller, & Linn, 2001; Sutton & Smith, 1999) brought attention to the role of bystanders in bullying. A study by Atlas and Pepler (1998) found that while bystanders are present for 85% of bullying episodes, they intervene only 10% of the time. Olweus and Limber (1999) name seven behaviors of bystanders in bullying: (1) initiate the bullying behavior; (2) actively support the bully; (3) less actively support the bully; (4) passively support the bully; (5) act as disengaged onlookers; (6) show disdain for the bully; and (7) defend the victim (cited in Jeffrey et al., 2001). Understanding the role of the bystander in bullying is thought to yield great potential in understanding how to prevent bullying behavior. Indeed, these roles are highlighted in Valley Middle School's bullying prevention program as the "circle of bullying" in the hopes that students will come to understand the public aspect of bullying and how peer intervention can help.

Bullying behavior can include verbal abuse in the form of racial and ethnic slurs, and can be centered in hate. This form of bullying can be especially toxic to students who are representative of cultural identities that are different from the mainstream. Adolescence is an important period of identity development. As middle school adolescents explore their unique identities they also begin to explore their ethnic and cultural identities (Gay, 1994; Tse, 1999). Tse identified four stages that diverse youth go through in the development of cultural identity:

1. Ethnic unawareness—during early childhood, characterized by little, if any awareness of ethnic differences;
2. Ethnic ambivalence—during late childhood and young adolescence characterized by avoidance of recognition of personal ethnic differences;
3. Ethnic emergence—characterized by experimentation with other ethnic identities, and also the beginning of acceptance of their ethnicity.
4. Ethnic identity incorporation—characterized by acceptance of their differences and the search for additional information about their ethnicity.

According to Brown and Leaman (2007), middle school adolescents that represent ethnic minorities are likely to be in the "ethnic ambivalence stage." The development of a strong sense of ethnic identity is important for a healthy self-concept in adolescent youth. This can become very difficult when middle school students attend schools such as Valley Middle School in which the majority of students represent White European American backgrounds. In addition, adolescents begin to understand elements of power structure in school and that there is a stigma attached to being ethnically "other" (Lee, 2005). This, especially when coupled with the absence of culturally relevant curriculum (Coulter & Smith, 2006; Fu, 1995), can render a student's ethnic identity invisible. For adolescents who are already ambivalent about their ethnic identity, this kind of environment is difficult to navigate. How can a middle school student develop a strong sense of ethnic identity within oppressive power structures, the absence of culturally relevant curriculum, and, on top of that, an onslaught of emotional and verbal abuse? Culturally and ethnically diverse adolescents who are subjected to bullying are particularly vulnerable because of the stages of ethnic identity development that they must pass through.

BULLYING AT VALLEY MIDDLE SCHOOL

Valley Middle School is making efforts to address issues of bullying. The adherence to team teaching and the focus on community building reflect a commitment to create a tenable middle school atmosphere for students. The Olweus program is an overt effort to address issues of bullying. It is a schoolwide program that involves faculty and staff at varying levels. It is a research-based program, and websites selling the program claim to reduce bullying behavior by 50% to 70%. The goal of this program is to incorporate bully-prevention discourse throughout the school.

At Valley Middle School, videos (which are created by faculty as an addition to the Olweus program) emphasize the "circle" of bullying which includes individuals who are the: (1) bully; (2) henchman/follower; (3) supporter; (4) passive bully; (5) passive supporter; (6) disengaged onlooker; (6) possible defender; (7) defender of the victim; (8) victim. Students are given language and concepts to help them understand that bullying is damaging, is a public process, and can be mitigated through peer support. The program itself has a strong foundation in the research of Olweus (Olweus, 1993a, 1993b; Olweus & Limber, 1999). The Center for the Study and Prevention of Violence at the University of Colorado, Boulder has named the Olweus program as a "model program." It is research-based, has undergone rigorous follow-up studies, and includes vital characteristics, such as a schoolwide emphasis and means for faculty and staff to address bullying on an ongoing basis. It should be noted that this paper explores subtle, complex aspects of bullying and is not meant to be a criticism of the Olweus program.

DESCRIPTION OF METHODS—COLLECTION AND ANALYSIS

I collected data for this study over a 2-year period. Data sources included observations, formal and informal interviews and discussions with participants and their parents, and school artifacts. Observations were conducted during extracurricular activities and events in which there was somewhat limited adult supervision. I was granted access to such events because I had a working relationship with the school. Formal interviews were audiotaped and transcribed. Informal interviews and ongoing discussions were noted and archived in a research journal and used as a foundation for follow-up interviews. Participants included three eighth grade immigrant girls: Bella, a second generation Persian American; Amy, a first generation Vietnamese American; and Shanti, a second generation Indian American. All three girls attended Valley Middle School. Ongoing drafts of vignettes underwent participant checks (Connelly & Clandinin, 1990), and revisions were made accordingly. Though there are trade-offs between validity and traditional generalizability, according to Becker (1992) and Stake (2000), because of the richness of data collected early on in the study I decided to focus on this research as a single case.

Data were analyzed using Ecker's (1966) process of qualitative problem-solving and Polkinghorne's (1995) narrative analysis in tandem. There are five phases in Ecker's process of qualitative problem-solving. First, as data are collected insights are scattered and don't congeal into a coherent whole. In the second phase, patterns emerge, but are still somewhat abstract. Writes Barone (2000) "tentative relationships between qualities are apprehended. These patterns of qualities present themselves as fractured fragments, but fall short of providing an ultimate theme or central set of insights around which the emerging story can be woven" (p. 195). In this phase, the researcher continues to read and reread data and reflect on the data, perhaps taking a shot at writing up a vignette or beginning a narrative construction (Barone, 2007). As the researcher continues to navigate the data, the third phase begins, and that is when a "pervasive quality" (Barone, 2000, p. 196), theme, or metaphor emerges. Data congeal and the researcher can begin to pursue story lines. In phase four the pervasive quality becomes what Ecker calls the "qualitative control" (cited in Barone, p. 196), and elements of stories can be worked into the construction or omitted, as needed. In the final phase of the process, the final story emerges, with the qualitative control tested through story elements.

In this study, once the qualitative control emerged from the data using Ecker's process, I began Polkinghorne's process. Reading and rereading the corpus of data, I began the storying process, configuring the data into a storied account. Thus, I began data analysis using Ecker's qualitative problem-solving process and then moved into Polkinghorne's process as I made recursive movements between the data base as a whole and the emerging story to check that there were no contradictions. Data that did not contradict the story, but that did not contribute to it were omitted. The following vignettes are a result of this process.

In addition to the narrative analysis and for the purposes of this chapter, I conducted an analysis that followed Erickson's (1986) modified analytic induction. For this phase of analysis the entire corpus of data was read and reread to generate assertions. Each assertion was subjected to a process of warranting, that is, weighing the evidence both confirming and disconfirming the assertion. Assertions that survived as stated or revised are listed in the next section along with discussion that demonstrates how each assertion is portrayed in the corresponding vignette. It is important to note that the presented excerpts do not represent the only confirming evidence for that assertion (Barone, 2000; Erickson, 1986; Graue & Walsh, 1998; Polkinghorne, 1995).

NARRATIVE CONSTRUCTIONS

The following narrative constructions emerged from the data collection and analysis procedures. Following the vignettes are the assertions that resulted from the Ericksonian analysis. The vignettes themselves are not meant to prove the assertions, but are offered as compositions (Barone, 2007) that resulted from the narrative analysis. Consult Chapter One of this volume for a thorough discussion of what constitutes narrative research and how a narrative construction counts as research.

Each vignette emerged from the data base as illustrative of the data. Again, each does not represent the *only* confirming evidence of assertions, but should be read as representative of all of the confirming instances. The vignettes are offered consecutively, without interruption or discussion, offering the reader the chance to transact (Rosenblatt, 1978/1996) with the stories. Following the vignettes are the assertions and discussions that will draw from the vignettes and the assertions that resulted from the analysis.

The vignettes that follow are faithful representations of the data. Faithful representations differ from literal representations. Faithful representations result from collaboration with participants in interpreting the data. Literal representations would be difficult to determine because there are as many different perspectives on any given event as there are participants. Instead, we strive for what Tim O'Brien, Vietnam veteran and author of the book, *The Things They Carried* (1990) calls the "story-truth." The story-truth is what brings the construction to life for the reader. O'Brien differentiates the story-truth from what he calls the "happening-truth":

> I want you to know why story-truth is truer sometimes than happening-truth. Here is the happening-truth. I was once a soldier. There were many bodies, real bodies with real faces, but I was young then and I was afraid to look. And now, 20 years later, I'm left with faceless responsibility and faceless grief.

> Here is the story-truth. He was a slim, dead, almost dainty young man of about 20. He lay in the center of a red clay trail near the village of My Khe. His jaw was in his throat. His one eye was shut, the other eye was a star shaped hole. I killed him. What stories can do, I guess, is make things present. (O'Brien, 1990, pp. 179-180).

Though all of the vignettes are, of necessity, faithful representations rather than literal representations--story-truth--the reader may be interested in knowing that all but the last vignette were stories that were recreated directly from single events described in interview data with participants and/or their parents or from observations. The last vignette is a composite of many different discussions and is composed to represent what participants expressed in interviews. All of the vignettes went through a series of participant checks.

Researcher bias is disclosed through how a narrative is constructed (Miller, 2005; Richardson, 1990). In the interest of literal transparency, however, I offer the following: Schools like Valley Middle School often cater to mainstream populations (Coulter & Smith, 2006; Fu, 1995). Schools that work actively toward cultural relevance in curriculum (Au, 1980; Ladsen-Billings, 2005; Olsen, 1997) as well as the wider school program (Ancess, 2003; Lucas, Henze & Dontao, 1990) do much to counter the perpetuation of negative stereotypes that can be so damaging to adolescent students (stereotypes that contribute to elements of bullying in middle schools). My bias as a researcher includes the notion that a pluralistic, inclusive, multicultural community (and curriculum) benefits all students.

The vignettes are presented in the next section and are followed by the assertions that were generated from the corpus of data as a whole (along with corresponding discussion).

BELLA: BACK TO SCHOOL SHOPPING

In back-to-school shopping trips for middle school students, parents are superfluous. Bella's mother has come to embrace her new role, and so on that hot August day she left Bella and her older sister to browse the huge section of backpacks in the center of the department store while she took her young son to the boys section to look at clothes. Thirty minutes later they made their way back to the backpack section. Bella was waiting for them, holding several in her hands.

"I've narrowed it down to these three," she said.

Her choices surprised her mother. If she had walked through the section and guessed on three that she thought Bella might pick, she would have guessed none of what Bella was holding.

"What?" Bella asked.

"Nothing … just … I'm surprised by your choices," her mother said.

"They aren't really my first choices," Bella admitted. Her mother was intrigued. Was Bella actually considering price?

"So, show me your first choices," she said.

Bella started leading her mother around the section. She pulled one off the rack.

"My first choice is this one," she held it up. Exactly what her mother would have thought she would choose … white with small hearts, part classy, part playful. She looked at the price tag. It was cheaper than the ones Bella was still holding.

"So why don't you get it?" Bella's mother asked.

"Because it's what the popular girls will have. If I choose that, I will look like a wannabe."

"Okay, so what's your second choice?"

Bella led her mother around the racks toward the opposite end of the display. She bent over and pulled one off a bottom rack. Different from the first, but a pattern and cut that looked like Bella's taste.

"I like this one, too, but this is what the Goth group would wear. The Goths are kind of druggies."

"Oh, so don't get that one," her mother said, taking it from her and hanging it back on the rack.

And so it went on. They looked through, discussed, and discounted backpacks based on where it would place Bella within the hierarchies and cliques of her eighth grade class.

"No offense, Bella, but do you think everyone at your school categorizes backpacks like this?"

"No offense, Mom, but duh," Bella answered.

In the end, Bella came out with two backpacks. One safe choice that she kind of liked and one over-the-shoulder bag that was a pattern she liked, but a little more risky in cut…not popular wannabe or Goth or anything else. Something not yet categorized. Her older sister, on the other hand, who was an early entrance community college student, picked a backpack in the color she liked, with an eye toward comfort and sturdy straps that wouldn't tear.

One thing was for sure: Eighth grade would be an interesting year.

XAVIER THE ROBOT

Xavier the robot is the star of the weekly Olweus videos at Valley Middle School. Every Wednesday morning a video featuring Xavier or some small cast of characters is shown. Then first period teachers are supposed to facilitate a discussion of the scenario in the video. Some teachers do it consistently, some now and again, and some not at all. Xavier and the Olweus program generate no small amount of ridicule from students. Wednesday lunch hours are a time to relive and joke about them. YouTube videos pop up on the internet, produced by students spoofing the videos. Students joke that Xavier has taught them new ways to bully. The video productions feature overdone special effects with an overused green screen and sterilized scenarios, such as a student grabbing another student's homework and refusing to give it back. Xavier the Robot is often the victim of bullying scenarios; bullies pick on him because he is different.

The Olweus program is designed to generate an awareness of bullying and procedures for response and prevention. A part of the program at Valley Middle School is the Bully Box. The Bully Box is a plastic tub that stays in the front office. When students have been a victim of bullying or have witnessed bullying, they write it down on a piece of paper and put it in the Bully Box. Faculty then respond accordingly. The Bully Box, too, is the object of ridicule. For one, it is rarely used to report bullying. Instead, it, too, is mocked. Friends who joke around with each other can be heard to say, "Stop it or I'll put you in the Bully Box!"

AMY: THE BULLY BOX

Bella and Taylor are sitting together in their computer class, when an office aide walks in with a message for the teacher.

"Do you know her?" Taylor asks Bella.

"Amy?" Bella asks.

"Whatever. She's like Chinese or something, right? She's weird." She says, spinning a bit of her blond hair around her finger.

"Vietnamese. Why do you think she's weird?" Bella asks. She lets her pencil drop on the worksheet they're working on and starts rolling it back and forth between her fingers, like a miniature rolling pin.

"She went to my elementary school last year. She was, like, obsessed with me. She like stalked me! She memorized my phone number and all of the numbers of my friends. She followed me around everywhere. One day I finally got annoyed with it and I told her I didn't want to be her friend. So you know what she does?" Taylor's hair was wound tight around her finger. She started unraveling it in circular movements.

"What?" Bella asks. She stops the pencil abruptly, then starts rolling it back and forth again between her fingers.

"She puts my name in the Bully Box! Can you believe it? The Bully Box!"

Bella bends down to pick up her pencil, which rolled to the floor. "What did the teachers do?"

"Are you kidding? The teacher read it and just laughed. I mean, the Bully Box. How pathetic."

SHANTI—THE BUS RIDE

Shanti dreads the bus most of all. On the bus she has no escape. On the bus there are no adults, except the driver whose attention is on the road, save for an occasional glance in the rearview mirror. On the bus she is confined under the radar of an overworked engine and the echoes of voices that sound brassy and shrill as they bounce off the aluminum walls.

It always starts the same. With Justin. She walks in and looks for an empty seat toward the middle of the bus. Not in the front with the Sevies, but certainly not in the back with the other eighth graders. She slumps off her backpack, hoping this will be one of the days he'll be distracted. Talking to his friends about pot or sex or some other victim. Some conversation that takes him in and makes him forget her. Renders her invisible, which is the best way to be. Not today. She's just sitting down on the sagging green seat when he speaks.

"Dude, she has a unibrow. Look at that thing, Connor!"

Nathan follows his lead, "Dude, why don't you shave? You've gotta shave that thing. Shave those legs and those arms and that unibrow. You're disgusting!"

Shanti closes her eyes and takes in a deep breath. The bus smells like sweat and peanut butter, with a slight twinge of urine ... probably some poor kindergartner from the elementary route who couldn't quite make it home.

"Hey, bitch! We're talking to you!" Justin seems especially persistent today.

"You know my name, Justin. And I'll shave if and when I want to."

"You want to *now*! Come on, it's disgusting. Like your face ... what's with that skin, anyway? It looks like a volcano went off in your head."

The targets are always the same. Her skin, her eyebrows, her hairy arms, her thick black hair, her weight. She can predict it ... could almost say the insults before they do. Her mother told her not to fight back. Just ignore it. But ignoring it only makes it worse. It becomes a game to them to taunt her until she says something. Explodes and says something that only serves to give them more material. So she has to balance on the tight rope between trying to defend herself without fighting and without saying anything.

"Whatever," she says, just to say something. Bella walks in and sits next to her. The driver swings the door shut and lurches the bus forward. Shanti looks at Bella and gives her a wane smile.

"Oh, no," says Bella. "Not again."

"Bella, don't sit next to her! You'll be puking all the way home if you have to look at all of that hair." Bella doesn't say anything. Shanti doesn't mind. If Bella speaks, if Bella defends Shanti, the boys will direct their attention to her.

The bus pulls away from Valley Middle School and both girls rummage around in their backpacks for their cell phones. Cell phones are the great escape. You can text, or call someone, or even just pretend to. You can be there without feeling like you're there. It's a new form of social saving grace. Shanti knows it's not over. But there is a chance, just a chance that the shifting bus will move the boys' attention to something else. It's a lucky day when that happens, because until Connor speaks up, it hasn't even really started. Connor stays quiet at first. He's the alpha, and he waits for his yapping hounds to tire the prey before he comes in for the kill. Justin starts it, Connor finishes it.

When Shanti hears his voice, she slips her phone back into her backpack. It's a lost cause.

"What is she," Connor says to Justin and Nathan, "a fuckin' Araaab?"

"No, she's a fuckin' Hindian," says Justin.

"Hey, Araaaab! You know, you'll have to shave off all your hair. Shave your unibrow, and your arms and your legs, and you'll have to shave your hairy vagina. You know boys don't like hairy Araaaab vaginas."

"Who cares?" says Shanti. She hates that she even has to reply. But it's all a dance. Give a little, a few generic protests to stave off the attack, nothing barbed to invite more.

"Who *cares*? You won't have a boyfriend with that hairy vagina, and you won't have any friends," Connor says.

Bella looks back at them. "I'm her friend."

All the boys laugh. That's it, Shanti thinks. Not Bella, too.

"You know what your problem is, Connor?" Shanti says.

"You and your unibrow?" Connor ventures.

"You're just mad that your mother's balls are bigger than yours!" Shanti hears some chuckles from the seats around her. She smiles a bit, though her hands are shaking.

"Yeah? Why don't you just go back to Arabia where women are hairier than men?" he replies. Then he turns to Justin and Nathan and their conversation continues, quieter now. Shanti still hears the mumbled taunts, but it seems that's the worst for today. She's not off the hook. She'll pay for that one later.

It's Wednesday. Just four bus rides left this week.

BELLA AND SHANTI: THE WALK HOME

One day Bella gets off the bus at Shanti's stop. She'll walk the rest of the way home. Shanti got off ahead of her and is walking quickly toward home, shoulders slumped against the weight of her backpack, head down. Bella steps off the bus and waits for it to pull away.

"Shanti?" she calls. Shanti stops and looks at her. "Wait up!"

Shanti waits while Bella catches up. She pulls on the straps of her backpack to move some of the weight off her shoulders. Bella catches up and they walk together, shoulder to shoulder.

"Do you want me to say something to them?" Bella asks.

"No. Forget it."

"Okay but ... why don't you tell your parents?" Bella asks.

"Are you kidding? My mother will ask me if I say something back to them, and then she will get mad. She says as long as I say something back to them, I'm a part of the problem."

"That sucks," Bella answers. The girls walk in silence for a bit. Shanti lets go of the straps, letting the full weight of her backpack fall back on her shoulders. When they get to the road that is the turn off for Bella, Shanti stops.

"Bella? I'm tired of fighting. I'm just going to ignore it. Okay? I'm just tired."

"Are you sure?" Bella asks.

Shanti nods and starts walking again. She turns back to Bella.

"Bella? Please don't tell. Okay?"

"Whatever. Bye, Shanti."

"Bye, Bella."

Bella starts walking down her street, turning for one more look at Shanti. She's walking forward like she did when she first got off the bus: shoulders slumped against the weight of her backpack, head down.

ASSERTIONS AND DISCUSSION

Assertion One: Valley Middle School is a Socially Stratified Middle School

The first vignette, "Bella: Back-to-School Shopping" introduces the first participant, Bella. Bella's role as a bystander to the bullying is highlighted throughout the vignettes. Bella's role as witness to bullying allowed for a protagonist within the vignettes that is neither victim nor bully, but a powerful observer. Therefore, Bella is present in most of the vignettes.

This vignette is also designed to give the reader some foreshadowing into the stratified social system at Valley Middle School that contributes to the issues of bullying there (in spite of the school-wide attempt at prevention). The vignette serves to introduce one participant, to give a sense of setting, and to give necessary context to the vignettes that follow. It is not meant to represent the only confirming evidence of the socially stratified norms at Valley Middle School.

Clearly, Valley Middle School, like most middle schools, is socially stratified. Students affiliate with cliques that delineate how they act, what they wear, who they can hang out with. In Bella's case, exactly when she is at the age in which she would begin to assert her sense of identity through her unique tastes and interests, she is compelled to fit within the norms of the social designations at Valley Middle School. It is an interesting intersection of conflicting needs: Adolescents need to assert their unique sense of self. At the same time, they need to have a sense that they belong. As in the case of Bella, oftentimes middle school students will subvert their emerging identities in order to conform and thus be accepted and gain a sense of belonging. For adolescent immigrants it is particularly troubling that they will subvert their sense of ethnic identity, so vital to a healthy sense of self, in order to belong.

Assertion Two: The Olweus Anti-Bullying has Been Coopted Into the Culture of Bullying at Valley Middle School

Much of the data collected centers around the contempt the Valley Middle School students feel toward the Olweus program. Discussions of bullying at Valley Middle School moved in nearly every interview to discussions of the videos, the teachers, and the counselors and their part in the Olweus program. Therefore, the second vignette, "Xavier the Robot" was designed to introduce Xavier the Robot and student perceptions of the Olweus program as expressed in the data. This vignette also provides some foreshadowing and a backdrop of irony to the next two vignettes. The vignette itself is more descriptive than literary, but it functions to connect the context to the stories. It also reflects instances in the data that represent ways in which the anti-bullying program itself was co-opted into the culture of bullying at Valley Middle School.

The vignette "Amy and the Bully Box" provides an example of how the Olweus program is coopted into the culture of bullying. Exclusion is a form of bullying. Amy tried to use the anti-bullying program at her school to get faculty support to help her with the exclusion she experienced. She took the Bully Box at face value. Instead of helping Amy and using the disagreement as an opportunity to support and protect Amy, the teacher humiliated her for using the Bully Box for its given purpose, laughing at her in front of the girls that bullied her. The episode follows Amy from her elementary school, which also uses the Olweus program, to Valley Middle School where Taylor continues to use it to isolate Amy. Hence, the vignette shows one way in which the program itself is co-opted into the culture of bullying at Valley Middle School.

It warrants noting that the choice of including Xavier the Robot in the videos is problematic. The premise is clear: Xavier is bullied because he is different. He is awkward and approaches school situations in a clumsy manner, true to his robot character. He is meant to represent those that are "other" at Valley Middle School. The choice of "Xavier" as a name connotes cultural heritage other than mainstream White European American. Bullying scenarios are created around him and his other-ness. For the creators of the videos (faculty at Valley Middle School) Xavier provides ample opportunities to depict bullying without stereotyping students based on differences such as ethnic identity or learning disabilities.

Look a little deeper, though, and the use of Xavier is troubling. Xavier is not a human being. To create a machine as a symbolic form of "otherness" not only insults students who represent cultures and ethnicities beyond the mainstream, but it also desensitizes those that bully them.

Assertion Three: There are Severe Episodes of Bullying at Valley Middle School

The vignette, "Shanti: The Bus Ride" is a literal story of bullying that was expressed in interviews. Though not the only story of bullying episodes at Valley Middle School, it represents one of the most severe because it constitutes bullying centered in hate. It also provides a backdrop to the culture of silence around bullying: Given the severity of this ongoing case of bullying (and the context of the bullying-prevention program) it is surprising that none of the children on the bus, including Bella and Shanti, know what to do to help. The boys themselves seem completely desensitized to the pain they are causing Shanti.

In this situation, Shanti is attacked on all levels: her ethnic identity, her physicality, her gender. Given what we know about adolescent development and ethnic identity, bullying such as what Shanti endures is extremely damaging. In order for adolescents to develop a strong self-concept, they need to be able to explore their own ethnic identity. For children who are emotionally and verbally abused based on their ethnic identity, that process is impaired. The resulting emotional scars can last a lifetime.

Assertion Four: There is a Culture of Silence Surrounding Bullying at Valley Middle School

Interview data reveals that telling on a bully makes things worse for victims. The victim or a bystander tells, the school is forced to respond, and the bully gets called to task. Then the bully gets back at the victim. The bullying gets worse. Though bystanders reported being concerned about Shanti, they also feared that if they informed school personnel, the whole school would think that it was Shanti that told and then everyone would hate her. According to participants, victims of bullying, like Shanti, would rather endure bullying episodes than experience large-scale exclusion. Another possibility is this: The counselor calls the bully and the victim to her office, where they are put together and forced to "work it out". It is better for the victim to simply try to ignore the bullying. Either way, if anyone tells school personnel, things get worse for Shanti. Shanti and her friends are effectively silenced and isolated, with little recourse but to try to ignore the abuse.

Though research indicates bystanders are a promising area for bullying prevention (Sutton & Smith, 1999), there is not much research on the affects of bullying on bystanders. Write Jeffrey, et. al (2001), "(b)ystander psychology is important because witnesses to bullying learn to be passive observers of the victimization of others, and this behavior is not in keeping with the democratic principles underlying public education. Bystanders who are helpless in the presence of another student's victimization learn passive acceptance of injustice" (p. 145).

While passive acceptance of injustice is detrimental to both individuals as well as the tenants of a democratic society, the damage does not stop there. Witnesses to bullying who are themselves navigating their own ethnic identity learn that it is not acceptable to represent cultures that are outside the mainstream. When Bella sees Amy and Shanti being bullied, she perceives that it is not okay to be Persian. For an adolescent already in the ethnic ambivalence (Tse, 1999) stage, this perception interferes with her development as a Persian American girl and, as a result, a positive self-concept.

Large-scale studies, such as those by the American Association of University Women (1993, 2001), reveal that large numbers of children have experienced some form of bullying. A study by Jeffrey, et al. (2001) shows that over time, children are increasingly desensitized to the feelings of the victims of bullying. Victims of bullying can carry scars for a lifetime (Sharp, 1995), and, according to Duncan (1999) bullies suffer long-term consequences of their own. Unfortunately, recent stories in the news include suicides that have occurred as a result of severe, ongoing bullying in school.

Further research on bullying and the implications for bullies, victims, and bystanders is needed. More, it is imperative that we understand the effects of bullying on adolescents of diverse cultural and ethnic backgrounds as well as how to support them through the difficult process of creating a positive, unique sense of identity.

Implications for Further Research

Amy's exclusion and the severe onslaught of racial slurs and sexual harassment that Shanti experiences beg the question: Is the Olweus program really working? The homepage of the Olweus program reports a drop in reported incidents by as much as 50-70%. This study is not meant to raise questions about the Olweus program. However, it shows that further research into the complexities of bullying, especially as these complexities intersect with cultural identity, is needed. In particular, qualitative and narrative research studies that engage participants in in-depth interviewing and field observations will help to fill out a research base that is largely survey driven. We need to understand the perspective of the bullies, the victims, and the bystanders, particularly as they intersect with cultural identity. We need to explore the implications of bullying on the development of ethnic identity of adolescent immigrant students. Further, it is vital that we continue to critically examine what works, and what does not.

REFERENCES

Ancess, J. (2003). *Beating the odds: High schools as communities of commitment.* New York, NY: Teachers College Press.

American Association of University Women. (1993). *Hostile hallways: The AAUW survey on sexual harassment in America's schools.* Washington, DC: AAUW Educational Foundation.

American Association of University Women. (2001). *Hostile hallways: Bullying, teasing, and sexual harassment in school.* Washington, DC: AAUW Educational Foundation.

Atlas, R., & Pepler, D. (1998). Observations of bullying in the classroom. *Journal of Education Research, 92*(2), 1-86.

Au, K. (1980). Participation structures in a reading lesson with Hawaiian children: Analysis of a culturally appropriate instructional event. *Anthropology & Education Quarterly, 11*(2), 91-115.

Barone, T. (2000). Beyond theory and method: A case of critical storytelling. In *Aesthetics, politics, and educational inquiry: Essays and examples* (pp. 191-200). New York, NY: Peter Lang.

Barone, T. (2007). A return to the gold standard? Questioning the future of narrative construction as educational research. *Qualitative Inquiry, 13*(4), 454-470.

Becker, H. (1992). Cases, causes, conjunctures, stories, and imagery. In C. Ragin & H. Becker (Eds.), *What is a case?* (pp. 205-216). Cambridge, England: Cambridge University Press.

Brown, D. F., & Leaman, H. L. (2007). Recognizing and responding to young adolescents' ethnic identity development. In S. B. Mertens, V. A. Anafara, V.A., & M. M. Caskey (Eds.), *The young adolescent and the middle school* (pp. 219-235). Charlotte, NC: Information Age.

Connelly, F. M., & Clandinin, D. H. (1990). Stories of experience and narrative inquiry. *Educational Researcher, 19*(5), 2-14.

Coulter, C., & Smith, M. L. (2006). English language learners in the comprehensive high school. *Bilingual Research Journal, 29*(2), 390-416.

Duncan, R. (1999). Maltreatment by parents and peers: The relationship between child abuse, bully victimization, and psychological distress. *Child Maltreatment, 4*, 45-56.

Ecker, D. (1966). The artistic process as qualitative problem-solving. In E. Eisner & D. Ecker (Eds.), *Readings in art education* (pp. 57-68). Waltham, MA: Blaisdell.

Erickson, F. (1986). Qualitative methods in research on teaching. In M. Wittrock (Ed.), *Handbook of research on teaching* (pp. 119-161). Chicago, IL: Macmillan.

Fu, D. (1995). *My trouble is my English: Asian students and the American dream.* Portsmouth, NH: Boynton/Cook.

Gay, G. (1994). Coming of age ethnically: Teaching young adolescents of color. *Theory into Practice, 33*(3), 149-155.

Graue, M. E., & Walsh, D. J. (1998). *Studying children in context: Theories, methods, and ethics.* Thousand Oaks, CA: Sage.

Jeffrey, L. R., Miller, D., & Linn, M. (2001). Middle school bullying as a context for the development of passive observers to the victimization of others. *Journal of Emotional Abuse, 2*, 143-156.

Kampulainen, K., Rasanen, E., Henttonen, I., Almqvist, F., Kresanov, K., Molanen, B., et al. (1998). Bullying and psychiatric symptoms among elementary school age children. *Child Abuse and Neglect, 22*, 703-717

Ladson-Billings, G. J. (1995). Toward a theory of culturally relevant pedagogy. *American Education Research Journal, 32*(3), 465-491.

Lee, S. J. (2005). *Up against Whiteness: Race, school, and immigrant youth.* New York, NY: Teachers College Press.

Lucas, T., Henze, R., & Donato, R. (1990). Promoting the success of Latino language minority students: An exploratory study of six high schools. *Harvard Educational Review, 60*(3), 315-340.

Miller, J. (2005). *Sounds of silence breaking: Women, autobiography, curriculum.* New York, NY: Teachers College Press.

O'Brien, T. (1990). *The things they carried.* New York, NY: Broadway Books.

Olsen, L. (1997). *Made in America: Immigrant students in our public schools.* New York, NY: The New Press.

Olweus, D. (1993a). Victimization of peers: Antecedents and long-term consequences. In K. H. Rubin & J. B. Asendorph (Eds,), *Social withdrawal, inhibition, and shyness in childhood* (pp. 315-341), Hillsdale, NJ: Erlbaum.

Olweus, D. (1993b). Bullying at school: What we know and what we can do. Oxford, England: Blackwell.

Olweus, D., & Limber, S. (1999). *Bullying prevention program*. Boulder, CO: Center for the Study and Prevention of Violence.

Polkinghorne, D. E. (1995). Narrative configuration in qualitative analysis. In J. A. Hatch & R. Wisniewski (Eds.), *Life history and narrative* (pp. 5-24). London, England: The Falmer Press.

Richardson, L. (1990). *Writing strategies: Reaching diverse audiences*. Newbury Park, CA: Sage Publications.

Rosenblatt, L. (1978/1996). *The reader, the text, the poem: The transactional theory of the literary work*. Carbondale, IL: Southern Illinois University Press.

Sharp, S. (1995). How much does bullying hurt? The effects of bullying on the personal wellbeing and educational progress of secondary aged students. *Educational and Child Psychology, 12*, 81-88.

Stake, R. E. (2000) Case studies. In N. Denzin & Y. Lincoln (Eds.), *Handbook of qualitative research* (pp. 435-454). Thousand Oaks, CA: Sage Press.

Sutton, J., & Smith, P. (1999). Bullying as a group process: An adaptation of the participant role approach. *Aggressive Behavior, 25*, 97-111.

Tse, L. (1999). Finding a place to be: Ethnic identity exploration of Asian Americans. *Adolescence, 34*(133), 121-138.

Whitney, I., & Smith, P. (1993). A survey of the nature and extent of bullying in junior, middle, and secondary schools. *Educational Research, 35*(1), 3-25.

CHAPTER 4

IT'S NOT BLACK AND WHITE

Stories of Lived Experience, Reading, and Assessments

Susan V. Piazza

This chapter weaves stories of lived experience into traditional literacy assessments and challenges "struggling reader" labels placed on many young adolescent Black males. The researcher narrates her own positionality and addresses how White female teachers might critically examine their own bias during assessments. Sociocultural theories and mixed methods provide a lens for analyzing interviews, assessments, and teachers' roles. Participants shared their views of masculinity, race, and "being cool" during reading, which contextualized retelling and comprehension assessments. Implications for practice include ways that other White female teachers might increase cultural competencies, work toward critical pedagogies, and build relationships with diverse students.

As a faculty member and supervisor of graduate students working in a large, urban after school reading program, I worked with primarily African American youth from lower socioeconomic and working class families. The reading program's goals included socially and culturally

Voices From the Middle: Narrative Inquiry By, For, and About the Middle Level Community
pp. 55–81

responsive instruction, but we found ourselves discouraged by the theoretical gap between recommended assessments and the sociocultural perspectives we held. Many of the common assessments used in after-school reading programs seemed problematic because they did not inform instruction in useful ways. Instead, they created hierarchies and labels. We wanted to work against labels and find new ways to approach assessments more productively. Would our student assessment outcomes differ across texts that mirrored their own social, cultural, and linguistic backgrounds?

During this time, I developed new understandings of sociocultural theories and antiracist pedagogies. This chapter explores my learning experiences as I worked with young adolescent Black males during an early career research project. It shares discoveries about my own beliefs as a White woman and the role I played during this study that examined how young adolescent Black males interpreted various multicultural texts. At the time, I wondered which text they would prefer. Would they relate better to texts that represented their own lived experiences? How would various assessments portray their thinking?

Concerns about literacy development and young adolescent Black males receive significant national attention. African American males have high dropout rates, and their experiences in schools between the ages of 9-13 can predict future income, college attendance, and jail time (Kunjufu, 2002). National Assessment of Education Progress (NAEP) statistics consistently point to achievement gaps between Black and White students (Vanneman, Hamilton, Anderson, & Rahman, 2009). Assessments are one of the primary means that educational systems use to set up and maintain these racialized disparities, which then perpetuate the social construction of Black males as *struggling readers*. Literacy development for young adolescent Black males is central to their academic and future trajectories; therefore, an accurate assessment of student thinking during reading would be a powerful teaching tool. In this chapter, reading is defined as social and cultural practices through which learners make sense of their developing identities and the world around them (Gee, 2000; McCarthey & Moje, 2002). Reading is about understanding and making sense of the world (Freire, 1973), rather than the application of skills alone. The terms Black and African American are used interchangeably in recognition that both terms are about equally preferred in our racialized national discourse. As well, the terms diversity and students of color are used to broaden the discussion when addressing ways that White educators can work toward equity and inclusiveness beyond Black and White issues.

This chapter describes my attempt at exploring the disconnect that exists between sociocultural theories of literacy and assessments in an effort to find more culturally sensitive ways to evaluate student thinking. First, the chapter begins with a narrative about my role as the researcher.

A methods section then provides background on participants, procedures, materials, and data analysis. The third section provides the theoretical framework used to conceptualize the study. Next, interview findings reveal the boys' prototypical masculine views of themselves; their uneasiness about discussing race with me, the White researcher; and, their attention to active play and "being cool." These discussions contextualized the assessments. The following section presents critical reflections on how my beliefs and practices changed over time as I reflected back on the study. The chapter closes with an examination of the implications for practice and suggests ways that other White female teachers might increase their cultural competencies, work toward critical pedagogies, and build relationships with diverse students.

RESEARCHER'S ROLE

It is important to reveal that I, as the principle investigator, am a White, middle-class female who is developing a critical pedagogy and incorporating antiracist practices into my teaching and research. My physical presence and the lack of shared lived experiences with the study participants were contributing factors in the outcomes. However, the design and context of the study purposefully represents actual occurrences in many classrooms across the United States since the majority of teachers are White, female, and middle class (Au & Raphael, 2000; Garcia & Guerra, 2004). Therefore, I chose to turn the lens on my own practice during this study with the boys who attended tutoring sessions during the prior year. Even though I was in a position of authority as the reading program supervisor, I felt largely underprepared to support fair assessments of their thinking and plan instruction in culturally relevant ways. As I conceptualized the study, I questioned my entitlement to research the literacy practices of African American males. I thought about ethical issues surrounding race, class, and power in the research design. I was unsure, but naïve enough to proceed.

Now that a few years have passed, I am better able to reflect on these issues. This retrospective analysis has helped me to come to terms with my own assumptions and biases about how to engage young Black adolescent males with texts and identify relevant instruction. These reflections led me to think more critically about how I work with graduate students in clinical settings around issues of assessment. It is my hope that this story will help others, especially White female teachers, join in the process of deconstructing their own assumptions about race and gender and explore alternative assessment practices that might better serve students unlike themselves.

With an overrepresentation of White, female, and middle-class teachers in increasingly diverse classrooms, there is a critical need to explore our social positionality in the teaching and learning process. Regardless of labels that position Black males as struggling readers, many scholars argue that it is more accurately a racialized society that created assessment practices in schools, which then creates and maintains these deficit labels (Ladson-Billings, 2006; Lewis, James, Hancock, & Hill-Jackson, 2008). If White teachers, like me, do not recognize their own social locations and influence on labeling Black males as struggling readers, then they will be unable to promote equity and dismantle social hierarchies in schools and society (Banks, 1996).

METHODS

Revisiting data from my earlier study (Piazza, 2006), a narrative inquiry approach (Clandinin & Connelly, 2000) was used to explore how Andre, Pablo, and Tony (all pseudonyms) talked about lived experiences in relation to reading multicultural texts. Interviews, oral retellings, and comprehension questions provided agency for the boys within an assessment context. When interviews are less structured and treated as conversations, narratives can emerge when least expected (Riessman, 1993). While many assessment settings maintain a positivist stance toward measuring the understanding of a reader, narrative inquiry shifts the emphasis to the teller's point of view and reveals, to the extent possible, how readers understand themselves and the world around them. In keeping with sociocultural perspectives, narratives allow tellers to share past experiences and relate them thematically to current events or phenomena (Alvermann, 2000), which in this case is reading.

An interpretive stance (Merriam, 1998; Wolcott, 2001) informed data collection, analysis, and reporting from a naturalistic perspective (Lincoln & Guba, 1985). Together, these mixed methods allowed exploration of alternative forms of data analysis and representation (Eisner, 1997). The centrality of student voices along with multiple data sources support credibility and trustworthiness in the representation of data and findings. As well, multiple sources of data helped to blur the boundaries between sociocultural perspectives on reading and the positivist stance of many assessments. First, a within-case analysis provided insight on the ways that each student responded to texts, followed by a cross-case analysis that helped identify three overall themes that were consistent across all three cases (Yin, 1994).

Participants

Participants were selected from a larger pool of candidates according to the following criteria: (1) 10 or 11 years old, (2) African American male, (3) participant in the literacy program, and (4) no formal reading disability. They were on the cusp of adolescence: Andre and Tony were 10, and Pablo was 11. Adolescent youth is generally recognized as ages 10 through 15 (Roney, 2001) and adolescence may begin as early as fourth grade (Moje, 2008). Often, awkward periods of transition from childhood to adulthood characterize adolescence, rather than the critical time in which social, cultural, and political influences help to construct their developing identities. Therefore, these young adolescents provide unique insights for educators about how they view themselves and their worlds, which then contextualize their understandings of texts.

During my supervision of the after-school reading program at the university, I established relationships with the boys over a period of 1 year, which provided prolonged engagement and built trust (Lincoln & Guba, 1985). Andre, Pablo, and Tony attended large urban public schools that consisted of approximately 98% African American students. Their families were working-class and demonstrated a commitment to literacy and the academic success of their sons. This was evident through interactions with the families and the boys' regular attendance. All three families talked with me about helping their sons avoid the "struggling reader" label. As well, they wanted to work against the "at-risk" factors attributed to large urban areas with violence and other social casualties due to geographic and economic conditions.

Andre described himself as a good reader who sometimes had "trouble." He shared stories of violence, guns, and drugs from his previous neighborhood. He said it was a "cool" place to live, but scary, too. His father was a police officer and moved the family to a "safer" and "nicer" neighborhood. Andre had a positive attitude and liked to tell jokes and laugh. He came to our first session neatly dressed, with a fresh buzz cut, and a great big smile. What impressed me most was his ability to think deeply about the readings and connect his own lived experiences to ideas in the texts. Andre was confident and clearly articulated his interests, thoughts, and feelings.

Pablo was soft-spoken and very polite. He demonstrated a desire to please adults and he identified himself as a "good" reader and a "good" student. Pablo paid close attention to details and illustrations in the texts. He was neatly dressed and wore his hair in short braids. He was enthusiastic during discussions. He was confident in his reading abilities, and made personal connections selectively. He did not reveal a great deal of lived experience in relation to the texts he read. Pablo's talk was controlled and academic and sometimes seemed superficial. I was cautious with questions in order to elicit his own thoughts instead of what he thought might be the correct answer. Pablo's case reminded me that my presence influenced the research process.

Tony positioned himself as a "good student" who read and understood texts, but also resisted the "good student" identity to be "cool." He clearly delineated the two by explaining he enjoyed books in school, but did not at home or with friends. The same applied to his friends. He had a great sense of humor and provided candid remarks. A lively personality and a no-nonsense approach during the interviews were the norm. Even though Tony offered to participate willingly in our research sessions, he often asked how many questions we had left and when we would be finished. He bantered with me on several occasions such as "Please don't ask me to explain," and "I knew you was gonna say that." While he may not have been completely comfortable with interviews and assessments, he provided straightforward remarks, which made his thinking more transparent than that of Andre or Pablo.

Procedures

Andre, Pablo, and Tony attended five individual sessions, one for each of the four texts, plus a summative session where follow-up questions explored earlier responses. I explained to them that they were helping me learn more about how they interacted with texts and that they were free to express anything about the texts or the research process. During each session, they listened to an audio recording of the book and followed along. This study did not focus on oral reading proficiencies; but rather, how lived experiences influenced thinking about texts. Therefore, the books were audio taped by an African American male voice for three reasons: (1) to control for oral reading proficiency, (2) to ensure an authentic reading of text written in dialect, and (3) to provide consistent delivery across four texts. After listening, the boys retold the story, answered 10 comprehension questions, and engaged in a semistructured, open-ended interview that elicited narratives about their lived experiences.

Selected Texts

Herein lies the heart of my story and my positionality as researcher. Two texts represented multicultural features and issues, which I perceived as good matches for the boys' developing identities: *Three Wishes* (Clifton,

Table 4.1.   Characteristics of Literature

| | *Literature* | | | |
Literature Traits	*Enemy Pie (Munson, 2000)*	*Three Wishes (Clifton, 1993)*	*The Best Friends Club (Winthrop, 1989)*	*Heroes (Mochizuki, 1995)*
Gender	• Male	• Female and male	• Female and male	• Male
Character ethnicity	• European American	• African American	• European American	• Japanese American and others
Linguistic format	• Standard English*	• African American dialect	• Standard English*	• Standard English*
Themes	• Friendship enemies	• Friendship luck/wishes	• Friendship rules	• Friendship/ enemies discrimination
Setting	• Suburban	• Urban	• Suburban	• Rural
Readability	83.7	85.3	82.2	83.1

*For lack of a more suitable linguistic term, "Standard English" represents the written language found in most printed texts.

1993) and *Heroes* (Mochizuki, 1995). Two texts featured White, middle-class characters: *Enemy Pie* (Munson, 2000) and *The Best Friends Club* (Winthrop, 1989). I perceived these texts to be very different from the boys' developing identities. At the time, I expected that Andre, Pablo, and Tony would connect better with texts that looked like and sounded like them. See Table 4.1 for a description of social, cultural, linguistic, and structural features of each text. Reading ease was determined with the Flesch-Kincaid formula (Barry, 1980). Minimizing differences in text structure and readability strengthened the credibility and comparison of sociocultural features.

Enemy Pie (Munson, 2000) is a book about two White middle-class boys in a suburban neighborhood. They begin as enemies, but through a scheme involving an "enemy pie," the two become good friends. The illustrations portray basketball, trampolines, tree houses, and other outdoor activities. *Three Wishes* (Clifton, 1993) is about a male-female friendship that falls apart over an argument about a lucky penny. A version of African American dialect and an urban setting are key features. *The Best Friends Club* (Winthrop, 1989) portrays a male-female friendship between two White, middle-class characters that create a list of club rules, which leads to the conflict and resolution of their friendship. The story is set in a suburban neighborhood. *Heroes* (Mochizuki, 1995) is set during the Vietnam War era and features a Japanese American boy who cannot prove to his friends that his family members are war heroes. His friends insist he looks like the enemy. They are ruthless in their teasing and pursuit of him as the enemy during war games. The story is set in a rural town and contains diverse characters.

Data Analysis

There were three data sources: interviews, oral retellings, and comprehension questions. The interviews were primary data sources because they contextualized participants' perspectives toward texts. Students provided open-ended retellings immediately following the reading (Goodman, Watson, & Burke, 2005). Then, I asked 10 comprehension questions modeled after the Qualitative Reading Inventory-4 (QRI-4) (Leslie & Caldwell, 2005).

Interviews

Andre, Pablo, and Tony's interviews were audio recorded and transcribed for accuracy with careful attention to any inflections, pauses, and variations found in oral speech (Riessman, 1993). To discover and clarify themes, I read and reread the transcribed data using a systematic and inductive approach (Mishler, 1991). Narrative analysis requires parsing units of speech into categories or themes (Gee, 1999; Riessman, 1993). These themes represent lived experiences as they relate to the four texts. Each case was analyzed to identify patterns, followed by a cross-case analysis to identify similarities across all three (Yin, 1994).

The following themes emerged as the most consistent across Andre, Pablo, and Tony's discussions: masculine views of themselves, uneasiness talking about race, and high levels of activity. I will limit discussion to these three, as they are the most salient themes related to the boys' lived experiences as connected to these texts. They are also the most significant in terms of how my beliefs influenced this study. For further information on themes such as linguistic differences, neighborhoods, violence, and conflict resolution, see Piazza (2006) and Hall and Piazza (2008). My attempt at representing the boys' narratives might not accurately represent their lived experiences (Denzin, 1989); however, flawed as these representations may be, they provide much needed insight into the positivist nature of most assessment approaches that do not include learners' narratives. Table 4.2 presents a few sample units of speech in each thematic category.

Table 4.2.   Thematic Units of Speech About Developing Identities

Theme	Definition	Sample Narrative
Masculinity	• Comments made about their gender or the character's	• "I don't got no girl shirt." [Looking at his own shirt] (Pablo)
Race/ethnicity	• Talk about skin color or lived experience.	• "No offense, but all these people in this book is light skinned." (Tony)
Activities	• Activities and events that are referred to as interesting and fun.	• "… they can be playin' video games or they can be shooting air rockets at each other." (Andre)

Oral Retellings

Two kinds of retelling analyses provided different ways to view this data. First, participants received a percentage score for correctly identifying story elements such as characters, events, plot, theme, and subtleties (Goodman et al., 2005). Second, a *text-related thinking* analysis (Feathers, 2002) parsed retellings into units of language that represented kinds of thinking, including, but not limited to, character description, thoughts and feelings, conditional statements, conclusions, evaluative statements, and levels of summarization. This protocol was much like narrative analysis (Gee, 1999; Riessman, 1993), but the taxonomy for kinds of thinking was predetermined and applied to the retellings of stories. For further information on this protocol, see Feathers (2002) and Piazza (2006). Interraters checked both retelling analyses and this check resulted in a reliability of 95%.

Comprehension Questions

Ten comprehension questions for each story produced percentage scores based on accuracy. These procedures were similar to Leslie and Caldwell's (2005) QRI-4 procedures. Each assessment consisted of five explicit and five implicit questions with predetermined answers. A group of 18 primarily White female graduate students worked together to create these questions for each text, in an effort to increase validity.

THEORETICAL FRAMEWORK

Sociocultural theories of literacy informed the methods and materials in this study. Within this framework, all language and literacy experiences have important social and historical origins (Bakhtin, 1986; Gee, 1999; Vygotsky, 1934/1962). Reading is a social and cultural act that helps students understand their developing identities and the world around them (Freire, 1973; Gee, 2000; McCarthey & Moje, 2002). There is ample sociocultural and critical research available on youth culture and out-of-school literacies that engage diverse learners at the middle level (Coiro, Knobel, Lankshear, & Leu, 2008; Lewis & Moje, 2009; McGill-Franzen & Botzakis, 2009); about boys' literacies (Newkirk, 2002; Smith & Wilhelm, 2002; Tatum, 2005); and specifically, on African American male literacy and achievement gaps (Tatum, 2005; Vanneman et al., 2009). There is also much available on the complex identities of adolescent learners and literacy practices in schools (Hall, 2007; McCarthey & Moje, 2002; Moje, 2008). However, there is scarce sociocultural research examining reading and assessment of middle level learners.

Developing Identities of Young Adolescents

Current theories around literacy development emphasize the situated nature of identities that change across activity, time, and place (McCarthey, 2002; McCarthey & Moje, 2002; Sarup, 1996). The idea of a static identity for young adolescents is problematic. McCarthey (2002) noted that traditional views of identity may be static, but more progressive views of identity are flexible and multiple. Students' backgrounds and lived experiences help them to filter their understandings of the world; including the texts they read (Bruner, 1986). Readers may position themselves in relation to texts based not only on how they see themselves, but also on how others see them (Tatum, 1997).

There is a recursive relationship between the way readers read themselves, read texts, and read the world (Freire, 1973). This relationship may explain how students enact certain identities during interactions with texts. Gee (2000) asserts that identity, as recognized within various communities or settings, influences the ways individuals choose to position themselves. Situated meanings in texts have powerful implications on the social worlds of readers in and outside of schools (Gee, 1999). The ways that learners experience texts and assessments in schools may not always reflect their social and cultural models of race, class, and gender (Compton-Lilly, 2004). Enacting sociocultural frameworks that value identities and lived experiences during interactions with texts may reveal new possibilities in meeting the needs of underserved students rather than simply ranking their performance.

Within a sociocultural framework, it is not appropriate to measure comprehension in one snapshot without regard to social, cultural, and historical influences on student thinking (Delandshere, 2002; Shepard, 2000). In today's accountability era, practitioners measure reading comprehension quantitatively to show growth on test scores. Whack's (2008) mixed-methods study revealed that young adolescent African American boys showed reading improvement only in qualitative measures when compared to quantitative assessments.

Assessment as Inquiry

Assessment as inquiry provides a framework for viewing student thinking with genuine curiosity, rather than as something tangible to measure. Powell and Van Zandt Allen (2001) argue that a problem for students in middle school is that they must answer questions they have not posed themselves. There are several naturalistic ways to uncover and contextualize readers' social constructions of themselves in relation to how they understand texts. Listening to students themselves, as they are the primary source, provides the most credible means to assess thinking. Retellings are another effective way to do this.

Reader retellings are a credible and valid means for evaluating understanding (Brown & Cambourne, 1990; Feathers, 2002; Goodman et al., 2005; Leslie & Caldwell, 2005). A single approach is never able to represent reader thinking; however, retellings are widely accepted because they elicit a narrative about the text from reader perspectives. Narrativization of lived experiences through oral retellings is a shared cultural practice often attributed to African American communities (Gee, 1989). Oral retellings as a form of assessment alongside other qualitative lenses can provide a culturally sensitive approach to research (Tillman, 2002) that examines the developing understandings of young Black males.

THEORETICAL REFLECTIONS ON INTERVIEWS

Readers tend to align or contrast their identities with others, including characters found in the texts they read (Mishler, 1999). As I conceptualized this study, I wanted to explore new understandings of sociocultural issues as they related to reading assessments. I understood that learners were marginalized when their identities were not valued during reading (Hefflin & Barksdale-Ladd, 2001). The interview narratives of Andre, Pablo, and Tony uncovered their specific views of themselves as urban, Black, male readers. The texts elicited narratives within a traditional assessment context in which power relations, gender differences, and cultural differences existed between students and researcher. This representation of the boys' narratives was only a slice of their realities. There was also the inevitable influence of my own interpretations. Further reflections on researcher bias will follow.

Cultural models serve as lenses through which readers perceive the world. Cultural models are the assumptions about what adolescents think is "normal" (Gee, 1999). Andre, Pablo, and Tony's interviews uncovered their cultural models of what it meant to be a young adolescent Black male as they discussed the texts. The following narratives reveal that Andre, Pablo, and Tony each talked about their lived experiences in prototypically masculine ways. Their cultural models of young adolescent masculinity remained consistent across all three boys. The following three themes appeared across all three participants: (1) prototypical masculine views, (2) uneasiness discussing race, and (3) high levels of activity.

Prototypical Masculine Views

One of the most surprising findings from my perspective was the fact that all three participants rejected texts chosen to represent diverse characters and issues. I thought the boys would most identify with *Heroes* and *Three Wishes* because I believed they mirrored the boys' realities. This was not the case. Pablo took issue with the male-female friendship and the main character's appearance in *Three Wishes* when he offered this opinion, "I'd change that boy to a girl cause he look like one … the light eyebrows and eyes, how they look (pointing to the curve in Victor's eyebrow) … and you know how girls be hangin' out together and stuff." According to Andre, Pablo, and Tony, the main character's behavior in *Three Wishes* was problematic because he had long talks with his female best friend and shared his feelings openly. Pablo indicated that only girls play with girls and it was unacceptable for him to play with girls. Andre shared, "I didn't like it very much … the part where they always talk and stuff, and they didn't do anything fun." While all of the books dealt with friendship, *Three Wishes* focused on friendship in a primarily female style, the interpersonal. Miller explains that this concept of masculinity stems from fear of looking or acting like a girl (cited in Pollack, 1998).

When talking about the main character in *Heroes*, Pablo talked about Donnie's "feminine" behavior with disapproval: "Well, if you don't get your way [you don't] just start to run away and stuff, when other people are bein' mean to you … he like whimpers when he don't get his way." I anticipated the boys would identify with Donnie's character because his friends treated him unfairly because of his ethnic background. Again, this was not the case. Andre, Pablo, and Tony shared the same prototypical male standard that Pollack (1998) describes as a burden that requires them to avoid shame such that, even when they are victimized, they must shrug it off and hide outward signs of being upset (Pollack, 1998).

Andre shared some lived experiences from his own neighborhood. In a quiet voice, he said, "They argue sometimes and…say, 'I gonna kill you.' They can threaten you … sometimes they be serious and they get a real gun and sometimes they will shoot you." Andre's cultural model of urban neighborhoods included violence as a norm. This unexpected narrative, from my perspective, about violent neighborhoods emerged during our discussions of war games and guns found in the *Heroes* text. Regarding his own experience, he said, "No, never, nobody *ever* bullied me … Nope, cause they won't … Cause they scared of me … because I'm big … [being] big makes a big difference … Yep. But the size don't mean nuthin'. That don't mean I can really fight." He also made sure that I knew he would never bully anyone else. Rather than perceiving the discrimination based on ethnicity, Andre thought that Donnie was bullied because of his small size rather than his Japanese American appearance and the social climate of that time. Brown (1999) documents the strong influence that Black males receive through multiple media in which hypermasculine gender roles are the norm. This is particularly true for young adolescent urban males who experience violence and must "take care of themselves." Hypermasculine and negative experiences found in urban neighborhoods often interfere with healthy development of adolescent Black male identities (Swanson, Spencer, Dell'Angelo, Harpalani, & Spencer, 2002).

Issues of Race

I recognize that as a White woman, regardless of prolonged engagement, I would not be the most natural choice with whom these boys would discuss race. However, one premise of the study was to examine how a teacher like me can learn from students' identities during reading and text discussions. I also recognize that race is a socially constructed idea that is systemic in the United States, particularly in schools and texts. In reference to Nobel laureate Toni Morrison, Ladson-Billings and Tate (1995) argue that the use of the term "race" is problematic and under-theorized, and it marginalizes individuals, yet its "metaphorical life is so completely embedded in daily discourse that it is perhaps more necessary and more on display than ever before" (p. 63). I did not initially understand this, and I still have not arrived at any final destination. I will always be constructing new understandings of racism, antiracist pedagogies, and culturally relevant teaching from a White woman's perspective. Tony was a very helpful informant that pushed my thinking on this issue.

"It don't make the story better ... I just don't like seein' light skinned people all the time. I wanna see my color, too," confided Tony after reading a story about two African American characters in *Three Wishes*. As we talked about the text, I asked if he read about many "dark skinned" characters before, and he responded, "When I'm in an animal book, I see dark skinned animals." I probed further about real people and he said, "Not so much." Tony's perception of racialized texts confirmed the cultural dissonance experienced by many students of color during reading (Hefflin & Barksdale-Ladd, 2001; Hornig, 2008; Sanacore, 2004). Tony was not privy to claims about the lack of high quality African American literature; however, he knew from lived experience that texts typically marginalize his "skin color."

Tony also shared, "That's just the way [books] are supposed to be." As a young adolescent, he was already positioning himself in ways that aligned with socially constructed patterns of race in America. His viewpoint positioned White characters as the norm and "dark-skinned" characters outside of the norm. The ways that readers see themselves within the context of reading is complex and not easily measured. Yet teachers and researchers often claim objectivity when measuring students' understandings of texts. While this might be Tony's perceptions about race, it is important that teachers and researchers not generalize, because there are many other factors that influence developing adolescents and their understandings.

Andre and Pablo were uneasy discussing race with me and only mentioned in passing their views on characters that did not look like them or live in neighborhoods like theirs. Rather than focus on skin color, Andre and Pablo were more concerned with what the characters wore, the games that they played, where they lived, and whether or not they were cool. These perspectives relate to their developing identities around class, gender, and race and are not mutually exclusive. As well, my presence and the context of our meeting was not an obvious space for discussing race explicitly.

Readers situate themselves and enact various identities depending on a particular place, time, and setting. Interactions with texts and surroundings are ambiguous and unstable and draw from the lived experiences that are rooted in homes and communities (Gee, 1999). Tony's connections to *Heroes* related to his attention to race and literacy. He indicated that Donnie was Chinese and said, "His face and his eyes ... his kind of skin, but no offense ... Chinese people have light skin." As he referred to Donnie's light skin, Tony was implicitly noting the difference between my light and his dark skin by saying "no offense." This led to a brief dialogue about discrimination based on appearance. I asked Tony if he had ever experienced anything like that and he said, "Like Martin Luther King?"

I said, "Yes, like him."

Tony thought for a moment and then in a very excited, almost inaudible voice said, "Ya'll, you … mumble … Yo skin was terrorizin' us!" and the following discussion occurred:

Researcher: What?
Tony: I don't know. Where you was born from? (still excited)
Researcher: In Canada.
Tony: My bad.
Researcher: Why? What were you gonna say, it's all right, go ahead.
Tony: Uh, go on.
Researcher: So, if I were born in America what would you say?
Tony: It was like, if you was born in America and you treated us like that, that wouldn't be fair. But it's all over now.
Researcher: You're right. I agree with you; it's not fair.
Tony: You wasn't even born back then, was you?
Researcher: I never saw it, but I did live in the South for a while where a lot of this bad stuff happened.
Tony: How long, when did all that bad stuff stop happening?
Researcher: They're still working on it, don't you think?
Tony: Hmm … You can go on, cause I don't really want to talk about this.

Even though this was uncomfortable dialogue for both of us, Tony was willing to discuss race with me, unlike Pablo or Andre. Tony referred to the legacy of racism attached to his skin color while again acknowledging my Whiteness. He acknowledged the power differential between us because he was sensitive about discussing critically sensitive issues with a White female researcher in a formal context. It was evident that race and power were at the forefront of Tony's thinking, which revealed to me his keen understanding of the racialized society we live in, its origins, and its influences on his developing adolescent identity. Regardless of my positionality as a researcher and authority in this setting, it was my awkwardness and inability to address my own Whiteness and talk with ease about power relations and race that prevented a more critical discussion. Had I been more aware of my own power and position, I may have facilitated a more open dialogue around issues of race past and present as it connected to the text. Nevertheless, Tony clearly felt strong personal, cultural, and historical connections to the issues elicited by the text. I walked a fine line between exerting my authority by inappropriately interrogating him, and my ethical obligations to respect his comfort level and willingness to discuss race with me. I respected his request to end it there and was grateful that he shared that much.

As Tony's example demonstrates, African American males have a greater chance of experiencing cultural conflicts with the texts they read (Delpit, 1995; Tatum, 2005). However, Andre, Pablo, and Tony demonstrated multiple kinds of cultural conflicts with texts, not simply based on race and/or gender, which is what I originally set out to explore. The relationship between reading and Black adolescent males has much room for improvement because traditional approaches have failed them (Tatum, 2005). The unstable nature of my dialogue with Tony demonstrated that we were both navigating new territory, and rather than ignore it completely, we ventured into dialogue and attempted to address the racialized society we live in, as well as the power relations between the two of us.

High Levels of Activity

The boys talked about outdoor activity and play as a prototype for all "cool" adolescent males, which, of course, is not every adolescent male's reality. Andre, Pablo, and Tony identified *Enemy Pie* as the "coolest" text due to its fun activities, interesting plot structure, and the devious nature of an "enemy pie." All three participants consistently talked about their own interests and neighborhood activities when discussing texts. In reference to *Enemy Pie*, Andre shared, "I like car racing, moto racers, drag racing ... and playin' Playstation, playin' Frisbee, playin' with [the] dog, talkin' to my dog, and takin' my dog for a walk." He also contrasted his interests with the activities in the text when he mentioned his favorite video game, Max Payne, which is a popular violent videogame with an urban setting. The trampoline in *Enemy Pie* elicited this experience: "Kids didn't play together sometimes ... but sort of in the back, out of the way ... there was always shooting guns on the fourth of July, which is really dangerous." The urban setting was prevalent across all participants' discussions, but Andre provided the most detail when he remembered his experiences with trampolines.

Andre and Tony both connected their interest in cool clothing when discussing *The Best Friends Club*, which is set in a White, middle-class neighborhood. Andre said, "Yeah, I would make one [character] 'Bullet.' I would name the girl 'Arius' and the boy 'Aaron' [after his cousins]." When I asked what these characters would look like, he said, "Well, Bullet would have a big old head and have on some sweet clothes ... They're sweet [high-pitched]! You have jeans and a jersey, watch, glasses, and a chain. There you go...and some Air Force Ones. Aaron would have a big head, kind of chubby, and some sweet clothes. Arius would be just regular with fashion." Andre was applying his cultural model of what cool adolescents might wear in his urban setting. Kirkland and Jackson (2009) address the notion of "coolness" in the lives of 11-14-year-old Black males in urban settings. They report that clothing is a large part of these boys' literacies because what one wears communicates developing identities and status, and clothing can subversively challenge negative stereotypes of Black males.

Participants shared their disapproval of feminine activities that were uncool. Unless the characters were engaged in outdoor activities, it seemed that the boys rejected the text. Pollack (1998) explains that boys show emotions, but through action-oriented play, such as climbing trees together, racing one another, or playing outdoor games. This perspective helps explain why my assumptions were off base. *Three Wishes*, which represented African American characters and dialect, contained the least activity. Andre said, "I didn't like it very much ... the part where they always talk and stuff...they didn't do anything fun!" Similarly, for *Heroes*, all three considered the main character, Donnie, "wimpy" because he cried when his friends bullied him into playing the enemy. Newkirk (2002) says that the constructs of such cultural understandings of masculinity can be resistant to change. Andre, Pablo, and Tony were candid about why they would not recommend the latter two texts to their friends. Tony shared that his friends would certainly not be interested in reading these books outside of school, and only if required during school.

THEORETICAL REFLECTIONS ON ASSESSMENTS

Assessments are cornerstones of the White middle-class cultural model of reading achievement. However, when young adolescent African American males' views of the world contextualize their reading, there is an opportunity to counter the images of failing and underachieving readers (Tatum, 2005). The narratives shared above lend a contrastive backdrop for presenting the assessment outcomes. This section briefly reports findings from the three assessments. For a lengthier discussion of assessments, refer to Piazza (2006).

Oral retellings aligned consistently with the boys' interviews, while the comprehension questions represented the boys in a way that contradicted their personal connections with texts. In all but their favorite text, *Enemy Pie*, the comprehension question outcomes were opposite when compared to the boys' retelling scores. The data from both retelling protocols triangulated with interview findings. All three data sources worked together to demonstrate how the boys' lived experiences and views of the world were central to their assessment outcomes.

Retelling Guide Analysis

The retelling guides aligned with the boys' personal narratives about masculinity and their acceptance and/or rejection of characters. Noteworthy were the lower scores found in the area of character description and details for *Three Wishes*, and relatively higher scores in the area of character description in *Heroes*. Table 4.3 displays the mean retelling scores across all texts. Analysis of interview data reveals that participants attended to details in *Heroes* because of the complex plot structure and outdoor activity, but did not attend to the details in *Three Wishes* because of their lack of interest. The boys' views of themselves toward the social, cultural, and linguistic features in *Three Wishes* influenced their retelling guide scores in a negative way, which aligns with interview data and second form of retelling analysis, Text-related thinking (TRT). As well, the mean retelling guide scores in *Enemy Pie* proved to be higher for all three boys.

Text-Related Thinking (TRT) Retelling Analysis

The TRT (Feathers, 2002) analysis resulted in findings that were similar to interviews and retelling guides. The TRT revealed cognitive ways in which the boys thought about texts. This approach provided a form of narrative analysis, which required parsing oral retellings into units of meaning. It did not rank or score the retellings, but instead provided a comparison of thinking across and within each text. Consistent with the interview data and retelling guides, *Enemy Pie* elicited a high level of personal connections evidenced by the higher number of units of causality, comparisons, conclusions, and speculation (higher levels of thinking). For

Table 4.3.   Mean Retelling Guide Scores

	Enemy Pie	*Three Wishes*	*The Best Friends Club*	*Heroes*
Characters	7.3	7	7	7.3
Character description	4	3.3	5	5
Theme statements	6.3	6.6	6.6	5
Plot statements	7	7.6	8	8.3
Events	17	14.8	14.8	15.8
Optional	7	2	6.3	4.3
Total mean scores	48.6%	41.5%	47.8%	45.8%

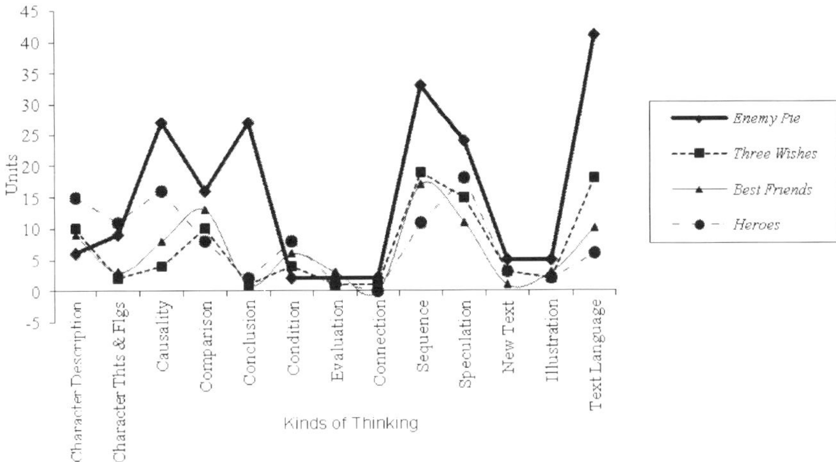

Figure 4.1.   Mean units of text-related thinking.

the most part, *Enemy Pie* elicited higher units of analysis across most categories of thinking. Notice how *Heroes* elicited more talk about character description, which related to interview data that focused on Donnie's wimpy behavior and inability to stand up for himself.

Not only did TRT remain consistent with interviews and retelling guides, it provided a comparison of character description items across both retelling protocols. The two retelling analyses together revealed detailed opportunities for instructional planning regarding character analysis, problem solving, alternative perspectives about masculinity, summarizing information, and critically examining texts. However, a limitation of many oral retelling guides is the quantitative value placed on recall. Lengthier retellings result in higher scores and brief summaries result in lower scores, regardless of personal connections. For example, Pablo's scores were higher than Andre and Tony's due to his attention to detail, and Tony's were lower because he provided higher levels of summary, as revealed in the TRT analysis. Figure 4.1 represents an overview of the units of narrative that described the boys' text-related thinking.

Comprehension Scores

The comprehension questions produced relatively lower scores for *Enemy Pie*, which was in direct contrast to the boys' connections and stories of lived experiences shared during interviews. However, all three boys

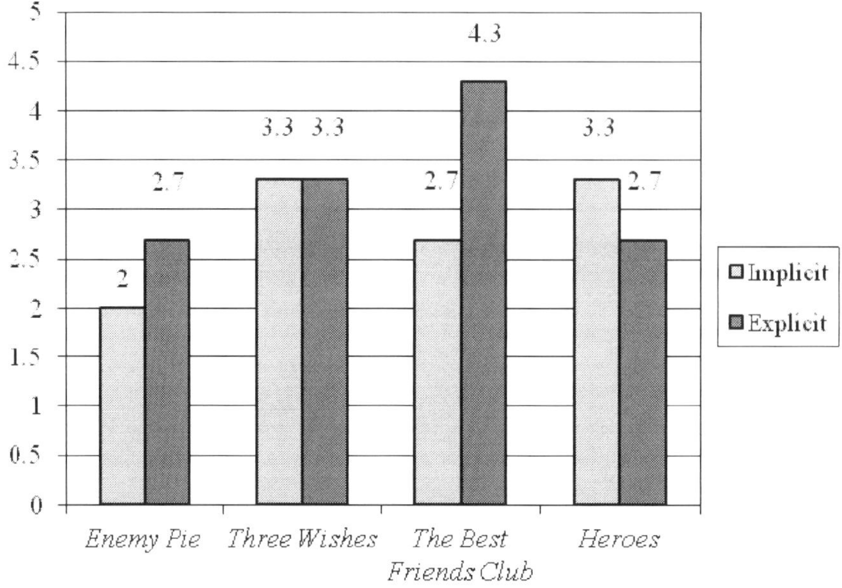

Texts

Figure 4.2.   Mean comprehension scores.

scored higher on the comprehension questions on the texts they considered less interesting and in which they had fewer personal connections. Figure 4.2 displays the mean comprehension scores across all three texts. Note the slightly higher scores in the texts that caused social and cultural dissonance for the boys' conceptions of masculinity, regardless of the multicultural representations in those books.

Comparing Assessments

Both retelling protocols provided interpretive data that consistently aligned with interview data, which would have been inaccessible without understanding how the boys' developing adolescent identities related to each text. When asked which assessment they thought was better at showing their understandings of each text, all three participants preferred retellings. Tony said, "[I like to] retell because it's like reading the story all over again." Retellings revealed how each participant retold details about characters, events, and subtleties. This assessment revealed how well each participant was able to summarize. In addition, retelling provided a lens into how each participant viewed the plots and themes of each story. There were many ways to determine instructional opportunities relevant to Andre, Pablo, and Tony's individual ways of understanding text. For example, all three focused less on character development than on events and activities. However, their attention to character details went up in the two stories that they rejected due to unacceptable feminine behaviors they perceived in the male characters. This relates to research that posits an overemphasis on masculinity in urban settings and youth cultures (Brown, 1999).

REFLECTIONS ON RESEARCH PROCESS

I began this study with the expressed intention of exploring the issues of race, gender, and language during reading assessment contexts. However, findings revealed a more serious need to understand how students narrate their lives during reading and thinking about texts. Retellings and interviews have the potential to help White female educators, and others, learn about students' perspectives, and they can help to interpret the instructional needs of diverse learners. Outcomes also validate retelling analysis as a credible and culturally sensitive way to assess thinking.

According to the comprehension scores, I might have assumed that students did not fully comprehend the texts that they most identified with. Instead, comprehension scores aligned with text features such as length and readability. I learned to question these traditional indicators of comprehension, which characterize so many assessments. It did not matter how participants' lived experiences connected to texts in this assessment, because answers were either correct or incorrect. Comprehension questions focus on predetermined answers and low levels of thinking such as basic recall, rather than higher levels of thinking. At the time, I knew that this assessment was the most traditional measure because predetermined answers essentialize one true meaning. However, I now recognize that the way questions were developed by primarily White middle-class female graduate students (for validity) also perpetuated the White middle-class bias that exists in so many reading assessments.

I continue to recognize new insights on my own bias, and the influence of Whiteness on everything I do. I hope that teachers and researchers will see my bias and examine their own, even if they think they have already arrived at an antiracist destination. The intersection of students' identities, text features, sociocultural issues, and assessments are complicated and nonlinear, just as teachers and researchers' beliefs are. Turning the lens on ourselves is a necessary precursor to helping all learners and working toward a more equitable pedagogy that might truly address achievement gaps. The contrast between lived experiences and assessments helped to identify multiple ways to engage in literacy instruction. As well, this approach helped confirm the heavy influence of social and cultural experiences on reading and meaning making. Their developing adolescent masculine identities proved to be powerful constructs that influenced thoughts about themselves during reading and assessments. As a female researcher, I completely underestimated the powerful role of gender and I was blinded by my own bias.

Teachers are always at risk of misunderstanding students' perspectives. To my surprise, the boys overwhelmingly preferred the texts that featured White, middle-class characters, which appeared counter-intuitive for me at the time. It was true that readers identified with texts that represented them, but on their own terms, and not based on race, class, or gender alone. While I was theoretically aware that all students see themselves in many different ways, this study provided a deeper understanding of those sociocultural complexities as a teacher and researcher. It helped me recognize my biased beliefs about what matters to students and who determines the interpretations of texts. Even though I defined reading as a transaction between readers' lived experiences and texts, it still took me by surprise that their interpretations were so different from my own. I understand more deeply my role, and teachers' roles, in the process of evaluation.

I learned that selecting texts based on race, gender, and language was, at best, superficial and, at worst, based on a subtle form of racism. In selecting the texts, I overemphasized physical appearance and socially constructed notions of dialect, and failed to account for the many complex ways that young adolescent Black males see themselves. If you asked me 3 years ago, I would have authoritatively responded with my interpretations of the outcomes at that time, which was that the findings were counter-intuitive because of gender. I, along with others, thought these were fascinating findings. My research earned a high profile award from an international organization; and even then, the bias, race, and power issues were not fully addressed and dealt with in a systematic way. Yet, it was only over time and through writing, rewriting, and much reflection that I recognized my role in the research process that influenced these outcomes. Ask me in another year, and I will likely have new interpretations of my Whiteness in relation to literacy learning, research, and my work with students of color. Teachers and researchers can learn from these boys' narratives that we must all turn the lens on ourselves if we are to live out critical pedagogies and become culturally relevant educators.

IMPLICATIONS FOR PRACTICE

There are no simple answers. We need to question and recognize our own beliefs, which will then inform how we respond to students' cultural models and lived experiences, and how these play out academically. Teachers can transform traditional assessments into open and naturalistic spaces by listening to students' perspectives. This will uncover tacit understandings about developing adolescent identities in relation to literacy. Infusing sociocultural perspectives into educational [and evaluation] settings can change the academic success and future trajectories of young adolescent Black males (Kunjufu, 2002; Tatum, 2005). This is especially important for teachers and researchers working with urban youth who are at greater risk of academic failure and prison (Tatum, 2005).

A significant outcome of this study was the inadvertent learning that helped me to see new ways of identifying natural opportunities for critical engagements with texts. As I parsed out Andre, Pablo, and Tony's tacit views of what it meant to be young Black adolescent males in this urban setting, I came to the realization that all educators must strive to continuously develop their critical teaching practices. In this study, the boys' overemphasis on masculine identities interfered with their ability to take a critical stance toward the texts. Had they assumed a critical stance, they might have challenged Donnie's friends in *Heroes* who treated him unfairly due to his ethnic heritage and physical appearance. They might have recognized that both multicultural texts purposefully challenged stereotypes and gender norms. Andre, Pablo, and Tony adopted the twentieth century portrayals of men who are "men or mouse, He-man or 98-pound weakling" (Brown, 1999). In order to address these flawed stereotypical or prototypical perceptions of themselves and others, it is important that teachers learn how to explore multiple perspectives and encourage critical examinations of texts (Hall & Piazza, 2008), regardless of their own backgrounds or beliefs.

Finally, teachers and researchers will never be culturally competent if their evaluations of students do not align with their sociocultural and/or antiracist beliefs. In order to address the achievement gap and positively impact the academic success of traditionally marginalized students, we must begin to assess thinking more naturalistically. In this way, teachers and researchers can assume an inquiry stance when working with diverse learners in order to plan appropriate instruction. This study reveals that evaluation needs to include a nuanced understanding of students' cultural models of the world in order to meet their instructional needs. Granted, instruction needs to include specific strategies and skills identified by assessments; however, assessments must not supplant our openness to students' identities as enacted during assessment contexts.

Teachers should avoid evaluation of student thinking with questions that have predetermined answers. Instead, middle level students need to answer questions related to their own lived experiences and interests (Powell & Van Zandt Allen, 2001). When we see students as informants instead of passive test takers, we begin to increase our cultural competence as teachers. Perhaps then, there is real potential for White female teachers to gain competency and more productively address the so-called achievement gap between young adolescent African American males and their counterparts.

REFERENCES

Alvermann, D. E. (2000). Narrative approaches. In M. L. Kamil, P. B. Mosenthal, P. D. Pearson, & R. Barr (Eds.), *Handbook of reading research III* (pp. 123-39). Mahwah, NJ: Erlbaum.

Au, K. H., & Raphael, T. E. (2000). Equity and literacy in the next millennium. *Reading Research Quarterly, 35*(1), 170-80.

Bahktin, M. M. (1986). *Speech genres and other late essays* (V. McGee, Trans.). Austin, TX: University of Texas Press.

Banks, J. A. (1996). *Multicultural education, transformative knowledge, and action: Historical and contemporary perspectives.* New York, NY: Teachers College Press.

Barry, J. G. (1980). Computerized readability levels. *IEEE Transactions on Professional Communication, 23*(2), 88.

Brown, J. A. (1999). Comic book masculinity and the new black superhero. *African American Review, 33*(1), 25-42.

Brown, H., & Cambourne, B. (1990). *Read and retell: A strategy for the whole language/natural learning classroom.* Portsmouth, NH: Heinemann.

Bruner, J. (1986). *Actual minds, possible worlds.* Cambridge, MA: Harvard University Press.

Clandinin, D. J., & Connelly, F. M. (2000). *Narrative inquiry: Experience and story in qualitative research.* San Francisco, CA: Jossey-Bass.

Clifton, L. (1993). *Three wishes.* New York, NY: Doubleday Books.

Coiro, J., Knoble, M., Lankshear, C., & Leu, D. J. (2008). *Handbook of research on new literacies.* Mahwah, NJ: Erlbaum.

Compton-Lilly, C. (2004). *Confronting racism, poverty, and power: Classroom strategies to change the world.* Portsmouth, NH: Heinemann.

Delandshere, G. (2002). Assessment as inquiry. *Teachers College Record, 104*(7), 1461-1484.

Delpit, L. (1995). *Other people's children: Cultural conflict in the classroom.* New York, NY: The New Press.

Denzin, N. (1989). *Interpretive biography.* Newbury Park, CA: Sage.

Eisner, E. W. (1997). The promise and perils of alternative forms of data representation. *Educational Researcher, 26*(6), 4-10.

Feathers, K. (2002). Young children's thinking in relation to texts: A comparison with older children. *Journal of Research in Childhood Education, 17*(1), 69-83.

Freire, P. (1973). *Pedagogy of the oppressed*. New York, NY: Seabury Press.

Garcia, S. B., & Guerra, P. L. (2004). Deconstructing deficit thinking: Working with educators to create more equitable learning environments. *Education and Urban Society, 36*(2), 150-168.

Gee, J. P. (1989). The narrativization of experience in the oral style. *Journal of Education, 171*(1), 75-96.

Gee, J. P. (1999). *Introduction to discourse analysis: Theory and method*. New York, NY: Routledge.

Gee, J. P. (2000). Discourse and sociocultural studies in reading. In M. L. Kamil, P. B. Mosenthal, P. D. Pearson, & R. Barr (Eds.), *Handbook of reading research III* (pp. 195-207). Mahwah, NJ: Erlbaum.

Goodman, Y., Watson, D., & Burke, C. (2005). *Reading miscue inventory: Alternative procedures*. Katonah, NY: Richard C. Owen.

Hall, L. A. (2007). Understanding the silence: Struggling readers discuss decisions about reading expository text. *The Journal of Educational Research, 100*(3), 132-41.

Hall, L. A. & Piazza, S. V. (2008). Critically reading texts: What students do and how teachers can help. *The Reading Teacher, 62*(1), 32-41.

Hefflin, B. R., & Barksdale-Ladd, M. A. (2001). African American children's literature that helps students find themselves: Selection guidelines for grades K-3. *The Reading Teacher, 54*(8), 810-819.

Hornig, K. T. (2008). An interview with Rudine Sims Bishop. *The Horn Book Magazine, 84*, 247-260.

Kirkland, D. E., & Jackson, A. (2009). "We real cool": Toward a theory of black masculine literacies. *Reading Research Quarterly, 44*(3), 278-297.

Kunjufu, J. (2002). *Black students. Middle class teachers*. Chicago, IL: African American Images.

Ladson-Billings, G. (2006). From the achievement gap to the educational debt. *Educational Researcher, 35*(7), 3-12.

Ladson-Billings, G., & Tate, W. (1995). Toward a critical race theory of education. *Teachers College Record, 97*(1), 47-68.

Leslie, L., & Caldwell, J. (2005). *Qualitative reading inventory-4 (QRI-4)*. New York, NY: Longman.

Lewis, C. W., James, M., Hancock, S., & Hill-Jackson, V. (2008). Framing African American students' success and failure in urban settings: A typology for change. *Urban Education, 43*(2), 127-153.

Lewis, J., & Moje, E. B. (2009). *Essential questions in adolescent literacy: Teachers and researchers describe what works in classrooms*. New York, NY: Guildford Press.

Lincoln, Y. S., & Guba, E. G. (1985). *Naturalistic inquiry*. Thousand Oaks, CA: Sage.

McCarthey, S. J. (2002). *Students' identities and literacy learning*. Newark, DE: International Reading Association.

McCarthey, S. J., & Moje, E. B. (2002). Identity matters. *Reading Research Quarterly, 37*(2), 228-238.

McGill-Franzen, A., & Botzakis, S. (2009). Series books, graphic novels, comics, and magazines: Unauthorized texts, authorized literacy practices. In E. H. Hiebert (Ed.), *Reading more, reading better* (pp. 101-117). New York, NY: Guilford Press.

Merriam, S. B. (1998). *Qualitative research and case study applications in education.* San Francisco, CA: Jossey-Bass.

Mishler, E. G. (1991). Representing discourse: The rhetoric of transcription. *Journal of Narrative and Life History, 1,* 255-280.

Mishler, E. G. (1999). *Storylines: Craftartists' narratives of identity.* Cambridge, MA: Harvard University Press.

Mochizuki, K. (1995). *Heroes.* New York, NY: Lee Low Books.

Moje, E. B. (2008). The complex world of adolescent literacy: Myths, motivations, and mysteries. *Harvard Educational Review, 78*(1), 107-154.

Munson, D. (2000). *Enemy pie.* Vancouver, BC: Raincoast Books.

Newkirk, T. (2002). *Misreading masculinity: Boys, literacy, and popular culture.* Portsmouth, NH: Heinemann.

Piazza, S.V. (2006). Case studies of transactions between boys' lived experiences and texts. *Dissertation Abstracts International, 67*(05). (UMI No. 3211018)

Pollack, W. (1998). *Real boys: Rescuing our sons from the myths of boyhood.* New York, NY: Henry Holt.

Powell, R., & Van Zandt Allen, L. (2001). Middle school curriculum. In V. A. Anfara (Ed.), *The handbook of research in middle level education* (pp. 107-24). Greenwich, CT: Information Age.

Riessman, C. K. (1993). *Narrative analysis.* Newbury Park, CA: Sage.

Roney, K. (2001). The effective middle school teacher: Inwardly integrated, outwardly connected. In V. A. Anfara (Ed.), *The handbook of research in middle level education* (pp. 73-105). Greenwich, CT: Information Age.

Sanacore, J. (2004). Genuine caring and literacy learning for African American children. *The Reading Teacher, 57*(8), 744-753.

Sarup, M. (1996). *Identity, culture, and the postmodern world.* Athens, GA: University of Georgia Press.

Shepard, L.A. (2000). The role of assessment in a learning culture. *Educational Researcher, 29*(7), 2-14.

Smith, M. W., & Wilhelm, J. D. (2002). *Reading don't fix no Chevys: Literacy in the lives of young men.* Portsmouth, NH: Heinemann.

Swanson, D. P., Spencer, M. B., Dell'Angelo, T., Harpalani, V., & Spencer, T. R. (2002). Identity processes and the positive development of African Americans: An explanatory framework. *New directions for youth development* (Fall), 73-100.

Tatum, A. (2005). *Teaching reading to black adolescent males: Closing the achievement gap.* Portland, ME: Stenhouse.

Tatum, B. (1997). *Why are all the black kids sitting together in the cafeteria?* New York, NY: Basic Books.

Tillman, L. (2002). Culturally sensitive research approaches: An African American perspective. *Educational Researcher, 31*(9), 3-12.

Vanneman, A., Hamilton, L., Anderson, J. B., & Rahman, T. (2009). Achievement gaps: How black and white students in public schools perform in mathematics and reading on the National Assessment of Education Progress. *National Center for Education Statistics.* Retrieved from http://nces.ed.gov/nationsreportcard/pubs/studies/2009455.asp

Vygotsky, L. (1962). *Thought and language* (E. Hanfmann & G. Vakar, Eds.). Cambridge, MA: M.I.T. Press. (Original work published 1934)

Whack, S. J. (2008). To grade level and beyond: A study examining the impact of intervention styles with fourth grade African-American males. *Dissertation Abstract International, 69*(7), 2654. Retrieved rom http://proquest.umi.com .libproxy.library.wmich.edu/pqdweb?did=1568973221&sid=2&Fmt= 2&clientId=32427&RQT=309&VName=PQD

Winthrop, E. (1989). *The best friends club.* New York, NY: Lothrop, Lee & Shepard.

Wolcott, H. F. (2001). *Writing up qualitative research.* Thousand Oaks, CA: Sage Publications.

Yin, R. K. (1994). *Case study research: Design and methods.* Thousand Oaks, CA: Sage.

CHAPTER 5

ADOLESCENT READERS' VOICES

Carole S. Rhodes

This chapter tells the story of 6 urban middle school students as they interact with a book and with each other. The study explores the multiple facets that adolescents exhibit in individual, same gender, and mixed gender group settings as they respond to a book. It reveals similarities and differences in responses and in the way that the students react and interact depending on the contexts. This study details the personal connections, the role of literature in readers' lives, and the issues that are at the forefront of their concerns.

More than a half-century ago, John Dewey recognized the importance of prior experience as it affects people's response to stimuli (1931-1932) Louise Rosenblatt (1938/1995), following Dewey, William James, and C.S. Pierce, related this to reading and proposed a theoretical framework for understanding the special relationship developed when a reader's mind intersects with a text. This transactional view of the literary experience, as Rosenblatt (1938) named it, attends to the reader and the text within the social context of the event. It acknowledges the relevance of the total experience. Unfortunately, much of the research in this area thus far has

Voices From the Middle: Narrative Inquiry By, For, and About the Middle Level Community
pp. 83–106

focused only on varying, often discrete, components within the literary experience. The research at times has concentrated on only one aspect of the engagement—text, reader, or context, while ignoring the total experience. The whole is lost to its parts. This study explored the responses of six young adolescents by looking at three dimensions together—text and reader in social context.

HISTORICAL AND THEORETICAL PERSPECTIVE

Early research on response to literature dealt with the degree to which individual readers were able to approximate what were considered "correct" reactions to a text. The background and experience of the reader were viewed as factors which might hamper and interfere with the reader's quest for correct interpretation (Richards, 1991). Rosenblatt (1938/1995) challenged this view as neglecting the element of the reader's psyche and she described the literary experience as one in which a "live circuit [is] set up between the reader and text: the reader infuses intellectual and emotional meanings into the pattern of verbal symbols" (p.25). Thus, according to Rosenblatt, the reader's past experiences, knowledge, and wisdom have great bearing on the meaning as suggested by the text. Meaning then is internally induced and generated by readers as they interact with the words on the page. The transaction between the reader and the text result in the "poem"—the personal meaning created by the reader (Rosenblatt, 1978/1994). Nearly 30 years after publication of *Literature as Exploration*, interest in readers and their responses burgeoned again (see, for example Galda & Liang, 2003; Hebert 2008; Rosenblatt, 2005; Serafini & Ladd 2008). Acknowledging the individual and the unique occurrence involving the mind and emotions of a particular reader is credited as being the incipient force in "reader-response" criticism.

READER, TEXT, CONTEXT

Much research thus far has focused on the reader, sometimes in relation to interacting with a text, but such research does not go far enough. For example, the reader's background knowledge and prior literary experience are seldom investigated. This aspect, almost universally overlooked by previous research, provides the major impetus for this study. The reader in interaction with a text was previously viewed as an isolated, separate entity—not as a part of a context. Thus, prior research is inadequate to answer the question of how readers' (particularly adolescents') prior life experiences, text, and context interact.

The text consists of a unique form and style which can affect a reader's expectations. These expectations can be altered during the reading experience. Thus, the text can guide the reader. Expectations formulated through life experiences as well as by previous literary encounters foster, modify, and enhance the literary experience. The context of response is crucial to the experience. The "cultural setting" (Rosenblatt, 1938/1995, p. 139) or the "interpretative community" (Fish, 1990) along with the reader and the text form a matrix.

Context for response includes the physical or social setting for the generation of the response as well as the context for the collection of response data. The formulation of response can be affected and influenced by the "community" in which the reader resides. The reader's schema is activated as the reader brings certain experiences and expectations to the literary experience. The manner in which readers are asked to respond, such as in individual or in group situations, influences their response.

The possibility of modifying responses in group settings is germane. It is often believed by those involved with adolescents that they are very often influenced by their peers. In examining youngsters' responses to literature in individual settings, then, we also need to investigate whether responses are modified in the "group community" and if they are, how and why this modification manifests itself.

Many psychological theorists note the importance of peers to adolescents (see for example Bosna & Kunnen, 2001; Kroger, 2004). Acceptance and support by their group matter intensely to children of this age. Peer groups provide adolescents with a basis for who they are and how well they do. They provide a forum for the youngster to try on and experiment with different identity roles. Groups can also exert powerful pressures to conform. This potential pressure, or lack thereof, must be studied when evaluating responses of young adolescents in a group setting or context. Costanzo's (1970) study of adolescent boys' responses to judgment questions indicated that almost one-half of the participants modified their responses to coincide with those that they were told had been offered by a group (which, unbeknownst to the respondents, was fictitious). Perhaps the most crucial finding was that the proportion of conformity among twelve and thirteen year olds was greatest. Readers displayed patterns of responses which appeared to be influenced by the contexts or "community" in which they were members. Patterns of responses as they were influenced by the social setting were also found in other studies dealing with adolescents. Particularly with young adolescents, the response offered in a group setting may be modified by that context. This possible modification becomes a much needed area for study.

More than 40 years ago Rosenblatt acknowledged the importance of knowing the reader prior to the literary experience. The question remains, though, whether this important facet in the matrix has been studied fully during the ensuing years. Clearly, it has not. Our understanding of how prior knowledge and experiences of these readers affect, modify, or color their response to a text is incomplete. The way people respond to a text is based on "who they were" prior to, during, and after the experience. Decades ago Rosenblatt (1978/1994) distinguished between the responses of adolescents who experienced disillusionment with friends as it affected their perception of and response to the relationship of Othello and Iago. We must now explore this intrareactional relationship more fully.

Little attention has been devoted to the special, interdependent relationships among the reader, the text, and context. This dynamic triad must be viewed wholly, with neither the reader, the text, or the context viewed as separate entities. Understanding these relationships would enhance our ability to facilitate meaningful encounters with literature. Such insight will bring about more complete understandings of why some children, particularly young adolescents, do not "connect" with books and how teachers might facilitate that connective process. Inherent in such an understanding is a respect for readers that acknowledges them as a crucial part of the matrix. Furthermore, it would help us to understand more clearly the impact of schools on the process of developing life-long readers.

The focus of this study was on young adolescents' responses to a particular novel in individual and group settings shortly after their reading and three weeks after the reading. The researcher looked at the reader, the text, and the context as they meshed to create a transaction. This study therefore investigated multidimensional aspects of readers' responses.

Setting and Participants

The setting for this investigation was a nonsectarian private school in an urban area. In the middle school (Grades 5-8), from which participants were drawn, class size varied from five to 14 students. The school community consisted of middle to upper middle class families. The children were predominately White but there was a small minority of Black children. According to Piaget, readers over the age of 12 are more likely to produce responses which are characteristic of formal operational thinkers. However, research dealing with these young adolescents' responses has been minimal. Literature-based studies focused on this age range have generally concentrated on the group's literary interests, attitudes, or preferences. This study begins to fill the void of response studies of young adolescents.

Procedure for Gathering Data

As part of the selection process, each student was interviewed individually and provided with the opportunity to practice reading a passage and to tape record their responses to written questions. During this interview, the text was given to the participants. Additional individual interviews were then conducted shortly after each student finished the text and three weeks after completion. The participants were interviewed in two separate same gender groups, and a whole group interview was conducted with each group.

Narrative inquiry, the process of gathering information for the purpose of research through storytelling, was used. Field notes, interviews, questionnaires, and orally told stories were used during the process of this narrative inquiry. This form of inquiry was used as a means to get inside the world of the middle school student participants and to hear their voices.

THE READERS

An author's words, like a chameleon, take on different meanings and identities depending on the reader of those words. Creating meaning is a collaborative effort culminating when a reader reacts with a text thus creating a work of art. This section provides profiles of the adolescent participants prior to the experiences initiated for this study. By first knowing them, we can more adequately interpret their ultimate responses. The sections that follow present an intensive look at the participants and their responses after reading a particular text. They reveal concerns of the readers, the role of literature in their lives, and the way the school influenced their interpretation of literature.

Melissa

Melissa, a 12-year-old champion archer, likes solitude. She is a straight A student who was offered a full academic scholarship for the ensuing 4 years of high school. While daydreaming in school, she imagines herself in some far off land, free to roam about and do as she pleases. She sometimes has to remind herself to "listen to the teacher, even if it is boring because I might have to take a test later, and I wouldn't understand how the teacher wanted me to answer." True to her archery skill, she aims for the focal point of what the teacher wants—she zeroes in on the particular point she thinks the teacher is looking for.

Melissa stated that recently she had trouble finding "a really good book that I really could get into and that I really liked." She wanted to participate in this study in the hopes that it would help her "get into reading again." Her favorite books included *Catcher in the Rye*, *To Kill a Mockingbird*, *Helen Keller: The Story of My Life*, and *The Diary of Anne Frank*. Melissa said that she enjoyed these books because she could relate to them. Of *Catcher in the Rye* she stated that she liked it so much because:

> he [Holden Caulfield] was just so different. He didn't care what anybody else thought. He was just all by himself sometimes but he had, well, I could sort of not relate to him but I could understand him. He just seemed so different from other characters who were so good and everything in the other books. He had faults ... he was real.

Keri

Keri, a vivacious 12-year-old, is studying to be an actress. She lives with her mother, a saleswoman in a boutique, and her stepfather, an artist. She sees her biological father once a year. Keri indicated that she generally did not like to read. "It's hard for me sometimes, it also depends on the mood I'm in. It really just depends on everything, the situation that I'm in or whatever." During our talks, Keri mentioned that she used to love to read "but then I stopped and when I tried to read again, I didn't like anything I read. So I just completely stopped and just read whatever I had to read for school—like for a book report or whatever I had to read that was assigned." Keri had no idea why she changed from someone who loved to read to one who now considers reading a chore to be done to satisfy school requirements. During a subsequent meeting, in discussing the kinds of books she would like to read, Keri stated:

> See, I was getting into this kind of teenage books about teenagers going out or whatever and my mother didn't like that because she said they're not, they're not real good books. They're not classics or anything so she wouldn't allow me to read them. So every day she said, "Every time you read a book it has to be approved by me because I don't want you reading junk like that.

Through careful tracing and chronological history, I discovered a distinct parallel between the time Keri started to dislike reading and the time her mother started to monitor her reading closely. This protectiveness and sheltering on her mother's part is even more interesting in light of the fact that Keri has more physical liberties than other students. She is allowed to travel at times and to places that others are not because of their parents' fears for their safety.

Keri discussed the books she did not like much more frequently than those she enjoyed. Keri frequently made reference to people forcing her to read. When she had to read a book she selected books that were short. She said that if she were to look for a book to read, she would "look for problems that may come up that I have; parents that maybe I wish my parents were a little like ... I also would want a book with a conflict that seems really tough and everything but in the end it gets figured out."

Sophia

Sophia, a mature 13-year-old, was able to participate in the study only by juggling her very busy schedule. Sophia felt that her family was "pretty normal. I'm at that stage where me and my mother don't get along fabulously but I think I'll pull through." Throughout our discussions, Sophia revealed a psychological insight that seemed mature for her years. She often used terms such as "underlying meaning," "repressed anger" or "deep-seated hostility." This apparently was due to the fact that her father was a therapist and she reported that they had "nice discussions" about things. Sophia felt that in order for books to be less superficial, they should be about "real problems like drinking or drugs." She said that she devoured the Agatha Christie mysteries and thought she enjoyed them so much because she and her father read the same books and then discussed them.

Evan

Evan was a 14-year-old whose parents were professional performers who appeared in numerous shows on Broadway. For the past 8 years, his mother taught in the school Evan attended, "Both my parents left acting because you can't make enough money to support a family." Evan was quite happy that his mother was not the teacher in any of his academic classes because "she wouldn't want kids to think she's easy on me so she'd be extra hard." During one meeting with Evan, his mother came into the room and asked if she could join us stating "Well I want Evan to know that I have read the book." When Evan asked why she read it, she said "Well, I read everything that you and your sister have to read. We're interested parents and we want you to know that we're interested." Evan said that it might be fun for his mother to join us for a few minutes. Although there was a distinct feeling of warmth and affection between Evan and his mother, I noticed that his mannerisms were modified by her presence. He sat up straighter and noticeably measured his words more carefully. During the minutes that his mother stayed, a dialogue ensued about the book they both read. Commenting on his mother's presence, Evan said "She's always really critical. Every time we see a movie she's very critical, she's always coming down on everything and not focusing on the good points." Later, he said that having his mother participate in the discussion made him uncomfortable. "She was talking away and not shy at all. It's not that easy." Evan describes himself as "a little conceited sometimes. I'm a little vain. Like I worry about my hair. I think I'm sort of fun loving, outgoing. I'm not shy at all." He stated that "I didn't like reading at all until I found out about fantasy. Now I read a lot because I found some great, exciting books that I like." Evan wrote his own book, a fantasy. He was quite proud of the fact that the book was almost two hundred pages long:

> It's long, but it's good. It's a fantasy. It's about a conflict between gods and the two opposing gods who have to pick the chosen ones between those on Earth and the mortals. And the point of view is from the good mortals and they eventually cross the world to the bad guys and kill them.

Ricky

Ricky, a 13-year-old boy, was one of the youngest in his grade. He was the only participant in the study who was Black. He was extraordinarily polite. Ricky was an only child who lived with his mother; his parents were separated for several years. Ricky, like Evan, was a student at the school for many years. "Well I've been here all my life and it's like a family to me." Ricky expected to complete all 12 years at the school but found out after our interviews that the school would not permit him to remain due to his D average.

Ricky did not appear to be shy. However, during our first meetings, Ricky maintained no eye contact with me. Whenever I asked him a question, he would look away; when he was ready to respond, he made strong eye contact. His responses to most questions were very short and terse. He often asked for clarification, at times asking "Well, how should I answer that?" Ricky and Evan were best friends. Ricky collected comic books. The other boys in the study often remarked about Ricky and his comics. Among the boys in the study, and apparently among the boys throughout the school, Ricky was famous for his collection of comic books. Ricky's favorite comics were from a series where "a group is going to save human

beings but the human beings don't like them because they're different."
Ricky could not recall a favorite book. The only memorable reading experiences he recalled involved his comics. He felt that the comics were:

> more exciting to me and I can collect them in a series. It's like a long story.
> Almost like a never ending story because it keeps going on like with comics
> it goes to number 200 then 201 and with books when you read a story, it's
> over.

Dan

Dan, a 6-foot-tall 14-year-old, was a self-proclaimed jock who loved
sports, particularly basketball. He, like Ricky, made little eye contact with
me during our meetings. Dan, more so than the other participants, carefully thought about most answers. He often needed a long time to
respond. Many times during our interviews, he interrupted himself or me
in order to respond to a previously unanswered question. Throughout our
meetings, Dan was interested in what the other participants said. During
each meeting he asked questions such as "Can you tell me who else is in
the study?" or "What did the other kids say?" He was particularly interested in finding out which girls were participating.

Dan lived with his parents and younger brother; two half brothers who
were more than 15 years older than Dan lived on their own. Dan's father
appeared to be much older than most of the other students' parents. During one interview Dan revealed that his father was the same age as some
of his classmates' grandfathers. Besides sports, Dan's favorite hobby was
writing but he admitted that he hardly ever wrote, "Even though I like to
write, I never feel that I have the time ... there's so much for a kid to do ...
I can't fit it all in."

THE READERS AND THE TEXT

The six adolescent readers who participated in this project indicated,
through the extensive interviews, a commonality of concerns and needs.
However, differences emerged, particularly between boys and girls. What
readers brought to the experience enabled them to form their own,
unique transactions with the texts. Under the guidance of the text, out of
his own thoughts and feelings and sensibilities, the reader makes a new
ordering, the formed substance which is for him the literary work of
art. The following analysis and synthesis presents the major themes

which emerged from individual discussions after the participants read the text.

The Text

Izzy, Willy-Nilly by Cynthia Voigt (1995) is a coming of age, realistic novel with a 15-year-old girl, Isobel Lingard, as the central character. The book opens with Isobel, a high school cheerleader, in a hospital. Through flashbacks the reader discovers the events that led up to the hospitalization. Izzy, as she is called, gets the chance many sophomores dream of—a date with a senior, Marco. Izzy does not really like Marco but she decides to go to the party in order to be noticed by the "in crowd." Marco drinks too much at the party. Izzy is offered a ride home by Tony, a boy she likes very much, but she refuses the ride. She fears that others at the party would view her as childish. On the way home from the party, with Izzy in the car, Marco crashes into a tree. Marco walks away from the accident unharmed and later denies remembering anything about the accident. Izzy's right leg is so badly damaged that it must be amputated below the knee.

Girls

Sophia said that at first she felt very "detached" from the book. She began to like the book, however:

> When I realized why she [Izzy] had her leg amputated, I realized that this could happen to anybody. It's not like one of those teenage novels where a boy meets a girl and they fall in love and someone comes in and blah, blah, blah. But it's like something that could actually happen. That's when I really got into the book.

Sophia's move from detachment to engagement with the book was evident as she related how she felt about some of the characters. Her conversation was laced with phrases such as "I could have killed Marco," or:

> I felt very close to Rosamunde, it was like she was one of my friends, I may not have agreed with how she acted all the time, but that's okay, she's a friend, and that's what friends do.

Sophia's engagement was with the characters. She continually focused on the traits of the characters as well as their deeds. Rarely did she discuss events. Melissa indicated that she felt "involved" in the book from the beginning. She specifically targeted the realism of the text:

> It was really realistic. It wasn't like at first I was thinking that she [Izzy] was taking it well and everything and then she broke down and I thought she's more real than I had thought because I thought that if I were in that situation I would have a hard time handling it so well. I really sat and thought about how I would feel … I'd be in a daze and in shock.

Melissa sometimes would "forget who I was when I was reading." "I could see the situations so clearly, it was like I was there." Keri didn't think she would like the book because "in the beginning it was about a drunken driver and I'm not really interested in that. So I thought it was going to be pretty boring but it came out pretty good. I liked it." Keri, unlike Melissa and Sophia, did not indicate any deep relationship with the text. She was detached. Throughout our discussions it became clear that Keri read for information, much like she reported having to do for her school assignments. Further it became evident that whereas Keri maintained a very distant view Melissa and Sophia placed themselves in the events portrayed in the text. Keri made a point of saying "It didn't mean anything to me" or "I didn't feel anything … it was just a book." Keri's "cool detachment" appeared to be a preordained posture that limited her reflective and evaluative processes. In listening to her and watching her, it became increasingly apparent that her distancing was a role she adopted. "I will never relate books to my everyday life. After I finish reading a book I don't think about it at all. I close the book; it's out of my mind." During this part of our conversation Keri's comments were terse and her body posture rigid and formal, almost regal. It seemed that she felt that in adopting this attitude, she set herself above others. When asked why she thought she never related books to her life, Keri replied:

> because I'm so into my own thing. I don't know why but a lot of times I notice that I open a book and I'll think about something totally different. I'm like reading it but my mind is somewhere else … It's like I have to read so I just read and study the answers … they're all just like textbooks.

Boys

Dan felt angry while he was reading *Izzy*. "I was really angry at what happened, the accident." The reported level of his anger seemed to have invaded his reading:

> I didn't get into the book at first, but then when I realized what happened, I
> wanted to find out more details about the accident. Then I really read fast
> and the faster and the more that I read, the more angry I got.

Dan focused on the details of the story. Few of his remarks were directed towards the characters but most related to events. When asked to describe the book Dan replied, "It's about someone who goes to a party and there's drinking going on. There's a car crash then the book tells about what happens." Dan depersonalized the text throughout our discussions. For example, he wandered off into irrelevant details such as "what kind of car it might have been" or "how many floors the school had." When asked to elaborate on what makes a book interesting, Dan replied, "It has to have good description of the events."

Evan, viewing the book from a writer's perspective, attended to details within the text. He reported: "Well, I thought the idea was good, like the plot, like how she [Izzy] deals with things but I would have done it differently." At another juncture, Evan said that when he reads a book "it takes me to different places. I leave myself and enter the book." Ricky, when first given the book, spent considerable time looking at its cover. Based on the fact that the picture on the cover portrays a girl sitting in a chair, he decided that the book would probably be "some romance book about this girl." He thumbed through the book and said he thought it was going to be "hard reading and very small print." He found this not to be the case, reporting:

> Once I started to read it, it was easy reading, it kept the pace. It had a good
> plot you know, about this ordinary girl whose life changed. And I thought
> that that could happen to me; I could relate to it.

Ricky's transaction with the book revealed issues of importance to him. In response to a question about how he would describe this book to a friend, he replied:

> I would just tell them that I read it and it was a nice book about a girl who
> was in a car accident and how she goes through being different. It was an
> abrupt change I think. I guess it would be almost like if I were a boy, I mean
> I am a boy, but if I was, for some strange reason like tomorrow I'd become a
> girl and having to do girl things, things that girls do, things that guys don't
> do. It would be like a very big change and hard to get used to. The stereo-
> types are different. Like I said, guys have a stereotype that the guys are
> much stronger than the women, more macho, stronger. The girls have to be
> ladies, perfect ladies, and nice women. It's like my being black, there's a ste-
> reotype that goes along with it and sometimes it's right and sometimes it
> wrong. I almost thought the book was about me getting accustomed to

things. Like I have to find a special way to fit in. Izzy didn't have one leg, and I don't have white skin.

THE ROLE OF LITERATURE IN READERS LIVES— TRYING ON LIFE THROUGH LITERATURE

The participants in this project exhibited various levels of involvement during the reading of *Izzy, Willy-Nilly*. Throughout the discussions it became apparent that books served specific purposes for these youngsters. All six readers indicated that books helped them "figure things out." During the group discussions this theme became even more pronounced. All participants indicated that this text enabled them to think about issues and confront problems which they might have to face. By placing themselves "in" the text and in the situations confronted by the characters, the youngsters were able to try on different identities and work out possible solutions to the problems they perceived. Sophia "tried to be Izzy at the party. I thought about what I should do. I was so confused. I wanted to be grown up and not appear to be a baby, so I was afraid to accept a ride from Tony." At another point in our discussions, Sophia expanded on this:

> It's like if you're going into a new situation and you really don't know what to do, you want some security, something to hang onto. If you're going into an unfamiliar place, you want someone with you. Izzy will go with me. It's like I had a chance to see the future and check out the place with Izzy.

Like Sophia, Melissa expressed a specific purpose which the reading experience fulfilled:

> It was interesting to think about all the things that happened. It was the kinds of things that I would want to go away and think about. I wanted to sort of close my eyes and imagine what I would do. There were so many different issues to have to deal with. It's just like us, we're trying to grow up and cope with all the stress and things that are ahead of us. It was easier to just read this book and imagine situations and problems. That way, if I mess up, I won't end up like Izzy. I can't truthfully say for sure that I wouldn't have acted like Izzy before, but now I sure wouldn't.

Five of the readers indicated that this reading experience provided them with an opportunity to ponder a situation before they might be confronted with it. The boys, like Sophia and Melissa, indicated that the book served a specific purpose, that of "forcing me to deal with an issue before it happened." "Facing up to the problems of growing up ... without having to experience the real screw up" (Dan). "Looking at what might confront me in the future…Thinking about the consequences ahead of time" (Evan). Laconic Ricky, usually not a man of many words, expressed a similar view of the role that this text played in his life.

> When I read the book and thought about what Izzy, and also Rosamunde and the others were going through, it really got me thinking. I imagined myself in the hospital when my friends would visit, how it would be when I went back to school, but mostly I thought about the party, and what I would do. It was scary and I realized that this probably would happen to me sometime in my life. I really thought about what I'd do. Now I'd do things differently because I had time to think about them.

Similar thoughts were expressed by five of the participants during individual sessions. Keri, the only participant who did not indicate a similar inclination during the individual interviews, changed in the group. Keri did not express any thoughts which indicated that books served any role in her life other than as "things she has to do for school." This changed, however, during our group meetings. During these meetings, Keri, too, indicated that the text served to help her think about situations which she will most likely have to confront in the future.

Summary

The participants' experiences with this text were ones of general involvement for five of the readers, Keri being the exception. The stance adopted by the participants enabled them to evaluate and respond emotionally while maintaining some distance from the events. They related the experiences portrayed in the text to their own lives. They often responded as though they were living the events vicariously. They viewed the text as a window to the future.

All participants indicated that they thought about issues evoked through this reading experience. Each reader's personal perspective on characters, actions, and events portrayed in the text was unique although some overriding themes emerged. Sophia, probing psychological aspects, sought the reasons behind actions which were portrayed. Melissa aimed for specific points, setting her sights on the realistic nature of the text. Keri adopted a detached role as she read. Dan, like a sportscaster, concentrated on details and specific action within the text while trying to figure out "hidden meanings." Evan, viewing the text from a writer's perspective, concentrated on characters and plot. Ricky, creating pictures in his mind, related closely to Izzy and the way she grappled with being different. Like Dan, he too searched for hidden meanings.

Many of these youngsters indicated that for them, this text provided a springboard for them to examine issues and to experience vicariously things which they may confront in the future. Through this reading, they explored a potential life in a safe harbor in a secondary world.

A DIFFERENT CONTEXT: THE GROUPS

The previous section provided a look at the readers' responses to the text during individual meetings. Since youngsters often respond to texts in group settings in school situations, these six youngsters also met to discuss their experiences in groups. The first group meetings included only the same gender participants, with subsequent group meetings including all participants.

The Girls

Sophia, Melissa, and Keri met as a group to discuss the book and their experiences. At first, Sophia and Keri monopolized the conversation. Melissa listened intently and only spoke when she had definite, firm thoughts and opinions. She dealt with direct issues, zeroing in on what her peers said. At first, I had to encourage her to "jump in." She said that she felt funny, just barging into the discussion. It was Sophia, ever the perceptive one, who managed to bring Melissa into the conversation. Sophia pointedly asked Melissa, "What did you think about Izzy's friends?" This apparently helped Melissa get over her initial hesitation and she then participated fully.

The students were generally helpful to each other. While Keri tried to dominate the discussion, Sophia tried to organize the group and provide a supportive environment. Sophia often asked for clarification or expansion of points which Melissa made but she rarely did this with Keri's remarks. Sophia responded and actively appeared interested in what Melissa had to say. This feeling seemed to be a mutual one. They both looked at each other as they spoke. When Keri spoke, there was a distinct change in their behaviors. Sophia, in particular, seemed to react negatively to the way Keri spoke. It appeared that Keri was once again playing a role, that of being aloof and mature. Sophia often grimaced when Keri responded. At one point Sophia mentioned that Keri "went into her act." After a while Sophia told Keri to "get real" and that seemed to bring Keri back to reality.

Focus of Attention: Teenagers and Drinking

The girls began by discussing whether or not they liked the book. "I didn't think I would like it in the beginning because it was about a drunken driver and I'm not really interested in that" (Keri). "I thought it would be boring like some of the books we read for school, but it came out okay. I like it" (Sophia). Melissa mentioned that she "loved the book, even though it was a little depressing at times." After a very short time in which they discussed various characters in general they concentrated on two issues almost to the exclusion of everything else. The issue of drinking dominated their discussion and led the girls towards intense contemplation of what they might have to confront in the future. The girls all mentioned that while they read and after they finished the book, they often imagined themselves as characters in the book, contented with issues which each character confronted. All three girls indicated that they thought about what they would do. The girls' personal involvement with the text increased as they related it more to what might happen to them. They spent long periods of time pondering what they would do in similar situations. They considered many possible actions.

The appearance of "being cool," as Sophia put it, was important to her and even more important to Keri. Although Sophia recognized the problems she would have to confront, she sought ways to deal with these problems, while, at the same time saving face in front of her friends. She sought a safe way out. Keri, on the other hand, did not consider multiple possibilities too often. She indicated that she would act in a manner which "was expected of me. I'm not a child and I won't act like one."

The girls contemplated their parents and friends' reactions if they called from a party and asked to be picked up. They attempted to grapple with real issues which would confront them. As they did during the individual interviews, they used the book as an enabler to help them "see what might happen in the future."

Involvement

The girls became involved in the events portrayed in the text and the level of involvement varied among them. Melissa identified closely with Izzy. Keri, the actress, often imagined herself as a character in the text. Sophia indicated a closer, personal relationship with the character. Although the level of involvement of these girls varied, there was a common thread among them. They each indicated that while they were reading they pondered various issues which may confront them later on. Melissa, near the end of our meeting, indicated that for her, the book served a specific purpose.

While I was reading, I had the chance to imagine myself in some of the situations, I thought about what I would do. It made a difference to me. I never really thought about what I would do at a party before. It never really occurred to me because I usually wouldn't be in that situation. But I think this helped me sort things out. Maybe Voigt saved my leg, or even my life.

The Boys

There was a warm feeling of camaraderie among these three boys. They were like a team, passing comments back and forth. With obvious affection, they often mocked one another. During the individual sessions, the boys, especially Ricky and Evan, occasionally spoke at length. Overall, though their comments and thus the duration of the interviews tended to be somewhat shorter than those of the girls, this difference was slight. A great difference emerged, however, when the boys met together. Whereas the girls in their group rarely responded with a phrase or a sentence, this was the characteristic pattern of response by the boys in the group settings. The comments of the boys were often very short and terse but they flowed continually. These boys were engaged in a dialogue. They required very little direction from me. They were generally supportive of each other.

Focus of Attention—Teenagers and Drinking

As with the girls, the topic of conversation rapidly shifted from the text to the issue of teenagers and drinking. This issue evoked more detailed responses from the boys. Evan said that he knew that some of his classmates drank. When this was challenged by Dan, Evan then responded "Well I mean I know kids who drink, not my age or anything." Dan, in particular seemed relieved to have Evan clarify his original statement. Later, Ricky brought up the issue of their peers' drinking and the boys agreed that they knew no one their age who drank. This was ironic in that during a school ski trip several months prior to the project, more than half of the students were found to have been drinking. When I brought this up, Dan said, "Oh yeah sure, but the ones who got caught weren't our friends." Evan then said, "See I was right. She promised that what we said would be confidential. I trust her."

While the boys spent considerable time discussing these issues, they did not relate back to the text. The girls, in discussing similar issues, pondered the issues within the context of the characters and events portrayed in the text. For the boys, the issue of drinking was abstract. Although the text precipitated the subject of attention, it was not referred to in the discussion.

Involvement

The boys did not exhibit a very strong level of internal involvement with the text. Each of them identified a level of engagement with the author rather than the characters or events which were portrayed. Evan, in particular, being an aspiring writer, scrutinized the manner in which the book was written. Realizing that he was not very involved in and with the text, Evan tried to figure out why. "That's why I couldn't put myself in that book. There wasn't a guy who did something really good. There wasn't a hero." The boys quickly moved from one issue to another, generally returning to discuss how the book was written or how it might have been written. Each time, this shift was initiated by either Evan or Ricky. Dan joined in quickly. The boys' remarks in general were critical. They were often judgmental. The issue of crying and showing emotions cropped up frequently. Each time, each boy indicated that it would be demeaning for them to cry or show their emotions. This was in direct opposition to what they indicated in the individual sessions. In this group setting, they seemed to want to protect and preserve an image. Whenever the conversation shifted to men showing their emotions, the boys changed the topic.

Boys and Girls Together

Group Dynamics

The whole group discussions stressed less of the personal aspects of the participants' engagement and more of the abstract, often impersonal nature of their transaction with the text. There were a few moments of silence before anyone spoke. The boys maintained a dialogue for a few minutes. Their comments were terse. They often challenged one another. It was Sophia who managed to break into this male- dominated dialogue. "Hey you guys, you know we're here too. We know you already; you don't have to show off." Sophia shifted the discussion to topics of interest to her. She tried to organize the group. She probed the multiple possibilities behind the events portrayed in the text. She solicited the opinions of Melissa and often asked her for clarification. "I'm not sure I understand what you mean... What are you leading to?" While Keri directed several comments towards the boys, Melissa sat quietly, almost meekly. Sophia seemed to take charge of the group. She shifted the topic of conversation from one which was male dominated to a more all inclusive one. "We know you think you're terrific, so can we talk about other things now. What did you think of the book?"

The conversation shifted. They talked about the text, concentrating on "the conflict and the resolution." Rarely did their comments reflect their own personal perspectives. They tried to recall events portrayed in the text. They "corrected" each other.

School Reading Experiences

Evan was the first to point out that in English classes he had to interpret books according to the teachers' standards. During this heated discussion, all six of the participants reported similar experiences. It became evident that although some of them had had different teachers, their experiences in English class were analogous. They complained about having to analyze books to death, having to read a specified amount of pages per night, and having many questions to answer about the chapters. They continued their discussion by trying to find ways in which English classes could be more interesting. Melissa wished, "that there was some way we didn't have to worry so much about interpreting it correctly." They all expressed worry over grades, fearing that their grade would be contingent on discerning the correct interpretation. Dan posed the question, "But how else can the teachers grade us, it's like remembering facts for history class. You just have to do it."

DISCUSSION

The Role of Literature in Readers' Lives—
Trying on Life through Literature

Melissa, Sophia, Dan, and Ricky all favored books which were realistic. Evan loved fantasy stories and Keri indicated that books should be about "make believe." Throughout the discussions it became apparent that for these youngsters, books served specific purposes. All six indicated that books helped them "figure things out." "The peculiar power of the literary work of art resides in its influence on an emotional level ... the very things most taken for granted in a work may have the most powerful influence on the adolescent reader" (Rosenblatt, 1978/1994, pp. 189-190).

Throughout the study it was clear that all participants viewed the text from their own personal perspective. The questions they had, the issues they raised were ones which had personal importance to them. The youngsters created and recreated the work as they attempted to grasp the significance of the text with their own lives.

Rosenblatt posits that a reader's response is altered and limited by the text. This was not true of this text and these readers. The youngsters used the text as a vehicle for them to seek out and search for their own identities. Their discussion involved less about the text and much more about the thoughts which the text helped evoke. Melissa said, "The book was just a book, but it really helped me begin to think about the problems I may have to face in the future." This manifestation of "selective attention" (Rosenblatt, 1989) was evident in the participants' emphasis on one issue—teenagers and drinking. This attention, according to Rosenblatt, "may be controlled or wandering, intense or superficial … and affect[s] the quality of the process under consideration…and is conditioned by multiple personal and social factors" (p. 157). The intense concern of these adolescents with drinking enabled them to live vicariously in a safe harbor while trying to grapple with issues which they were sure would confront them in the future. They pondered actions and consequences.

The readers, particularly Melissa, Sophia, and Ricky, evidenced an increasing sense of identity of a real character, one who, during the reading they had become and one who they may have to become in the future. The reading then for them served the purpose of being a trial run for real life. This trial enabled them to try on several identities to see which one "felt right" and which ones they could hope to aspire to and internalize. The students identified with varying and various characters in the text. They indicated that at points, they felt that they were the characters. They felt the anger, the passion, the remorse and the frustration of Izzy and her friends. The readers, while identifying with the characters, tried on the roles which were portrayed. They hypothesized as to what they would do in a given situation depicted in the novel. They thought about how different actions and reactions would result in varying situations and behaviors. They seemed to expect to learn from the experience of reading.

These six adolescents are preparing to face the world, armed with the strength they had when they embraced the heroes of Cynthia Voigt's book. They tried on roles, became the hero or villain in the safe harbor of a novel. Will they someday have the courage to walk home rather than accept a ride with a drunken friend? Will they live by their beliefs that they should not date a friend's friend? We may never know the answers to these questions but we can rest assured that they have grappled with these decisions as they read Cynthia Voigt's novel.

Context

The responses of the participants in this study varied within the individual and group contexts. During the individual sessions, the respondents stressed personal issues which they found important. They expressed the role literature played in their lives. The overriding issues were personal. While commonalities existed, each discussion took on a unique form centering on each individual's particular concerns. During the group sessions, however, the responses were more superficial with two strong common themes emerging.

Two topics which were previously discussed by each participant tangentially became central in the group discussions. Even though the participants first met as two separate groups based on gender, the issue of teenagers and drinking dominated each group's discussion. During the whole group discussion this prevailed. The group responses paralleled those which each youngster had offered during the individual sessions. This contradicts some commonly held notions regarding the influence of the group on adolescents' responses.

The influence of the group seemed to have its most profound effect on the offering of response as opposed to the generation and formulation of response. During the individual sessions, the youngsters did not have to compete for speaking time with anyone else. No limitations were placed on the time for each session. Participants were free to contemplate their responses. The group setting, by its very nature, did not encourage this leisurely, reflective mode. The dynamics were such that the participants, although allotted time for the generation of response, did not have the luxury to muse on their thoughts as they had been afforded in the individual settings.

Another strong group common theme which had been minimally discussed in individual settings but which greatly pervaded the group setting was the participants' school experiences with literature. The respondents used the group situations, more than the individual context, to expand upon their dissatisfaction with the ways in which their English teachers handled the study of literature.

Even though these youngsters came from varying backgrounds and had different school experiences and different teachers, there seemed to be a strongly held notion that they must react to and interpret text in a manner which is in accord with a preordained idea of their teachers. This is especially peculiar in light of the fact that this school prides itself on being one which encourages children to think for themselves. Their prior experiences in this school, involved six different teachers, all of whom describe themselves as teachers who encourage children to think. The English teachers boast that their classroom environments are conducive to the generation of response and ones which respected each individual's ability to respond. Although I did not have the opportunity to speak with teachers from the other schools which some of the youngsters attended, it became clear that in these instances, too, children had to "find the one true meaning in a text."

The differences in reading a book for school and the experience of having participated in the study were expressed more vociferously by those youngsters who were no longer avid readers. Those who considered themselves "readers" likened this situation to that of reading a book at home for their own pleasure. Although all six discussed much more positive feelings about this type of experience as opposed to their typical school experiences with books, the children who indicated at the beginning of the study that they were not avid readers were the most vocal in terms of their distaste for reading books for school. It was almost as if the school experiences tainted reading for them. The two youngsters who were not as adamant about the differences were Sophia and Evan, both of whom indicated during the initial phase of the study that they enjoyed reading more than the other participants. Sophia indicated that she and her father often talked about and recommended books to each other. Evan's mother, although he expressed displeasure at her "butting into almost everything I do," often read the books he read and that precipitated family discussions about the books.

Sophia's and Evan's positive home experiences with books seemed to have countermanded the negative experiences they encountered in school. This was not the case for the other four participants.

CONCLUSIONS

Within the transactional framework readers construct *their* own knowledge. This active process is initiated and propelled by the reader. During this study, it became increasingly apparent that when these readers were given the opportunity to initiate and design (direct) their experiences, these experiences became more meaningful and richer for them. They called upon their prior life and literary experiences to begin and propel the process of response. That this process is cyclical and ongoing, with each experience modifying and helping the reformulation of new experiences, was evident.

The readers' minds were engaged. They were in the process stage of formulating their response. That this response could be modified and reformulated enabled the readers to generate and explore multiple possibilities of responses which were evoked by and during the reading experience. Teachers must allow and use this process stage in order to help their students achieve their maximum potential.

The findings of this study indicate that youngsters offer different responses in different contexts, specifically, more personal responses are generated by individuals in individual sessions; that patterns of responses exist, and that responses offered in a group context are consistent among the individuals across contexts.

Implications

Human experience involves transaction. In the reading experience discussed here, the transaction involved the individual readers, a text, and an environment all providing input into the matrix that was formed. Any element within the matrix can inhibit or foster the experience. Further studies need to focus on these elements in varying contexts and with varying texts. Obvious questions emerge: Are these stances chosen by a particular reader and maintained throughout all reading experiences? Can the adoption of particular stances be fostered or inhibited by teachers? Are there key features within texts or individuals which trigger modification of stance?

Teachers need to look at their own teaching to ensure that they are teaching in ways that foster connections with their adolescent students. Educators must look at students through a more holistic lens in order to fully see the potential and the accomplishments of middle school students. For example, Ricky showed great insight and thought. His intellectual growth and development even during the short time we worked together was evident to those research reviewers (all teacher researchers) who first read the data transcripts and then the data analysis. They all indicated that Ricky, in particular, evidenced tremendous insight and intelligence. This was in direct opposition to the school grades and the opinions of the school administrators. Much information about students' abilities can be gained from looking beyond typical test scores. By understanding adolescent readers and by listening to their voices, we are better able to teach and reach them.

> Present in every human being [is] ... the desire to make new secondary worlds of our own, or if we cannot make them ourselves, to share in the secondary worlds of those who can. (Auden, 1968, p. 49)

This reading experience provided a secondary world for these youngsters and enabled them to vicariously face new worlds and interpret new experiences. This secondary world enabled them to embark on new journeys, create new adventures, or escape from their own existence. It enabled these youngsters to imagine multiple possibilities and potentialities. The readers saw a light emerging from an abyss:

> We have not even to risk the adventure alone, for the heroes of all time have gone before us. The labyrinth is thoroughly known. We have only to follow the thread of the hero path, and where we had thought to find an admonition, we shall find a god. And where we had thought to slay another, we shall slay ourselves. Where we had thought to travel outward, we will come to the

center of our own existence. And where we had thought to be alone, we will be with all the world. (Campbell, 1985)

REFERENCES

Auden, W. H. (1968). *Secondary worlds*. New York, NY: Random House.

Bosna, H. A., & Kunnen, E. S. (2001). Determinants and mechanisms in ego identity development: A review and synthesis. *Developmental Review, 21*, 39-66.

Campbell, J. (1985). *The power of myth*. New York, NY: Doubleday.

Costanzo, P. (1970). Conformity development as a function of self blame. *Journal of Personality and Social Psychology, 14*, 366-374.

Dewey, J. (1931-1932). *The middle works, vol. 6*. Carbondale, IL: Southern Illinois University Press.

Fish, S. (1990). *Doing what comes naturally: Change, rhetoric, and the practice of theory in literary and legal studies*. Durham, NC: Duke University Press.

Galda, L., & Liang, L. (2003). Literature as experience or looking for facts: Stance in the classroom. *Reading Research Quarterly, 38*(2), 268-275.

Hebert, M. (2008, July). *Evaluate the quality of collaboration and talk in peer led literature discussions*. Paper presented at 22nd World Congress on Reading: International Reading Association, Costa Rica.

Kroger, J. (2004). *Identity development through adulthood*. New York, NY: Routledge.

Richards, I. A. (1991). *Richards on rhetoric: I.A. Richards, selected essays 1929-1974*. New York, NY: Oxford University Press.

Rosenblatt, L. (1995). *Literature as exploration* (5th ed). New York, NY: The Modern Language Association. (Original work published 1938)

Rosenblatt, L. (1994). *The reader, the text, the poem: The transactional theory of the literacy work*. Carbondale, IL: Southern Illinois University Press. (Original work published 1978)

Rosenblatt, L. M. (2005). *Making meaning with texts: Selected essays*. Portsmouth, NH: Heinemann.

Serafini, F., & Ladd, S. M. (2008). The challenge of moving beyond the literal in literature discussions. *Journal of Language and Literacy Education* (online), *4*(2), 6-20. Retrieved from http://www.coe.uga.edu/jolle/2008_2/challenge.pdf

Voigt, C. (2005). *Izzy, Willy-Nilly*. New York, NY: Simon & Schuster.

CHAPTER 6

FROM LOATHING TO LOVE

Sandy's Reading Journey

Mary Beth Schaefer

This study represents the findings of 1 teacher researcher who used narrative inquiry as a way to help her understand and negotiate the literacy needs and desires of her young adolescent readers in a middle school language arts classroom. The study, contextualized with a personal and pedagogical story of literacy, draws on fieldnotes, reflections, student journals, transcripts of classroom discussions, and open-ended interviews to describe the journey of 1 reluctant reader and her teacher. Using a model of effective middle school teaching, the author examines how the process of inquiry helped improve her pedagogy and the reading achievement of one reluctant reader.

NARRATIVE INQUIRY IN MIDDLE SCHOOL: SANDY'S READING STORY

I fell deeply in love with books in the second grade, but it was not love at first letter. Every night my mother would set a timer and demand that my three older brothers and I read for 20 minutes. Our prize was the timer

Voices From the Middle: Narrative Inquiry By, For, and About the Middle Level Community
pp. 107–125

going off and the TV going on. I remember struggling through *Little House in the Big Woods* (Wilder, 1932/1959), sad that my mother's favorite book bored me.

I accepted her gift of the next book in the series with resignation and slowly opened it exactly at the moment the timer began to tick off 20. But this time, something happened. I was finally leaving the Big Woods of Wisconsin. Ma, Pa, Mary, and I had just crossed the ice. I was asleep in a strange place when I was scared awake by the sound of pops like gunfire. Pa assured me it was only the ice cracking. What if the ice had cracked while we were crossing? Did we have to cross another frozen river tomorrow? The chapter ended with our safe arrival in Kansas. Only then did I pull my face away from the book. My brothers were already watching TV. The room had a strange light and seemed bigger. I felt dazed and a little scared. Blinking rapidly helped to reposition the living room, but something in me was profoundly changed: I looked forward to the next night of reading when I would cross the raging creek.

I never heard the timer again.

I tell this story to acknowledge how my early reading experiences play a central role in the following narrative inquiry. As Clandinin and Connelly (2000) explain, "These narrative beginnings of our own livings, tellings, retellings and relivings help us deal with questions of who we are in the field and who we are in the texts that we write" (p. 70). My experience of falling in love with reading was emotionally powerful. Many voracious readers have a similar story of that first book that pulled them in and held them in thrall, but for some children, that book never arrives. When I became a middle school reading teacher, I resolved to find a way to woo my most reluctant readers into the pleasures and rewards of reading. This chapter presents the stories of two middle school students, both reluctant readers and recipients of my determination to find the book that would positively impact their attitude towards reading, and by extension, their reading ability (Wilhelm, 1997).

INTRODUCTION

These are not stories of personal pedagogical success. Indeed, pedagogical failure marks the first of the two student stories I tell in this chapter. The first, Matt's story, I constructed from my memory. This story marks a time before I used narrative and practitioner inquiry, yet in its telling, I can look back, rethink, and reassess the classroom environment and my role in it (Cochran-Smith & Lytle, 1993). My personal preamble, a brief discussion of narrative inquiry and Matt's story serve to contextualize Sandy's story. Her reading journey was chronicled as part of a larger dissertation study that used both narrative and practitioner inquiry. Sandy's story is important because it is at once about Sandy and about issues and stories that impact the middle school English classroom. As the teacher orchestrating these elements to support readers and improve her own practice, Sandy's story is also mine.

WHY RESEARCH AND WRITE NARRATIVELY?

While my personal vignette and Matt's story follow the conventions of narrative, described by Gordon, McKibbin, Vasudevan, and Vinz (2007) as a "way of recounting, constituting, representing and constructing the story" (p. 327), Sandy's story follows the conventions of narrative inquiry, which "has a narrator/researcher who is the medium for storying the research journey and the understandings that emerge along the way…[it] is interpretive and situated research activity, and the story exists as data or artifact of this engagement" (Gordon et al. 2007, p. 327). My vignette and Matt's story help forge a link to the narrative inquiry methods I use in the more formal research study. I see narrative as a way of understanding experience so that "stories lived and told educates the self and others" (Clandinin & Connelly, 2000, p. xxvi). Narrative engages us in learning about life (Bateson, 1989) and narrative inquiries teach us about life in and out of the classroom (Chan, 2006; Clandinin & Connelly, 2000; Coulter, Michael, & Poynor, 2007; Moss, 2004; Schaafsma, Pagnucci, Wallace, & Stock, 2007).

The decision to do research through a narrative lens also means to write from a vulnerable, reflexive position. As Behar (1996) says, "when an author has made herself or himself vulnerable, the stakes are higher: a boring self-revelation … is more than embarrassing; it is humiliating" (p. 13). An interesting narrative, on the other hand, gives the reader what Schaafsma and Vinz (2007) describe as "a door to open and walk through" (p. 277). I invite you to enter Matt's story first. His name has been changed, but I, the teller, remain vulnerable.

MATT'S STORY: THE LESSON

When students hate to read, much of school becomes a game of watching the reading timer. As a language arts teacher of large seventh grade classes in New York City, it was difficult for me to understand why individual students resisted reading, but when I moved to Texas and became a middle school reading teacher, I realized that my small classes of 12-15 students had serious reading issues: Some lacked fluency, others had little comprehension of what was read, and many could not draw conclusions or make inferences. It was quickly apparent, however, that all of them shared one characteristic. They did not read for pleasure.

Determined to woo my students to reading, I searched for high interest, low level texts. They wrote letters to me that reflected personal responses to their self-selected books, and I answered with encouragement and questions. For most students, this strategy worked; they wrote frequently and read without resistance. Their scores on practice exams for the Texas Assessment of Academic Skills (TAAS) improved steadily. But every time I picked up Matt's journal, I read a different story.

Matt, a seventh grader, was often teased for his small size, soft blond curls, and thick-rimmed glasses. He tended to lash out at the teacher or other students during classroom lessons. His voice, often filled with anger and frustration, had a gravelly, low pitch and nasal-infused monotone. The voice was perfect for delivering a punch line or pithy observation, and Matt was smart and witty enough to do both. But his reading journal was a mess of scratched out words and graffiti doodles. One day all he wrote was, "I am bord [sic]." Another day he wrote, "IHATE REDING [sic]." Sometimes he erased or crossed words out with such fury that the paper gaped and ripped. I brought him books on his reading level but he rejected them as too babyish. I got him a biography of his favorite heavy metal rock group. He looked at the pictures but would not read the text. I knew he was fascinated by horror and suspense so I found stories for the class based on true-life mysteries and real-life crime. Although he occasionally followed along in class readings, he read nothing independently.

One day while my students were reading and I was somewhat absorbed in a Steven King novel, Matt stopped doodling and came over to my chair. "Hey, can I look at your book?" Surprised, I handed it over. He wandered back over to his table and read for the next 20 minutes. I worried, briefly, that the book was too far above his reading level, but when the bell signaled the end of class, Matt approached me and asked to take the book home. Of course, I let him.

When Matt returned to school the next day, he handed me the book with a note inside. His parents were on their way to see me. They showed up furious and outraged. "We don't allow Matt to read this trash," the father growled, gesticulating angrily toward the book.

"We try to guide him toward healthy books," his step-mother explained.

"Why did you give my son a book about the devil?" the father demanded. I explained that the story was not about Satan, but about the struggle between good and evil, love and selfishness. Matt's father opened the book with a flourish and pointed to a tagged section of the book. Sure enough, the devil was in the details.

"This was the only book in 3 months that has piqued Matt's interest," I explained. "He won't read other texts. Right now I'm just trying to get him engaged in a book."

"There's no problem with that," the father said. "The problem is with this." He pressed his finger on the book. "*We* will find appropriate reading material for our son."

When Matt came to school the next day, I asked him if he had gone to Barnes & Noble or perhaps Borders.

"Nope," he said, throwing himself into a seat.

"Well, do you have something to read?"

"Yup." Matt threw down a stack of booklets, all religious tracts. I watched him scowl through the pictures, and by the next day he had lost most of them. My efforts to engage him in another book were half-hearted. I really didn't think he would like *Sounder* (Armstrong, 1969) but I knew his parents would approve. Things did not improve after the holiday break. Matt blamed me for his Christmas present—the latest edition of "Hooked on Phonics."

I never again saw Matt voluntarily select a book or get lost in a text. At first I blamed his parents, but over time, I realized that the blame belonged to me. My vision of developing literacy was too limited; I saw my classroom as a kind of enclosed context within which I was responsible for all aspects of literacy learning. An effective middle school teacher understands that it is important to form critical relationships (Roney, 2001) with a "circle of allies" (p. 87). Cultivating these relationships helps reading teachers understand how to negotiate the multiple social systems (Casey, 2008/2009) that impact adolescent literacy development in order to support reluctant or struggling readers. I did not understand Matt's social systems. I failed Matt because I failed to see and understand the ways in which literacy extended beyond my classroom. Was literacy for Matt tied up in religion? Was he forced to read the Bible at home? Was his rejection of reading a reflection of his resistance toward his parents? My feelings of failure fed my questions, and although Matt left me at the end of the semester, the questions did not.

THE NARRATIVE INQUIRY

Research Question and Site

Several years and many miles later, I was ready to begin fieldwork for my dissertation. My overarching research question turned on how, as a teacher, I might negotiate among the different literacy needs and desires that middle school students bring to the English language arts (ELA) classroom and improve my pedagogy and students' literary understandings. I decided to teach and research simultaneously. For my research site, I chose a middle school in New York City. This middle school opened in 1979 with a special mission--to bring together an ethnically and academically diverse group of children and teach them in classes that reflected this heterogeneity. The school served approximately 1,200 students in Grades 6 through 8 and represented over 70 ethnic groups.

Methods for Collecting, Recording, and Analyzing Experiences

From the beginning of October, 2001 until the last school day in June, I was an unpaid ELA teacher for a class of 30 seventh-grade students for 43 minutes a day. The previous teacher for this class had no ELA certification and gladly gave me complete charge of this one class. I wrote daily field notes, analytical memos, and personal reflections. I conducted open-ended interviews, analyzed reading journals and students' stories, and taped/transcribed classroom discussions. Following Clandinin and Connelly (2000), my notes were filled with details of place, thoughts about time, and on-going reflections. Data were analyzed using open coding, axial coding, and selective coding (Strauss & Corbin, 1998). I searched for patterns, narrative threads, tensions, and themes not only among students, but in my own field experience (Clandinin & Connelly, 2000). As patterns of literary understanding emerged from conceptualization and classification of codes, I used the comparative method (Charmaz, 2000) to make emerging theories and patterns denser and then shared my interpretations with students. For example, in my *Fieldnotes and Reflections*, (March 19) I marked 19 classes as having qualities of intense participation. When I went back through my notes and transcripts of these classes, I was struck by the subject matter. Half of the classes were about stories and life. The other half were about reading skills and strategies. I was surprised that skills and strategies would engage students' interest and response, but in fact, my emerging theory of reading showed that they found pleasure in learning discrete reading skills. When I took this finding back to the class for a member check, they explained that the emerging pattern made perfect sense. There was a high-stakes citywide reading exam they had to take in April. Doing well on that test meant getting into a good high school. Doing well gave them pleasure.

The Reflective/Reflexive Teacher Researcher of Sandy's Story

To capture and examine the experience of education, my researcher role was that of narrative interpreter (Gordon et al., 2007). Every day I reflected on my practice in my journal, and the next day I shared my interpretations and assumptions with my class. This activity functioned not only as a member check, but as a way to encourage and promote active participation and response among students over time (Clandinin & Connelly, 2000). Constructing knowledge with students through their words and stories and using these multiple perspectives placed me at a fruitful boundary between narrative inquiry and teacher research. This data-gathering method also became a way for students to see their thoughts and words honored. Through inquiry into my own and my students shared experiences, I tried to improve my pedagogy (Conle, 2003) and by extension, my students' experiences of literacy in the classroom.

In her research on the characteristics of effective middle school teachers, Roney (2001) found that the most had qualities that may be subsumed under four themes: They understood the transitions of the young adolescent, they developed personal qualities, they developed critical relationships, and they organized the learning environment. In his study of middle school teacher qualities, Vagle (2007) reexamined Roney's themes through a phenomenological lens and, following Beane (1997), suggested that an effective middle school teacher "integrates these characteristics" (p. 326). Vagle's challenge was how to study this integration, because it was "difficult to access in practice" (p. 326). An interesting aspect of the following narrative inquiry is that through the lens of Sandy's developing awareness of her literacy and reading attitudes, we can see how Roney's themes are integrated into my teacher researcher role. Sandy's story, as an artifact of my narrative inquiry (Gordon et al., 2007), is also my story.

Sandy's Story

Buses, yellow, grinding and ubiquitous, begin queuing up in front of the school at 7:00 A.M. Students run though the diesel fumes and into the front door, unsteady under the weight of their backpacks. They dart through the hallways with excited, high pitched voices. Thirty of these students line up outside of my classroom. I haven't taught in several years. It has taken me longer than anticipated to obtain permissions for my study, so it is already the beginning of October. I am an outsider and I am terrified. A set of high windows on one side of the classroom allows me to peer out into the hall. I see faces and heads popping up. These are my future students, beginning to signal their impatience to get into the room by hitting each other.

I open the door and smile as they shove past me. How could I have forgotten the energy and living bliss that many middle school students embody? They sit on top of desks and chat. Didn't they see me? Should I clap? Count? Flick the lights? I look across the room and feel a strong absence of warmth and affection for these students. I do not know or love them, nor they me. My first inclination, in fact, is to take that joy, vitality, and zest that imbued their physical and socioemotional developing selves and push it right into their seats. Finally, they notice me.

"I don't like you," I start.

They stare.

"… in rows." I finish. They laugh and quickly help me arrange the desks into groups of four, perhaps relieved that their new teacher seems to have the requisite sense of humor.

Gradually we developed a routine. Daily lessons usually began with a five minute discussion about assignments and activities or shared reflections/interpretations of the events of the previous day. A minilesson and whole class discussion then ensued, and a 15-20 minute group activity sometimes followed. This was the basic structure that I envisioned, but often our whole class conversations were just too interesting to stop, or we had to begin class with unfinished group work. Students were especially interested in how I interpreted their thoughts, actions, or journals from the day before.

Fridays were our independent reading days. As I watched students fall into the private places of their books, I noticed Sandy. When I smiled at her and gestured towards my book, indicating that she should join in the independent reading, she grimaced. Her eyes moved to a book on her desk, but soon I saw her looking at me again. Everyone else was focused on their books. Sandy was quiet. She seemed bored. I felt the specter of Matt enter the classroom.

Sandy intrigued me. One of the six students in my class with an Individual Education Plan, she shared an aide with another girl in the class. The aide occasionally tried to help Sandy with her writing, but Sandy loudly proclaimed that she preferred to work alone. A pretty girl with long dark hair who identified her ethnicity as "Dominican," she appeared to be two different learners: Her writing was atrocious. Her essays ignored margins and paragraphs. Her handwriting was large and bubbly. She scored a level one, the lowest score possible, on her sixth grade citywide reading test. She disliked reading intensely and did not enjoy writing either. Having to write about her reading in a reader's journal was doubly torturous to her. She could not read her journal responses aloud. Even to herself, her writing was jumbled and incoherent. Nothing about Sandy the Writer matched Sandy the Thinker.

I first became aware of Sandy's distinctive and powerful thinking during class discussions. During a conversation about how to read for social studies and other content areas without falling asleep, Sandy first listened to other students talk about how they took notes, read slowly, asked themselves questions, and read the subtitles. Then, she commented, "Usually I notice that our textbooks aren't really textbooks. They're opinions that are presented as facts." Every head swiveled to the back of the room. I asked her to explain, but she just shrugged. Sandy was still sitting in the back of the room at this point.

I soon learned to call on Sandy if I wanted conversations to move in more thoughtful and provocative directions. As I shared my observations and reflections with the class, I quoted Sandy quite often and she gradually emerged as a lead thinker in the class. This was a very new and different position for her. One day in January she paused outside the classroom and waited until I had said goodbye to everyone.

"You are the first person to call me smart," she said. "No one ever said I was smart. No one ever said I was a good thinker."

Startled, I told her the truth: "You have a brilliant mind," I said, "and you make us all smarter." Sandy stared down at the floor. She seemed upset.

Without lifting her head, she leaned toward me and whispered, "I was left back in second grade. That really made me think I was stupid."

I bit my lip and touched her arm. "You are anything but," I assured her.

In the social context of classroom learning, Sandy's voice emerged as authoritative and influential, and this seemed to positively influence her attitude in my class (Galda & Beach, 2001; Ivey & Broaddus, 2001, Johnston, 1987; Moller & Allen, 2000; Van Horn, 2000). Through this private conversation, Sandy helped me understand that she was transitioning to a new position in the classroom.

The next day Sandy asked to be moved to the front of the room. This is how I remember her—eyes focused and attentive, hand up, mind open, book closed. As smart as I found her, she was also failing my class. Her reading journal was missing entries. She continued to hate to read and was often negligent in turning in written assignments.

Sandy enjoyed writing to me in her reading journal about other things, such as what she did over the weekend or while on vacation. I encouraged this writing because it helped me understand what she found important in her life—friends, family, and traveling—and it gave her opportunities to practice penning her thoughts. More importantly, I gradually gained a greater understanding of the larger context of Sandy's life and the critical relationships (Roney, 2001) that informed it. I learned that Sandy spoke only Spanish at home, could not read at all in that language, came to the United States in kindergarten not speaking English, and had a sister who borrowed her clothes without asking. She had an aunt whom she loved, an uncle who drank too much, parents who worked constantly, and a grandmother who recently died from cancer. Sandy knew I read, studied, and responded to her journal carefully. I believe Sandy appreciated the fact that I was genuinely interested in her life and her unique transitions (Roney, 2001). She responded by trying every independent reading book I selected for her.

To appeal to Sandy's intellect and willingness to write about her life, I thought she might enjoy *Anne Frank: The Diary of a Young Girl* (1952/1993) or *The Lovely Bones* (Sebold, 2002). Sandy sometimes wrote about how she struggled with her role as a Latina girl in a traditional family, so I gave her books by Sandy Cisneros, Pam Munoz, and Julia Alvarez. My experience with Matt reading something of interest but above his reading level led me to recommend Laura Esquivel. Sandy also wrote and spoke about the importance of friends in her life, so I asked her to try Jerry Spinelli, S.E. Hinton, and Ann Brashares. She politely tried the books and returned them all. Mindful of the Sandy's critical relationships (Roney, 2001), I encouraged her to borrow books from friends.

When Sandy saw how hard I worked to find a book that might pique her interest, she began to help me. She tried to understand what actually happened when she sat down to read. In her journal, she wrote, "I always watned [sic] to do something alse intead [sic]. I think that what made read so boring and unpelsureble [sic]" (*Reading Journal*, December 15).

Meanwhile, during our class discussions, students would often describe their experience of reading as "stepping into" or "entering" a story. Sandy listened attentively to these conversations. When she reflected on her own reading, she seemed to feel a sense of loss. In January she wrote, "What I leaned [sic] about myself the last few entries is that my reading history is very sad. If I dont [sic] start reading for peleasure [sic] right now I wont [sic] read for peleasure [sic] ever in my life" (*Reading Journal*, January 29).

About a month later she was still trying to figure out what happened when she tried to read: "When Im [sic] reding [sic] I feel like Im [sic] going to fall asleep and I rader [sic] do everything alse [sic] beside read. I always say that if someone culd [sic] write a book that would hold my attention for 5 seconds Id [sic] pay him/her" (*Reading Journal*, February 29). Encouraging self-reflection, as a way for students to understand their own and other's literary identities, was an organizing principle of my classroom environment (Roney, 2001). Through her self-reflection, Sandy constructed and interpreted herself as a reader who was bored, but longed to find a book that would "hold" her attention. The difficulties of friendship and transitioning emotionally and physically were themes that Sandy understood and this helped her finish Judy Blume's (1970/1986) *Are You There God, It's Me, Margaret*:

> The story that am [sic] reading is about 5 girls specially one girl who moved from New York to New Jersey. But luckily she meet [sic] 4 girls. If she does

good socially she's not doing very [well] emotionally sometimes it can be hard to talk about with your friend so the girl so [sic] one else to talk to G-d. (*Reading Journal*, February 8)

Sandy expresses concern with the character's socioemotional development. Her observation that "sometimes it can be hard to talk … with your friend" indicates a kind of empathetic understanding. Sandy clings to these kinds of connections and finishes the book in just under two months. Then, in a journal entry on March 30, I notice the first sign that Sandy's attitude toward reading might be changing:

I hope you liked my Idia [idea] for the reached [research] project I hope it not inproper [sic] because to tel [sic] you to trueth [sic] a was secptacal [sic] about telling you my Idia [sic] because I was inbarest [sic] to say in fornt [sic] of the class. Write back to me as soon as you can Your Students + [sic] friend Sandy (I hate to read even if now it [sic] more fun).

I almost missed this last line about reading. While Sandy clings to her identity as one who "hate to read" she also acknowledges "it more fun." Acknowledging this seems to allow her to "enter" a story more fully as she seems to do here, as she writes about a book recommended by a friend. This is Sandy's longest response yet:

I read a book called the pact it is about this boy and girl who were best friends when they got oder [sic] they became more the [sic] that thought [sic] the book the girl got pregnant and did not what [sic] to discriseasce [disgrace] famaliy [sic] so she told her boyfriend she was going to kill herself but said I am going to kill myself is you do he relly [sic] did not think he was going to tue [sic] with it. One day she killed herself [sic] and they aquest [accused] her boy of the marder [sic]. (*Reading Journal*, May 4)

Sandy shows that she understands a few things that make me think that she might be "inside" of the story. She introduces both of the characters in terms of the trouble they get into. She writes vividly about the central problem of the story and describes the plot. It is also important to note that a classmate gave Sandy this book, further supporting the idea that creating a comfortable social environment for middle school readers (Wilson, Jewett, & Vanderburg, 2008) is an important quality of effective middle school teachers (Roney, 2001).

By June, Sandy's journal contains three pages of letters about a book called *The Princess Diaries* (Cabot, 2000), yet another book given to her by a classmate. Not only has she read the first book in the series, but she has finished the second and most of the third. I interview Sandy at this point to ask her to explain how she managed to read nearly three books in 3 weeks when before it had taken her 2 months to read one. I share large segments of this interview, because it shows how Sandy the Thinker has intersected with Sandy the Writer to become Sandy the Reader.

> Sandy: I read a *lot* more than I used to before I took your class.
>
> MB: Why?
>
> Sandy: I don't know! You made me think about it. I just thought before, when I was younger and before I took your class, I just thought it was something you did because you *had* to do it. Like it was people reading a story…people just reading a story that was a bunch of words put together to make sense. That's what reading was to me. And like you made me think about it more, like I never thought about reading as much as I do when I'm in your class, or because I think you made me look at reading from a totally different point of view. I didn't know that it could be so creative. And fun. And that you could really understand what they're trying to say, and really, uh, get it. Really *get* what they're trying to say. I never did that before. That's why I had problems with reading comprehension because I never really thought about what I was reading—I was just reading a bunch of stuff put together. I really wasn't thinking about what the author was trying to say. You know, there were a lot of questions on the standardized test that said, "what do you think the author was trying to say" like, in this paragraph or in this sentence. And I just had trouble with those questions. I could never understand what was going on, but now I can, and that's why I think I did really well on the test, because every time I came upon one of those questions I could answer like this [snaps fingers], 'cause I already knew what was going on. I understood it better. And I think that's why reading is more fun now.
>
> MB: I'm blown away by what you just said. Because you never understood the *question* you never did well on those tests or because you never knew what the heck they were talking about?
>
> Sandy: No, it wasn't the question. I understood the question. I just never got it right because I never *thought* about reading, I never analyzed it.
>
> MB: I see!

Sandy applies her formidable thinking and developing inquiry skills to her reading and gradually understands not only what the author was saying, but why and how the author was saying it. These insights affect her recreational reading and her understanding of the high-stakes standardized reading test that she took at the end of April. She realizes and appreciates the author's point of view and purpose. These understandings lead to greater comprehension, and for the first time ever, Sandy believes (correctly) that she has done well on a standardized test. She goes on to explain how reading has finally become "fun."

MB: And you never had—I just heard this word peek into your conversation just now—fun. You just said "fun."

Sandy: Yeah!

MB: What's fun?

Sandy: What is fun, fun is that now when I read I kind of picture the book in my head and I like, I have a really good imagination … and I can like, and now I can read a book and really get into it—like I can't get "into" it—I just *see* it in my head. And I pretend that I'm part of the story.

MB: Has that ever happened to you before?

Sandy: No! This is the first time it happened! And I felt so weird when it happened, I was like, "whoa!" It's just so cool, because I can picture it, I can make pictures in my head about what's going on, and if the reader is describing somebody, I can picture that person exactly how the author is describing him.

In order to understand Sandy's involvement in the story, I probe more deeply into her reading experience. Both of us cite thoughts from other students in the class to help us explain and describe her experience with reading. This referencing of others' insights helps illustrate the co-constructive nature of our classroom environment:

MB: When you picture yourself in the story, do you picture yourself as one of the characters or do you see yourself as, um, somebody who is with them but invisible? How do you see—

Sandy: Yeah, it's kinda like, like what Brittany said? A window? It's like looking "in." I'm not really part of the story, I'm just looking into the story to see what's going on. It's like watching a movie.

MB: Right.

Sandy: But in my head.

MB: But in your head. God that's so cool! I have learned so much from the different people in the class—some people like Mike and John—they actually *become* the character. And can you imagine that? They participate in the story *as* the main character.

> Sandy: I don't do that, I kinda look like, I watch it, like a movie, like looking through binoculars to see exactly what's going on.

I struggle mightily at this point during the interview to control my emotions. Sandy is so excited and vocal about her experience and I am deeply moved by her passion. My next question is an attempt to understand the extent of Sandy's newfound interest, and when I find out just how involved she has become in books, to the point where she prefers the book to the movie, I reach for a tissue:

> MB: That's so cool, Sandy. That's so cool. So, are you reading a book now?
>
> Sandy: I'm reading the third *Princess Diaries* book. That's the book that kind of got me started, 'cause I saw the movie and the movie did not do the book justice, I think. I was really mad about that. The movie was nothing like the book!
>
> MB: Really!
>
> Sandy: Nothing at all. It didn't really do it justice at all and I was so mad. I mean, I love the movie but the book is so, way way better. It's more like, detailed. It's so cool.
>
> MB: Oh Sandy, I'm gonna cry!

The transcript cannot capture the animation and excitement Sandy expressed as she spoke of being "inside" the story, watching the characters, and being part of the action. The stunning contrast between the sullen, defiant, challenging stance she'd taken towards reading at the beginning of the school year and the enthusiasm and joy with which she spoke about reading now transfixed me. I felt incredibly privileged to witness such a transformation, and it was at this point among a tissue, the tape-recorder, and Sandy's joy that I experienced a convergence of the themes that I helped orchestrate as a teacher researcher. I understood Sandy's transitions because I shared them. Through this sharing I developed new personal qualities as a teacher, including an ability to empathize deeply with Sandy.

Following this interview, I knew Sandy's feelings about reading had taken a dramatic turn, but her writings from June demonstrate new understandings of her reading preferences: "The book has got to be a Love story on something kind of grily [sic] books for me to like it" (*Reading Journal*, June 6) and the idea of reading as a new leisure activity: "Now Am [sic] read Prices [sic] Diarys #2 I finished #1 it was great but it was nothing like to movie it was better I can't wait to read #3 #4 #5 … I love to meet Meg Babbet [Cabot] … my friends are going to see her and maybe get ordergraphe [sic]" (*Reading Journal*, June 1).

Once Sandy said if anyone could write a book that could hold her interest she would give that person a million dollars. It is, therefore, not surprising that Sandy reveres the author of her favorite series enough to try and get her autograph. Sandy's confidence in her new reading abilities were also well founded: On the seventh grade citywide reading test, she earned the sixth highest score in the class and placed in the top 16% of all students in New York City.

CONCLUSION

All three stories converged in this one middle school English Language Arts classroom and had deep and lasting influences on my pedagogy. Participating in Sandy's journey helped me orchestrate the social, emotional, personal, and cultural elements that came together in this classroom. To foreground how these elements converged, it is helpful to revisit Roney's (2001) descriptions of the four themes of effective middle school teachers.

Roney's (2001) first theme, "Understanding the Transitions of the Young Adolescent," described effective teachers as having a "fundamental love" (p. 82) for youths. This love and abiding interest fed the process of narrative inquiry as I listened to, taped, transcribed, and reflected on my students' thoughts, feelings and stories. I also sought to understand students by asking and responding to probing questions in their *Reading Journals* and classroom conversations. Sandy's *Reading Journal* helped me understand more of her family life. Matt's journal was empty and so remained my contextual understanding of his life.

The second theme, "Developing Personal Qualities," dovetailed importantly with the process of narrative inquiry. I shared my own developing thoughts and insights with students, and Sandy especially responded to this intimacy, writing about her life and speaking freely with me after class and during interviews. We both wanted to understand *why* Sandy did not like to read. Appreciating her journey created such a strong sense of empathy that when she finally experienced a love for books, I shared her joy in a way that brought tears to my eyes.

The third theme, "Developing Critical Relationships," was completely lacking in my experience with Matt. How might Matt's outcome in my class have been different if I had cultivated a relationship with his family early on? At the same time, I had little contact with Sandy's family. Neither parent spoke English and I had a limited understanding of Spanish. I did, however, understand that Sandy's peers were another important aspect of her critical relationships, and ultimately Sandy's friends were the ones who handed her the books that catapulted her into the world of the story.

Roney's (2001) fourth theme, "Organizing the Middle School Environment" underscores the importance of teacher research and narrative inquiry. As an organizing principle in my classroom, inquiry meant that students' stories and thoughts were central to classroom knowledge and discussion. I had, perhaps in part because of this emphasis, few discipline issues. If we understand what is commonly called "adolescent rebelliousness" as, following Nakkula and Toshalis (2007), an "ongoing construction and interpretation of the developing self-in-the-world" (p. 3), then our classroom, through narrative inquiry, provided a place where students were invited to construct themselves as readers and help me interpret what that meant. Inquiry helped me understand my students' developing literacies and enabled Sandy to explore her emerging identity as a reader.

Educational Significance

Matt and Sandy's stories help us understand the importance of recognizing the teacher's role in the social community of the middle school language arts classroom. When access to learning about students' lives and interests is limited (as I allowed it to be when Matt refused to write in his journal) so too is the teacher's participation in the classroom's social community. The process of inquiry creates many opportunities for educators to understand students. The narrative interpreter gathers students' thoughts and stories and constructs knowledge in a transparent way. Students see their voices honored as their words are placed at the center of inquiry. Sandy's frequent and profound participation in classroom conversations enables entry into her social worlds and a more complete picture of her reading needs and desires is gained through other conversations, shared stories, and the reading journal.

In Matt and Sandy's stories, we see how access to diverse classroom conversations about reading impacts the social community. Matt's placement in a class with students identified as needing "reading improvement" limits his access to a community of avid readers. Sandy, on the other hand, participates in a mixed ability class with many voracious, hungry readers who enjoy articulating their pleasurable reading experiences. In the social community of the mixed-ability class, students' conversations about reading pleasure deeply affect reading attitude. Sandy wants to read the books her friends read and experience the reading world that they enjoy. We know that it is important to encourage students to read for pleasure, even in school. What this study helps us see is how, through a commitment to narrative inquiry and participation in the social community of the classroom, the teacher creates an environment that invites all students to read for pleasure.

Final Thoughts

Sandy and Matt helped me become a more reflective practitioner and effective teacher. Critical relationships helped Sandy find compelling reading material, and the classroom environment, characterized by self-reflection and inquiry, gave Sandy the space to think, learn, and transform her literacy. Sandy helped me see myself as a teacher who needs to develop awareness of ways to orchestrate the myriad stories that students embody, stories that converge in the classroom. Through Sandy's story, I see my own.

REFERENCES

Armstrong, W. H. (1969). *Sounder.* New York, NY: Harper Collins.

Bateson, M. C. (1989). *Composing a life.* New York, NY: Plume.

Beane, J. A. (1997). *Curriculum integration: Designing the core of democratic education.* New York, NY: Teachers College Press.

Behar, R. (1996). *The vulnerable observer: Anthropology that breaks your heart.* Boston, MA: Beacon Press.

Blume, J. (1986). *Are you there God? It's me, Margaret.* New York, NY: Random House. (Original work published 1970)

Cabot, M. (2000). *The princess diaries.* New York, NY: Harper Teen.

Casey, H. (2008/2009). Engaging the disengaged: Using learning clubs to motivate struggling adolescent readers and writers. *Journal of Adolescent & Adult Literacy, 52*(4), 284-294.

Chan, E. (2006). Teacher experiences of culture in the curriculum. *Journal of Curriculum Studies, 38*(2), 161-176.

Charmaz, K. (2000). Grounded theory: Objectivist and constructivist methods. In N. K. Denzin & Y. S. Lincoln (Eds.), *Handbook of qualitative research* (2nd ed., pp. 509-535). Thousand Oaks, CA: Sage Publications.

Clandinin, D. J., & Connelly, F. M. (2000). *Narrative inquiry: Experience and story in qualitative research.* San Francisco, CA: Jossey-Bass.

Cochran-Smith, M., & Lytle, S. L. (1993). *Inside/outside: Teacher research and knowledge.* New York, NY: Teachers College Press.

Conle, C. (2003). An anatomy of narrative curricula. *Educational Researcher, 32*(3), 3-15.

Coulter, C., Michael, C., & Poynor, L. (2007). Storytelling as pedagogy: An unexpected outcome of narrative inquiry. *Curriculum Inquiry 37*(2), 103-122.

Frank, A. (1993). *Anne Frank: The diary of a young girl.* New York, NY: Bantam Books. (Original work published 1952)

Galda, L., & Beach, R. (2001). Response to literature as a cultural activity. *Reading Research Quarterly, 36*(1), 64-73.

Gordon, E., McKibbin, K., Vasudevan, L., & Vinz, R. (2007). Writing out of the unexpected: Narrative inquiry and the weight of small moments. *English Education, 39*(4), 326-351.

Ivey, G., & Broaddus, K. (2001). "Just plain reading:" A survey of what makes students want to read in middle school classrooms. *Reading Research Quarterly, 36*(4), 350-377.

Johnston, P. (1987). *Social scenes of reading: A study of eighth-graders' talk about books.* Unpublished doctoral dissertation, University of Pennsylvania, Philadelphia.

Moller, K. J., & Allen, J. (2000). Connecting, resisting, and searching for safer places: Students respond to Mildred Taylor's *The Friendship. Journal of Literacy Research, 32*(2), 145-186.

Moss, G. (2004). Provisions of trustworthiness in critical narrative research: Bridging intersubjectivity and fidelity. *The Qualitative Report, 9*(2), 359-373.

Nakkula, M. J., & Toshalis, E. (2006). *Understanding youth: Adolescent development for educators.* Cambridge, MA: Harvard Education Press.

Roney, K. (2001). The effective middle school teacher: Inwardly integrated, outwardly connected. In V. A. Anfara (Ed.), *The handbook of research in middle level education* (pp. 73-105). Greenwich, CT: Information Age.

Schaafsma, D., Pagnucci, G. S., Wallace, R. M., & Stock, P. L. (2007). Composing storied ground: Four generations of narrative inquiry. *English Education, 39*(4), 282-305.

Schaafsma, D., & Vinz, R. (2007). Composing narratives for inquiry. *English Education, 39*(4), 277-281.

Sebold, A. (2002). *The lovely bones.* New York, NY: Little, Brown and Company.

Strauss, A., & Corbin, J. (1998). *Basics of qualitative research: Techniques and procedures for developing grounded theory* (2nd ed.). Thousand Oaks, CA: Sage.

Vagle, M. D. (2007). Middle school teacher qualities: Looking for signs of dignity and democracy. In S. B. Mertens, V. A. Anfara, & M. M. Caskey (Eds.), *The handbook of research in middle level education* (pp. 73-105). Greenwich, CT: Information Age.

Van Horn, L. (2000). Sharing literature, sharing selves: Students reveal themselves through read-alouds. *Journal of Adolescent Literacy 43*(8), 752-763.

Wilder, L. I. (1959). *Little house in the big woods.* New York, NY: Harper Collins. (Original work published 1932)

Wilhelm, J. D. (1997). *"You gotta BE the book:" Teaching engaged and reflective reading with adolescents.* New York, NY: Teacher's College Press.

Wilson, J., Jewett, P., & Vanderburg, M. (2008). A whole-school "read" creates a reading community. *Middle School Journal, 40*(1), 4-11.

CHAPTER 7

"THIS IS THE WAY IT IS"

The Experiences of Preservice Middle School Teachers Integrating Instruction With High Stakes Test Preparation

Steven L. Turner

This chapter is the narrative of the experiences of 3 middle school student teachers learning to teach in an era of standardized testing. These preservice teachers' experiences, voices, and stories anchor a narrative examination of life in today's middle schools and address an important question in the current era of accountability. To what extent is it possible to integrate instruction and high stakes test preparation strategies?

INTRODUCTION

Teachers and parents of young adolescents are well aware that students in Grades 4-8 disproportionally bear the brunt of educational accountability (Anderson, 2009; Lipka, 2004). Young adolescents are among the most tested group of students in our nation's schools (Anderson, 2009), and middle school teachers often report the demand for accountability influ-

Voices From the Middle: Narrative Inquiry By, For, and About the Middle Level Community
pp. 127–150

ences how and what they teach (Faulkner & Cook, 2006). While Anderson (2009) and Faulkner and Cook (2006) explored the encroachment of high stakes testing on teaching in middle school, less is known about the experiences of preservice middle school teachers and how they manage instruction within a high stakes testing environment. This chapter presents the narratives of three student teachers who are learning to teach at a time when standardized test scores are highly valued, often at the expense of student learning (Erb, 2003; Popham, 2008). These preservice teachers want to leave students with experiences that inspire and motivate, but their stories, told here, reveal the often complex and contradictory challenges of the teaching profession. The experiences are, in part, a story of No Child Left Behind (2002) and the explicit pressures of accountability. The narratives also provide affirmation for the reasons why middle schools were first established and offer support for why middle grades teachers need to be specially prepared to support young adolescents' learning and development.

Amid calls for increased accountability and more rigorous standards, the middle school movement now finds itself under a spotlight of intense scrutiny (L'Esperance, Strahan, Farrington, & Anderson, 2003). High stakes testing, and to some extent, high stakes test preparation has become an inescapable reality for most middle level teachers (Erb, 2003; Turner, 2009). Is integrating test preparation into the curriculum good instruction? The answer may be moot. In the current age of educational accountability, good instruction, by default, has come to be defined as whatever raises student test scores (Grant, 2000; Rex & Nelson, 2004). When preparing students for high stakes exams, a central question most middle school teachers ask is whether they can prepare students for high stakes standardized tests without setting aside what they know to be true about effective teaching and learning (Faulkner & Cook, 2006; Turner, 2008, 2009). This is not just an issue for experienced teachers. Preservice middle school teachers, must also effectively gauge how to prepare students for high stakes tests without shortchanging meaningful instruction.

BACKGROUND AND OVERVIEW

This study utilizes a narrative inquiry lens to present the experiences of three middle level preservice teachers who learn to teach in an era of standardized testing. This study expands our knowledge about the ways preservice middle school teachers negotiate the pressure of accountability and middle school philosophy. By sharing these preservice teachers' experiences, I hope to offer insight into middle level instruction and high stakes test preparation as informed by these future middle school teachers' lived experiences.

Portraits of the Participants: The three participants involved with this study, Lara, Will, and Maria were part of a larger cohort of 20 student teachers in the final semester of an undergraduate initial teacher licensure program in middle childhood education at a large university in the Midwest. Each participant spent 12 weeks student teaching. Ten of those weeks were spent as the full-time teacher with full responsibility for instruction. Prior to student teaching, each participant had three 4-week clinical field experiences working in middle grade classrooms. To maintain confidentiality, all names are pseudonyms and identifying characteristics have been masked.

Lara, Will and Maria: Teaching in an Era of High Stakes: During clinical experiences prior to their student teaching semester, Lara, Will, and Maria expressed concern about the extent that high stakes testing conflicted with middle school philosophy. Prior to student teaching, the three teacher candidates met with me to discuss what they saw as an encroachment of test prep on instruction. Their purpose in meeting was to debate the positive and negative aspects of high stakes testing and brainstorm strategies for preparing students for the tests that were not just isolated drill and practice. Sensing their interest in exploring the topic further, I suggested during student teaching that each of them keep a journal of their student teaching experiences and record their attempts to integrate ethical high stakes test preparation and maintain meaningful instruction. Lara, Will, and Maria agreed to write about their experiences. They turned in their journals after completing student teaching and I did not grade the journals as part of the course.

Lara: Lara described her experiences teaching language arts and social studies in a rural middle school. Lara's school was on "academic watch" because the previous year almost thirty percent of the seventh grade students did not pass the standardized tests for social studies. Due to this unsatisfactory academic performance, Lara reported the curricular pacing and content decisions for her 12 weeks of instruction had already been made by the planning team prior to her arrival. Rather than feel burdened by decisions that were out of her hands, Lara embraced the planning team's philosophy and went into student teaching believing this would be the year her students passed the standardized tests.

Will: Will completed his student teaching in a suburban middle school (eighth grade science and math). Will considered himself a "hands on," student-centered teacher, preferring to create lessons and activities that were authentic and designed to engage students as active participants in learning. There was a strong focus at his school to prepare students for the upcoming second semester high stakes tests, which most students passed the previous year. Early in the semester, Will wrote that he was determined to maintain a balance between direct instruction and inquiry learning.

Maria: Maria student taught in a suburban seventh grade social studies and language arts classroom. The students in Maria's school generally did well on high stakes tests and the milieu of her school was heavily steeped in high stakes preparation. Each quarter her students took a battery of exams formatted to resemble the standardized tests they would take the following term. The students were tested in language arts, social studies, mathematics and science. Early in her student teaching, Maria reported that if there was a concept she wanted to teach and it was not a state standard, it was unlikely it she would be allowed to teach it.

Thinking about high stakes tests. Before student teaching began, the student teachers were asked to discuss their perspectives about high stakes tests. In her journal, Lara wrote:

> Keeping a positive attitude will not only motivate me, but also the students. What student would want a teacher to begin a lesson by saying "I know you all hate the high stakes test, I do too, but let's begin class with another boring activity...?" Making lessons engaging and interesting to students is what they will appreciate the most. They may not even consciously realize that they are preparing themselves for large tests that impact them significantly.

The pressure to prepare students to perform well on high stakes tests was the foremost concern for Will as his placement began:

> As a teacher in this new era of accountability I feel as though I should be "teaching to the test" to make sure my students achieve high scores, however, I know that would hinder my students' learning experiences ... I will continue to base my lessons on constructivist approaches in favor of student-centeredness ... to help my students as learners and test-takers.

Maria attended her school's professional development workshops and went into her student teaching experience aware of the importance the administration placed on successful student performance on high stakes tests and how that emphasis influenced instruction:

> The school district is very thorough in making sure students are well prepared in content and test-taking skills ... all of my lessons were based around content and school standards before I even went to look at [the specific topic] of the lesson I was teaching.

A summary of the student teacher demographics is shown in Table 7.1.

Table 7.1.   Summary of Student Teacher Demographics

Student Teacher	Grade	Subjects Taught	District	Class Previously Passed Tests in Licensure Area
Lara	7th	• Social studies • Language arts	Rural	No
Will	8th	• Science • Math	Suburban	Yes
Maria	7th	• Social studies • Language arts	Suburban	Yes

METHODOLOGY: TOOLS TO REVEAL THE NARRATIVE

Teachers lived experiences can be translated into illuminating narrative stories (Rushton, 2004). In narrative inquiry, the sense of the whole is built from rich data sources that create narrative strength (Connelly & Clandinin, 1990). A narrative inquiry design promotes open investigation of the participants' perceptions of the issues under study and narratives present a record of participant experiences and understandings. Journals created by participants and analysis of those journals are a useful narrative inquiry tool to investigate a contemporary phenomenon such as high stakes testing within its authentic context (Connelly & Clandinin, 1990; Creswell, 2008).

Journals

For this study, participant journal entries were chosen as a data source to explore the three student teachers' experiences with high stakes tests. The student teachers were asked to use journals as a place to record and explore their experiences with high stakes test preparation strategies.

Before student teaching began, I provided the student teachers with several high stakes test preparation strategies as a framework to investigate the extent to which high stakes test preparation could be integrated into their lessons without short-changing meaningful instruction. In their journals, the participants discussed which strategy (if any) they were able to integrate into the normal course of instruction. Specifically, for this study:

- The student teachers participated in two small group discussions with each other and the author, investigating the extent high stakes tests may align with goals of middle level education. The first discussion occurred the week before student teaching began. The second took place during the fifth week of teaching. Both occurred at the end of student teaching seminar class meetings.

- The student teachers submitted a cumulative, 12 week journal documenting their experiences with the five strategies. In the journal, students first reported, then offered reflection on their classroom experiences as they integrated strategies or implemented instruction that was geared toward preparing students for high stakes tests.

A Closer Look: Ethical High Stakes Test Preparation in Middle Schools

A meta-analysis and review of high stakes testing literature indicated that teachers, researchers, and measurement specialists identified several significant high stakes test preparation practices. These practices, if implemented appropriately and ethically, can help teachers demonstrate professional knowledge and support student learning during stressful instructional situations and high stakes testing (Gulek, 2003; Miyasaka, 2000; Turner, 2009; Volante, 2006). The five most-often cited high stakes test preparation practices in the literature were: (1) teaching to the curriculum and integrating test content; (2) integrating high stakes test assessment approaches and item formats; (3) reviewing test-taking strategies; (4) judicious timing of test preparation, and (5) successfully engaging students' motivation (Turner, 2009). Table 7.2 presents a detailed summary of the five strategies.

Analysis of Student Teachers' Journals

A content analysis was completed for all three student teachers' cumulative journals detailing their experiences with the five high stakes test preparation strategies. The data were reviewed in three steps. First, I read the journal entries individually, and then reread them together. The second step involved creating a large spreadsheet of each student teacher's experiences and comments taken from each of their journals. The comments and experiences from the journals were analyzed for common elements and broad similarities and differences across the three journals. This process was repeated by a peer to confirm agreement. Once agreement was achieved, two broad themes emerged:

Table 7.2.   Five Often Cited High Stakes Test Preparation Practices

Strategy	Description in Practice	Specific Example
Teaching to the curriculum and integrating expected test content	Teaching to the curriculum means a middle level teacher's instruction should closely follow the district's curriculum guide and provide students with the knowledge and skills on which they will be tested.	Using instructional compacting (focusing on concepts and content students have not yet mastered).
Integrating high stakes test assessment approaches and item formats	Middle school students will need opportunities to learn and practice a variety of assessment approaches likely to be on high stakes tests, including multiple-choice, short answer, extended response, vocabulary, word attack skills, and performance and computational tasks.	Providing multiple assessment methods (story form, short answer, fill-in-the-blank, true-false, presentation, written essay responses).
Reviewing test-taking strategies	Teachers can assure students are familiar with test-taking skills such as correctly marking answer sheets, strategies for making optimal guesses on certain types of items, and carefully allocating test-taking time	Skipping difficult items and creating a marker to return to them later. Creating a web or outline for written essay responses.
Judicious timing of test preparation	Suggested intervals for test preparation occur throughout the year and some scheduled review in close proximity to the test.	At the beginning of the year, align curriculum and class assessments with test assessment formats.
Engaging student motivation	When middle grade students are not sufficiently motivated to take high stakes tests, they often mark answers randomly, engage less in critical thinking and complete test items quickly without really trying or thinking about their answers.	Briefly review the importance of the tests and establish learning goals that are codeveloped by teachers and students.

1.   How and to what extent the strategy was attempted or integrated; and

2.   To what extent the strategy was reported to support or disengage students.

These themes were developed into coded categories. The total data set was further evaluated and grouped to determine whether implementing (or declining to use) the strategy aligned with the student teachers' stated beliefs about teaching. In sum, the student teachers' experiences with the five high stakes test preparation strategies were analyzed by documenting how each strategy was integrated, examining the extent each strategy was reported to engage students and identifying whether a belief about teaching was expressed through explanation of the use or nonuse of a strategy.

FINDINGS AND RESULTS

Teaching Young Adolescents and Teaching Ourselves

This section is organized around the five high stakes test preparation strategies and the student teachers' experiences with each one. The findings are presented individually and in summary form (see Table 7.3) to communicate the multiple perspectives of the study.

Teaching to the curriculum and integrating expected test content. Each of the three participants identified teaching to the district curriculum as an important task and indicated doing so was a significant element of their instruction. This strategy was reported by all participants as the easiest to integrate and was considered the most effective of the suggested strategies. The administration at Lara's school made it clear that all her lessons were to be aligned with curriculum and content standards students would later be tested on:

> I planned my lessons in social studies through a professional learning community. In this group of other eighth grade social studies teachers, we reviewed the standards that we needed to focus on, created a test directly based on those standards, and decided how we were going to implement this content into the classroom.

Lara felt additional pressure to focus on the district's curriculum since the students she worked with had struggled to pass the high stakes tests for social studies:

> The seventh grade has not been successful in passing the social studies [standardized tests]. In the back of my mind, I know that this could be the year the seventh grade social studies students pass their [state tests] and it is very important that I remain focused on what's significant.

Lara noted she reviewed seventh-grade content standards with her mentor teacher and made sure, while teaching, never to stray far from that content:

We reviewed the standards that we needed to focus on and created tests directly based on those standards and decided how we were going to implement content into the classroom … if I led a class discussion I made sure that I was using vocabulary and language that students may see on the tests. Activities that I planned all had a purpose and followed the content standards.

Will also made certain his students had ample opportunity to learn the content they would later be tested on, but he was determined not to allow the high stakes test to significantly alter his instruction or prohibit learning experiences he felt his students needed:

I didn't "teach to the test," but instead I found appropriate activities that supported the content that my students are expected to master by the end of the year … I have made it my mission to incorporate creativity and hands-on activities into my lessons that allow my students to explore and become active participants in their learning process. I believe that my students need a good balance between direct-instruction and inquiry learning, so I must make sure that both are incorporated in my lessons.

Additionally, Will reported the use of content differentiation and standards by pretesting students and focusing more instructional time on concepts students were unfamiliar with and less time on concepts students understood. This allowed him to intentionally plan instruction to focus on concepts his students were least familiar with:

At the beginning of each unit I provide my students with a pre-test so I, the teacher, can see what my students already know and what they have not yet mastered about the given content … since standardized tests are based on academic content standards, the pre-tests allow me to direct my instruction to the various parts of the curriculum that my students are not fully competent in while preparing them with the content knowledge they need to achieve high scores on standardized tests.

Maria spent a great deal of her student teaching struggling with the concept of "teaching to the test." There was not a day in the 12 weeks she was teaching she did not feel pressure to cover more concepts from the curriculum. If there was a possibility a concept might be on the test, Maria felt it was her duty to teach it. Maria learned to approach instruction thoughtfully or the idea of only covering what is likely to be on the test could overtake her intentions for instruction:

I have often found myself tempted to fall into the gap of teaching to the test. It is easy to have students day after day open their text book and read new information, while hoping they are able to soak up enough of the information to [repeat] back on a standardized chapter test … however, my cooperating teachers and I have each challenged ourselves by breaking away from the norm … often my cooperating teachers and I would sit down and pull out the school's curriculum and the state standards and figure out what concept we were to cover and how to best [engage the students on the topic involved].

Integrating assessment approaches and test item formats. Each student teacher wrote about attempting to integrate varied assessments and different assessment formats. Lara reported that she occasionally modified assessment approaches and was extremely conscientious about including assessment formats that were likely to be on high stakes tests. She wanted to be certain if her students did not do well on the standardized exams it would not be because they were unfamiliar with the format of the test:

> Assessment approaches in social studies were very much aligned to the state tests that my students will take…every small detail is considered, from the word choice of questions, the way the state test is formatted, including font, spacing, directions, etc. I worked really hard to make sure that all social studies tests that I gave looked like what the students would receive when it came time for them to take the [standardized tests].

Lara believed integrating assessment approaches and item format was smart teaching and openly wondered if there would be an opportunity later to complete a test-item-analysis to see if students scored higher on test-item formats they had been exposed to before the test:

> I feel that this strategy supports student learning [because] students will become comfortable and familiar with each type of format. It will be interesting to compare test results from this year to other years based on test format and question practice implemented in class.

Not all responsibility for familiarizing students with test approaches or formats was left with the student teachers—Lara noted her school administration took matters into their own hands:

> [Our school] recently has implemented the usage of a test scan machine. Students now make marks on a bubble sheet and answer short and extended questions on an answer document, just like the [state test].

Reviewing test-taking strategies. Just as they ensured their students were familiar with the types of assessments on standardized tests, the three student teachers reported that middle-level students needed to know how to take tests. All three indicated they consistently integrated wise test-taking strategies into their instruction. There was little drill reported. The student teachers indicated they presented test-taking strategies to their students in the context of sharing ideas to help students succeed on the test.

Will discussed his belief that reviewing test-taking strategies was akin to setting his students up for success:

> As an educator, it is my job to help students learn content, but it is also extremely important to guide them through test-taking strategies that will help them keep a steady pace, minimize errors, remain focused, and feel confident in themselves ... I taught students how to recognize and eliminate incorrect answers to help them minimize their options and make it easier to identify the correct answer. Just by the way my class ran, my students understood that they should always make an educated guess instead of skipping a tough question.

Students were explicitly taught test-taking strategies at Lara's school. For example, since short answer questions was an area where her students struggled, the teachers Lara worked with developed a strategy to help students monitor their written responses on tests and quizzes:

> Test taking strategies are reviewed and used throughout the year to help students practice skills to use on their achievement tests whether students know this or not. One way that we have already began to execute strategies in short answer and extended response questions is through the usage of the acronym IDEA. The acronym stands for the following: I - Include the question in your answer; D - Use descriptive vocabulary words in your writing; E - Explain or provide examples in your response. A - Answer each part of the question ... using the acronym helps students to organize their thoughts and provides them with a checklist when they read over their responses. It has so far been effective for all students.

Maria concluded her units of instruction with broad content reviews and reteaching challenging content, but as the weeks passed, she felt her students' grades did not accurately reflect their knowledge and understanding. She narrowed the problem to strategies the students used (or did not use) while taking a test:

> As I started getting deeper and deeper into my student teaching experience I could tell a difference in the responses I was getting back on assessments and evaluations I was giving to the students. Starting out, I focused on reviewing material students were about to be quizzed or tested on, and often times that helped, but I soon learned that it was not enough. If a student knew the information but was lost on how to go about taking a test correctly, then content knowledge was going to be of no assistance to them. My cooperating teacher and I sat down and created a workshop for students focus-

ing on the best strategies to use when attempting to take any kind of tests. Students had the opportunity to learn how to correctly set up a short answer response, how to read through a multiple choice question to identify the best answer, and also [other] reading strategies that assist in comprehension.

In Maria's view, what started as a review of test-taking strategies, essentially transformed into an opportunity to engage students' metacognition, improve strategic thinking and provide Maria with greater insight into the teaching and learning process:

As the students and I progressed through this test-taking workshop, it was easy to see the difference in students' thinking processes by the end of the week. Yes, they were still quick to pick a multiple-choice answer, still making other simple mistakes when reading a selection, but they were able to identify these simple mistakes after making them. They could tell me the steps they should take when going about reading, and they knew how to break apart a multiple choice question. However, now it was up to them to take these skills and slow down to apply them as they took their exams. Overall, after grading the exams I could tell the students did just that, and those who had previously struggled on multiple question tests were improving.

Judicious Timing of Test Preparation. The timing of test preparation was cause for anxiety and concern—how much is too much? The student teachers indicated there was a fine line between preparation and pressure, and admittedly, they sometimes crossed it. Research indicates that in schools where students tend to perform above expectations on high stakes tests, review of specific test taking strategies is ongoing and purposely integrated into day-to-day curriculum (Johannessen & Kahn, 2001; Langer, 2001). Rather than set aside specific days or times, Will ensured his high stakes test preparation took place continuously, throughout the year:

Cramming in standardized test strategies and content right before a test is not as helpful as frequent preparation throughout the school year. As an instructor, I try to incorporate as many test preparation strategies as possible in my lessons without the students realizing that they are preparing for a test.

Consensus on whether it is ethical to use previous year's test questions as preparation for high stakes tests is not to be found in the literature (Gulek, 2003; Miyasaka, 2000; Popham, 2008). Should the practice of using old test questions be considered "good" teaching? Will explained his rationale for using previous test questions in his instruction:

I occasionally like to give my students a [standardized test] question from previous tests as a bell work problem. These questions will usually be aligned to the content from the previous day to see if they can apply what they learned. I never tell my students that this is a [standardized test] practice question but instead I call it a challenge or problem of the day…. my students are exposed to standardized test questions and formats without even realizing they are.

Test preparation was approached differently in Lara's class. Many of her students failed the social studies test last year and the school's faculty implemented several test preparation strategies with the hope of engineering a more positive result the semester Lara student taught:

Test preparation for my students has been occurring since basically the beginning of the school year. Everything that we do in the classroom is a piece of the [high stakes standardized test] puzzle that gears them towards a passing score … students are also well aware that some of the activities that we practice in class or what I had them do at home was practice for the [high stakes standardized test] … making students aware of the test earlier gives them time to prepare and work hard over an extended amount of time … I felt that this strategy supported student learning because … instead of cramming at the last minute, students have taken weeks, even months to prepare.

Test preparation was often a collaborative activity between Lara and her students. She gave students multiple opportunities through the year to assess their own work and become comfortable with assessments—both formal and informal:

In both of my classes, students were given rubrics along with some of their major assignments or projects. They were able to assess their own work before turning it in and also were able to ask questions about what they would be graded on. Formative and summative assessments were [woven] into both social studies and language arts units. I also implemented quick check and exit tickets to gauge student comprehension and learning. After reviewing each assessment, I provided students with feedback and gave them their assessment as a study tool for not only their unit exams, but also the high stakes tests.

Maria and her teaching team planned mid-term tests in the style of the standardized tests her students would later be taking:

Each quarter students would receive tests formatted like the standardized tests they would be seeing the following year. The students are tested in language arts, social studies, mathematics and science. There are two or three days given in certain subjects to review the main concepts of the quarter, but mostly it is an opportunity to see what the students retain, and how well they are able to set up their own study skills to review information previously presented to them.

The impending high stakes tests presented an interesting dilemma for Maria and her team. If students did not do well, there were likely to be unfortunate consequences for students, teachers and the school. What did this mean in practice? Maria indicated in her social studies and language arts classes, this meant turning to a method of high stakes test preparation that was not widely supported (Faulkner & Cook, 2006; Popham, 2008): Giving full class periods over to test preparation:

> Before standardized testing was to occur … we set aside a part of class to go over test-taking skills and review [content], then as the tests came closer we would spend full class periods reviewing material. It was never a case where the tests came as a surprise to students, nor were they expected to manage all the preparation for a test on their own.

Engaging student-motivation. Each student teacher reported they used a combination of personal enthusiasm and authentic instruction to engage student motivation to increase the learner's personal connection to curriculum. Will explained how he honored his students for their humanity before he approached them as learners:

> I try to create a classroom environment where my students feel comfortable enough to make guesses and are not afraid to make mistakes. One student in my sixth grade classroom stated that one of my teaching strengths was "making you think you could do it and not laughing if you got something wrong." This statement shows the classroom environment I established for my students [was one] where they felt motivated and encouraged to succeed. This environment provided my students with a safe place to learn and gave them the much needed [belief] they can pass any standardized test because they are capable of succeeding in anything they put their minds to.

Will indicated his way of knowing and his teaching philosophy were essential to his students' personal development and academic achievement:

> I believe that students learn more by discovering concepts through their own experiences. Using their personal experiences to recall information is a great skill that will help students succeed on standardized tests.

Maria worked to establish a classroom community where learning goals were codeveloped by teachers and students:

In preparation for standardized testing of students in my language arts classroom, my cooperating teacher and I had students set a personal goal that they hope to achieve ... students responded well to this and seemed to take more pride in the work they were doing, all while holding themselves responsible for their own success.

Maria and her mentor searched for a way to increase student engagement. Toward the middle of the semester, they presented the students with an idea:

My mentor teacher explained to students that instead of complaining and groaning every time they were forced to take another state standardized test, they should instead look at it as an opportunity to prove their intelligence. She would constantly tell them "I've always known I was smart, now here is my chance to prove it to the world." This speech would always have the students building up excitement and the confidence to take the test without letting doubt and dread cloud their abilities.

Lara also found ways to motivate students in her social studies classes, the subject her students struggled with most on high stakes tests, by integrating more open-ended questions and including more activities asking students to make decisions and explain why and how they answered as they did:

I felt that it was in my best interest to motivate students to stay positive and engaged in what they were doing. For example, I used "Think Tank" prompts in my classroom. One example of an opening prompt that I used asked students to explain what a compromise was and to provide an example of when they had to make a compromise in their life. This Think Tank was relevant to our content because students were learning about the Constitutional Convention that took place in Philadelphia and the compromises that were discussed at this meeting amongst the delegates. Think Tanks like these eased students into the main goal or objective of the lesson. Students were motivated by Think Tanks because they were able to make connections to their life and share with their peers.

A summary of how each student teacher implemented the five strategies is presented in Table 7.3.

Middle Level Teaching and High Stakes Test Preparation

Lara and Will concluded their journals by indicating they expected to begin their teaching career in middle schools figuring out ways to combine instruction and test prep. Will, whose journal indicated he was gen-

Table 7.3.   Summary of Student Teachers' Test Preparation Practices

Strategy	Lara	Will	Maria
Teaching to the curriculum and integrating expected test content	• Taught lessons aligned with the curriculum and content student would be tested on. • Integrated vocabulary students were likely see on tests.	• Embedded content students would be tested on in creative inquiry-based lessons. • Pretested students to differentiate content.	• Focused instruction on the most important concepts and standards. • Collaborated with mentor to plan engaging activities
Integrating high stakes test assessment approaches and item formats	• Every teacher-made test was modeled after the format of state tests. • Students were made familiar with a broad variety of assessments.	• Students were made familiar with a broad variety of assessments. • Extended response questions modeled after the format of state tests.	• Held bimonthly assessments for students using a broad variety of assessments, including multiple choice, short answer and extended responses.
Reviewing test-taking strategies	• Taught test-taking strategies and provided opportunities to use them in class. • Offered students strategies to monitor their own performance.	• Reviewed and taught test-taking strategies and provided opportunities to use them in class.	• Held test-taking strategy workshops. • Offered students strategies to individually monitor their own performance.
Judicious timing of test preparation	• Gave test practice activities in school and as homework. • Collaborated with students to practice ways to individually monitor their own performance on assessments.	• Regularly incorporated test preparation activities throughout the year.	• Gave students mid-term test formatted like standardized tests. • Set aside full class periods for reviewing content expected to be on the standardized tests.
Engaging student motivation	• Gave students opportunities to connect learning to their personal experiences.	• Sought to create a safe class environment where students were willing to make mistakes. • Encouraged students to connect learning to their personal experiences.	• Collaborated with students to set personal learning goals. • Explained high stakes tests as an opportunity to show how much they have learned.

erally upbeat throughout his student teaching experience, admitted some tension about high stakes testing in his final entry.

> I do feel pressured to make sure my students do well on these tests, but at the same time I feel if I teach my students all they need to know and provide them with support and confidence, they will succeed … I definitely think these tests put a lot stress on teachers and students but I must remember not to lose all the effective teaching strategies I have learned … and continue to base my lessons on constructivist approaches in favor of student-centeredness to help my students as learners and test-takers.

Lara concluded her journal with thoughts toward a future career as a middle school teacher that would almost certainly include high stakes tests:

> In the future I know testing will continue to be one of the biggest concerns. I will hold on to what I have learned throughout student teaching about how to weave test preparation into lessons and how to motivate students to be triumphant in the content that they must learn. It is important to stay grounded as a teacher when considering [high stakes] tests … teachers need to take one day at a time.

Common Patterns Across Narratives

Although it may appear the narratives of the three student teachers resist easy categorization, four issues emerged that link the student teachers' experiences.

1. *Increasing students' academic achievement is a priority.* The student teachers' experiences essentially present a pattern that was common to the three of them. They all taught using learning experiences that were largely developmentally aligned with middle-level philosophy and were infused with strategies designed to increase student scores on standardized tests. Some of the developmental middle level practices noted were differentiation, connections made to students' personal experiences, and the use of a wide variety of assessment approaches.

2. *Some measure of test preparation may be warranted and appropriate.* All three student teachers reported it was their duty to prepare students to take high stakes, standardized tests. For two of the student teachers, most of the test preparation occurred in daily instruction. One instituted test-prep workshops and used student data gener-

ated by the workshop to plan specific instructional interventions in advance of the high stakes tests.

3. *Students must be engaged in the learning process.* All three student teachers at some point in their journals advocated for authentic instruction or active engagement of the students. They recognized that students did not try their best on standardized tests nor any other academic task if they were not sufficiently engaged in their work.

4. *Student teachers experience pressure with regard to high stakes tests and seek to integrate some measure of test preparation.* The five high stakes test preparation strategies were suggested as a guide, to see to what extent they could be integrated while maintaining meaningful instruction. All three student teachers embraced each strategy and wrote about the extent to which each was implemented. Pressure to prepare students for standardized tests existed in all three narratives, regardless of whether or not the student teacher taught in a high performing or a struggling school.

DISCUSSION AND IMPLICATIONS

Increasing students' academic achievement has always been an important goal of middle level instruction, but is integrating test preparation into the curriculum good instruction? All three student teachers integrated high stakes test preparation into their instruction, and one in conjunction with her mentor teacher, focused a significant part of her instruction and academic learning time on increasing students' preparation for standardized tests. Given the complexity of issues related to accountability and how measures of student achievement are used, it is not completely unexpected that middle school student teachers would report that they provided instruction that prepared students for standardized tests.

What Current Research Says

Over the last decade, high stakes test preparation has gradually infiltrated the inventory of developmentally responsive middle level instructional practices (Erb, 2003; Faulkner & Cook, 2006, Turner, 2009). Teachers and student teachers report pressure from school administrators, policymakers, and the media to improve test scores (White, Sturtevan,t & Dunlap, 2003). Unfortunately in the current culture of testing and accountability, for many educators, teaching for higher achievement has come to be synonymous with teaching to the test (Haney, 2000; Nichols &

Berliner, 2005). In the experiences of the student teachers presented here, there was an emphasis on test preparation and providing students with opportunities to learn concepts and skills that students would later be tested on. This practice aligns with current research findings—middle level teachers consistently report accountability has led them to emphasize specific information that will be tested and to neglect material involving higher-order thinking and problem-solving (Anderson, 2009; Faulkner & Cook, 2006). Should the goal of earning higher standardized test scores be a driving force in our nation's middle-level instruction? Some have argued for dismantling the middle school model, claiming it is not structured to focus on achievement (Manzo, 2000a, 2000b). Monty Neill, a national advocate for open and fair testing warns:

> The higher the stakes, the more schools focus instruction on the tests. Whole subjects, such as science, social studies, art, or physical education may be reduced or eliminated if only language arts and math are tested. Even in tested subjects many important topics or skills that are not covered by the exam are not taught. Instruction starts to resemble the tests. (Neill, 2006, p. 30)

The news is not all negative. Recent reports note the positive influence high stakes testing can have on increasing the general quality of teaching—including deepening instruction, more closely aligning instruction with standards, and increasing opportunities for professional development (Darling-Hammond & Rustique-Forrester, 2005). Middle level teachers who follow curriculum aligned with state standards and use test data as feedback on instruction have reported positive effects on high stakes test performance (Anderson, 2009). High stakes test preparation, done ethically and appropriately, does not have to detract from meaningful teaching and can instead be a significant tool to aid genuine understanding and learning (Gulek, 2003; Volante, 2006). However, the student teachers' narratives recounted here suggest the need for preservice teachers to develop a more systematic understanding of the difference between teaching for greater student achievement (test prep in the hopes of higher test scores), and teaching for greater student understanding (stronger comprehension, transfer and application of ideas and concepts).

One area of limited research is our understanding of the impact that accountability and the culture of testing has on preservice teachers' and beginning teachers' beliefs about teaching and pedagogy. In this study, we can infer beliefs about teaching from the narratives of the three student teachers, but there were few instances where the student teachers questioned high stakes tests or questioned the appropriateness of dedicating significant amounts of class time to prepare for them.

Is it even appropriate to assume current preservice middle school teachers, most of whom recently experienced a high stakes testing environment during their 6th-12th grade years, are capable of critically questioning the impact of high stakes testing on the middle school classroom? Will beginning middle school teachers push back against the emphasis on standardized testing they have become acculturated to as both a student and a teacher? Should they? Answers to those questions will have a clear impact on the professional practice of middle school teachers. These questions need further study.

Implications for Middle School Teacher Preparation Programs

The issues raised by these narratives have implications for mentoring, professional development and the design of middle level teacher preparation programs. Teacher education conceptual frameworks, which are already inundated with licensure and accreditation requirements, must also offer opportunities for preservice teachers to investigate how the intense pressure on students and teachers created by assessment driven reforms may influence their classroom instruction. Other steps middle level teacher preparation programs can take include:

- Inviting experienced middle school teachers to speak to preservice teachers about the challenges and rewards of teaching in an era of accountability as defined by NCLB or value-added measures.
- Providing opportunities for preservice teachers to study, challenge, and articulate their beliefs regarding high stakes standardized tests and their impact on teaching and learning in the middle grades.
- Developing partnerships of sustained engagement with local school districts and providing consultation and leadership on issues related to middle-level testing, especially effective instructional practices and strategies for improving student achievement.

Implications for Middle Level Research

In pursuing this line of research, it became clear that there is considerably more to learn regarding the relationship between high stakes tests, test preparation, and middle school philosophy. One area that requires more investigation is the extent to which the vision of middle schools as developmentally responsive, academically challenging, and socially equitable, is supported or undermined by high stakes tests, test preparation, and how test data is used. Though previous attempts to ascertain the relationship between middle level practice and student achievement have produced ambiguous and conflicting results (Anfara & Lipka, 2003), it is an endeavor worthy of further study. Another area important for middle-level researchers, teachers and administrators to address in future work are longitudinal studies evaluating the impact preparing for high stakes tests has on preservice and beginning teachers' instruction, beliefs about student learning and their understanding of middle level philosophy. Long-term studies are needed because instructional practices used by preservice and beginning teachers' may influence their instructional decisions for many years following (White et al., 2003).

Current systems of educational accountability are tied to high stakes testing, and the middle school movement has struggled with poor performance of students on national and international eighth grade assessments (Anfara, 2009). Future research is needed that surveys middle level teachers whose students tend to perform well on high stakes tests; specifically, what are those teachers' instructional practices that address high stakes tests, and to what extent do those practices maintain meaningful learning in the middle grades? Additionally, the voices and perspectives of early adolescents regarding high stakes tests and their experiences with test preparation need to be documented and disseminated. Future middle level research on high stakes test preparation should present both national and international perspectives.

Conclusion: This Is the Way it Is

What do these stories from the newest members of our profession tell us about life in middle schools in an era of accountability? We know that for these preservice teachers, when given ethical and appropriate test preparation strategies, they can plan instruction that integrates excellent ideas for test prep. But should excellent test preparation be the aim of middle school educators? Lara, in her final journal entry, puts the matter into perspective:

> I think all teachers essentially worry about their students passing [high stakes tests], some are just better at hiding their worries than others ... testing preparation is basically built into the curriculum [here], teachers make it very clear that their students need to pass this test. In my three months working in this environment, I have never heard one student complain about the test, make any negative comment about activities that were implemented in the classroom, nor challenge my mentor teacher or I in the activities that we planned. I think that many students have come to the realization that this is the way it is ... and [many] already [have] been greatly

exposed to this type of atmosphere, where many activities revolve around test prep.

Somewhere in the discussion about high stakes test preparation, accountability, and its effects on the educational experiences of young adolescents, a debate about the aims of middle school instruction and the purpose of education should occur. Is education the process of shaping the skills and intellect of our children and inviting them into the great conversations of our nation's cultural and intellectual life? Or is education a student's accumulation of a discreet set of knowledge and skills that can be measured with standardized tests of general competence (Neil, 2003, 2006; Sadker & Zittleman, 2004)? Both points of view exist simultaneously, and each view has arguments that are extensively documented and persuasive. Yet the increase of instructional time given over to high stakes test preparation in middle grades is an educational benchmark that cannot and should not be ignored. This trend has an impact on middle school curriculum and student promotion rates. As an unintended consequence of accountability, middle school students are among the most tested group of students in our nation's schools (Anderson, 2009). It may be a disservice not to offer middle school students some form of high stakes test preparation. Integrating test prep into instruction is a choice many preservice and middle school teachers' must make. I am not sure that a preservice teacher's choice to integrate test preparation methods, even test preparation methods identified as ethical, is a good choice. Hopefully, discussion about high stakes test preparation and high stakes tests will continue to address what it means to be a middle school teacher in the current era of accountability. The outcome of this discussion represents one of the best hopes we have that the standard for educational accountability may evolve to truly reflect what young adolescents need to know, understand, and be able to do.

REFERENCES

Anderson, L. W. (2009). Upper elementary grades bear the brunt of accountability. *Phi Delta Kappan, 90*(6), 413-418.

Anfara, V. A., Jr. (2009). Changing times require a changing middle grades research agenda. *Middle School Journal, 40*(5), 61-68.

Anfara, V. A., Jr., & Lipka, R. P. (2003). Relating the middle school concept to student achievement. *Middle School Journal, 35*(1), 24-32.

Connelly, F. M., & Clandinin, D. J. (1990). Stories of experience and narrative inquiry. *Educational Researcher, 19*(5), 2-14.

Creswell, J. W. (2008). *Educational research: Planning, conducting, and evaluating quantitative and qualitative research.* Upper Saddle River, NJ: Pearson.

Darling-Hammond, L., & Rustique-Forrester, E. (2005). The consequences of student testing for teaching and teacher quality. In J. L. Herman & E. H. Haertel (Eds.), *Uses and misuses of data for educational accountability and improvement, 104th yearbook of the National Society for the Study of Education, Part 2* (pp. 289-319). Malden, MA: Blackwell.

Erb, T. O. (2003). Achievement: What tests test or something grander? *Middle School Journal, 35*(1), 4.

Faulkner, S. A., & Cook, C. M. (2006). Testing vs. teaching: The perceived impact of assessment demands on middle grades instructional practices. *Research in Middle Level Education Online, 29*(7). Retrieved from http://www.nmsa.org

Grant, S. G. (2000, February). Teachers and tests: Exploring teachers' perceptions of changes in the New York State-mandated testing program. *Education Policy Analysis Archives, 8*(14). Retrieved from http://epaa.asu.edu/epaa

Gulek, C. (2003). Preparing for high stakes testing. *Theory into Practice, 42*(1), 42-50.

Haney, W. (2000). The myth of the Texas miracle in education. *Educational Policy Archives, 8*, 41. Retrieved from http://epaa.asu.edu/epaa

Johannessen, L. R., & Kahn, E. A. (2001, October). *How to prepare students for high-stakes tests and still live with your conscience!* Paper presented at the annual fall conference of the IL Association of Teachers of English, Elmhurst, IL.

Langer, J. A. (2001). Succeeding against the odds in English. *English Journal, 91*(1), 37-42.

L'Esperence, M. E., Strahan, D. B., Farrington, V., & Anderson, P. J. (2003). *Raising achievement: Project genesis, a significant school model.* Westerville, OH: NMSA.

Lipka, R. L. (2004) High stakes testing. *Middle Level Education Research Policy Brief,* 1-3. Retrieved from http://www.rmle.pdx.edu/

Manzo, K. K. (2000a). Missed opportunities. *Education Week, 20*(5), 15-19.

Manzo, K. K. (2000b). The weak link. *Education Week, 20*(5), 3-8.

Miyasaka, J.R. (2000, April). *A framework for evaluating the validity of test preparation practices.* Paper presented at the annual meeting of the American Educational Research Association, Chicago, IL.

Neill, M. (2003). The dangers of testing. *Educational Leadership, 60*(5), 43-46

Neill, M. (2006). The case against high stakes testing. *Principal, 85*(4), 28-30, 32.

Nichols, S. L., & Berliner, D. C. (2005). *The inevitable corruption of indicators and educators through high stakes testing.* Retrieved from http.www.asu.edu/cduc/epsl/

No Child Left Behind Act of 2001 (H.R.1), Title II. Public Law 107-110 (2002). Retrieved from http://www.ed.gov/policy/elsec/leg/esea02/index.html

Popham, W. J. (2008). *Classroom assessment* (5th ed). Boston, MA: Pearson.

Rex, L. A., & Nelson, M. C. (2004). How teachers' professional identities position high-stakes test preparation in their classroom. *Teachers College Record, 106*(6), 1288-1331.

Rushton, S. P. (2004). Using narrative inquiry to understand a student-teacher's practical knowledge while teaching in an inner-city school. *The Urban Review, 36*(1), 61-79.

Sadker, D., & Zittleman, K. (2004). Test anxiety: Are students failing test—Or are tests failing students? *Phi Delta Kappan, 85*(10), 740-751.

Turner, S. L. (2008). Moving beyond teaching to the test: High stakes test preparation and middle school instruction which supports young adolescents' learning. *Ohio Middle School Journal, 31*(2), 4-9.

Turner, S. L. (2009). Ethical and appropriate high stakes test preparation in middle school: Five methods that matter. *Middle School Journal, 41*(1), 36-45.

Volante, L. (2006). Toward appropriate preparation for standardized achievement testing. *Journal of Educational Thought, 40*(2), 129-144.

White, C. S., Sturtevant, E. G., & Dunlap, K. L. (2003). Preservice and beginning teachers' perceptions of the influence of high stakes tests on their literacy-rated instructional beliefs and decisions. *Reading Research and Instruction, 43*(2), 39-62.

CHAPTER 8

RECLAIMING CAMELOT

Capturing the Reflections of Exemplary, Veteran Middle School Teachers in an Age of High Stakes Testing and Accountability Through Narrative Inquiry

Nancy Fichtman Dana, Darby Claire Delane, and Paul George

The purpose of this study was to understand the ways that the current era of high stakes testing and accountability affected and shaped the experiences of 8 outstanding middle-school team leaders over the past 3 decades. Through phenomenological interviewing and narrative analysis, these exemplary educators' perspectives and experiences over the years are captured by utilizing a jigsaw puzzle metaphor as a way to: (1) explain what the participants refer to as the Camelot era of middle school education, (2) explain how the vision and practices of this era were directly affected by the intrusion of the era of accountability and a loss of local, school-based control for educating early adolescents, and (3) illustrate how middle school leaders might "reclaim Camelot," as they seek to effectively negotiate the tensions between the middle school reform of the Camelot era and that of high stakes testing and accountability.

Voices From the Middle: Narrative Inquiry By, For, and About the Middle Level Community
pp. 151–172
Copyright © 2010 by Information Age Publishing

SETTING THE STAGE

With the changing of the guard in the U.S. Executive Office, many political and media analysts draw parallels between Barack Obama and John F. Kennedy, spinning the new presidency as an opportunity to reclaim the "Camelot years." The Kennedy era is often remembered for its domestic focus on collectivity, civil rights, a call for innovation and new ways of thinking, and the reenvisioning of responsible leadership. President Kennedy, like many in the early 1960s, was a great fan of the Broadway musical, "Camelot," which told the hopeful story of King Arthur's transformation into leadership marked by service and a commitment to building a unifying identity. Kennedy's favorite song from the musical included these lyrics:

> Don't let it be forgot
> That once there was a spot,
> For one brief, shining moment
> That was known as Camelot (Lerner & Loewe, 1960).

Middle level education experienced the shining moments of a Camelot era in the 1970s, a period characterized by such practices as teaming, exploratory programs, thematic curriculum, small group advisement, and block scheduling (George & Alexander, 2003). These signature practices of exemplary middle school education seem to have been all too brief. There is evidence that core middle school practices have gradually waned over the subsequent decades (George, 2008). This diminution was particularly stark around the turn of the twenty-first century when the implications for an age of accountability and high stakes testing gripped middle school education at the ground level. At a time when the "essential components of effective middle school programs began to disappear from the daily experience of educators and students" (George, 2008, p. 1), it may be time to tap into the collective expertise of the teachers who lived in the Camelot era, make sense of what happened to core middle school practices since the era of increased accountability, and attempt to repaint a portrait of what Camelot could mean for middle schools today.

We embarked on this narrative study of middle level educators in a district known widely for its exemplary implementation of the middle school concept. We targeted teachers with 20-40 years of teaching experience in order to capture their reflections on their careers and the changes they experienced as middle school educators over time. In particular, since a signature feature of middle level education during the Camelot era was teaming, we focused on middle school teachers who served in the role of team leader during the 1970s, 1980s, and 1990s. While the importance of interdisciplinary teaming in supporting effective middle school education has long been established (Boyer & Bishop, 2004; Clark, 1997; Flowers, Mertens, & Mulhall, 2000; Husband & Short, 1994; Lee & Smith, 1993; Pounder, 1999), few studies have focused on how these practices are affected by the current era of No Child Left Behind.

The purpose of this study was to understand the ways that the current era of high-stakes testing and accountability affected and shaped the experiences of outstanding middle-school team leaders over the past three decades. By gaining the historical perspectives of veteran middle school educators through narrative, we hope that the practices that hall-marked middle school reform in the decades leading up to the reauthorization of the No Child Left Behind Act of 2001 will be more closely re-examined through the lenses of practitioners at the school level.

METHODOLOGY

The eight participants in this study were selected through purposeful sampling, which involves seeking "information-rich cases" for in-depth study (Patton, 2002). We sought to find and interview 5-10 middle school educators who taught for over 20 years, served in the role of team leader during the late 1970s, 1980s, and/or 1990s, and had an established reputation for being exemplary, innovative middle school practitioners. We began by inviting a recent National Middle School Association's Distinguished Educator Award winner to participate in this study. From her recommendations we used snowball sampling to find seven additional participants. These participants came from a wide variety of schools and educational contexts within a single school district serving approximately 30,000 K-12 students, and containing seven middle schools (and one K-8 school) that represented a spectrum of socioeconomic, cultural, and geographic contexts, ranging from rural, to urban, to suburban settings. An individual 60- to 90-minute interview was conducted with each participant, and each interview was audio-recorded and transcribed verbatim in order to capture the collective wisdom, experience, and reflections of these veteran middle level educators. Pseudonyms were assigned to each participant.

The interviews were modeled after Seidman's (1991) phenomenological interviewing process. This interview method assumes that an individual's stories are of interest "because they are of worth" (Seidman, 1991, p. 3), and phenomenological interviewing is consistent with narrative inquiry. In phenomenological interviewing, researchers frame interview questions for the participants with three separate emphases, each building upon the other.

The first emphasis is on the life history of the participants. The goal of these questions are to put the participants' experiences in context by learning as much about them as possible in terms of their middle school teaching experiences up until the present time. The second emphasis is to ask participants to reflect on experiences in middle level education. Questions with this emphasis are structured in order to create a space for the participants to tell stories of their work as middle level educators through the years. The third emphasis is reflection, where participants are asked questions that help them synthesize, articulate, and make meaning of their life and experiences as middle school professionals. Through questions that focused on these three emphases (life history, experiences, and meaning-making), the participants in this study were asked to describe what it was like to serve as middle school educators and team leaders over the span of their careers with special emphasis on their observations and experiences of how middle school practices and goals changed in the last decade. Table 8.1 summarizes the questions that were asked of each participant.

Table 8.1.   Interview Protocol

Emphasis	*Interview Questions*
Life history	1. Tell me the (insert name of person) story.
	2. How did you come to your career in education?
	3. How did you come to be a middle school educator?
	4. How did you define the work of a middle school teacher?
	5. You've been identified as an exemplary teacher leader by your colleagues—how do you (or did you) define your role as a middle school teacher leader?
Experiences	6. Give me a feeling for what it was like when you served a teacher leadership role as a teacher in the middle school. What kinds of experiences, stories, or situations might you share about being a middle school teacher leader?
	7. I'm going to ask you to reflect on *being a team leader* in the 1970s, 1980s, and 1990s. I'll ask you what your goals, your roles, and your responsibilities were as a team leader, as well as how your teams were organized. First, how were teams organized at that time?
	8. What would you say were your primary goals as a team leader in the 1970s, 1980s and 1990s?
	9. What would you say were your primary roles and responsibilities as a team leader in the 1970s, 1980s, and 1990s?
	10. What might a typical work week or work month look like as a middle school team leader at that time?
Meaning making	11. I would like you to reflect on your observations and experiences on how middle school team leadership has changed and/or stayed the same over time. First, how have you seen team leadership change over the span of you career?
	12. In what ways has it stayed the same?

Data analysis consisted of many readings and rereadings of the data set (verbatim interview transcripts from each participant) by two members of the research team individually, during which time we independently coded the data for themes and patterns. A three-hour research meeting was then held, creating the space for two of us to share, discuss, and debate patterns and themes emerging from our initial review of transcripts. When we agreed on patterns, a second round of transcript readings were conducted to look for confirming and disconfirming evidence to support patterns (Erikson, 1986). To ensure trustworthiness of this study, we then reported and discussed these patterns with a third member of our research team, a university colleague with over 30 years of experience researching and writing on middle level education, to engage in the process of "peer debriefing" (Creswell, 2007; Lincoln & Guba, 1985; Maxwell, 1996; Merriam, 1998). This colleague reviewed our analysis to help us test working hypotheses, play devil's advocate, and relate emerging themes to current literature on middle level education. In addition, member checking (the verification of data and interpretations with the study participants) was conducted. Hence, analyst triangulation, peer debriefing, and member checking enhanced the trustworthiness and credibility of this study (Patton, 2002).

After completing the data analysis process described above, we captured these exemplary educators' perspectives and experiences over the years by utilizing a jigsaw puzzle metaphor as a way to (1) explain the Camelot era of middle school education, (2) explain how the vision and practices of this era were directly affected by the intrusion of the era of accountability and a loss of local, school-based control for educating and meeting the unique needs of early adolescents, and (3) illustrate how middle school leaders might reclaim Camelot, although in a new, hybrid form, as they seek to effectively negotiate the tensions between the middle school reform of the Camelot era and that of high stakes testing and accountability.

Although we have attempted to preserve each of these teachers' voices through inclusion of transcribed recordings of our interviews, these stories are still embedded within our own story as the researchers. According to Connelly and Clandinin (1990):

> One of the tasks of writing narrative accounts is to convey a sense of the complexity of all of the "I's" all of the ways each of us have as knowing. We are, in narrative inquiry, constructing narratives at several levels. At one level it is the personal narratives and the jointly shared and constructed narratives that are told in the research writing, but narrative researchers are compelled to move beyond the telling of the lived story to tell the research story…. This telling of the research story requires another voice of the researcher, another "I." In this latter endeavor we make our place and our

voice as researcher central … In some ways the researcher moves out of the live story to tell, with another "I," another kind of story. (p. 10)

Hence, as suggested by Connelly and Clandinin (1990), we moved out of the narratives of experiences reported by each individual participant in this study to create a collective narrative, storied by the researchers. This grand narrative is reported in the remaining portions of this paper utilizing the jigsaw puzzle metaphor to explicate the Camelot years, the ways the Camelot years were affected by the era of high-stakes testing and accountability, and the ways middle level educators might "reclaim" Camelot.

THE CAMELOT PERIOD: 1970S–1990S

The eight veteran middle school educators who participated in this study included five women and three men who ranged between 43 years old to near retirement age. Each of these educators valued their diverse teaching backgrounds as far as the content areas and student populations that they taught over the years. Today one of these educators is a reading coach, three are principals, two serve district-level roles, and two are still teachers and team leaders. All of these teacher leaders, except for two, came to teaching middle school from either a high school or elementary school teaching background. Many were initially reluctant when recruited to teach middle school, only to become passionate about their new charge after seeing how upholding the practices of the middle school concept impacted student learning.

These eight middle school teachers took a historical look to the 1970s when many traditional junior high schools were reorganized into "middle schools." The rationale behind middle school reform was to allow a fundamental shift in teacher focus from a particular content area or subject to that of the whole student, taking into consideration the social, emotional, intellectual, and physical dimensions of early adolescents in a way that fostered a more effective transition from elementary to high school. Rather than treating middle grades only as a preparation for the structure and demands of high school (Cornelius, 1993; George & Alexander, 2003), the middle school reform movement dedicated itself to a focus on the unique developmental and affective needs of young adolescents through reconceptualizing building design, student and teacher organization, curriculum and instruction, and governance (George & Alexander, 2003). Student-teacher relationships, rather than departmental disciplines, became the center of school organization (Pounder, 1999).

This new vision for the education of early adolescents led to structural and organizational changes that fostered the critical need for relationship building for students and their teachers. Some of these features included an exploratory curriculum, block scheduling, schedules and building spaces organized as small schools-within-schools, and small, interdisciplinary teams of teachers that worked for the heterogeneous and inclusive grouping of students (George & Alexander, 2003). As can be imagined, reorganizing middle schools to incorporate these features took a tremendous commitment from legislative and district-based leadership in order to make such a reform viable. The teachers interviewed for this study fondly referred to this period of middle school reorganization as Camelot. Dan, currently a principal, described what he and his colleagues meant by this:

> The '70s were the Camelot years…. That's when you [had] a strong vision from the superintendent … there was a sense of singular focus in this district I think…. Then the PRIME legislation came in … that dealt with just middle school education…so it was like a huge movement … [focusing] on the whole concept of teaming, of affective education, of advisor/advisee, [which we] had … for 30-35 minutes every day.

Perhaps even more critical was the fostering of collective, school-based leadership that the districts nurtured and supported. According to the participants in this study, implications for this courageous re-visioning of horizontal teacher leadership had a tremendous impact on the efficacy of middle school teachers and their students. Kelly, a former language arts teacher and current district leader in professional development, elaborated on this experience:

> It was almost like Camelot. I mean people just loved working [in our middle school], teaching there—it was such an exciting place to be. You just got up every morning and were glad to go to work and it was fun. But the leadership was exemplary, too, and I'm sure that's part of it. We all worked hard together and they, [the administration], trusted us, [the teachers], to do what we knew was right for our kids…. It was just … a truly unique educational experience and one that I will value forever. I mean it was just wonderful.

According to the veteran middle school educators interviewed, three major characteristics defined the middle school of the past resulting in the common threads that tied together all the participant stories. Evidence of each characteristic came out as a major theme in each participant interview. Together these three characteristics served to define what many of them called "the Camelot years." First, there was a clear focus on understanding, nurturing, and then integrating the affective dimensions of early adolescents into the daily school experience. This is how Odanda, an eighth grade Spanish teacher and team leader put it:

> Kids are not just content. Kids have emotions, they are people … [if] you don't build any type of relationship or ownership … are you going to be happy at your job? Are you going to be curious and continue to grow? Are you going to want to keep coming back? You're not. So I think [meeting the affective needs of adolescents] is good for kids' growth, as well as for *our* growth as teachers … as a community of learners … everybody—all of us.

Second, these affective needs anchored school organization, allowing for an interdisciplinary, exploratory curriculum to emerge that teachers created to meet the needs of young adolescents. Sherrie, a former home economics teacher, explained:

> We had flexible block scheduling where we could actually, as a team, decide we want to do these activities and so we are going to rearrange our schedule … we were able to do activities with the kids as a family and then as a sixth grade team we would come together and do things as well. That was incredible.

Dan elaborated on this idea:

> I mean you teamed … everybody did interdisciplinary units. Not just interdisciplinary teaching, but units. You would sit down [together] and you would write a unit on global warming.

The final characteristic served to link meeting the affective needs of young adolescents to the exploratory curriculum. This characteristic was a laser-like focus on building relationships between students and students, students and adults, and faculty and administration. Odana described it this way:

> I think the original focus of middle school education was creating a *team* of teachers working with a *team* of students.… We wanted to create relationships between the kids and the teachers, but also the administration and the teachers. We were encouraged to work together as a team to do a lot more interdisciplinary units and activities as a team … and as a team our goal used to be building relationships. I think that was our goal in the middle school before FCAT, the state achievement test. And yes, teaching academics … but I think it was definitely more focused on building relationships, building an accepting environment and getting the kids to have a smoother transition between elementary and high school.… Now I think the goal is just making the school run so that we can meet FCAT scores.

Deidre, now a reading coach in a small, rural middle school, emphasized how important relationships once were in defining middle school education:

I used to have the same homeroom for three years in a row ... you bond with those kids like you can't imagine…you just grew up with them ... you just watched them grow physically and mentally and emotionally and it was very powerful ... I'm still close to those kids today. Graduation day was so emotional. It was to the point of traumatic ... you know the gains we made with those kids because they loved us and worked for us and trusted us and they worked their butts off for us, and I think today ... you just get to know the kids ... and they're gone—boom, they're just gone.

Each of the eight middle school educators brought forward stories that contained degrees of what they felt to be the same three hallmarks of middle school education: meeting the affective needs of early adolescents, relationship building, and the exploratory curriculum. Three components complete and perfect the jigsaw puzzle (see Figure 8.1). The three pieces of the puzzle fit together to create the Camelot years so fondly recalled by the eight participants in this study.

Feeding the Two Monsters: Camelot Comes Under Duress in the Late 1990s

When participants in these in-depth interviews reflected on the era of Camelot in their middle schools, they spoke with passion and enthusiasm, pointing out that they worked above and beyond normal work hours and

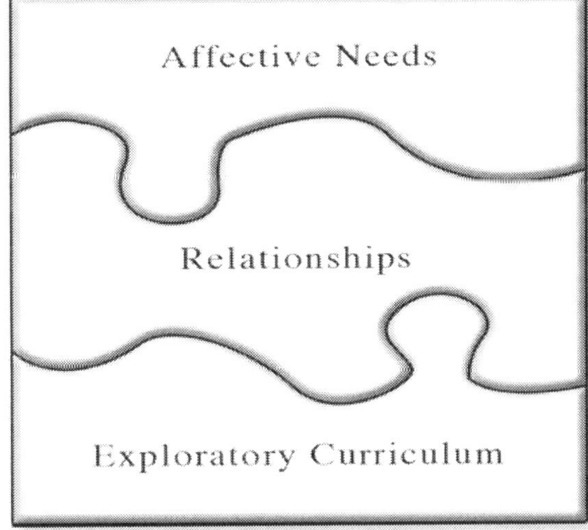

Figure 8.1.   The Camelot years.

nothing could have stopped them from doing so during this time. Dan's narrative is an example of how the pay-offs for their students and for the work environment were irresistible to all of these educators:

> (It was) a lot of work for teachers ... I taught every subject. It was just what you did.... There was no money, no stipends (for performing extra roles) back in those days. You just did them because you...wanted the concept to move forward. For example, at my middle school for a couple of years in a row, we gave up our planning periods to build the elective base, so we all taught special interest high need courses.... And you know when you see teachers doing that voluntarily, you know that you've got something right going on, so that was really a fun part of it, but it was a lot of work. I remember I would get up just about every morning at 5 or 5:30 and work for an hour before I went to school ... but it was just part of the job...it was also fun, and then the creativity part—creating things, because we didn't just use text books you know. We wrote and used a lot of resources, putting together exciting kinds of learning for kids.

However, when shifting their focus to their current working conditions in the middle school and the implications for their students, these educators spoke with disheartenment and frustration. They lamented the many shifts away from the exemplary practices that characterized the Camelot years, due to the era of high stakes testing and accountability. The shifts mentioned by one or more of our participants fell into three categories (organization of time and space, curriculum, and governance). These are summarized in Table 8.2.

Table 8.2 indicates that, over the several decades of their careers, the teachers in this study observed the loss or significant decrease in interdisciplinary team organization, flexible block schedules, exploratory programs, heterogeneous grouped classes, and advisor-advisee programs. According to our participants, these losses or decreases resulted from a litany of state and federal mandates that continually tugged at the fabric of the Camelot era. Dan illustrated it this way:

> [Before] you didn't have senior management saying you have to do this and that. [Then there were these] certification rules. Then you get into pieces of legislation ... course code directories ... that say you've got to cover this material ... and then of course in the 90s you've got the Sunshine State Standards, and then you've got the No Child Left Behind and it's like every time you turn around there's something that is yanking at the fabric of this thing.

As state and federal mandates tugged at the fabric of signature features of exemplary middle school practices, the teachers in this study experienced frustration in trying to balance academic rigor and emotional/

Table 8.2.   Comparison of Middle School Education: Past and Present

Camelot *(1970s–Mid 1990s)*	*Today* *(Late 1990s–Present)*
Organization of Time and Space • Block scheduling (80-100 minute classes) and decreased teacher-student contact (1 teacher: 60-80 students) • Schedules driven by student needs; • Teams of teachers and students in common area of the building • Common teacher planning periods and space in the building—schedule determined by teams • Team leader supervises scheduling to meet needs of unique students and teachers	**Organization of Time and Space** • 6-7 period days (43-50 minute classes) and increased teacher-student contact • Schedules driven by state-defined curriculum • Teams of teachers and students not necessarily in the same area of building • Teacher planning periods determined by overall school schedule, driven by different programs and tracked classes • Computer programs lead scheduling to meet demands of accountability
Curriculum • Robust/diverse exploratory curriculum • Many extracurricular activities and field trips to build sense of team community and support social-emotional growth • Weekly Advisor/Advisee programs and curriculum • Interdisciplinary curriculum designed and assessed by school-based teams • Provision of equitable and positive experiences for all students' social and emotional growth • Focus on "whole child"	**Curriculum** • More limited "elective" classes • Little time or money for field trips or activities • Elimination or reduction of Advisor/Advisee programs • Insulated curricula prescribed by state mandates and textbooks and assessed by standardized tests • Positive experiences reserved for only some students due to tracking • Focus on data and content/skills (especially reading)
Governance • Democratic, horizontal leadership anchored by strong vision by administration • Small, interdisciplinary teams (2-4 teachers) • Team meetings focus on individual students and on interdisciplinary units • Teacher as team member and collaborative team player	**Governance** • Vertical, top-down governance guided by external definitions of accountability • Large, grade level teams • Team meetings function to implement mandates, do paperwork, and follow district and state procedures • Teacher as isolated entity

affective development for young adolescent learners under the new constraints of accountability. In the words of Diana, a former special education teacher who is now a principal:

> You really can't have one … without the other … so, we're trying to feed both of those monsters. It's almost like you snatch from one to give to the other and then you snatch back.

The fact that the affective and intellectual needs of early adolescents are spun by this middle school educator as demanding, hungry "monsters" illustrates how desperate and out of balance veteran middle school educators felt in maintaining quality education for middle school students in the face of top-down mandates that came from outside of the school walls. At different middle schools, there are varying degrees of how these two "monsters" have been more or less effectively dealt with, but in every case the effects of the high stakes testing era on the daily, lived experiences of teachers and students left its mark (see Table 8.2), and resulted in a dramatic decrease in time and space to develop the critical relationships needed to balance affective and intellectual needs. Odana put it this way:

> We're not building the relationship with each other as teachers—and more and more you see that [in all schools]—we're not building those relationships as people.

Returning to our jigsaw puzzle metaphor, the era of high-stakes testing and accountability created a fissure in the perfect piecing together of academic and affective goals for young adolescents, attained through the development of strong relationships between and among the adults and young adolescents in the middle school characteristic of the Camelot era (see Figure 8.2).

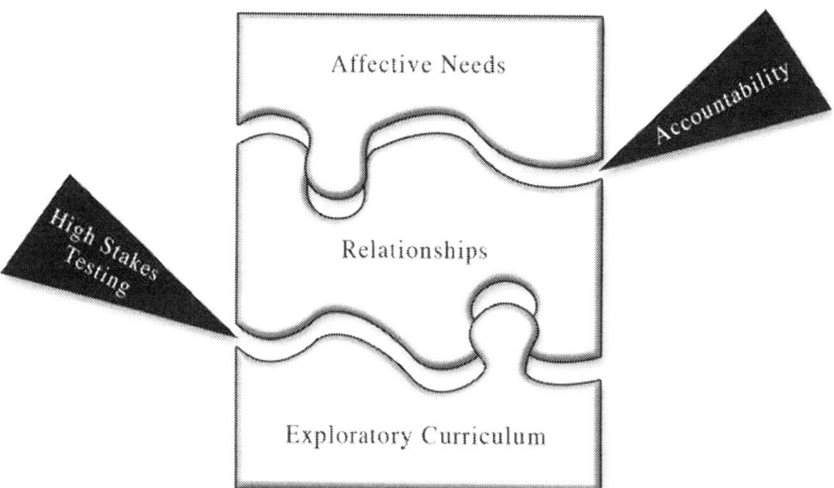

Figure 8.2.   Era of high stakes testing and accountability.

Reassembling the Puzzle to Reclaim Camelot: Where Do We Go From Here?

While it is easy to focus on what is lost in middle level education due to the disassembling of the Camelot puzzle, it is important to note that the teachers we interviewed did not describe the era of accountability as inherently bad. For example, Deidre shared that the use of data to make more refined instructional decisions for students was a positive outgrowth of the era of accountability:

> Now there is a different focus, there's a new direction, and it's eye opening for educators to have data [because] we have to look at it to know where to go ... for the kids' benefit. Now we know what [the students] need and how to get them to that point ... We have to look at data ... I mean it's your road map, and if you don't have a road map you're just going in circles.

To reclaim Camelot, middle level educators must regroup, take inventory of the losses and gains since the advent of No Child Left Behind, and assemble a new puzzle. This new puzzle may include a fourth piece termed "accountability" that encapsulates the good that came from this era, such as the focus on data to gain insights into student learning as indicated by the quote above. Accountability must become an integral and important piece of the exemplary middle school puzzle in a way that it no longer drives a wedge between meeting the affective and academic needs of young adolescents (see Figure 8.3).

It is important to note however, that with the current public emphasis on standardized test scores, such assessment measures can often be the first and only type of data practitioners think about in today's middle schools. There are many additional sources of data that can provide tremendous insights into middle school teaching and learning. These might include student work, artifacts and portfolios, field notes, interviews, digital pictures, videos, reflective journals and/or surveys (Dana & Yendol-Hoppey, 2009).

While standardized test scores can provide valuable "pictures" of learning trends that happen in the middle school, this single form of data can never be expected to fulfill the information needs held by all audiences interested in measuring learning. These diverse audiences include the public, administrators, policy makers, teachers, parents, and students (Farr, 1992). For example, while administrators may find criterion-referenced, performance based assessments most helpful when comparing individual or class-based student performance to a specific curriculum used in a school, parents may want information that allows them to compare their child's performance to national norms. Teachers, on the other hand, may need information that can shed light on the

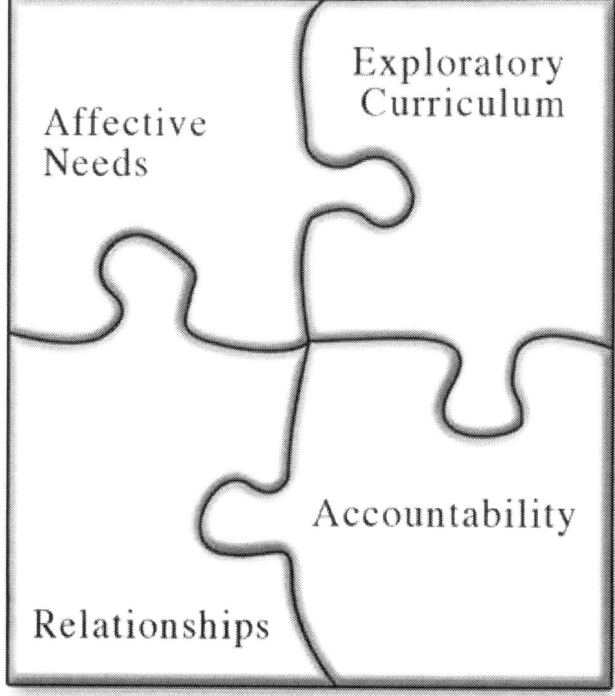

Figure 8.3.   The new middle school puzzle.

day-to-day decisions that they need to make for instruction. Therefore, middle school teachers may need to be cautious when using standardized test scores to define student learning. Being cautious means understanding what the assessment data is designed to measure, what its limitations are, and how to balance these measures with other assessment forms to build a more comprehensive picture of student learning. Failure to use standardized assessment data appropriately can have dire consequences.

Consider the following scenario depicting a superficial use and reliance on standardized test score data reported by Love (2004):

> When educators in one Texas high school saw African American students' performance drop slightly below 50% on their state mathematics test, putting the school on the state's list of low-performing schools, they reacted quickly.
>
> Decision makers immediately suggested that all African-American students, whether or not they failed the test, be assigned peer tutors (Olsen, 2003). Based on one piece of data and one way of looking at that data, these

decision makers made assumptions and leapt to action before fully understanding the issue or verifying their assumptions with other data sources. They ignored past trends, which indicated that African American students' scores were on an upward trajectory. They failed to consider that the decline was so small that it could better be explained by chance or measuring error than by their instructional program. They considered only the percent failing without digging deeper into the data to consider what students needed. Finally, they proposed intervention targeting only African Americans students, while overlooking Hispanic and White students who also failed the test (p. 22).

To guard against interpretations of middle school test scores as described above, it is important for middle school teachers to interpret these data carefully. It is also important for middle school teachers to consider other data sources to create a richer picture of all the complexity that occurs within the place we call middle school each day. The complexity of teaching middle school results from two factors. First, middle school students have entered an age of sociability and activity, exploration, and risk-taking. Second, middle school teachers know that most young adolescents find traditional schooling, which often includes solitary reading, pouring over texts, and exploring the world of the mind in a passive manner, does not match the energy, passion, adventurousness, romanticism, and yearning to be grown-up that characterizes their age group (Sizer & Meier, 2006). These two factors intertwine to make teaching the middle school child an inherently complex endeavor. Because of this complexity, any one data source such as student performance on standardized achievement measures only provides one "take" of what is occurring in a middle school.

Good schools invoke multiple sources of data to accomplish what qualitative researchers refer to as "triangulation" (Creswell, 2007; Patton, 2002). Using multiple sources of data can better inform the middle school teacher's understanding of the young adolescents they teach as they gain different perspectives from different types of data. Hence, relying on multiple data sources helps the middle school teacher create a more complete puzzle picture.

How do today's middle school educators build this new puzzle of exemplary middle level practice for the twenty-first century, one that includes affective education, academic rigor, relationships, and accountability achieved through reliance on multiple types of data? Diana leads a faculty which is committed to the ongoing gathering and use of a variety of data sources to make decisions to meet school-wide, classroom-based, and individual student needs. She framed the challenge this way:

> It can all mesh really well with the accountability system, I think … That to
> me is the challenge. How to use that wonderful middle school philosophy to
> bring about increased achievement … It's not a separate thing. You can't
> have one without the other.

Drawing on the wisdom and experience of the teachers interviewed in this study, it is clear that four roles for middle school teachers need to have the space and support to emerge in order to create this new vision for middle level education: (1) middle school teacher as decision maker, (2) middle school teacher as teacher educator, (3) middle school teacher as researcher, and (4) middle school teacher as political advocate (Frankes, Valli, & Cooper, 1998).

Middle School Teacher as Decision Maker

The middle school teacher as decision maker was well developed in the Camelot years, but underwent a significant decline. Participants in this study articulated that the nexus of decision making has now "bumped up" one level for every area of middle school business. For example, where small teams once decided on scheduling, now administrators oversee that task.

Where administrators once had the flexibility to decide where to assign teachers to specific courses, now state mandates dictate these decisions. The results are the same in each case. As educators lose control over decision making for their students, fewer and fewer choices can be made that honor the specific needs of specific students in specific contexts. This makes it more difficult to provide appropriate, sensitive, tailored school experiences for early adolescents and increases the difficulty of fulfilling the core mission of middle school—transition—effective for all learners.

We know that moving from elementary to less directly supportive middle schools is associated with decreases in self esteem, and declines in academic performance and motivation, creating life trajectories after this point that are very hard to "undo" (Juvonen, Le, Kaganoff, Augustine, & Constant, 2004). This makes success for *all* students in this age range no less than a social justice issue for middle school educators (Jackson & Davis, 2000). The middle school teacher as decision maker may need to be given the space, time, and leadership to revitalize.

Middle School Teacher as Teacher Educator

Several of the middle school teachers in this study made poignant the urgency for developing the role of teacher as teacher educator in the middle school. They shared their realization that the incoming generation of new middle school teachers and principals have little to no preparation for the unique context of middle school and little to no knowledge of core middle school practices and philosophy, such as interdisciplinary teaming, exploratory curriculum, and small group advisement. Some of the teachers in this study, including Odana below, go so far as to blame themselves for not being able to uphold the middle school vision under the monumental pressures of No Child Left Behind:

> But [the connections and vision] used to *be* there … [we] had bought into that.… Today nobody knows. You know? Because we haven't done anything to teach the new, incoming teachers … [and], like me—you get pulled by the crowd.… What's really sad is that some of those teachers … who had really truly bought into the middle school concept, now are older—even older than me … and they're like just wanting to get done and get retired.

Unless veteran middle school teachers like the ones in this study take on the role of teacher educator, the middle school vision risks being lost, perhaps forever. This study suggests that middle school educators who experienced the best years of middle level education may need to assume responsibility for somehow preserving the precious insights that were developed during those years.

Middle School Teacher as Researcher

One of the positive outcomes of the era of accountability is the availability of multiple forms of data collected through such mechanisms as progress monitoring tools and state mandated testing. These data can provide additional insights into student progress over time. However, in many cases, and particularly since the advent of No Child Left Behind, the meaning and use of these data have been defined by state departments and district administrators who are far removed from the middle school student and sometimes have little knowledge of exemplary middle school practice. These officials are used to *telling* teachers what they must do rather than *including* teachers in the data analysis process. In many other cases, the misuse of these forms of data led to overly simplistic practices in the effort "to raise student achievement."

These practices include assigning grades to schools, threatening teachers, homogenizing the curriculum, turning curriculum into test preparation, tracking students, or even taking over schools by state departments of education (Guthrie, 2002; Sleeter, 2005).

Alternatively, middle school teachers may develop their role as action researchers. The process of action research includes naming a question or wondering, collecting, and analyzing data to gain insights into that wondering, sharing results with other teachers, and taking action to change and improve teaching practice based on what was learned (Dana & Yendol-Hoppey, 2008, 2009). In this way, middle school teachers may take charge of their own professional development. Rather than data being analyzed by others and subsequently used to tell teachers what they must do, teachers analyze data themselves in relationship to pertinent questions they have emerging from the four walls of their classrooms.

One of the participants in this study capitalized on the notion of teacher as researcher at her middle school. Through ongoing action research, her faculty demonstrated that high academic rigor can be maintained even though a large proportion of their time is devoted to interest clubs, special activity days, and advisor-advisee programs. Subsequently, this middle school faculty made the case to keep this sacred time in the curriculum.

Middle School Teacher as Political Advocate

While an understanding of the political nature of schooling is not commonly taught in teacher preparation programs, becoming a political advocate for middle level education can have far reaching effects. For example, Charles, now a middle school principal, reflected on the strong commitment at his school to fostering the role of teacher as political activist by placing some of his best teachers strategically in leadership positions at the local and state level:

> It was really important that I got [one of my best teachers and friends] in a powerful position.…   I hated it, and I wished I could have had another year with him, and he did too, but we had enough time together and will still keep in touch … I helped him take over as the regional director for the Florida League of Middle Schools.

In placing teachers from their faculty in strategic positions, this middle school protected their small, interdisciplinary teams of two and three teachers, heterogeneously grouped classrooms, democratic faculty governance, block scheduling, and their exploratory program. The academic performance of their students continued to win the respect of the local school district and the state for almost ten years. This made it very difficult to argue the choices this faculty made "against the grain" of district, state, and federal pressures to abandon their middle school core practices in the name of increasing student scores on standardized tests.

In addition to the four roles middle school teachers must enact to create this new vision for middle level education, drawing on the wisdom and experience of the teachers interviewed in this study, it is also clear that there are implications for two other important groups—policymakers and middle school researchers.

Implications for Policymakers

Well-intentioned actions by state and federal governments have mixed, if not negative, results on middle school practices. In Florida, for example, the Class Size Reduction Amendment of 2002 was put into place to reduce student-teacher ratios so that teachers could improve their responsiveness to individual students, but, since it often meant teachers needed to pick up an extra class and lost common planning time with their colleagues, this amendment ended up eradicating teacher teaming efforts (George, 2008).

Similarly, we learned from the participants in this study that legislation intended to improve the learning and achievement of middle level learners can actually have the opposite effect. Policymakers need to be aware of the ways that policies in practice can actually lead to the erosion of core concepts associated with middle schools. They also need to listen to the voices of middle school teachers and administrators to adjust policy decisions to maximize the good intentions of the legislation and minimize unforeseen negative consequences.

Implications for Middle School Researchers

This research study illuminated a problem, accountability practices diminishing the middle school concept, and the possible solution, balancing the components of accountability and developmentally responsive pedagogy in middle schools. Now, research efforts are needed to study how this balance can be achieved. Future research should focus on the ways some middle schools navigate the tensions between core middle school concepts and high-stakes testing.

One of the participants in this study lamented that middle school teachers new to the profession are often not fully knowledgeable about core middle school concepts. Future research should focus on the social ization of new middle school teachers into the profession. Such research could focus on understanding the ways these professionals, key to the future of the middle school movement, make sense of melding the history of the middle school movement and the Camelot era with contemporary issues of accountability that they face when they begin their teaching careers.

CONCLUSIONS

With a new administration heading our national government, one elected to office on a vision of hope, there seems to be no more urgent time than now to reclaim Camelot in middle school education. While this dream is entirely possible, as President Obama said the night he was elected, "The road ahead will be long. Our climb will be steep" (YouTube, 2008). According to Kelly, one of the exemplary veteran middle-school educators in this study, we cannot, and should not return to Camelot, but:

> What I would love to see is a school that takes into account all the external barriers and things that seem to be hindering what we are doing, but finding a model for still putting the developmental needs of the young adolescent at the core of the program with relationship building at the heart of it, using some of our old middle school components, but then rethinking and realizing that, you know, it's not the same in 2009 as it was in 1970, or 1980, or 1990.

Charles likened the reclaiming of Camelot to the work of Darwin and the notion of survival of the fittest, pointing to the need for educators to be able to sustain this vision of middle school education by adapting it to the ever-changing political, economic, and social landscape:

> Darwin said that the key to a successful species are those who can adapt. And that's what we constantly have to learn how to do in education. We've got to constantly keep our eye on what's good for kids and what works for kids, and as the climate changes or the context changes, we have to figure out how to adapt so we don't lose those really important pieces . . . If middle schools don't have the ability to adapt, then, we're going to lose any progress that we have made.

In order not to lose the progress made by middle schools, it is important to remember the Camelot years. The purpose of this paper was to recall those years through the voices of those that lived them, so they are not forgotten. By developing the roles of decision maker, teacher educator, researcher, and political advocate, middle school teachers may ensure that the progress of the middle school movement will not be lost in the era of accountability and high stakes testing. To inspire action, we end this chapter as we began it, with the lyrics to the Broadway musical's title song:

> Don't let it be forgot
> That once there was a spot,
> For one brief, shining moment
> That was known as Camelot (Lerner & Loewe, 1960).

REFERENCES

Boyer, S., & Bishop, P. (2004). Young adolescent voices: Students' perceptions of interdisciplinary teaching. *Research on Middle Level Education Online, 28*(1), 73-76.

Clark, S. (1997). Exploring the possibilities of interdisciplinary teaming. *Childhood Education, 73*(5), 267-271.

Connelly, F. M., & Clandinin, D. J. (1990). Stories of experience and narrative inquiry. *Educational Researcher, 19*(5), 2-14.

Cornelius, M. (1993). The middle school concept within the United States. *Contemporary Education, 65*(1), 47-49.

Creswell, J. W. (2007). *Qualitative inquiry and research design: Choosing among five traditions* (2nd ed.). Thousand Oaks, CA: Sage Publications.

Dana, N. F., & Yendol-Hoppey, D. (2008). *The reflective educator's guide to professional development: Coaching inquiry-oriented learning communities.* Thousand Oaks, CA: Corwin Press.

Dana, N. F., & Yendol-Hoppey, D. (2009). *The reflective educator's guide to classroom research: Learning to teach and teaching to learn through practitioner inquiry* (2nd ed.). Thousand Oaks, CA: Corwin Press.

Erickson, F. (1986). Qualitative methods in research on teaching. In M. Wittrock (Ed.), *Handbook of research on teaching* (3rd ed., pp. 3-36). New York, NY: Macmillan.

Farr, R. (1992). Putting it all together: Solving the reading assessment puzzle. *The Reading Teacher, 46*(1), 26-37.

Flowers, N., Mertens, S., & Mulhall, P. (2000). What makes interdisciplinary teams effective? *Middle School Journal, 31*(4), 53-56.

Frankes, L., Valli, L., & Cooper, D. (1998). Continuous learning for all adults in the professional development school. In D. J. McIntyre & D. M. Byrd (Eds.), *Strategies for career-long teacher education* (pp. 69-83). Thousand Oaks, CA: Corwin Press.

George, P. (2008). *Special report: The status of programs in Florida middle schools.* Gainesville, FL: School of Teaching and Learning.

George, P., & Alexander, W. (2003). *The exemplary middle school* (3rd ed.). Belmont, CA: Wadsworth/Thomson Learning.

Guthrie, J. (2002). Preparing students for high-stakes test taking in reading. In A. E. Farstrup & S. J. Samuels (Eds.), *What research has to say about reading instruction* (pp. 370-391). Hillsdale, NJ: Erlbaum.

Husband, R., & Short, P. (1994). Interdisciplinary teams lead to greater teacher empowerment. *Middle School Journal, 26*(2), 58-61.

Jackson, A., & Davis, G. (2000). *Turning points 2000: Educating adolescents in the 21st century.* New York, NY: Teachers College Press.

Juvonen, J., Le, V., Kaganoff, T., Augustine, C., & Constant, L. (2004). *Focus on the wonder years: Challenges facing the American middle school.* Santa Monica, CA: Rand Corporation.

Lee, V., & Smith, J. (1993). Effects of school restructuring on the achievement and engagement of middle-grade students. *Sociology of Education, 66,* 164-187.

Lerner, A., & Loewe, F. (1960). Finale Ultimo (Camelot Reprise) [Recorded by Richard Burton]. On *Camelot: Original Broadway Cast* [CD]. New York, NY: Columbia.

Lincoln, Y. S., & Guba, E. G. (1985). *Naturalistic inquiry.* Newbury Park, CA: Sage Publications.

Love, N. (2004). Taking data to new depths. *Journal of Staff Development, 25*(4), 22-26.

Maxwell, J. A. (1996). *Qualitative research design: An interactive approach.* Thousand Oaks, CA: Sage Publications.

Merriam, S. B. (1998). *Case study research in education: A qualitative approach.* San Francisco, CA: Jossey-Bass.

Olsen, L. (2003, May 21). Study relates cautionary tale of misusing data. *Education Week, 22*(37), 12.

Patton, M. Q. (2002). *Qualitative research and evaluation methods* (3rd ed). Beverly Hills, CA: Sage Publications.

Pounder, D. (1999). Teacher teams: Exploring job characteristics and work-related outcomes of work group enhancement. *Educational Administration Quarterly, 53*(3), 317-348.

Seidman, I. E. (1991). *Interviewing as qualitative research: A guide for researchers in education and the social sciences.* New York, NY: Teachers College Press.

Sizer, T., & Meier, D. (2006). Foreword. In the Education Alliance at Brown University & EEI Communications (Eds.), *Breaking ranks in the middle: Strategies for leading middle level reform* (pp. vii-viii). Reston, VA: National Association for Secondary Principals.

Sleeter, C. (2005). *Un-standardizing curriculum: Multicultural teaching in the standards-based classroom.* New York, NY: Teachers College Press.

YouTube. (2008, November 4). *President-elect Barack Obama in Chicago* [video]. Retrieved from http://www.youtube.com/watch?v=q5Xx9Q0JtQQ&eurl=http%3A%2F%2Fchange.gov%2Fnewsroom%2Fentry%2Fpresident_elect_obama_speaks_on_the_eve_of_this_election%2F&feature=player_embedded#t=322

CHAPTER 9

TEACHING TO THE MIDDLE IN AUSTRALIA

Four Teachers Tell Their Stories

Nan Bahr and Donna Pendergast

This chapter explores the perceptions of middle years specialist teachers in the contemporary Australian schools context. Written narratives were obtained from 4 Australian teachers. Each has followed distinctly different paths to teaching in the middle years. However, each has a high leadership profile in the general schooling sector assumed relatively early in their professional careers. These teachers were asked about their entry into teaching, the pathways they pursued to teaching at the middle level, opportunities and limitations experienced for them in schools, and their conceptions of the future of middle years reforms in Australia.

INTRODUCTION

Middle years of schooling (MYS) reform has colored the landscape of education in Australia for little more than a decade (Pendergast, 2009). There was a season of rather frenetic policy writing in each Australian

Voices From the Middle: Narrative Inquiry By, For, and About the Middle Level Community
pp. 173–191
Copyright © 2010 by Information Age Publishing
All rights of reproduction in any form reserved.

state and territory in the mid-1990s. Since then there has been an era of reform that has seen the traditional schooling structures creak and has been buffeted by gusty winds of change to effectively accommodate MYS, and alongside it, specialized middle years teacher education. Policy associated with middle years' school education has been driven largely by isolated state and territory based initiatives. Yet, the Ministerial Council on Education, Employment, Training and Youth Affairs' (MCEETYA) *Melbourne Declaration on Educational Goals for Young Australians* (MCEETYA, 2008, p.10) identifies one of its eight interrelated action areas as "enhancing middle years' development." In the commitment to action, the elaboration provides the following explanation:

> The middle years are an important period of learning, in which knowledge of fundamental disciplines is developed, yet this is also a time when students are at the greatest risk of disengagement from learning. Student motivation and engagement in these years is critical, and can be influenced by tailoring approaches to teaching with learning activities and learning environments that specifically consider the needs of middle years' students.

However, change has not been embraced, nor has it been sustained. Only three teacher preparation institutions (out of the nation's 38) currently offer target programs for the development of middle years specialists. Even these three are under threat. School principals are not convinced of the merits of MYS, school structures are unyielding, and the level of attention showered on MYS in the 1990s has faded. And yet, there are still champions for MYS and pockets of reform.

This chapter explores four stories of engagement with MYS by four teachers. They share a commitment to MYS, but their stories relate and capture diverse perspectives on the resistance, challenge, opportunities, and possible future for MYS in Australia. The chapter draws on the narrative research approach to highlight the complex dynamics that surround MYS reform, with particular emphasis on the demands for teacher education and teacher professional development.

MYS IN THE AUSTRALIAN CONTEXT

To properly understand the impact of MYS, we provide an overview of traditional and typical schooling structures and systems in Australia. The Australian education systems are governed principally by state parliamentary authorities. However, there are increasing movements toward a more centralized oversight of curriculum. Federal statutory authorities have been investing considerable development work around establishing and implementing a national curriculum (Ingvarson, 2009), a national framework for teacher professionalism (Teaching Australia, 2009), and a national accreditation process for teacher education programs (Ingvarson, 2009). However, State governments remain as the delegated authorities for funding, resourcing, and policy design and implementation. While they are currently the key authorities for education in their regions, this is a highly politicized space.

A recent trend in Australia has been the move to more aligned practices between the states/territories, a national approach, nearly. This is a hotly contested move with each individual state and territory arguing to maintain governance of their schooling sector and resisting the move to federal level central policies and funding. For the most part, schooling in Australia is compulsory between the ages of 5 and 16. Typically, children begin their schooling at the age of 5. After prep they enter Grade 1 and typically spend 7 years in a primary school, followed by 5 years in a secondary school. Secondary, or high schools, are usually separate school communities, situated on their own campuses. As many as seven or more primary schools are "feeders" to the usually large and comprehensive district high school. Typically, children transition from primary to secondary school at the age of 12 and graduate high school by the age of 17. This pattern is considered the traditional model of Australian schooling.

Traditional Australian primary schools generally are arranged around class groups of approximately 30 children who are taught for a complete year by a single teacher, "their" teacher. This teacher is responsible for student learning of every endorsed discipline area. As such, they are generalist primary teachers. Specialist teachers support study areas such as music and physical education.

Traditional Australian secondary schools are organized differently. Students gather into class groups, and generally pass from teacher to teacher for discipline area studies. In most schools an additional teacher is allocated for pastoral care, which often exists as one class session per day. Pastoral care refers to support and care given to each child for their general well-being. The pastoral care class session often includes activities to assist students with vocational guidance, resilience building, and general life skills. Teachers who engage in pastoral care, are called "home" teachers and they may or may not teach their class group for any subjects across the school timetable. Although there are some variations on these designs, these descriptions remain the predominant approach to schooling in traditional schools. Most Australian schools keep the tradition. Middle schooling models disrupt this pattern.

Schools that have adopted a middle schooling philosophy have reformed practices that keep the students in a single home area, a "pod," with a small teaching team of two or three teachers who work together to lead students for all the discipline studies in the program. This teaching team stays with a group of students for a three year period, that is, each student will be allocated to their class group and remain with those teachers for 3 years. The class group will gradually change over the 3 years as students move out of middle school into higher grades, and as younger students move in. These teachers provide the pastoral care for the students in the pod. The middle schooling pod becomes a close knit community of learners with a strong sense of belonging and shared experience. Unlike traditional schooling, the middle years reforms promote cohesive frameworks between disciplines, an interdisciplinary curriculum, and a free flowing timetable organized around the nature of the learning activities rather than block rigid schedules.

All schools in every state and territory have been guided to their MYS reforms by policy frameworks developed separately in each State/Territory (Pendergast, 2007), and by alternate systemic schooling organizations, for example the Brisbane Catholic Education Office (2004). Not all schools have successfully adopted reforms consistent with MYS policy. The schools that have embarked on reform have attempted to respond to young adolescent needs through the adoption of MYS signature practices (Middle Years of Schooling Association [MYSA], 2008). These signature practices include:

- higher order thinking strategies;
- integrated and disciplinary curricula that are negotiated, relevant and challenging;
- heterogeneous and flexible student groupings;
- cooperative learning and collaborative teaching;
- small learning communities that provide students with sustained individual attention in a safe and healthy school environment;
- emphasis on strong teacher–student relationships through extended contact with a small number of teachers and a consistent student cohort;
- authentic and reflective assessment with high expectations;
- democratic governance and shared leadership; and
- parental and community involvement in student learning (MYSA, 2008).

Even with this as a foundation, middle schooling does not conform to a single template, and these signature practices have been adopted in schools to a lesser or greater extent depending on local circumstances. Middle schooling is an evolution of traditional primary and secondary schools. Middle schooling is an approach to teaching and learning that differs from traditional secondary and primary schooling, and relies heavily on coordination and communication across the boundaries of these traditional structures. In Australia, we do not have stand alone middle schools, so this investment to erasing the boundaries between traditional primary and secondary schools has relied upon the ingenuity and commitment of innovative teaching staff and school administrators. A few examples, secondary schools with multiple feeder primary schools may only have the capacity to provide limited interdisciplinarity, and even then only for students in their first year of secondary schooling (12-year-olds). Secondary schools that share a fence line with a primary school may be able to link some activities across the shared border, but students will not maintain a relationship with a core group of staff across their MYS. Some P-12 schools (many private schools and some state schools) have greater capacity, but are hamstrung by inflexible facilities that force students into tightly constrained timetabling. MYS is, therefore, more of a philosophy of schooling that drives practice rather than a template for staffing, curriculum, pedagogy, and schooling structures.

In the preservice arena, many teacher preparation institutions continue to offer discrete primary and secondary teacher preparation which overlap the middle years. They do not treat MYS as a specialized field of knowledge and practice. In terms of pedagogy and curriculum, teacher preparation courses focus around the needs of younger children or senior syllabus requirements. Graduates are not prepared for the particular needs of early adolescents. In 2002, the first cohort of students commenced their study in a unique, specialized preservice middle years' dual degree teacher education program. This bachelor of education MYS offered by The University of Queensland has to date graduated six cohorts and a total of 276 novice teachers from the program. Extensive details of the conceptual foundations of the program have been outlined elsewhere (e.g., Garrick, Pendergast, Bahr, Dole, & Keogh, 2008; Hunter et al., 2004; Keogh et al., 2004; Mitchell et al., 2003; Pendergast, Whitehead, De Jong, Newhouse-Maiden, & Bahr, 2007). Two of the four middle years teachers' voices that will be heard in this paper graduated from this program. Furthermore, the philosophy underpinning the curriculum development in this program of study mirrors the characteristics that will be valued from graduates of the program and reflects current research related to preservice teacher education for MYS. The principles are outlined in Table 9.1.

The curriculum and its modus operandi set out to model what it means to work in a MYS context (see Table 9.1). Importantly, the underpinning conceptual understandings of the program were strongly informed by the United States's National Middle School Association. In a position statement on the professional preparation of middle level teachers for the United States, the organization outlines what it considers are essential ele-

**Table 9.1.   Principles Underpinning
the MYS Teacher Preparation Program**

Negotiated learning paths	• Students commence in the program after completing two years of a dual degree or as graduate entry from an approved program—based on their previous experience and interest. They elect an English or mathematics pathway, combined with a focus in studies of society and the environment.
Integration	• The program is multidisciplinary, utilizing multiple pedagogical practices and catering to multiage groupings.
Team work	• Students conduct much of their teaching practicum and major learning activities in teams of varying sizes and with varying expertise across key learning area fields.
Collaboration	• Students work together with team members comprising university colleagues, university lecturers, classroom teachers, and community bodies, creating a community of learners. This leads to the development of attitudes of democratic governance, where families and communities are inextricably linked.
Flexibility	• The program allows for the development of expertise in literacy or numeracy, along with the key learning area focus, study of society and environment. Students prepare to teach across all other key learning areas.
Technological literacy	• Students are engaged in flexible learning practices and are encouraged to develop skills in flexible delivery modes.
Student ownership	• Student ownership is evident as students are able to map learning paths that best suit their needs, depending on their companion degree and other life learning.
Specialist knowledges	• Students gain specialist knowledge and an understanding of adolescents and their learning styles, with the development of concomitant pedagogical practices. • Students gain specialist knowledge and an understanding of diversity and development of attitudes to embrace diversity and change, and the implications for pedagogy. • Specialist understanding of reforms in middle years in terms of curriculum, pedagogy and structures
Extensive practicum experience in MYS contexts	• Students have the opportunity to observe and interact with expert teachers in a number of settings.
Deep/higher order/ enhanced learning	• Students actively engage in deep learning, developing skills of critical and reflective practice through complex tasks.
Expert-novice approach to learning	• Students are encouraged to adapt a philosophy of learning where they are expert at learning anew and continuously, leading to a commitment to life-long learning.
Authentic learning experiences	• Students negotiate topics of interest to them, in real contexts and applications.

Source: Adapted from Carrington et al. (2001).

ments of MYS teacher preparation programs: collaboration in teacher preparation with school-based faculty; study of young adolescent development and needs; study of middle level philosophy and organization; study of middle level curriculum organized around and emphasizing interdisciplinary and integrative approaches, approaches that also incorporate young adolescent interests as starting points for curriculum planning; broad academic background, including concentrations for at least two teaching fields; systematic study of planning, teaching and assessment, and practice in authentic settings; early and continuing field experiences in middle schools; and opportunities for preservice teachers to understand and experience the collaborative role of middle level teachers (National Middle School Association, 2001).

All students enrolled in the program had the opportunity to participate in a longitudinal study entitled Creating Teachers for New Schooling Contexts: A Longitudinal Study Involving the Middle Years of Schooling Teacher Education Program (Pendergast et al., 2009). The study contributes to our understanding of: why participants are interested in the MYS; the ways in which the middle years are conceptualized by the research participants; the impact on the student teachers' practice; and the implications of the program for teacher education reform at the regional and national levels. This attempt to build better evidence-based understandings around middle years teacher education is the first of its kind, with scholars such as Luke et al. (2003, p. 138) supporting the need for such research:

> What is needed is medium-duration longitudinal studies of teacher problems, strategies and pathways from various kinds of training into and through the middle years in the schooling sector. This would set the conditions for a much better sense of what really counts as excellent middle years teaching practice.

In this chapter, the use of narrative research adds a new layer to the largely quantitative studies that have been conducted since the program commenced. Its use is appropriate to build insights into the lived experiences of teachers who are graduates of the specialized middle years teacher education program. As Moen (2006, n.p.) has noted,

> Narrative research is increasingly used in studies of educational practice and experience, chiefly because teachers, like all other human beings, are story tellers who individually and socially lead storied lives. Narrative research is thus the study of how human beings experience the world.

Of interest in this paper is how two of the graduates of the specialized middle years program experienced their world as teachers, through the telling of their own story. This will be combined with the stories of two middle years teachers who entered middle years teaching after a switch from traditional primary or secondary level teaching.

METHODOLOGY

For this research, four teachers were asked to relate their journeys into MYS, and to track their experience to their current position as leaders of MYS, or in their active practice, as a school leader, and/or as a tertiary teacher educator. We call them Karen, Tony, John and Leo (pseudonyms). These teachers were selected from a list of active members of an Australian professional association for middle school teachers based on their currency in school practice, their leadership positions in schools, and the relative recency of their graduation from preservice preparation (within 5 years). Moen (2006) describes collaboration as the "main characteristic" of narrative inquiry and suggests the use of the term participants, rather than informants or respondents. Therefore, we refer to the four teachers involved in this research as participants.

Participants were contacted by email and were asked to respond to key themes by reflecting on their own experiences, incorporating illustrative stories where possible. As they told their stories they were asked to consider retelling any potent experiences about MYS reform. This approach is consistent with narrative research where stories are presented about remembered events and how these were experienced (Sandelowski, 1991). No limits were prescribed for their written responses. They each provided their own written narrative regarding their experiences of:

- entering middle years teaching,
- beliefs and attitudes about the middle years,
- beginning as a middle years teacher,
- middle years reform, and
- the future of middle years in Australia.

These became the themes and organizers for retelling the stories in this research. Each participant produced a written document (1,000-2,000 words) submitted by email to the researchers either as attachment or in the text of the message. After 1 week, each participant was contacted again and was asked to peruse their submission and add any further detail that had come to mind. Two of the participants came back to the researchers with additional written recollections offered in support of their first submission.

Introducing Karen, John, Tony, and Leo

Karen

Karen completed the dedicated middle years preservice teacher education course described above. She came to teacher education as a career change mature age student. She spent an extended period of time at home with her young children, after a career in small business. She chose MYS for her teacher education enrolment and, on completion, was in the rather unique position of entering her first school as a beginning teacher filled with the agenda to drive MYS reform for an urban school. Five years after completing her first teaching qualification, Karen is a tertiary teacher educator, specializing in MYS preservice teacher education.

Tony

Tony, like Karen, was a mature-aged, middle years preservice teacher. He was a father of four and explored many occupations before settling on teaching as a career. On completion of the same course as Karen he was employed at a large private P-12 school that had a middle school. As a beginning teacher, Tony led the region to establish a support cluster for MYS teachers and is currently an assistant principal for a P-12 school, only 4 years since graduation from his teacher preparation course.

John

John was not initially formally prepared as a MYS teacher. John was already a secondary teacher in a traditional school before becoming attracted to MYS. He pursued his passion through higher degree studies in MYS and is a recognized state leader for MYS reform.

Leo

Leo was mature aged when he entered undergraduate study at university, having worked as a health insurance salesman. He first studied a liberal arts degree and then followed into a 1-year graduate diploma of education program which prepared him for secondary teaching. As a beginning teacher he quickly formed an interest in MYS and has since completed postgraduate higher degree courses focussing on MYS. Within 5 years of completion of his first teacher qualification, he was appointed deputy principal (middle years) at a large independent school. He was made a head of curriculum (middle years) in his second year in the profession.

Karen, John, Leo, and Tony's Stories

The four participants provided personal stories related to the five themes: entering middle years teaching; beliefs and attitudes about the middle years; beginning as a middle years teacher; middle years reform;

the future of middle years in Australia. It is important to note that not all participants provided a story for each of the themes.

Selecting MYS

Each of the participants' stories reveals what was the unique set of circumstances leading to their choice of the middle years teacher education program. For Tony, difficulty choosing between the traditional primary and secondary options played a part, but more importantly, the connection to his own previous failure in these traditional contexts particularly influenced his choice. Tony wrote:

> I felt at the time, very unsure as to whether I wanted to be in a primary or secondary setting ... the middle years of schooling degree enabled me to work in either setting so I had the opportunity to experience both areas. The real selling factor though was the focus on student centred learning, having failed Year 12 (17-18 year olds), due to disengagement, this seemed a great way to make a difference in regards to how teaching COULD meet the needs of students as opposed to the boring didactic approach I had to succumb to.

For Leo and John, the pathway to working in the middle years was somewhat different. As a secondary trained teacher, Leo became interested in the middle years in his first year of teaching, writing:

> My journey into the middle years began in my first year of teaching. I had both senior phase student classes as well as middle phase students. I quickly started to enjoy the connection I was making with these students and the freedom to make the curriculum learning relevant and interesting to them. The freedom allowed me to focus on developing student skills such as literacy and numeracy with an interesting pedagogical approach that younger students could connect with.... I believe that for a long time that the students in the middle years have been the forgotten group of learners with much attention given to early and senior year students. However, this apparent neglect also allowed for the growth and empowerment of cutting edge development and focus by a growing group of dedicated teachers, researchers, and academics across Australia, of which I am proud to be associated with.

Likewise, John "had already been a secondary teacher for a few years when [he] became interested in middle years teaching". His interest was driven by a shift from a small rural to a large urban school and with it a change in school culture and student engagement and learning outcomes. John explains:

> I returned to the city to continue my career and found that I no longer enjoyed the same level of rapport with my students. This was due in part to me being a new teacher in a large urban high school. The culture of the school was different too—it was unheard of to offer an after-hours tutorial to students. I discontinued this practice. I began to realize that in some of my classes there were students who were simply not learning anything from being there. More than this, I found myself accepting a tacit "mutual non-aggression pact" with these students, by which I mean we agreed not to bother one another so long as the rest of the class could run smoothly. I liked these kids and they liked me, but I wasn't teaching them anything.

Karen was not initially vocationally oriented toward the middle years, but selected it based on its presumed marketability:

> To be honest the initial impetus was marketability. Coming in to education in midlife, I was conscious that I was competing with contemporaries with up to 20 years experience. Middle schooling was new and there wasn't many, if any, middle years trained teachers... My theory proved to be true as I was offered a job prior to graduation in a private middle school. (Karen)

Tertiary educators often assume that applicants to preservice programs are drawn almost naturally to particular programs as a part of their sense of vocation. The comments from all of these teachers have shown that MYS did not loom as a discrete career option in the minds of applicants as they started the course shopping process. There was a tendency to select traditional options (primary or secondary) and then convert into a MYS specialist, or select MYS as a side door to primary and secondary specialization. Karen says:

> Also by being trained middle years, it gave the option of primary, secondary and P-12 schools.... I didn't know the first thing about middle schooling when I started the course. I was converted along the way and am now a strong advocate.

The fact that these teachers now find themselves at the forefront of this field has been a process of career development that started for some of them in their preservice programs.

For the authors of this paper, both involved in preservice teacher education and in particular middle years preservice teacher education, the stories about the selection of the middle years as a program of study resonate with their experience of typical reasons for students to choose this pathway. Essentially operating from a deficit model, three of the four stories highlight the need for a new approach to the middle years with a chance for change. Tony points to "mak[ing] a difference"; Leo to middle years students being "the forgotten group of learners" and John realized that students were "simply not learning." Karen's selection of the program as "new" and marketable is also typical, though less common.

Developing Beliefs and Values About the Middle Years Through Preservice Education

The participants were asked to tell stories about how their beliefs and values about middle years students and the middle years as a site of teaching and learning were impacted by their formal teacher education program of study. Tony revealed much in his story about preservice education, including what he regarded as his greater expertise in middle schooling than his supervising teachers. Tony wrote:

> Often ... I was far more prepared than my supervising teachers ... in most cases this was great, but when students respond to you better than their own teacher and make this quite obvious ... it can be a little difficult.

The schooling contexts in Queensland and Australia lagged behind the initiatives of the teacher education program and this upset the balance of expertise in the practicum setting and in the early stages of the profession. It is possible that Tony's sense of accomplishment, preparedness to teach, and possession of unique skills and knowledge sets helped him to find a leadership niche in a school long before this would normally have been the case. Tony participated in an extended internship and revealed the following about this experience:

> It was a great opportunity to learn how to hook into kids to get them to want to learn ... I utilized a range of activity based learning strategies that got students out of the standard classroom environment. This was very well received and helped develop trust and a working relationship with students ... they enjoyed coming to class ... hell isn't that a start? If they enjoy coming to class and are learning at the same time ... you're on a winner.

So Tony was excited to teach and was given considerable autonomy perhaps due to his perceived specialization in early adolescence. Karen also felt positioned to make a significant impact from her very first practicum experiences. She wrote:

> My strongest impression, and the one that stays with me, was how much the middle schooling course made you aware of the deficit model and negative thinking towards adolescents. How many times we just see what they don't or can't do instead of seeing their potential and how much they have to offer in terms of their own education.... By spending a whole term just studying adolescents, it made you think about them in a whole new light. Then you could rethink your approach to education, starting with the adolescents, their developmental stage and their interests.

Karen explains how this orientation to adolescence through her MYS program alerted her to different aspects of the classroom experience that actually set her apart from other teachers. This self perception as a unique/different type of teacher, an early adolescence specialist, launched these beginning teachers into their teaching career with particular beliefs about the place of teachers in adolescent lives.

Perhaps unsurprisingly, when reflecting upon these participant stories, there appears to be a strong connection between their beliefs and values about the middle years that can be directly connected to the philosophy underpinning the program of study, as outlined in Table 9.1. It is of interest to hear the participants mirroring this philosophy in their stories.

Beginning Teacher Stories

For the MYS trained teachers, the stories of their entry into the school contexts focus on the issues surrounding curriculum, rather than their developing pedagogical content knowledge and disciplinary expertise. When participants were invited to tell stories that were particularly potent for them in their early days of teaching, a wide range of stories were revealed. Tony showed how emotionally vulnerable teachers can be. He reported:

> I worked in an all boys' school that had a "zero tolerance" for bullying, yet I felt administration contributed to the low self-esteem some boys were experiencing. Boys who played rugby were revered, those who didn't ... well, if you were academic you got the occasional mention but those in between often felt like they didn't belong. One lad I worked with ... was an international student, he was often very alone and isolated from his peers. I managed to coax him down to the gym, an environment that really suited this lad as he was able to really get into it and challenge himself. He literally (over 2 years) went from around 50 kilos to a monstrous 80 kilos of muscle. Unfortunately he contracted leukaemia and died about 12 months after I left the school. I have found that each school offers a variety of challenging opportunities to learn from, in this instance I felt a real connection with this lad as I was able to help him personally and socially despite a situation that was challenging for the both of us. It also highlighted that despite the boundaries you put up to protect yourself as a professional, some kids will get to you - both positive and negative.

This powerful story reveals that the challenges and dilemmas of being a teacher *do* impact on the emotions of teachers, regardless of the stance of professional distance being advocated as appropriate. Coming into the lives of young people, influencing their development, literally encouraging them in certain directions, and providing opportunities for growth and challenge can quickly be replaced by shock and loss when circumstances such as this occur. Teachers touch the lives of young people, and young people touch the lives of teachers, as this story of a beginning teacher clearly reveals.

Leading MYS Reform in the School Setting

John's story revealed much about the teaching strategies and successes he experienced as the middle years leader in his school. He wrote:

> I used to get a lot of complaints because of the noise my class made. We were in a room that was not properly sealed with a complete wall, so lots of sound carried. This was difficult for me, because there was a sense that my personal crusade to find a way forward was coming at the cost of other people trying to teach their classes next door. I also used to worry about the quality of maths teaching my students were getting, as the maths program at the school was pretty much based on the textbook.

His story reveals much about the successes of middle years reform, but also the challenges he faced. This was quite often interrupted with indicators that he was succeeding, as John explained in the following paragraph:

> I found that within the class, kids actually believed they could learn. I was touched by a letter I received from a parent whose child was moving school saying that she felt it was against her better judgment and that for the first time she felt her son really felt positive about himself as a learner. Other students who had well-developed "traditional" academic talent sought out "less capable" kids to join their group because they recognized these kids could provide insights that their own way of thinking prevented them from seeing.

He also shared his frustration at the difficulty of enabling others to adopt middle years practices. In John's words:

> One wise colleague pointed out to me that I had won my understanding through very hard work over a long period of time and that it might be unreasonable for me to expect others to develop this same understanding overnight. Looking back I now wish I had the skill back then to assist others in their understanding of what teaching can be. My own ideas were still not formed (to an extent they still aren't—I just am more comfortable with managing the tensions) and I was still getting the odd complaint about my noisy class. However, all of these lessons have served me well in the time since.

Tony told his story of establishing a professional network to assist his initiatives in the middle years. He wrote:

> I got involved straight away with the Middle Years Association and established a group meeting in my district as one didn't exist. It was very well

received and teachers from an array of schools attended regularly to toss around ideas. I found it difficult to convince the oldies in the profession that student centred learning was farmer beneficial than chalk and talk. Some saw the benefits; others maintained that it gave students too much freedom and they lost respect for the teacher.

Tony also shared his visions for reform in his current school, writing:

> As an administrator, I am looking at implementing an array of middle schooling strategies into the school. This has begun with the establishment of a middle schooling coordinator (also a MYS graduate) and beginning the process for an integrated curriculum for Years 6-9 (10-13 years old). We are looking closely at structural changes across the school to support middle schooling concepts and frameworks with greater zeal. This involves changing mindsets of staff and a culture that has been in place for some time.

Karen felt she had been introduced to the school as the platform for MYS reform. She noted:

> It was a bit daunting as I was introduced as the middle schooling "expert." At this school the middle school was only a year old and it was still evolving in both physical buildings and philosophy. One particular staff member who had been at the school for some time and had been involved in the inception of the middle school was maybe uneasy? threatened? by this. Her opening statement when we first met and the head of the school said I should have a lot to offer was that "the curriculum was pretty much set for this term." She made life very unpleasant for me the whole time I was there to the degree I transferred to their primary school. Others were much more open and appreciated a sharing of expertise where I could contribute a middle schooling perspective and they contributed years of experience and depth of content.

This attempt by schools to seed the agenda for MYS development through staffing initiatives has been particularly problematic especially since specialization in the MYS is currently a "new" area and is predominantly dominated by early career professionals. Karen is now a lecturer in the tertiary sector and contributes to the conduct of preservice programs preparing MYS teachers. It is interesting that she soon abandoned her place as a classroom teacher due to her feelings regarding the conflict between her being perceived as a beginner in the profession as well as a specialized expert.

Visions of the future for MYS in Australian Schools

When invited to consider what the future holds for MYS, the participants typically reflected on their own stories and projected the main issues as they saw them. For Tony, this was within his school and was about changing 'mindsets' and staffing issues. Tony wrote:

> Often staffing issues are an issue. Middle schools need the right teachers. These are not always that easy to come by. I have introduced practical placements at my school (never done before). This is to give opportunities to prac teachers to experience a very different teaching setting, but also to enable staff to experience new students, their enthusiasm and motivation as this can often be contagious in the right environment…. It just means changing mindsets and this is slow ESPECIALLY with older staff in a secondary environment.

For Leo, the future for middle years reform is promising. He wrote:

> At this point the middle years at this school has the greatest opportunity to develop the principles of middle schooling that has been advocated by MYSA and myself for many years. Many changes to the teaching and learning environment have been made (including a 1-to-1 laptop program) that will benefit the students and place them in good position for a successful future in the senior years.

For John, who is currently involved nationally in guiding policy around middle years, expectedly a broader perspective was shared. John wrote:

> In Australia generally, I think there are some mixed messages. National documents sound promising in some areas (like the National Goals that explicitly recognize middle years as a concern) and discouraging in others (such as centralized literacy and numeracy tests). At the moment, MYSA is well positioned to make some noise about middle years concerns in an emerging National Curriculum but the current political climate has a strange fascination with particular kinds of data. For middle years to flourish, there is a need for research to demonstrate clear links between specific kinds of practices with both positive development AND "performance." Now this research might exist, but it needs to be in the context of the present climate, high-functioning middle schools need to be shown to be achieving this today. A research model that shows links between practice, development and achievement would very neatly fit the messages from authorities which recognize the need for particular kinds of citizens as well as particular kinds of knowledge.

Karen explained that the developing agenda for defined curriculum in Australia will place direct pressure on MYS and reforms. She noted:

> I think middle schooling is under threat … with the emphasis on assessment, reporting and narrow measurable outcomes, there is a danger that the less measurable aspects of middle schooling such as pastoral care will be

set aside as "not the teacher's responsibility as they don't have time." This despite the numerous research studies that show adolescents won't learn while they are stressed or dealing with other issues. I'm concerned that you will end up back at a curriculum that is not engaging but is measurable!

The visions offered by the participants reveal some of the wider challenges facing the middle years reforms in the Australian context. Broad agendas of accountability and high stakes testing for instance, evident in the widespread introduction of external testing regimes particularly targeting literacy and numeracy standards, have placed agendas focussing on pedagogy in jeopardy. The immediate response to these imperatives has been to develop skills associated with the testing genres and to ready students by "teaching to the test." This has relegated reform agendas with a broader social and pastoral mission, such as middle years reform, in the margins.

REFLECTION AND DISCUSSION

This paper explored, through the use of narrative inquiry, how two of the graduates of the specialized middle years program and two middle years teachers who entered the field through an alternate path, experienced their world as teachers. Their experiences, captured through their story retelling provided insight to the challenges and opportunities that face the development of cohesive MYS contexts, and the contribution possible through specialized preservice teacher programs.

The four participants in this narrative inquiry each shared their lived experiences of becoming and being middle years teachers, and of speculating about the future for middle years. For each, the journey was unique; however, this study also reveals common issues across participants.

At the individual teacher level, along with the school and wider systemic levels, middle years reform is a challenging and exciting place to be in the Australian education system. Each of the participants is convincing and unswerving in their commitment to the value of and need for MYS reform. The stories reveal the need for cautious experimentation and robust research about the benefits of middle years reform. Yet, it is apparent from the stories that none of the story tellers have been readily accepted into the traditional primary and secondary schooling contexts. Their teaching practices have been challenged and scrutinized, as have their abilities to engender an interest and capacity for middle years reform in their fellow teacher colleagues. This raises a serious issue for middle years reform—is it the responsibility and task of middle years teachers to continually argue the benefits of middle schooling and to professionally develop colleagues with few specific skills in this area?

In an American study of the status of middle schooling programs in Florida, three elements were deemed essential for success: clarity of mission, authentic commitment, and skilful execution (George, 2008/2009). In the Florida scenario under investigation, it was resolved that there was "critical insufficiency in each of these three essential areas" (George, 2008/2009, p. 9). The report criticized the lack of support for middle years reform, yet pointed out that the:

> decade-long record of outstanding academic achievement attained by Florida middle schools (much more positive than either elementary or high schools), even with severely truncated program components, may lead to a new consensus about the requirements for highly effective middle level education. (George, 2008/2009, p.1)

In other words, though lacking comprehensive support for middle years implementation, there are still clear benefits for students in middle school programs. George (2008/2009, p. 9) makes many claims about where efforts are required to ensure middle schooling benefits prevail, but notes that "one of the most significant of these is the dearth of either preservice teacher or administrator preparation." This narrative inquiry similarly points to middle years teacher specialist and middle years leaders as key drivers of middle years reform.

REFERENCES

Brisbane Catholic Education Office. (2004). *Pathways for middle schooling: Walk the talk. A position paper and self audit process.* Brisbane, Australia: Author.

Carrington, V., Pendergast, D., Bahr, N., Kapitzke, C., Mayer, D., & Mitchell, J. (2001). Education futures: Transforming teacher education. In: M. Brennan (Ed.), *Education futures and new citizenships: Proceedings of the 10th national biennial conference of the Australian Curriculum Studies Association.* Deakin, Australia: Australian Curriculum Studies Association.

Garrick, B., Pendergast, D., Bahr, N., Dole, S., & Keogh, J. (2008). Researching the construction of middle years teacher identity: A study of graduates. In T. Aspland (Ed.), *Teacher educators at work: What works and where is the evidence. Conference proceedings: The Australian Teacher Education Association (ATEA)* (pp. 253-271). Sunshine Coast, Queensland, Australia: Australian Teacher Education Association.

George, P. (2008-2009). *Special report: The status of programs in Florida Middle Schools.* Sarasota, FL: Florida League of Middle Schools.

Hunter, L., Patel Stevens, L., Pendergast, D., Mitchell, J., Bahr, N., Carrington, V., & Kapitzke, C. (2004, July). *Finding sustainable spaces for young people in middle schooling: an historical and theoretical enquiry into adolescence.* Paper presented at The Australian Teacher Education Association (ATEA) making spaces: Regenerating the profession, Annual Conference, Bathurst, Australia.

Ingvarson, L. (2009). A partnership whose time has come: *National curriculum and national professional teaching standards.* Melbourne, Australia: Centre for Strategic Education.

Keogh, J., Bahr, N., Hunter, L., Stevens, L., Wright, T., Pendergast, D., & Rohner, C. (2004, December). *Three years on: Growing teachers for the middle years.* Paper presented at Australian Association for Research in Education (AARE) 2004 International Education Research Conference, Doing the Public Good: Positioning Education Research, Melbourne, Australia.

Luke, A., Elkins, J., Weir, K., Land, R., Carrington, V., Dole, S., & Stevens, L. (2003). *Beyond the middle: A report about literacy and numeracy development of target group students in the middle years of schooling* (Vol. 1) Brisbane, Australia: JS McMillan Printing Group.

Ministerial Council on Education, Employment, Training and Youth Affairs. (2008). *Melbourne declaration on educational goals for young Australians.* Retrieved from http://www.mceetya.edu.au/verve/_resources/National_Declaration_on_the_Educational_Goals_for_Young_Australians.pdf

Middle Years of Schooling Association. (2008). *MYSA position paper. Middle schooling: People, practices and places.* Brisbane, Australia: Author.

Mitchell, J., Kapitzke, C., Mayer, D., Carrington, V., Stevens, L., Bahr, N., & Hunter, L. (2003). Aligning school reform and teachers education reform in the middle years: An Australian case study. *Teaching Education, 14*(1), 69-82.

Moen, T. (2006). Reflections on the narrative research approach. *International Journal of Qualitative Methodology, 5*(4), Article 5.

National Middle School Association. (2001). *NMSA's position statement on the professional preparation of middle level teachers.* Retrieved from http://www.nmsa.org/news/middlelevelteachers.htm.

Pendergast, D. (2007). Middle years schooling. In N. Bahr & D. Pendergast (Eds.), *The millennial adolescent* (pp. 204-228). Canberra, Australia: Australian Council for Educational Research.

Pendergast, D. (2009). The success of middle years initiatives: Some important considerations. *Professional Voice—Australian Education Union, 6*(3), 13-18.

Pendergast, D., Keogh, J., Garrick, B., Reynolds, J., Dole, S., & Bahr, N. (2009, June). *Synergies between the MYSA position paper and preservice middle years teacher education: A case in point.* Paper presented at the meeting of Australian Teacher Education Association, Albury, Australia.

Pendergast, D., Whitehead, K., De Jong, T., Newhouse-Maiden, L. & Bahr, N. (2007). Middle years teacher education: New programs and research directions. *The Australian Educational Researcher, 34*(2), 73-90.

Sandelowski, M. (1991, Fall). Telling stories: Narrative approaches to qualitative research. *IMAGE: Journal of Nursing Scholarship, 23*(3), 161-166.

Teaching Australia. (2009). *Standards for accomplished teachers and principals: A foundation for public confidence and respect.* Western Australia, Australia: Author.

CHAPTER 10

REFLECTIONS ON SHARED MIDDLE LEVEL EXPERIENCES

A Case Study

**Shirley M. Matteson, Richard M. Fletcher,
Tamera Tidwell, and Doris I. Garrett**

There is a need for qualified individuals who can fill middle level teacher educator positions. This study investigated work environment characteristics that motivated middle school teachers to pursue doctoral degrees. The narratives of 4 middle school teachers were examined to determine what specific factors from their shared teaching experiences were motivational. The analysis of the narratives suggests that positive and negative experiences with campus leaders, and the subsequent changes in campus climate, were motivational factors with these teachers. A second motivating factor was the development of professional relationships.

This We Believe (National Middle School Association [NMSA], 2003) divides characteristics of middle schools into two parts. One part focuses on aspects of school culture, while the other addresses what successful schools should provide. Several important characteristics of school culture are addressed in this study, including:

Voices From the Middle: Narrative Inquiry By, For, and About the Middle Level Community
pp. 193–212

- courageous, collaborative leadership,
- an inviting, supportive, and safe environment, and
- high expectations for every member of the learning community (p. 7).

This narrative inquiry relied on personal reflections, written by four middle school teachers who taught together in the same middle school for a number of years, to provide the basis for an *instrumental case study* (Stake, 2003). The intention of this inquiry was to examine which aspects of middle school shared experiences shaped teachers' attitudes and subsequently influenced career goals. This study sought to answer the question, "What characteristics of the work environment motivate middle school teachers to pursue advanced degrees?"

PROVIDING A VOICE

The participants in this inquiry were intentionally chosen to represent a population whose voices have been silent in educational research literature—that of middle school teachers who have chosen to pursue doctoral degrees. This study reveals that elements of middle level philosophy and practice may have played a unique role in prompting these four teachers to seek terminal degrees. Pragmatically, the voices of the four teachers in this study may be representative of teachers of all grade levels engaged in such a pursuit.

Why should the voice of those pursuing doctoral degrees be heard? Understanding why some middle level teachers pursue doctoral degrees might lead to the development of support structures, which, in turn, might increase the number of individuals seeking and earning terminal degrees. This could result in more highly qualified teachers working with middle level students. In addition, there would be a larger pool of qualified candidates for teacher education faculty positions. Many teacher education positions have remained unfilled due to a nationwide shortage of qualified candidates (e.g., Wolf-Wendel, Baker, Twombly, Tollefson, & Mahlios, 2006). Some areas, such as mathematics education and special education, are experiencing severe shortages (Wolf-Wendel et al., 2006). There is a need for veteran middle school educators who are (1) familiar with the characteristics of adolescent learners, (2) well acquainted with the ideals incorporated within *This We Believe*, and (3) conducting research on middle school issues. These individuals are needed at the university level to instruct the next generation of middle school teachers and middle school teacher educators.

The National Center of Education Statistics (NCES) report entitled *Digest of Education Statistics: 2007* (NCES, 2008) noted that in 2003-2004 master's degrees were held by 40.9% of the nation's public school teachers and 1.2% held doctoral degrees. A comparison of the master's degrees earned by elementary and secondary teachers found 40.6% of elementary teachers held master's degrees to 41.3% of secondary teachers. For those holding doctoral degrees, the percentage of elementary teachers was 0.8% while secondary teachers was 1.7%. Some states, such as Texas where the four middle school teachers in this study worked, have reported lower percentages. In this state only 21% of public school teachers hold a master's degree and half of 1% have earned a doctorate (Texas Education Agency, 2008).

Why do teachers hesitate to earn advanced degrees? Sometimes there are no advantages to earning advanced degrees. Texas teacher salaries are based on the number of years of service, not on coursework or additional degrees. However, Texas educators who hold certificates issued after September 1, 1999 "are subject to a 5-year certificate renewal period, with a 150-hour continuing professional education (CPE) requirement" (Texas Classroom Teachers Association [TCTA], 2008). States that require master's degrees usually do so for tenure or salary purposes. Upon earning a master's degree, teachers in many states are required to complete additional hours of professional development. Texas teachers do not earn tenure and teacher unions are not permitted to negotiate for teacher benefits. There is a state minimum salary schedule for public school teachers, although individual school districts may choose to pay teachers above the state salary schedule (Texas Education Code, 2008). The lack of either tenure or pay incentives are prevalent reasons that discourage the pursuit of master's or doctoral degrees.

Since over 40% of the nation's teachers already hold a master's degree, what other factors prevent individuals from pursuing doctoral degrees? Obtaining a doctoral degree is an arduous and expensive task. Individuals may not live near institutions that grant doctoral degrees, although online programs could be pursued. Many educators are not financially secure enough to add the expense of graduate studies to the family budget. Others do not want to endure the hours of research and writing that completing a dissertation entails. Veteran educators do not want to lose the benefits of tenure, longevity, or change retirement plans.

The sharing of the reflections of four middle level educators who pursue doctoral degrees may provide insights into the factors that influenced their decision to undertake a terminal degree. Additionally, reading about their experiences may serve to motivate others who have considered pursuing such a path, but believe that only a specific type of individual embarks on such an endeavor.

METHODOLOGY

This qualitative study examined the narratives of four middle school teachers who worked in the same building during several overlapping years. Narratives supply "the context for making meaning of school situations" (Connelly & Clandinin, 1990, p. 3). Narrative inquiry is well suited to investigating the dynamics of the school structures of people, place, and time (Powell, 2005). In fact, Clandinin and Connelly (1994) have noted that "time and place, plot and scene, work together to create the experiential quality of narrative" (p. 416).

Participants

I, Shirley, invited several former colleagues already enrolled in doctoral programs to write narratives for this study. Richard and Tamera accepted my invitation. Doris was included in when another individual declined to participate. I was middle school Team 6A's leader when Richard joined us as a student teacher and was designated as Tamera's "buddy" when she joined the faculty. Tamera was on Team 6B, the other sixth grade team. Teachers new to the district, but not new to teaching, were assigned buddies to help in learning campus and district policies and procedures. Doris was the last one of the group to be hired as a faculty member at the middle school. As an elective teacher, she worked with both sixth grade teams.

During our time at the middle school campus, the four of us shared common experiences such as teaching on block and traditional schedules and changes in campus administration. Additional insights into our professional selves were revealed by relating events that occurred prior to being hired as a faculty member at the middle school.

Shirley: I hired into the district immediately after earning my master's degree in music education, which I obtained after 3 years of classroom experience. I remember briefly considering becoming a principal, but couldn't imagine leaving the classroom to deal with primarily administrative duties or disciplinary issues. I was a restless educator and thrived on change or challenges, such as teaching a different subject or grade level.

Before I transferred to the campus from another district middle school, I had worked on 11 different campuses within the district and added several certifications to my résumé. My initial teaching certification was all-level music and I had held positions as a high school and middle school band director and elementary general music teacher. In addition, I had earned elementary generalist and secondary English language arts certifications and had several years of teaching experience in sixth and seventh grade language arts before landing in sixth grade mathematics. My various teaching experiences had shown me I enjoyed working in middle schools the most, and could be content no matter what subject area I was asked to teach. I was excited about the opportunity to experience block scheduling and intrigued with the possibilities for students in receiving mathematics instruction during a longer block of time. That was my major reason for requesting a transfer to the district's newest middle school.

Richard: I was about midway through my 20-year military career when I had an "ah-ha" moment that led me into education. In the mid-eighties, I met my wife who, at the time, was a speech and language pathologist. One day, while she and I were watching television, there was a knock on the door. When I opened the door, there stood a young Marine looking resplendent in his Marine Corps dress blue uniform. This young man, who stuttered, had been one of my wife's students in high school. On his first leave home, he had taken time to seek her out. He wanted to thank her for equipping him with speech techniques that allowed him to be successful in the military. He smartly snapped to attention and gave her the hand salute, an honor held by military personnel worldwide as a sign of respect and one often reserved for those of higher rank.

At that moment, I saw the pride my wife felt while tears simultaneously filled her eyes. I wondered how it felt to know you had that much influence on a young person's life. I found myself momentarily reliving my own school experiences and realized I, too, had an educator who had influenced me in much the same way. A science teacher named Mr. Vereen refused to give up on a tough talking kid from inner-city Detroit because he saw something in me I did not see in myself at the time. Mr. Vereen taught me science at my first elementary school, which housed kindergarten through grade three, and then at my next elementary school for grades four through six. Mr. Vereen transferred to the new junior high school I attended and again taught me science from seventh to ninth grade. The citywide technical high school I attended for grades ten through twelve was incorporated into a new neighborhood high school. Mr. Vereen, whom I thought I had finally left behind, transferred to the new school and became my teacher for the final 3 years of my public school career. I met Mr. Vereen one last time when he pulled into the gas station where I was working. He asked me what I was doing back in Detroit working at a service station. He had been told I had been off at college, but that I had left after my first year. Three weeks after the encounter, I received a letter from a prestigious private Detroit university stating Mr. Vereen had personally recommended me for, and I had been awarded, an academic scholarship to attend the university. My high school musings mingled with wanting to feel the pride I could see welling up in my wife. That event prompted me to immediately decide that I was going to become an educator when I retired from active duty. This is a decision I have yet to regret.

My middle school campus story begins when, nearing completion of a second bachelor's degree, I was offered a job as a behavior management teacher on another district campus. The personnel office told me if I accepted the position I would have to abandon the work I had completed toward my secondary education social studies degree. Instead, I would need to complete an extra 21-hour deficiency plan to become special education certified. I had completed all the degree requirements except student teaching and was torn between my wanting to work (being paid) with special needs students, but having to do this at the expense of abandoning the undergraduate work I had already completed. Alternatively, I could complete my social studies degree by student teaching (without pay) and hope to find work as a secondary history teacher.

My soon-to-be supervisory teacher called me before the semester began. She urged me to complete my student teaching and argued that I would see enough disciplinary issues as a sixth grade history teacher to decide if I wanted to become a behavior teacher. I joined team 6A at the middle school as a student teacher, but was introduced to students as a cooperating teacher to help cement my authority in the classroom—a technique I subsequently used with student teachers in my role as an administrator.

Tamera: I was the first in my family ever to graduate from college. My mother quit high school in the tenth grade to marry my father. My father finished high school, but college was not in his plans. My parents, especially my mother, valued education. My family did not have the means to send me to college, but I was fortunate to earn an academic scholarship to a local university for a 4-year undergraduate degree. I spent another year in a teacher certification program, and in the mid-eighties landed a wonderful teaching position in California.

After I married, we moved and I was able to continue my teaching career in Texas. A few years later, a military transfer relocated us to North Carolina. The local district was different from what I was used to; a priority was placed on participation in professional academic organizations. I enrolled in a university to take advantage of free graduate courses that were offered to only science and math teachers. These courses did not require acceptance into a formal graduate program, but did provide an enriching staff development opportunity. The coursework was rigorous, but enjoyable. The experienced instructors provided opportunities for excellent discussions and stimulating debates.

The experience got me thinking "If this is so much fun, why not enroll in the Master's program full time?" The degree program I chose would accept the courses I had already taken. I hired my neighbor to babysit my son, who was not even a year old. Twice a week I took evening classes after teaching school during the day. This was a demanding schedule, as my husband was deployed overseas. I doubled up on summer courses and was able to finish in a couple of years. I earned a master's degree in middle grades education, with an endorsement to teach reading and English language arts at the middle level. I had previously been restricted to teaching only through grade six because of my elementary certification.

Eventually, our family was transferred back to Texas. I was very excited about my new degree and the possibilities of teaching up through grade eight in reading and English language arts, so I sought a position to utilize those skills. That did not happen, as I was hired to teach sixth grade mathematics. I met Shirley, Richard and, several years later, Doris joined the grade level.

Doris: I entered the field of education by chance. After starting college as a business major, I switched to education after my friend suggested teaching—he was pursuing teacher certification. I had a young child and knew there would be several benefits to becoming a teacher. My friend suggested that I first substitute teach to determine if I liked the experience. This would also help me determine what grade level(s) I felt most comfortable teaching. I recalled a former high school teacher of mine who compared his life to that of his sister, who was a business executive. He mentioned how often she traveled, the 60-plus hour work week, and the amount of time it took for her to advance towards her current position. Since his sister had not married or had children, this career choice fit her lifestyle. However, my teacher was married and had a baby for whom he had to provide. He had decided that a teaching career better suited his family's needs. This made me reflect on my own life, and I decided a career in education best suited the needs of my family.

I began substitute teaching and found that I enjoyed the campus environment and interactions with the students. After subbing in various grade levels, I found middle school to be the best fit for me. My first substitute teaching experience was actually the school at which Shirley, Richard, and Tamera worked. At the time, this campus followed a block schedule, which I thought might be difficult for a sub, but I had no problems. I came to like this model and was disappointed to find it had returned to a traditional model by the time I was hired as a faculty member.

The campus was actually my second choice for employment. Though I subbed there frequently and was familiar with many staff and faculty, I had hoped to get a teaching position at my middle school alma mater across town. I had also subbed there frequently and even completed my student teaching at that campus. However, upon finishing my degree, my alma mater had no immediate openings. I found myself contacting the principal at my second choice, as I had developed a positive rapport with the administration and staff. To my delight, I interviewed the following day and was then offered a position.

Table 10.1 is included to assist readers in quickly identifying the four participants.

Data

The participants (see Table 10.1) were asked to share whatever impressions of being on the campus they wanted to discuss, and to elaborate on their doctoral pursuit. A chronological format was used in writing the ret-

Table 10.1.   The Participants at a Glance

Participant	*Brief Biography*
Shirley	6th grade mathematics, team leader, and mathematics department chair. Transferred to the campus from another district middle school. Earned PhD in 2007 and is on faculty at a state university as a middle level teacher educator.
Richard	6th grade social studies. Retired military. Student taught and first teaching job at the campus. Currently a high school administrator, pursuing an EdD.
Tamera	6th grade mathematics. Prior teaching experiences in various states before being hired for the campus. Working on an EdD with emphasis in curriculum while teaching 5th grade mathematics.
Doris	6th grade elective teacher and girls athletics. Substitute teacher and first teaching job at the campus. Pursing a DMgt while working in educational service center.

rospective narratives. Some chose to write a year-by-year account, while others delineated time by referring to specific events (e.g., dropping off the block schedule) or individuals (e.g., administrator changes). Clarification or additional information was requested as needed. In essence, each wrote an abbreviated professional autobiography. There was also a transparent element in collecting the data in that everyone had the opportunity to read the others' narratives.

Data Analysis

Data analysis and collection for qualitative studies frequently utilize either an emic, etic, or negotiated perspective (Drew, Hardman, & Hosp, 2008). The emic perspective considers data collection and/or analysis from the participants' viewpoint, the etic perspective considers the researcher's viewpoint, and a combination of the emic and etic perspectives results in a negotiated perspective. A negotiated perspective was used for the analysis of data, as I was both a participant and the primary researcher.

In narrative inquiry the participants and researcher mutually construct a story. "Narrative is a way of understanding one's own and others' actions, of organizing events and objects into a meaningful whole, and of connecting and seeing the consequences of actions and events over time" (Chase, 2005, p. 656). Multiple analytic lenses were used in the analysis, including considering the narratives as (1) a way of making meaning, (2) verbal action, (3) stories that are both enabled and constrained, (4) socially situated interactive performances, and (5) interpreting situations

(Chase, 2005). In my dual role I narrate, speak as an individual, or serve as an "interpretive authority" (p. 662).

Theme Development

The initial intent was to frame the analysis of the narratives around topics such as (1) characteristics of those who pursue terminal degrees, (2) the role of mentors in this journey, (3) levels of engagement in professional development opportunities, and (4) the influence our actions had upon our peers (S. Matteson, personal communication, November 11, 2008). However, after the first reading of the narratives, the initial list of topics was discarded. Several themes were considered. These themes were shared with Richard, Tamera, and Doris and supporting sections of the narratives that illuminated the analysis of specific situations (Chase, 2005) were selected. During subsequent drafts changes in wording of the themes and edits to supporting narrative sections were negotiated. The themes of campus leadership and climate and professional relationships were selected due to their influence on our decisions to pursue doctoral degrees.

Trustworthiness

One criticism of the data is that there were no other sources for triangulation. Although there had been infrequent visits, emails, and phone calls between the four of us, other written documents were not available. Polkinghorne (2007) has argued "that different kinds of knowledge claims require different kinds of evidence and argument to convince readers that the claim is valid" (p. 474). In order to ensure accurate representation and interpretation of the data, each participant was asked to check the manuscript for clarity and accuracy in interpreting events and reflections. Numerous drafts were sent back and forth and everyone's suggestions were considered, a further example of the negotiated perspective of analysis (Drew et al., 2008).

Generalizability and transferability

Generalizability and transferability remain major issues of concern in qualitative inquiries. Some disapprove of case study research because "the results are not widely applicable in real life" (Tellis, 1997, p. 2). However, case studies can be deemed trustworthy if the narratives "resonate experientially with a broad cross section of readers" (p. 2). The results of this study are believed to be more transferable than generalizable.

Contextual Setting

The following subsections provide a detailed description of the middle school at which the four of us taught. Information about aspects such as the school's location, layout, schedule, and leadership might assist readers in determining whether the conclusions of the study are logical. Readers may recognize several of Powell's (2005) characteristics of a true middle school within the following subsections.

Location

The middle school at which we worked opened in the mid-1990s and included students from Grades 6 through 8. The building was strategically placed as the focal point in a growing new subdivision. Seventh and eighth grade students were rezoned to the campus in order to relieve two overcrowded middle schools. Two elementary feeder schools, including one that housed the district's only Spanish bilingual program, provided the majority of the sixth grade student population.

School Layout

The middle school's physical design became the prototype for at least two subsequent district middle schools. The main core of the building housed the administrative offices, nurse and counselor area, cafeteria, library, and rooms for programs that serviced many grade levels of students—such as art, theater arts, and special education. There was a music/athletics wing and three grade level wings. The sixth grade wing was the furthest away from the administrative offices and music/athletics wing, so in a sense the sixth grade students and teachers were isolated from the rest of the campus. A shared area of lockers and restrooms separated the two academic teams, Team A and Team B, in each grade level wing. Construction of new classrooms, although disruptive, became warranted. Within 5 years of opening the building, the campus student population increased to 1050, 300 more than the original capacity. After the new classrooms were added, team locations were reassigned. Teams became located on sides of the hallway instead of at the ends. This configuration placed teachers of the core classes directly across from each other. The change was positive for teachers as they could communicate easier with their subject colleagues. However, the configuration was negative for students, as they moved from classroom to classroom in close proximity, which facilitated interdisciplinary activities. Collaborative instructional efforts among team members became more difficult to manage and there was a decreased sense of belonging to a smaller group for the students. Unfortunately several teachers, usually teachers who did not teach the core subjects, still traveled every period.

Staffing and Schedule

The first principal of the middle school was a veteran district educator who had a vision for the middle school. He carefully "robbed" gifted groups of middle level educators from other middle school campuses in the district and filled some positions with first year teachers or teachers new to the district. During staffing interviews he informed all interviewees of the intent for this school to open using a traditional format, but to follow an alternating block schedule the next year, a move supported by the district administration. Mathematics and language arts/reading classes met for 85 minutes every day, with science, social studies, and other courses meeting every other day on an A/B schedule. As the first middle school in the district on such a schedule, the campus was under a great deal of scrutiny. A local university conducted studies concerning the implementation of the block schedule in partnership with the campus for a number of years.

The transition to the block schedule required teachers to update and extend teaching skills. Content areas conducted special sessions that emphasized hands-on activities and/or cooperative grouping strategies. Faculty members were encouraged to go in-depth in each respective subject area. The block schedule affected staffing allocations. Due to classes meeting every day, a greater number of mathematics and language arts teachers were hired, as each teacher in those subject areas had usually around 60 students. The teaching load for core teachers was three double-blocked sections with one extended conference/team period. Team members generally taught the same set of students, which sometimes strained the campus schedule. Some special classes, such as advanced classes, resulted in cross teaming of students. The school board returned the campus to a traditional schedule the year after the campus received the state's *Recognized* status for increasing student scores on the state standardized assessments. Block scheduling resulted in benefits as well as many concerns. However, the board's decision was based on financial considerations.

Team Organization and Responsibilities

Under the block schedule, teams consisted of six teachers (two mathematics, two language arts, one each of science and social studies). Several teams created specific team member roles such as team leader, discipline secretary, team minutes secretary, liaison to other building staff, student special needs, and esteem builder. The esteem builder organized celebrations of adult and student birthdays, recognized accomplishments of students and staff, and organized social events such as an end of the year pool party for team members, their families, and other invitees. Teams were allowed a great deal of flexibility in meeting student needs. The first building principal believed the team would take greater responsibility in mentoring individuals if they were involved in the hiring process, so the team interviewed candidates for team vacancies. Hiring recommendations were coordinated with the various department chairs and campus administrators.

Department Organization

All core subjects held departmental meetings. Elective teachers were encouraged to meet together as a department, but many also joined specific teams. Several teachers held positions on district curriculum, technology, or assessment committees. The campus mathematics department became the model for implementing hands-on mathematics instruction within the district.

This contextual setting provides a foundation to readers for understanding the excerpts from the narrative reflections. Readers may wish to refer back to various sections as they consider the themes presented in the following section.

FINDINGS

The question that framed our study was "What characteristics of the work environment motivate middle school teachers to pursue advanced degrees?" The themes that emerged from the narratives addressed the campus leadership and climate and our professional relationships. Imbedded within those themes are the ideals of a courageous, collaborative leadership; an inviting, supportive, and safe environment; and high expectations for every member of the learning community (NMSA, 2003).

Campus Leadership and Climate

The campus principal "influences student achievement and teacher effectiveness by advocating, nurturing, and sustaining an effective instructional program" (NMSA, 2003, p. 10). Richard focused on the leadership style of the first principal.

> Richard: I must talk about the working environment of the school under the school's first principal, the innovative educator that Shirley described earlier. He staffed the campus with a group of like-minded, self-actualizing, motivated, and innovative educators—and gave us the freedom and support to do what was right and in the best interest of the students. This is a leadership style I have continuously striven to emulate since becoming an administrator 6 years ago.

Staff and faculty members spent many days prior to the opening of the school in professional development meetings and collectively embraced the vision of an inviting, supportive, and safe environment for the campus (NMSA, 2003). Fortunately this principal was not intimidated by our strong personalities. He was confident in his leadership capabilities. He had a reputation for deliberately surrounding himself with capable individuals and letting them do their jobs without interference.

We experienced many changes during our years at the campus, including returning to a traditional eight period schedule. Shortly after the first principal retired, several faculty positions were eliminated. Teachers had to adjust to teaching on a traditional schedule, which several faculty members had never experienced. The pace of the campus seemed hurried and the campus climate was not as inviting. We did not have time to develop relationships with students, parents, or new colleagues. Subsequent campus leaders were not as supportive of the faculty. Since I taught at the campus longer than Richard, Tamera, or Doris, I experienced several cycles of administrators.

> Shirley: During pursuit of my doctoral degree, the campus administration changed three times. With the first change, a different campus climate emerged as the new leadership emphasized developing their individual résumés, not addressing student needs. Negative attitudes surfaced in the building. We felt micromanaged and overburdened with useless initiatives. Then the campus was led by an interim principal for a semester while another instructional leader was found. This next principal was supportive, which really helped me focus on my final courses and dissertation. My teaching schedule was arranged so that I had the last period of the day as a planning period, thereby lessening commuting concerns—it was a two hour commute just to get to the university. My principal, under the impression that I needed to have "family" present, even drove over with me one afternoon when I was recognized for a research award that was directly linked to improving our students' mathematics performance. I found myself spending a great deal of time seeking her advice as my studies progressed and the reality of completing my doctorate started to sink in.

The positive atmosphere of the campus was decimated within a relatively short time frame. Many of us who had emerged as teacher leaders were perceived as a "threat" to insecure administrators. I grew restless and decided to start a doctoral program. I relinquished several leadership positions to focus on my studies. The campus leadership changed several times within a short amount of time and the campus climate somewhat stabilized.

> Doris: Changes in campus leadership my second year of teaching affected employee morale. Though many staff remained another year, people were unhappy and the level of camaraderie that existed before was not as significant. I tried to transfer, but was unsuccessful. Because I had witnessed many

poor decisions and lack of courage among administration, I became motivated to become a model campus leader. By this time I was halfway through my master's degree in education administration. At the end of my third year of teaching I began seeking an assistant principal position. I wanted to be in a position to have a greater impact in education for all of its stakeholders.

Many of the faculty made decisions similar to Doris's. As a traveling teacher and coach, Doris was aware of the morale throughout the building. Her experiences served as a catalyst to completing her degree in educational administration. She, like Richard, had a vision of an effective campus leader. Several faculty members chose to pursue master's degrees in educational administration in order to secure instructional specialist or assistant principal positions at other campuses.

Professional Relationships

Teaming allowed a strong sense of community to develop. Deep relationships formed within the teaching staff. We allowed specific colleagues to hone our professional personas as we embraced the ideal of high expectations for every member of the learning community (NMSA, 2003).

Richard: From the first day on campus, I was embraced as an equal by my fellow team members and encouraged to share ideas and experiences with them, thus causing me never to feel like a student teacher. Once my supervisory teacher, who was completing a master's in education administration, felt comfortable with me as a teacher she began transferring more and more lesson-planning and teaching duties to me. She gave me the freedom to develop a teaching style of my own, but would review and coach my lesson planning and delivery method offering "suggestions" for improvement. In retrospect, I believe our talking about her reasons for pursuing a postgraduate degree and her nurturing supervisory style planted the early seeds for my eventual postgraduate studies. History was not her first teaching field, and at the end of my student teaching assignment she volunteered to move to an English language arts opening. Her decision allowed me to become the team's social studies teacher.

Richard was accepted by the team right from the start. In contrast to his military career, he did not need to earn his way up the ranks in order to become a full-fledged team member. All of us enjoyed the freedom of developing our individual teaching styles.

Shirley: Tamera was one of several colleagues who assisted me in the National Board certification process. She read my submissions and helped me select videotape segments for analysis. I was grateful to find out Tamera knew of the rigor of the process due to the assistance provided to National Board candidates in North Carolina. Members of my team and the mathematics department supported my endeavor.

Achieving my National Board certification was a collaborative effort. As a team and department leader, my role was to support my colleagues. Now our roles were reversed. I did not realize how becoming a National Board Certified Teacher would later impact my career.

The Doctoral Pursuit

Just like our middle school students, we matured during the years we spent as teachers on the middle school campus. The themes of campus leadership and climate and professional relationships impacted each of us in different ways, and ultimately inspired us to embark on our doctoral journeys. Extended portions of our narratives reveal what prompted us to start our doctoral degrees and what we hope to accomplish in the future.

Richard: The entire campus resonated with a collegial atmosphere where everyone, students and staff alike, were encouraged to enrich their own academic pursuits and become lifelong learners. I credit the first principal with creating the scholarly and Socratic environment that encouraged each of us to improve our content knowledge and question our methodology and expertise. This, to me, is what made the middle school so ripe with educators going on to pursue terminal degrees. It was shortly after a new principal took over and began changing the school climate that frustration levels increased. We began to talk more earnestly about earning terminal degrees. Such a degree would enable us to become educational leaders and influence preservice and in-service teachers and would increase the number of students we touched directly and indirectly. This talk persisted and intensified even after I left the middle school to become an administrator in another district. Had I not had the experiences I did while at the middle school, I would not have been as confident or willing to walk the educational path I am on now. I have incorporated the practices of collaborative collegiality and servant leadership practiced at the middle school into my leadership style, and encourage my subordinates and colleagues to further their educational pursuits.

My desire to reach as many students as possible is not for any monetary gain or positive tributes. Rather, I wish to serve as a positive adult role model, teacher, mentor, and empathic ear to an expanding circle of students. This is the very thing Mr. Vereen had seen in me—but something I had not yet seen until that point in my life. Despite my having spent these past 5 years as a high school administrator, I feel this goal lends itself best to middle school where teachers can still exert influence, positive and negative, on their students. Although I am not a special education teacher I have always wanted to work with special needs students. Earning an Ed.D. with an emphasis in special education should open doors. I could become a district level director of special education or teach special education classes as an adjunct university level instructor.

Tamera: While at my former campus, I discovered I had a keen interest in being involved with district level committees and working with curriculum. I was especially interested in positions and programs that had a direct impact on beginning teachers. In a new district, I learned how to look at testing data differently by using software that disaggregated subpopulations and objectives to show areas of potential growth. This was exciting to me. The information provided me a way to fine-tune what was being accomplished in the classroom. I then became the campus math coach with teaching duties, which included all the campus at-risk students.

Since coming to my current district, I have been invited to plan and teach staff development days for summer in-service. I served as a consultant for staff development at a neighboring district, and have been encouraged to apply for a couple of district level math positions that have been related to my grade level expertise. I was offered a central office position in another neighboring district not for just a few grade levels, but an entire district in the subject area that I love. Unfortunately, I had to decline the offer, but that vote of confidence gave me the push I needed to make the decision and commitment to apply for an EdD in curriculum and teaching.

Doris: I left the school district to work at an education service center. I saw the position as a way to gain more administrative skills and experience. I felt this was an opportunity to broaden my scope of influence within the realm of education. As an education specialist, I trained and monitored interns in the alternative teacher certification program. I also had the opportunity to help manage the newly created principal alternative certification program.

My experience at the education service center broadened my perspective of roles that can significantly impact all stakeholders in education. While working at this organization, its culture and climate helped renew my interest to earn a doctoral degree. I sought a program that would combine my work experiences to date and help me in future endeavors. I was only employed there for a year before military orders moved our family to Missouri. Prior to moving, I stumbled upon a management program that met my needs and was ecstatic when I learned of my acceptance. I look forward to opportunities that foster and encourage the positive development of youth and professionals. I aspire someday to open a creative, diverse learning facility for children.

Shirley: I believed I would just continue teaching in the district until my retirement, but after earning my NBCT certification, I grew increasingly frustrated at the lack of professional recognition for educators. Having been professionally reinvigorated while seeking my certification, I needed to channel my frustration into something productive. I had achieved recognition as an "accomplished" mathematics educator by district personnel, mathematics teachers at other campuses and parents. I considered two different avenues: (1) to become a state recognized master mathematics teacher or (2) take courses that would lead to a district level position in mathematics curriculum and instruction. However, the latter was largely an administrative position and I preferred working with students and colleagues. I deliberately sought out universities offering a doctoral degree in curriculum and instruction with an emphasis in mathematics education. I knew I still had much to learn about mathematics education, but I was inspired by others' confidence in me.

The idea of training the next generation of mathematics teachers was appealing. I was often assigned as a mentor to new teachers and talked with many veteran educators at professional development workshops I conducted. I was starting to network at the university level when presenting at research conferences. I began to realize my sphere of influence would be much larger at the university level and I could continue to work with public school students and both preservice and in-service teachers.

The themes of campus leadership and climate and professional development permeate our reflections and have continued to play an important role in shaping our professional lives.

REFLECTIONS

Connelly and Clandinin (2006) state that "people shape their daily lives by stories of who they and others are and as they interpret their past in terms of these stories" (p. 477). The four of us acknowledge the uniqueness of our shared experiences—not every middle school teacher has the opportunity to be part of an innovative and dynamic campus, which values collaboration and empowerment. Our work environment changed dramatically when we returned to the eight period traditional schedule. After reading sections of our narratives, many would agree that there are certain aspects of our shared experiences that could have contributed to the setting of the goal of earning a doctoral degree. We understand that others may hold a different interpretation than ours, as that is the nature of qualitative inquiries. However, we are comfortable with the themes that emerged during analysis.

We acknowledge that there are limitations of the inquiry. Besides the limited data sources, there was an absence of perspectives from individuals teaching other grade levels. Researchers would be prudent to compare narrative themes from individuals who have taught in what would be referred to as junior high school settings to those of "true" middle schools (Powell, 2005). Narratives collected from various regions of the nation could provide additional insights as to which characteristics of the work environment motivate middle school teachers to pursue advanced degrees.

Readers must ultimately decide if our quests for doctoral degrees are dependent on our individual ambitions or if it was the middle level campus leadership and climate and professional relationships that strongly influenced our pursuit. However, there were several important lessons that we learned along the way.

First of all, we believe in the importance of setting high expectations for every member of the learning community (NMSA, 2003). Teachers need to have high expectations set for them, as well as set high expectations for themselves and others. Even novice teachers should be encouraged, with guidance available, to undertake leadership roles. Phil Schlechty reiterated in *Working on the Work*, one of his favorite slogans, "Every teacher a leader, every leader a teacher, and every child a success" (Schlechty, 2002, p. 59). When teachers understand and embrace that they are educational leaders, putting this belief into action can have a profound effect on the culture and climate of the school.

Secondly, we believe in collaboration as it "supports the professional empowerment of teachers and fosters and builds upon qualities of openness, trust and support between teachers and their colleagues" (Acker-Hocevar & Touchton, 1999, p. 14). Collaboration is critical to middle school reform and results in empowerment. An empowered faculty contributes to the blurring or elimination of hierarchies within the school building. Everyone, no matter their campus position, should understand that they contribute to the effectiveness of the school.

Lastly, it is my belief that an emphasis needs to be placed on recruiting middle school teachers into doctoral programs. The current focus has been on designing effective middle grades teacher preparation programs. More importantly, courses in those programs must be "taught by professors who had/have practical experience in middle level education" (Roney, 2001, p. 91). When one looks merely at the statistics, there are many potential doctoral candidates. Somehow we must encourage and support effective middle school teachers to pursue doctorates. We need qualified middle level teacher educators instructing the next generation of middle school teachers.

REFERENCES

Acker-Hocevar, M., & Touchton, D. (1999). *A model of power as social relationships: Teacher leaders describe the phenomena of effective agency in practice.* Paper presented at the annual meeting of the American Educational Research Association, Montreal, Quebec, Canada. Retrieved from ERIC database. (ED456108)

Chase, S. E. (2005). Narrative inquiry: Multiple lenses, approaches, voices. In N. K. Denzin & Y. S. Lincoln (Eds.), *The Sage handbook of qualitative research* (3rd ed., pp. 651-680). Thousand Oaks, CA: Sage.

Clandinin, D. J., & Connelly, F. M. (1994). Personal experiences methods. In N. K. Denzin & Y. S. Lincoln (Eds.) *Handbook of qualitative research* (pp. 413-427). Thousand Oaks, CA: Sage.

Connelly, F. M., & Clandinin, D. J. (1990). Stories of experiences and narrative inquiry. *Educational Researcher, 19*(5), 2-14.

Connelly, F. M., & Clandinin, D. J. (2006). Narrative inquiry. In J. L. Green, G. Camilli, & P. Elmore (Eds.), *Handbook of complementary methods in education research* (3rd ed., pp. 477-487). Mahwah, NJ: Erlbaum.

Drew, C. J., Hardman, M. L., & Hosp, J. L. (2008). *Designing and conducting research in education.* Thousand Oaks, CA: Sage.

National Center for Education Statistics. (2008, March). *Digest of education statistics: 2007, table 65.* Retrieved from http://nces.ed.gov/programs/digest/d07/tables/dt07_065.asp?referrer=report

National Middle School Association. (2003). *This we believe: Successful schools for young adolescents.* Westerville, OH: Author.

Polkinghorne, D. E. (2007). Validity issues in narrative research. *Qualitative Inquiry, 13,* 471-486. doi: 10.1177/1077800406297670

Powell, S. D. (2005). *Introduction to middle school.* Upper Saddle River, NJ: Pearson.

Roney, K. (2001). The effective middle school teacher: Inwardly integrated, outwardly connected. In V. A. Anfara, Jr. (Ed.), *The handbook of research in middle level education* (pp. 73-105). Greenwich, CT: Information Age.

Schlechty, P. C. (2002). *Working on the work: An action plan for teachers, principals, and superintendents.* San Francisco, CA: Jossey-Bass.

Stake, R. E. (2003). Case studies. In N. K. Denzin & Y. S. Lincoln (Eds.), *Strategies of qualitative inquiry* (2nd ed., pp. 134-164). Thousand Oaks, CA: Sage.

Tellis, W. (1997). Application of case study methodology. *The Qualitative Report, 3*(3), 1-17. Retrieved from http://www.nova.edu/ssss/QR/QR3-3/tellis2.html

Texas Classroom Teachers Association. (2008). 2008-*2009 survival guide: Educator certification.* Retrieved from http://www.tcta.org/publications/survival_guide/Certification.htm

Texas Education Agency. (2008). *Academic Excellence Indicator System, 2007-2008 State Profile Report,* Section II, pg. 2. Retrieved from http://ritter.tea.state.tx.us/perfreport/aeis/2008/state.html

Texas Education Code. (2008). Section *21.402(c) - Minimum salary schedule for certain professional staff.* Retrieved from http://www.statutes.legis.state.tx.us/?link=ED

Wolf-Wendel, L., Baker, B. D., Twombly, S., Tollefson, N., & Mahlios, M. (2006). Who's teaching the teachers? Evidence from the National Survey of Postsecondary Faculty and the Survey of Earned Doctorates. *American Journal of Education, 112*, 273-300.

CHAPTER 11

THE MIDDLE LEVEL LITERACY COACH

Navigating Multiple Roles in Context

Antony T. Smith

This chapter explores the topic of literacy coaching, an innovative model of professional development for teachers. It examines the literacy coaching process across middle level contexts, telling the story of a representative day in the life of Grace, a middle school literacy coach. Her story describes her literacy coaching roles and responsibilities in school and classroom settings. Drawn from observation field notes and interview data, the chapter discussion examines themes that emerge from the narrative and considers implications for the future of literacy coaching efforts in middle level settings.

INTRODUCTION

Literacy coaching is an increasingly popular model of professional development that continues to evolve as it expands across diverse school settings (Marsh et al., 2008; Walpole & Blamey, 2008). The goal of literacy coaching is to help teachers build knowledge of effective practices in reading and

Voices From the Middle: Narrative Inquiry By, For, and About the Middle Level Community
pp. 213–235
                213

writing, improve instruction, and increase student achievement (Deussen, Coskie, Robinson, & Autio, 2007). The appeal of this professional development model is its promise to provide reflective learning opportunities, over time, within school contexts (Poglinco et al., 2003). Encouraged by the relatively widespread implementation of coaching in early elementary grades (Moss, Jacob, Boulay, Horst, & Poulos, 2006), literacy coaching has spread upward to the middle level, a phenomenon that has outpaced research on coaching effectiveness (Neufeld & Roper, 2003). The International Reading Association (IRA) responded to this development by establishing a set of standards for middle and secondary level literacy coaches (IRA, 2006). Noting the paucity of research on coaching, the IRA recommends researching existent literacy coaching efforts, asking questions important to practitioners, and relating findings to inform practice (2006). These recommendations are particularly salient to middle level coaching, as little research has examined the work of literacy coaches in relation to the unique features of middle level settings. Recognizing the need to describe middle level literacy coaching in context, I conducted a case study guided by the following research questions:

- What roles do literacy coaches play in different middle school settings?
- In what ways do contextual factors, and the coaches themselves, affect these roles?

In this chapter I explore these questions and share the story of Grace (all names are pseudonyms), a literacy coach who participated in this case study. Her narrative gives voice to the themes and challenges that emerge when literacy coaches work in middle level settings.

REVIEW OF LITERATURE

Literacy in Middle Level Contexts

The middle school years represent a shift in the teaching of reading, from an elementary level focus on learning to read toward an emphasis on reading to learn and understand subject-specific texts (R. Brown, 2002). Young adolescents engage in a variety of literacy experiences in middle level settings, including direct instruction in reading classes, reading and writing instruction as part of a language arts block, and the application of literacy skills in content area classes. While students may be involved in literacy related activities throughout the day, language arts teachers carry much of the responsibility of teaching reading:

Although literacy growth might be recognized as important, many schools do not include reading instruction in the curriculum for all students. Language arts teachers often have sole responsibility for guiding students' reading growth while still being held accountable for covering a literature program, teaching grammar, offering personal advisory programs, and so on (Moore, Bean, Birdyshaw, & Rycik, 1999, p. 4).

Beyond language arts classes, middle school students are often expected to use reading and writing skills to understand content in other subject areas. These expectations may not be supported by the kinds of instruction students experience in these classes (Beane & Brodhagen, 2001). Irvin (1998) points out the difficulty of balancing content focused and reading related instruction, noting, "Sole emphasis on content leaves students with isolated information and without strategies for learning new content; sole emphasis on reading process leaves students with little about which to think or write" (p. 241). Without this balance, students may be assigned literacy tasks without sufficient instructional support to make learning possible (Fisher & Frey, 2008). A number of factors, from content area teachers' limited familiarity with research-based practices in reading instruction to a reluctance to spend time teaching reading and writing skills, add to the challenge of teaching literacy in a range of middle level contexts.

Across content areas, higher-level thinking is emphasized as a crucial element of an authentic middle level curriculum (Caskey, 2002). Yet reading, when it is taught in middle schools, tends to address lower-level skills in isolation rather than higher-level thinking and reading skills (Langer, 2001). Reading comprehension strategies may not be taught at all (Dole, 2000). Moore, Bean, Birdyshaw, and Rycik (1999) acknowledge the urgent need for quality literacy instruction, noting the range of reading and writing skills among adolescents: "Even with the best instruction early on, differences magnify as students develop from year to year" (p. 4). Across middle level settings, the literacy needs of adolescents are considerable and diverse.

Literacy Coaching

Coaching holds promise as a way to facilitate teacher learning in the context of ongoing reflective practice (Ball & Cohen, 1999; Roney, 2001). The ways literacy coaching might effectively support teacher learning is an issue of interest to researchers. Emerging research on literacy coaching has focused primarily on elementary level coaches in an effort to identify the types of activities that comprise a coach's work (Deussen, et al. 2007; Walpole & Blamey, 2008). The results of an initial survey of elementary level coaches (IRA, 2004), for example, suggest coaches engage in a variety of activities from informal conversations with colleagues to formal procedures such as observing in classrooms and modeling lessons.

This range is reflected beyond the elementary level in the IRA standards for middle and secondary literacy coaches, with the four identified standards evenly split between two major responsibilities: teacher mentoring work aimed at helping teachers improve classroom practice and literacy advocacy work focused on schoolwide literacy goals and professional development (IRA, 2006). These responsibilities are supported by the literature on coaching. Mentoring is emphasized by Toll, who defines a literacy coach as "one who helps teachers to recognize what they know and can do, assists teachers as they strengthen their ability to make more effective use of what they know and do, and supports teachers as they learn more and do more" (2005, p. 4). Dole (2004) agrees with this focus on mentoring, emphasizing classroom observations, feedback on lessons, and teaching demonstrations.

Other researchers emphasize literacy advocacy coaching responsibilities. Sturtevant (2003) stresses schoolwide leadership, defining coaches as "master teachers who provide essential leadership for the school's entire literacy program" (p. 11). Walpole and McKenna (2004) share this perspective, identifying school-level planning and curriculum implementation as crucial elements of literacy coaching.

Although the literature suggests literacy coaching is a combination of mentoring and school-advocacy responsibilities, the balance between these responsibilities is not clear. How a literacy coach might manage to work effectively as both schoolwide literacy advocate and classroom-level teacher mentor remains an open question. This question is particularly relevant to coaches working in middle level settings, which have received little attention in research on coaching. Commenting on literacy instruction for adolescents, R. Brown observes, "We cannot automatically assume that what works for elementary or high school students will work for middle school students" (2002, p. 346). The same may hold true for literacy coaching. With this instructional observation in mind, the study described here was designed to contribute to clarifying knowledge about this issue of balancing literacy coaching responsibilities in middle level contexts.

CONCEPTUAL FRAMEWORK

The conceptual framework for this study is based on theories of teacher learning and forms of teacher knowledge. These are essential elements of quality teaching, which is "characterized by educators who recognize the importance of deep understanding of content knowledge and appropriate uses of research-based instructional strategies" (Hirsch, 2004, p. 219). At the middle level this quality teaching would perhaps occur within the context of a program with features such as a relevant integrative curriculum, multiple teaching approaches, and a supportive learning environment (National Middle School Association, 2003). As the goal of the literacy coach is to foster quality teaching through changes in classroom practice, the means of affecting these changes are supporting teacher learning and facilitating teacher knowledge development while also considering the contexts in which teaching and learning occur.

Teacher Learning

Teacher learning is situated within the larger concept of teacher change. Change efforts in education traditionally moved in discrete, linear steps from research to change agents to practitioners (Richardson & Placier, 2001). An alternative is the normative-reeducative change process (Chin & Benne, 1969), which emphasizes the needs of the individual, collaboration between change agent and individual, and the selection of resources to address issues identified through this process. Professional development efforts grounded in the normative-reeducative process emphasize changes in beliefs as well as practice, the development of a change orientation, and the growth of dialogue and community as important elements of teacher change (Chin & Benne, 1969).

The situated learning perspective aligns with the normative-reeducative change process by emphasizing context as an integral element of learning (Putnam & Borko, 2000). From this perspective, teachers are encouraged to enhance and change beliefs through inquiry, reflection, and the formation of learning communities. In school settings, learning communities are a component of communities of practice (Wenger, 1998), where teachers are engaged in networks and interactions beyond the relative isolation of the classroom. At the middle level, such communities of practice might include small learning communities or study groups, collaborative teams, and schoolwide advisory committees (National Middle School Association, 2003). Seen from the situated learning perspective, effective professional development for facilitating teacher learning would need to be embedded in context, collaborative in and across learning communities, and ongoing in nature to sustain growth in teacher learning and create change in practice (Darling-Hammond & McLaughlin, 1996; Garet, Porter, Desimone, Birman, & Yoon, 2001).

Teacher Knowledge

Literacy coaching, by emphasizing ongoing teacher learning across contexts, addresses multiple forms of teacher knowledge. The metaphor of the professional knowledge landscape (Clandinin & Connelly, 1995) serves as a way to organize forms of knowledge in relation to teachers' experiences. This landscape, existing at the intersection of theory and practice, is comprised of classroom and out-of-classroom places:

> The classroom place on the landscape is a place of teaching activity and interwoven stories of these activities. The out-of-classroom place on the landscape is one of abstract talk about abstract policies and prescriptions. These abstract policies and prescriptions are fed into the landscape via a conduit that connects the world of theory with the world of practice. Dilemmas are created as teachers move back and forth between the two places on the landscape. (p. 67)

Literacy coaching has the potential to bridge the gap between places on the landscape, helping teachers deepen their knowledge and apply new knowledge to practice.

Several forms of knowledge prominent on the professional knowledge landscape are particularly relevant to middle level literacy coaching. Subject matter knowledge, consisting of factual information, central concepts, and organizing information (Grossman, Wilson, & Shulman, 1989), is key in terms of specific content areas. The transformation of subject matter knowledge into something teachable defines pedagogical content knowledge, which is, "in a word, the ways of representing and formulating the subject that makes it comprehensible to others" (Shulman, 1986, p. 9). This process of knowledge transformation would be of central importance to coaches working with teachers to learn and implement literacy skills and strategies across middle level settings.

Practical and personal practical knowledge, two additional forms on the professional knowledge landscape, appear relevant to literacy coaching. Practical knowledge bridges thought and action, connecting pedagogical content knowledge to a teacher's wealth of experience working with students and managing classroom logistics (Elbaz, 1983). Practical knowledge is an important element of enacting new learning in classroom contexts, with variation from teacher to teacher (Lampert, 1985). Personal practical knowledge is described as a way to capture the idea of experience in order to talk about teachers as knowledgeable and knowing persons (Connelly, Clandinin, & He, 1997). This form of knowledge is found in practice, bringing together subject matter, practical, and even personal knowledge on the professional knowledge landscape. Literacy coaches, working with middle level teachers individually and in communities of practice across a variety of settings, would need to address these multiple forms of knowledge to affect teacher learning and support instructional change, moving toward the ultimate goal of boosting student achievement.

METHODOLOGY

To examine literacy coaching in middle level settings, I conducted a case study with a multiple case structure (Yin, 2003) that allowed me to examine similar and contrasting themes across the cases of three middle level literacy coaches in two large districts in a western state. This study was designed to explore the experiences of these coaches as they interacted with teachers, administrators, and students across a range of middle level contexts. Taking the stance of participant observer (Patton, 2002), I observed the coaches as they went about their work, participating in discussions only as much as necessary to help participants feel comfortable with my presence as researcher and former classroom teacher. My goal was to describe the experiences of the coaches as they assumed a variety of roles and to consider the ways their work played out in middle level contexts.

Participant

This chapter focuses on one coach, Grace, whose experiences are representative of the coaching themes and challenges that emerged from the larger case study. Grace was in her second year working as literacy coach at Adams Middle School, an urban school with over 40 certificated teachers and approximately 750 students. She had previously worked as a district-level curriculum specialist in writing and as an elementary level teacher. Additional informants from Adams Middle School were approximately 30 individuals who worked with Grace on an ongoing basis, including a language arts teacher named Amanda and the building principal, Judith.

Procedures

Data collection occurred over a 5-month period, with follow up interviews conducted 2 years later. I observed Grace for three 1-week visits, with a break of at least one week between visits. During these observations I shadowed Grace throughout the day as she interacted with students, teachers, administrators, and district personnel. I took field notes during these observations, focusing on roles she assumed and the variety of contexts in which she went about her work.

Scheduled interviews provided a second source of data. At the beginning of the first visit, I conducted a semi-structured intake interview. Throughout my visits I conducted frequent conversational interviews exploring coach reflections on daily work activities. An exit interview was conducted at the end of the data collection period, and a follow-up interview focusing on changes in coaching work over time was conducted two years later.

To explore multiple perspectives, I selected two classroom teachers from Adams Middle School to participate in the study. These teachers had worked with Grace on a regular basis. I conducted semistructured interviews with these teachers and observed them working with Grace as well as teaching students without the coach present. I interviewed the principal of Adams Middle School, Judith, to get a sense of her perspective on literacy coaching. All data sources were transcribed and coded for analysis.

Data Analysis

The narrative inquiry perspective was essential to this study of coaching. It enabled me to analyze and present data in a manner that focused on the story of Grace in context (Chase, 2005; Clandinin & Connelly, 2000) and aimed to provide coherence and continuity in communicating themes and findings (Lieblich, Tuval-Mashiach, & Zilber, 1998). The narrative construction process I used is conceptually grounded in the professional knowledge landscape metaphor. It is an adaptation of *composite biography* (Connelly, Clandinin, & He, 1997), a narrative inquiry process used to combine experiences of multiple participants to portray forms of teacher knowledge across contexts. I also sought to combine multiple perspectives, including those of teachers and principals. Unlike composite biography, however, the narrative construction process I utilized kept the focus of the story on the individual coach in order to examine the specific contexts in which she worked. Sikes (2005) notes that narratives are particularly useful when describing settings that are generally unfamiliar to readers. The daily work of a middle school literacy coach represents such a setting.

The process of constructing a coaching narrative from case study data involved four phases: Coding, framing, writing, and verifying. In the first phase I coded and clustered data segments around common themes that had emerged (Miles & Huberman, 1994). Through this process I developed a set of 36 codes in five thematic categories: classroom practice, coach background, coaching roles, social contexts, and teacher learning. Each thematic category contained a number of codes, some broadly defined and some very narrow in scope. Clustering the coded segments around these five themes helped establish the building blocks for constructing a narrative.

In the second phase, framing, I identified episodes from the data clusters that clearly illustrated some facet of the five thematic categories, determining through this process a set of 16 codes that provided a basic outline of the types of tasks and interactions that made up the daily experience of a middle level literacy coach. Using Atlas.ti (Version 5.0) as a filtering tool, I compiled roughly 60 coded data segments to form the outline of a 2-day narrative. These segments were sorted into two categories aligned with the major responsibilities of the literacy coach identified in the literature and with classroom and out-of-classroom places on the professional knowledge landscape. The first category, *classroom instructional*, included work that focused on classroom level instruction and practice. The second category, *school-related*, contained a broader range of activities including team meetings, professional development sessions, and other school-level work. Sorted data segments in these categories were then arranged to be temporally and proportionally representative of the data set while also forming the outline of a cohesive narrative. Specifically, the amount of time dedicated to each episode in the narrative equaled what was observed in the field, giving the narrative temporal accuracy. Additionally, the percentage of coach time spent in either classroom-instructional or school-related episodes was calculated so that this number accurately reflected what was observed in the field. These calculations helped balance a compelling story with consistent representation.

The third phase of the process, writing, was informed by rhetorical criteria identified by Lincoln and Guba (2002), with a particular emphasis on craftsmanship. This rhetorical criterion focuses on the process of transforming data into a cohesive story. Power and elegance, a specific element of craftsmanship stressing a powerful and thoughtfully written story, had a direct impact on the narrative writing process and helped me transform a logical series of events into an engaging story. Another craftsmanship criterion, of being open and problematic, helped me address underlying themes by adding two sections: a reflection section between days and a discussion of issues after the end of the second day. These added sections helped portray the exploratory and problematic character (Lincoln & Guba, 2002) of the coaching experience.

The fourth phase, evaluation, involved examining the draft narrative in terms of validation and trustworthiness (Riessman, 1993). To address persuasiveness and coherence, two elements of trustworthiness, I analyzed the constructed draft for alignment between episodes in the 2-day narrative and major issues raised in coaching reflections, assessing the ways multiple perspectives were represented and the degree to which themes were supported by evidence from the data. Correspondence, an element of trustworthiness that emphasizes gauging the researcher's interpretations, was addressed in two ways. First, information from member checks conducted throughout the data collection process was incorporated into the narrative construction process. Second, perspectives and emerging themes were discussed in the coach follow-up interview, allowing me to align the narrative with coach perspectives over time. While the element of correspondence was addressed in these ways, it must be noted that the narrative construction is my own. As Riessman acknowledges, "In the final analysis, the work is ours. We have to take responsibility for its truths" (1993, p. 67).

The goal of this four-phase narrative construction process was to tell a story of the literacy coaching experience, across middle level contexts, in a trustworthy and compelling manner. The next section contains an excerpt from Grace's constructed narrative. This excerpt illustrates her efforts to find balance between teacher mentoring and schoolwide literacy advocacy work. I chose to share a substantial excerpt from Grace's narrative in order to illustrate the experiences of one coach in detail, creating for the reader a vivid sense of time and place (Sikes, 2005) essential to narrative inquiry. Grace's excerpt is followed by a discussion of issues raised in her narrative.

ANALYSIS: DAY IN THE LIFE OF A MIDDLE SCHOOL LITERACY COACH

Introduction

Grace was a literacy coach at Adams Middle School, an urban school with an ethnically and socioeconomically diverse population. A large number of students were considered at-risk for academic failure. Teachers were organized into teams, mostly by subject area, and were encouraged to take part in professional development opportunities aligned with the school's curriculum integration and improvement plan. Grace's goal as the literacy coach was to increase reading achievement by improving literacy instruction. Her focus the previous year was to work exclusively with sixth grade language arts teachers on process writing and reading comprehension strategies. For the current year, Grace's responsibilities expanded beyond sixth grade, but her specific work assignment was at the discretion of Judith, the building principal. Judith decided that Grace should concentrate her work on four teachers at different grade levels while also assisting with administrative tasks. Table 11.1 outlines day one of Grace's narrative, with episodes included in the excerpt indicated in bold. Also shown are the name, time, duration, and type of each episode (classroom instructional or school-related) in the narrative.

Table 11.1.   Grace Constructed Narrative Day One

Episode	Time	Minutes	Type
Office work	7:30	60	School
Planning with Amanda	8:30	30	Instructional
Principal meeting	9:00	60	School
Summer planning	10:00	120	School
Office work	12:00	60	School
Coaching Amanda	1:00	80	Instructional
Record-keeping argument	2:20	10	School
Science rubric work	2:30	60	Instructional

Narrative of a Day

7:30 A.M. Office Work

Grace spent the first hour of her day working in her office, reading email, looking through books on literacy instruction, and organizing piles of assessment and professional development papers. This quiet work was interrupted by a number of surprise visitors. The first was a language arts teacher who stopped by to pick up a set of test preparation booklets for an upcoming state test. As this teacher left a moment later, Judith came into Grace's office, threw herself into a chair, and talked excitedly about an upcoming conference on schoolwide data interpretation. Moments later she bolted off, and just as Grace was settling back into her work, Stephen, the vice principal, came in, asking, "Grace, what size of T-shirt do you wear?" She answered and he left, not saying why he asked. Grace sighed and went back to work, trying to get everything in order before Amanda arrived for her planning meeting.

8:30 A.M. Planning With Amanda

Amanda, in her second year teaching seventh-grade language arts and social studies, was assigned by the principal to work with Grace and was meeting with her throughout the school year to work on a few goals they identified together: teaching writing, planning writing units, and developing instructional techniques and approaches. Amanda was struggling to develop integrated language arts and social studies units that addressed the needs of her students and met the objectives of the school's learning plan.

This morning, Amanda came to Grace's office during her preparation period to work on a plan for a coaching and observation session later in the day. She rushed in, fifteen minutes late, sat while catching her breath, and began telling Grace about her recent attempt to teach introductory paragraphs to her students. It had not gone very well. Amanda found her students reluctant to critique their own work and she was not sure what to do next:

> Amanda: So what should I work on now?
> Grace: Introductions. I would teach them how to write a good topic sentence.
> Amanda: Write a topic sentence and then think of ways to make it better. Do we do this together?
> Grace: I would model and do guided practice together. Take ideas and synthesize them into an introductory paragraph.
> Amanda: How do I ask for suggestions to make it better?
> Grace: Guided practice. They're trying out this skill. Think aloud first. What do you think? As a group, working together, or independently.
> Amanda: Their points are there but they're missing examples. There's not enough behind what they're trying to say.
> Grace: There needs to be practice. Group practice on a common topic, local restaurants, for example. Kids could add to a main topic by adding details. "for example..." Every point needs elaboration. The idea is to make ideas as clear as possible to the audience.

Amanda had a clear idea of her students' struggles and tried describing these to Grace to get recommendations on what to do next. Grace responded with conceptual phrases, talking for some time, uninterrupted, while Amanda sat and nodded, listening but looking nervous by the way she fidgeted in her chair. She finally interrupted Grace, asking:

> Amanda: Where do we start?
> Grace: Topic, ideas, bare bones topic sentence, go from there.
> Amanda: Embellish the topic sentence first?
> Grace: Yes, you could start there. Get beyond the formula and the dead writing, no student voice in it. Create a fluent, consistent voice—but that's revision. I have a good packet on openings and closings.

In this conversation, Grace offered advice moving from specific to broad, while Amanda kept asking questions to move the discussion from broad to specific. For example, Amanda expressed that she wanted to know what to teach and did not want to talk about the conceptual picture of how to teach the entire writing process to a group of reluctant adolescents. With time running out, they used the last few minutes to come up with an action plan for that afternoon's demonstration. Grace volunteered to teach a lesson on topic sentences and supporting details, using a prompt that would ask students to write a letter explaining why their community was a good or bad place to live. Amanda agreed with this idea, asking Grace to come at 1 o'clock to teach the writing lesson to her second block language arts class. With this tentative plan in mind, Amanda rushed out of Grace's office and back down the hall to her room, just in time for her next class.

1:00 *P.M. Coaching Amanda*

At 1 o'clock, after spending four hours on school-related tasks such as talking with Judith about assessment issues and planning a summer workshop with another literacy coach, Grace headed down the hall, arriving at Amanda's room just as she was finishing a 10-minute homework review. Grace went right to the front of the room, said a few words to Amanda, and immediately began teaching her lesson. She started by setting the purpose, which was to write better and prepare for the upcoming state literacy test. Grace displayed a prompt about why a neighborhood might or might not be a good place to live, and after students had read the prompt, she asked them, "What is it you're being asked to write about? Will you focus on the good or the bad? So what are you supposed to write about?"

Students provided a range of somewhat random answers to these questions. While none of their responses addressed the main idea of the prompt, they indicated engagement with the task. Almost all of the 26 students seemed to pay attention, and several raised their hands, waiting for Grace to call on them. She redirected the conversation, reminding students of TAPF (Topic, Audience, Purpose, Form), a writing model that Amanda introduced to the class earlier in the term. Grace pointed out that the topic was why their community was a good place to live and that the audience was adults. "What does that tell you about the language you should use?"

Students responded (some in unison) that proper language with respect was in order. Drawing their attention back to the prompt, she asked them what the purpose of their writing would be. After a few more random answers, she introduced the word "expository," pointing out that it meant "to explain something."

It seemed that students were following along, despite their seemingly tangential answers to her questions, but at this point Grace suddenly moved in a different direction by introducing and explaining the term, "anecdote," a word that students clearly did not know. She defined it as a story that relates to an example or detail, and offered two examples to illustrate the concept: a romance story like *Romeo and Juliet*, and a pink dress the color of cotton candy. Amanda stood in the back of the room, looking puzzled. Grace commented, "I kind of got off on a tangent, but it was a good one."

Grace continued her lesson by offering the class an example topic sentence: "Amanda is the best teacher in the world because she is funny, smart, and generous." Using this sentence, Grace talked with the class about how each of those points would need to be supported by details, using anecdotes to illustrate Amanda's funniness and smartness. Suddenly Grace commanded, "Say, 'I must prove it!'" She pounded her fist on the table while saying this. "Prove it!" everyone shouted. They agreed that the purpose of this writing was to prove that their neighborhood was a great place to live. Grace finished this part of the lesson by saying this writing assignment needed to be in the form of a letter, and students grudgingly admitted that the letter would need to be several paragraphs long. "So we're writing about why our community is a good place to live," said Grace. "The next thing we'll do is brainstorm on this topic: 'Good things about our community.' What is a good thing about a community?"

Students came up with a list of topics, including: no gangs; no violence; safe school, good teachers who can provide a good education; places to hang out; a community center, basketball; a play area for little kids; a supermarket; restaurants. Students seemed engaged, drawing upon knowledge of their neighborhood and features they and their parents either used or wished they had. Grace worked to focus this brainstorm, asking students to think about things that made the area convenient, adding, "So one of the things we could say is that these things are convenient and make life easier. So let's do a bubble map and come up with some adjectives."

Grace began writing on the overhead, but Amanda, looking puzzled, suddenly called for a break. While students milled around, Amanda talked with Grace, expressing confusion over Grace's use of the terms *example*, *detail*, and *anecdote*. Amanda wanted to know the ways in which these terms were different and whether or not that was important. It seemed that Grace was using them somewhat interchangeably, and this bothered Amanda, who did not see them this way. They had not talked about these terms in their morning planning session. Although Grace tried to explain her thinking, the few minutes at break were not enough to resolve the issue.

Once students were back in their seats, Grace reviewed the bubble chart with students and asked them to vote on the ones they thought might make the best case for their neighborhood's attractiveness as a place to live. Ruby, an African-American girl who had been sitting quietly, seized the conversation, firmly stating, "Parents aren't looking to have fun in the neighborhood. They're looking for convenience. My mom always says stuff like that." The energy level in the room increased and the vote discussion moved toward chaos, but with a little facilitation from Grace and lots of lobbying by Ruby, the class chose convenience over clean. Grace wrote on the board, "There are three reasons why I believe my community is a great place to live. It is safe, convenient, and friendly."

Grace moved the lesson forward by telling students that writing each of the paragraphs was simple. According to her, all that remained for students to do was add details to each of the three reasons the class picked. She asked students what they thought might be convenient about their neighborhood, and they came up with a list of examples including grocery stores, coffee shops, gas stations, and restaurants. Happy with their ideas, Grace said, "This is the basic setup for it. See what we did—a brainstorm about community, then 'How can I describe my community.' Then we picked out the three best ones."

After observing quietly for almost an hour, Amanda, from the back of the room, asked: "Should they have the reasons in the introduction?" Grace replied, "Later. Right now, it's barebones to get the structure in place. From my intro, the reader knows I will be talking about fun, safety, and convenience."

Grace finished the lesson by describing the conclusion to the letter and how it would contain the same points outlined in the introduction. Her final comment was, "We'll go over it again next time and work on the middle part, then work on different ways of beginning and ending a paper." She and Amanda walked around the room for about 10 more minutes, until class was over, helping students write their ideas from the prompt and reminding them to copy the introduction that Grace had written with their input.

2:30 P.M. Record-Keeping Argument

The plan for the remainder of Grace's workday was to reflect on the demonstration lesson and figure out what to work on next with Amanda's class. But this did not happen. Instead, Grace found herself involved in an argument with several teachers in person, over the phone, and via email about test score recording forms and how to properly fill them out. Many teachers seemed to think Grace was the person in charge of this assessment, while she saw herself as a resource person and considered test administration to be a compliance issue with principal oversight. One teacher in particular did not share Grace's point of view, taking her perspective public via email to gain support. Other teachers replied to this provocative message, siding with the author and claiming they had not been trained on how to complete the test-reporting forms in dispute. After reading this series of messages, Grace sighed in frustration. Looking a bit defeated, she pointed out to me that while she was to provide support to teachers giving the test, it was the job of the school administrators to ensure that teachers completed testing on time and turned in the proper scoring forms. Grace decided this issue was out of her hands, acknowledging the sense of resentment a number of teachers had toward her for not "pulling her weight" by teaching classes or tutoring students. This was part of a school climate with an undercurrent of negativity, and Grace decided that she did not want to think about such issues today. Focusing her attention elsewhere, she spent the rest of the afternoon constructing a writing rubric for a science teacher.

Coaching Issues and Perspectives

Split between whole-school tasks and mentoring work with teachers, Grace seemed to struggle with her multiple coaching roles. From her own perspective, she saw her work as valuable, but at the same time acknowledged the perception held by some that her position was a waste of resources. Although she attempted to work with her four identified teachers on classroom related issues of literacy instruction, much of her work ended up focused on other concerns such as standardized test administration and scoring. She had little success working with teams of language arts teachers and struggled to establish contact with teachers in other content areas. Her focus was reading and writing instruction, but not specifically in relation to the diverse needs of adolescent students or the particular middle level contexts in which she worked. Her general approach to literacy coaching did not appear to be aligned with the specific needs and challenges of middle level teachers.

Ultimately, Grace defined her role as a "questioner," someone whose work was to help people think about best practices in literacy and the future value of instructional choices. When Grace did not feel successful in this role, she found herself asking questions about the qualities it would take to make a good teacher, wondering, "Can you teach an adult to be intrinsically motivated? Some people are simply miscast for the job." Grace said she was willing to coach teachers, to help them learn and implement new instructional strategies. But she did not consider everyone worthy of being helped, and she seemed to have an idea of where to draw the line. Coaching, apparently, had its limitations.

DISCUSSION

Literacy Coaching Roles

Grace assumed a surprising number of roles as she worked across middle level contexts. While these roles appeared to be aligned with the responsibilities of teacher mentoring (Dole, 2004; Toll, 2005) and literacy program advocacy (Sturtevant, 2003; Walpole & McKenna, 2004), they did not play out well in practice. This multiplicity of roles, influenced by contextual factors such as school structure, scheduling, and principal support, contributed to a fragmentation of the coaching process, bringing into question the viability of a middle level coaching model that emphasizes two sets of responsibilities.

The responsibility of mentoring teachers (Dole, 2004; Toll, 2005) proved difficult for Grace to fulfill. While previous research suggests power in mentoring-related coaching roles (Ballard, 2001; Hasbrouck & Christen, 1997), such research has typically focused on an established set of goals in specific contexts. In this study, Grace's classroom instructional roles related to mentoring were numerous, but only a small number of these involved ongoing conversations with teachers on issues of practice. Grace's work with Amanda exemplifies such a conversation; but as illustrated in the narrative, this mentoring work was problematic. Although the two met and talked, their conversations focused only tangentially on the issues of instruction that Amanda considered important. She expressed frustration over these mentoring sessions, wanting the coaching process to involve more action and less talk. While Grace tried to model effective teaching in her demonstration lesson, her approach was somewhat disconnected from the instructional needs of Amanda's adolescent students. Effective middle level practices such as collaborative small group learning and active discourse patterns (D. F. Brown, 2002) were left out of the coaching process. The responsibility of mentoring teachers appeared challenging for Grace to implement.

The schoolwide literacy advocacy responsibility appeared problematic as well, consuming large amounts of Grace's time. In the example narrative and across all of her observed experiences, she spent a majority of time on schoolwide activities rather than mentoring individual teachers, a finding echoed in a recent study of Florida middle level reading coaches (Marsh et al., 2008). These activities had little apparent connection to the goal of improving classroom practice, limiting her opportunities to facilitate teacher learning through mentoring or work with teacher learning communities. Overall, the sheer number of roles Grace assumed, the sorts of tasks she ended up performing within these roles, and the disproportionate amount of time spent on schoolwide activities, contributed to a fragmentation of the coaching process.

Literacy Coaching in Middle Level Contexts

Middle level contextual factors such as structure, school climate, and the role of the principal affected the literacy coaching process. The complex structure of the middle school impacted Grace's efforts to work with teachers. She struggled to address literacy instruction across content areas, attempted to navigate stacked class schedules and combined language arts and social studies blocks, and was prevented by the daily schedule from finding regular times to meet with even the four teachers (two of whom had been assigned to her by the principal) at the center of her coaching efforts. Additionally, Grace had limited interactions with teacher communities of practice (Wenger, 1998) functioning within the school. Language arts team meetings frequently occurred without her, for example, and she had limited success engaging with groups of teachers in other content areas. Between the layered structure of the school, a complex daily schedule, and numerous teacher communities of practice, Grace ended up with disjointed chunks of time in which to try to affect teacher learning among the small number of teachers willing to work with her.

School climate influenced Grace's efforts. The working context of a negative climate discouraged collaboration and made it more difficult to access classrooms. Teachers' communities of practice appeared to contain elements of mistrust and suspicion, traits at odds with the inherently collaborative nature of coaching (Joyce & Showers, 2002). In Grace's case, teachers at Adams Middle School resented her position and were not afraid to voice their opinions. Without communities of practice willing to work with a literacy coach, it was a struggle for Grace to establish a level of trust and rapport necessary to address teacher learning.

The middle school principal was another factor in the ways literacy coaching played out in practice. It appears that if the principal has a clear vision of the purpose of coaching and is willing to support the coach's efforts, the coach may have greater success working as a teacher mentor and literacy advocate across middle level contexts. Without direct support from the principal, the coach may struggle to connect with teachers or schedule even informal observations. This was the case for Grace, who was treated by Judith as a confidant and an assessment director. To a number of teachers, Grace was the one who collected test scores. Without clear support for her focus on improving literacy instruction, she struggled to engage teachers in an ongoing process of change.

Coaching and the Professional Knowledge Landscape

While coaching holds promise as a way to bridge the conceptual divide between classroom and out-of-classroom places on the professional knowledge landscape (Clandinin & Connelly, 1995), the work of the literacy coach appears to be only partially aligned with elements of this landscape. Three factors appear to influence this misalignment. First, although classroom instructional and school-related roles relate to teachers' classroom and out-of-classroom places, these terms are not synonymous. Classroom instructional roles, as observed, did not often lead to helping the teacher translate new knowledge into practice. Observing a teacher, for example, puts the coach in a classroom instructional role. But it only aligns with the classroom place on the landscape if the teacher and coach have the opportunity to meet and discuss the observation, thereby connecting to instruction. Without these connections, the observation is an isolated event that may not lead to change. Grace attempted to focus her classroom-instructional work on supporting teacher learning, but this proved difficult to orchestrate.

Similarly, school-related roles did not align with the out-of-classroom place on the knowledge landscape. While Grace worked on a variety of school-related tasks, this work did not often relate to issues of teacher knowledge. Grace's effort to coordinate schoolwide reading assessments is an example of this misalignment. This work was necessary, but it did not relate to Grace's literacy coaching goals, and she ended up being perceived by teachers as a test administrator rather than a resource for improving literacy instruction. Grace's experience suggests coaches may be kept busy with a wide range of work and activities that are fundamentally disconnected from the central coaching goal of helping teachers transform knowledge into practice.

Finally, the literacy coach herself appears to impact the coaching process and its alignment with teachers' professional knowledge landscapes. What Grace brought to the position, from literacy knowledge to teaching experience and personal interests, influenced the ways she engaged individual teachers and addressed schoolwide literacy issues. The literacy coach appears to draw upon her own knowledge and interests when working with teachers, adding to the complexity of implementing literacy coaching across middle level settings.

CONCLUSION

Grace's narrative illustrates a gap between literacy coaching in general and middle level settings in particular. Her story suggests that while coaching may have potential as a means of professional development, research is needed to identify ways to integrate literacy coaching with the particular learning needs of young adolescents and the specific features of effective middle schools. Future research needs to consider questions such as: In what ways might the middle school literacy coach work with content-area teachers to integrate research-based reading and writing strategies with subject area instruction? How might the coach work as literacy advocate to effectively support the ongoing learning of middle level teacher communities of practice? What are the perspectives of middle level teachers on the purposes of literacy coaching and the ways in which a coach might best support ongoing teacher learning and professional development?

Addressing the process of teacher learning, Darling-Hammond and McLaughlin observe, "Like students, teachers learn by doing, reading, and reflecting; collaborating with other teachers; looking closely at students and their work; and sharing what they see. This kind of learning enables teachers to make the leap from theory to accomplished practice" (1996, p. 204). Grace's story suggests the potential of literacy coaching to help teachers make this leap, but her struggles raise issues to be considered in terms of coaching program implementation and efficacy in middle level settings. Coaching holds promise as a way to improve literacy instruction and student achievement, but without sufficient alignment between literacy coaching and middle level settings, the potential of this professional development model may not be realized.

REFERENCES

Ball, D., & Cohen, D. K. (1999). Developing practice, developing practitioners: Toward a practice-based theory of professional education. In L. Darling-Hammond & G. Sykes (Eds.), *Teaching as the learning profession: Handbook of policy and practice* (pp. 3-32). San Francisco, CA: Jossey-Bass.

Ballard, T. I. (2001). Coaching in the classroom. *Teaching and Change, 8*, 160-175.

Beane, J. A., & Brodhagen, B. L. (2001). Teaching in middle schools. In V. Richardson (Ed.). *Handbook of research on teaching* (4th ed., pp. 1157-1174). Washington, DC: AERA.

Brown, D. F. (2002). Culturally responsive instructional processes. In V. A. Anfara, Jr., & S. L. Stacki (Eds.), *Middle school curriculum, instruction and assessment* (pp. 57-73). Greenwich, CT: Information Age.

Brown, R. (2002). Straddling two worlds: Self directed comprehension instruction for middle schoolers. In C. C. Block & M. Pressley (Eds.), *Comprehension instruction: Research-based best practices* (pp. 337-350). New York, NY: Guildford Press.

Caskey, M. M. (2002). Authentic curriculum: Strengthening middle level education. In V. A. Anfara, Jr. & S. L. Stacki (Eds.), *Middle school curriculum, instruction and assessment* (pp. 103-117). Greenwich, CT: Information Age.

Chase, S. E. (2005). Narrative inquiry: Multiple lenses, approaches, voices. In N. K. Denzin & Y. S. Lincoln (Eds.), *The Sage handbook of qualitative research* (3rd ed., pp. 641-679). Thousand Oaks, CA: Sage.

Chin, R., & Benne, K. (1969). General strategies for effecting changes in human systems. In W. Bennis, K. Benne, & R. Chin (Eds.), *The planning of change* (2nd ed., pp. 32-59). New York, NY: Holt, Rinehart & Winston.

Clandinin, D. J., & Connelly, F. M. (1995). *Teachers' professional knowledge landscapes.* New York, NY: Teachers College Press.

Clandinin, D. J., & Connelly, F. M. (2000). *Narrative inquiry.* San Francisco, CA: Jossey Bass.

Connelly, F. M., Clandinin, D. J., & He, M. F. (1997). Teachers' personal practical knowledge on the professional knowledge landscape. *Teaching and Teacher Education, 13,* 665-674.

Darling-Hammond, L., & McLaughlin, M. W. (1996). Policies that support professional development in an era of reform. In M. W. McLaughlin & I. Oberman (Eds.), *Teacher learning: New policies, new practices* (pp. 185-202). New York, NY: Teachers College Press.

Deussen, T., Coskie, T., Robinson, L., & Autio, E. (2007). *"Coach" can mean many things: Five categories of coaches in Reading First* (Issues & Answers Report, REL 2007-No. 005). Washington, DC: U.S. Department of Education, Institute of Education Sciences, National Center for Education Evaluation and Regional Assistance, Regional Educational Laboratory Northwest. Retrieved from http://ies.ed.gov/ncee/edlabs

Dole, J. A. (2000). Explicit and implicit instruction in comprehension. In B. M. Taylor, M. F. Graves, & P. van den Broek (Eds.), *Reading for meaning: Fostering comprehension in the middle grades* (pp. 52-69). New York, NY: Teachers College Press.

Dole, J. A. (2004). The changing role of the reading specialist in school reform. *Reading Teacher, 57,* 462-471.

Elbaz, F. (1983). *Teacher thinking: A study of practical knowledge.* New York, NY: Nichols.

Fisher, D., & Frey, N. (2008). What does it take to create skilled readers? Facilitating the transfer and application of literacy strategies. *Voices from the Middle, 15,* 16-22.

Garet, M. S., Porter, A. C., Desimone, L., Birman, B. F., & Yoon, K. S. (2001). What makes professional development effective? Results from a national sample of teachers. *American Educational Research Journal, 38,* 915-945.

Grossman, P. L., Wilson, S. M., & Shulman, L. S. (1989). Teachers of substance: Subject matter knowledge for teaching. In M. C. Reynolds (Ed.), *Knowledge base for the beginning teacher,* (pp. 23-36). Oxford, England: Pergamon Press.

Hasbrouck, J. E., & Christen, M. H. (1997). Providing peer coaching in inclusive classrooms: A tool for consulting teachers. *Intervention in School and Clinic, 32,* 172-177.

Hirsh, S. (2004). A new vision for professional learning. In S. C. Thompson (Ed.), *Reforming middle level education: Considerations for policymakers* (pp. 205-229). Greenwich, CT: Information Age.

International Reading Association. (2004). *The role and qualifications of the reading coach in the United States* (Position statement). Newark, DE: Author.

International Reading Association. (2006). *Standards for middle and high school literacy coaches.* Newark, DE: Author.

Irvin, J. L. (1998). *Reading and the middle school student: Strategies to enhance literacy.* Needham Heights, MA: Allyn & Bacon.

Joyce, B., & Showers, B. (2002). *Student achievement through staff development.* Alexandria, VA: ASCD.

Lampert, M. (1985). How do teachers manage to teach? Perspectives on problems in practice. *Harvard Educational Review, 55,* 178-194.

Langer, J. A. (2001). Beating the odds: Teaching middle and high school students to read and write well. *American Educational Research Journal, 38,* 837-880.

Lieblich, A., Tuval-Mashiach, R. & Zilber, T. (1998). *Narrative research: Reading, analysis, and interpretation.* London, England: Sage.

Lincoln, Y. S., & Guba, E. G. (2002). Judging the quality of case study reports. In A. M. Huberman & M. B. Miles (Eds.), *The qualitative researcher's companion* (pp. 205-215). Thousand Oaks, CA: Sage.

Marsh, J. A., McCombs, J. S., Lockwood, J. R., Martorell, F., Gershwin, D., Naftel, S., et al. (2008). *Supporting literacy across the sunshine state: A study of Florida middle school reading coaches.* Santa Monica, CA: RAND.

Miles, M. B., & Huberman, A. M. (1994). *Qualitative data analysis* (2nd ed.). Thousand Oaks, CA: Sage.

Moore, D. W., Bean, T. W., Birdyshaw, D., & Rycik, J. A. (1999). *Adolescent literacy: A position statement.* Newark, DE: International Reading Association.

Moss, M., Jacob, R., Boulay, B., Horst, M., & Poulos, J. (with St. Pierre, R., et al.). (2006). *Reading First implementation evaluation: Interim report.* Washington, DC: U.S. Department of Education.

National Middle School Association. (2003). *This we believe: Successful schools for young adolescents.* Westerville, OH: Author.

Neufeld, B., & Roper, D. (2003). *Coaching: A strategy for developing instructional capacity: Promises and practicalities.* Providence, RI: Annenberg Institute for School Reform.

Patton, M. Q. (2002). *Qualitative research and evaluation methods.* Thousand Oaks, CA: Sage.

Poglinco, S. M., Bach, A. J., Hovde, K., Rosenblum, S., Saunders, M., & Supovitz, J. A. (2003). *The heart of the matter: The coaching model in America's choice schools.* Philadelphia, PA: Consortium for Policy and Research in Education.

Putnam, R. T., & Borko, H. (2000). What do new views of knowledge and thinking have to say about research on teacher learning? *Educational Researcher, 29,* 4-16.

Richardson, V., & Placier, P. (2001). Teacher change. In V. Richardson (Ed.). *Handbook of research on teaching* (4th ed., pp. 905-947). Washington, DC: AERA.

Riessman, C. K. (1993). *Narrative analysis.* Newbury Park, CA: Sage.

Roney, K. (2001). The effective middle school teacher: Inwardly integrated, outwardly connected. In V. A. Anfara, Jr. (Ed.), *The handbook of research in middle level education* (pp. 73-105). Greenwich, CT: Information Age.

Shulman, L. S. (1986). Those who understand: Knowledge growth in teaching. *Educational Researcher, 15*(2), 4-14.

Sikes, P. (2005). Storying schools: Issues around attempts to create a sense of feel and place in narrative research writing. *Qualitative Research 5*(1), 79-94.

Sturtevant, E. G. (2003). *The literacy coach: A key to improving teaching and learning in secondary schools*. Washington, DC: Alliance for Excellent Education.

Toll, C. A. (2005). *The literacy coach's survival guide: Essential questions and practical answers*. Newark, DE: International Reading Association.

Walpole, S., & Blamey, K. L. (2008). Elementary literacy coaches: The reality of dual roles. *Reading Teacher 62*(3), 222-231.

Walpole, S., & McKenna, M. C. (2004). *The literacy coach's handbook: A guide to research-based practice*. New York, NY: Guilford Press.

Wenger, E. (1998). *Communities of practice: Learning, meaning, and identity*. Cambridge, England: Cambridge University Press.

Yin, R. K. (2003). *Case study research: Design and methods* (3rd ed.). Thousand Oaks, CA: Sage.

CHAPTER 12

MIDDLE LEVEL EDUCATION THROUGH THE WINDOW OF A WRITER'S WORKSHOP

Developmentally Responsive Education

Rita S. Brause

As a tenured professor, I return to teach in a middle school program and reflect on my experiences there. I carefully selected the middle school based on its reputation as an effective, "good" alternative, public school. My goal was to determine the qualities which contributed to its effectiveness. When assigned to teach writers workshop, I found myself focusing on the subject matter I believed was implicit in a writers' workshop curriculum to the virtual marginalization of the focus on individual development, self-efficacy, responsibility, independence, and autonomy. My actions conflicted with the implicit philosophy of the school's program, contributing to my constant and ongoing struggle. I continue to question the organization for instruction and the content of instruction based on this intensive reflection.

Middle schools view preadolescents as increasingly responsible as learners and as social beings. While some schools choose to keep these two ele-

Voices From the Middle: Narrative Inquiry By, For, and About the Middle Level Community
pp. 237–257

ments separate by focusing on the academic content in traditional school time (9 A.M.-3 P.M, Monday-Friday) and advocate for students to participate in new activities outside of the school day, some intentionally create communities in the school building which address both of these concerns. The Center Place program is an exemplar of the latter concern. The administrator and teachers carefully construct the school program to integrate social development with the academic curriculum. And parents and students elect to attend this "choice" school.

Middle schools have historically been settings of great concern for educators, parents, and students. There are not many stories of school districts highlighting the effectiveness of their middle schools. Rather, more frequently we hear of people who are delighted with elementary and high school programs while distraught with the prospect of sending their children to the middle school. Although some settings may exude harmony and industry, others are battlegrounds. I sought to discover the factors which contributed to the harmonious community prevailing at this alternative middle school, The Center Place. I wanted to discover the ways in which the participants in this setting created their community as a basis for informing the development of other middle school settings. Ultimately, I realized that the Writer's Workshop was an ideal context for addressing many middle school concerns.

THE SETTING

At a local, alternative, urban, public middle school I was assigned as leader for a writers' workshop which met three times each week for approximately 45 minutes at each session. As part of the language arts curriculum every student every year (Grades 5-8) was assigned to writer's workshop. By design, there was cross-grade groupings resulting in students in all four grade levels assigned to the same workshop. There were three major selection criteria for placement in a particular workshop:

- Size restricted to 12 participants;
- All four grade levels needed to be represented among the participants;
- Participants only met in this setting, not in any other course/subject;
- Participants are new to the teacher as writers' workshop leader.

In contrast to middle school settings where students move as a cohort, maintaining integrity as a "class," this setting focused on individual students, and sought to insure that each student had class with every other student in the school. The design was intended to create a context where different perspectives, strengths, and interests would become starting points for continued learning and friendship of the students. Despite the complexity inherent in arriving at this distribution among the students, the director's commitment to this design and its intended purpose of meeting students' uniquely developing personalities was paramount in her devotion to this time-consuming design, particularly noting its evolution early in the days of computer programming. And this design was reconfigured three times during each academic year, shuffling students into new settings with new teachers.

Data and Analysis

It was in the capacity as workshop leader that I discovered many of the nuances of the organization of the school program as these were realized in one particular but common experience. To document the experience as a basis for reflecting and learning from my experiences, I collected a wealth of data during the actual time the workshop was operant. I aggregated a wide range of data which included:

- A collection of all the documents which students and I created and used in these sessions;
- Notes on conversations with colleagues at the school and at the university, telling stories of what was happening while seeking advice and counsel for ways to proceed throughout the term;
- Notes on conversations with doctoral students who were also teaching in middle school, to share what was happening and to obtain ideas for improving my professional practice as well as to interpret my experiences with different perspectives;
- Notes of students' informal comments to peers and to me, capturing the gist of the message as I understood it;
- Jottings from my middle of the night awakenings/nightmares on understandings of students' actions in response to my actions and statements;
- Creating, distributing, and discussing anthologies of student work;
- Copies of comments on student report cards from students, coteachers, student teachers, and parents as well as my statements;
- All official school documents including statements made at end of the year closing ceremonies by students and colleagues;

- Drafts of my conference proposals and manuscripts to help me to better understand my experiences as well as to share these with interested colleagues.

From these accumulated data, I slowly became aware of the complex and multifaceted experience, particularly becoming sensitive to the many voices which needed to be considered. I was not the sole interpreter. Many voices helped me to construct numerous interpretations of my experiences and the experiences of the students assigned to the writer's workshop which is the main focus for my data.

Analysis of my data was slow. Initially, I was reluctant to review my boxes of data, in part being intimidated by the quantity, but also reluctant to uncover my many inadequacies. Although there were many positive outcomes from the experience both for my students and for myself in the main, I found myself being supercritical and judgmental about many problems during my time at the Center Place. My reflections on these individual and collective elements contribute to knowledge generation and theory regarding middle school practices (Clandinin & Connelly, 2000; Cummins, 2009). My experiences as a classroom teacher and researcher have informed my growing understanding of the challenges and compromises (along with the rewards) facing middle school teachers and the teacher educators who seek to support their work. Continued reflection on my experiences for class presentations, conference presentations, and for this chapter, for example, have enabled me to obtain multiple perspectives on the myriad activities and outcomes which were connected with the writers' workshop experience.

I identified one major issue in the life of this middle school program, namely the bifurcation of academic and social concerns. While students referred to academic subject names as they moved throughout the day ("I'm going to math now."), the emphasis for most of the students was on who they would meet in the hall and who would be sitting next to them in their next classroom ("I'll see Jaime and tell him about my dream."). While the teachers were nominally charged with an academic curriculum, they were mindful of the importance of engaging the students' social beings as participants in useful conversations. For example, I was encouraged to engage students in conversation as a launching pad for identifying some issues and events to write about (Kutz, 1997; Wilson, 2009). Students' writing after these conversations seemed more authentic in that the writers seemed interested in their evolving texts, in contrast to their responses to nonnegotiated "required" writing.

Unusual elements which characterized Center Place (a pseudonym) became apparent as I immersed myself in the setting, with the responsibility of conducting a writers' workshop three-times weekly. It was in this capacity as an instructor that I observed and participated in the daily activities of Center Place. Since Center Place is known as an "alternative" public school, all who participate in its activities elect to be here.

The Context and Individual Stakeholders

The school was created for students in Grades 5-8. As part of the entrance process, all candidates complete an application process including visiting the school for a day with their parents and 1:1 interviewing with current students and staff. There are twice as many students seeking to attend this school as there are available openings. Although success on standardized tests was valued, there were no academic criteria for admission. The program was committed to enrolling students with a wide range of achievements on standardized measures. This resulted in a wide achievement and age range in classes. Ethnic diversity was a hallmark of the school. Thus, students mixed with different peers as they went through the day. This process enabled them to become familiar with students in all four grades represented in the program, and the possibility of adopting, negotiating, or at least trying on different identities as they traveled through the day and the 4-year program. In addition to the courses, several schoolwide activities (i.e., school trips and stage presentations) created opportunities for interaction. The students were active participants in selecting the site of the school trip, preparing for the visit, and reflecting on their return. Thus, school trips became integral to the educational goals of the program and important markers for all involved in promoting the development of a wide range of social and academic skills, concepts, and competencies.

Report cards were created in collaboration with the students. The adolescents commented on the teacher's documentation of their achievements and evaluation thereof, with both statements being presented on the same document to the parents. Neither numerical nor alphabetical grades were used. Narratives were crafted for each student with some common statements explaining general course activities (see Figure 12.1; note that all identifying features on all figures have been blocked out).

There were no bells marking the end of a class period. Rather, from the chatter in the hall, or the teacher's or student's concluding comment, or a glance at the clock, the teachers and class knew it was time to move on. The halls were filled with conversations, enthusiastic greetings (high-fives and hugs), and missteps. Adults, as they traveled to their next location, also monitored the safety of the students and frequently stopped to converse with students or peers as they moved from room to room. Students were implicitly responsible for their own safety and appropriate behavior.

Student: _Michael_ ▮▮▮▮▮▮
Advisor: ______________
Teacher: Ms. Brause

Writers' Workshop

Students in this Writers' Workshop were engaged in a variety of activities, all designed to enhance their skillfulness in writing, collaborating, and observing. Specifically, each chose the topic and form for each piece of writing. Each selected a New York West Side highlight (Museum of Natural History, Hayden Planetarium, Central Park, Children's Museum of Manhattan, Intrepid Air and Space Museum or Lincoln Center). We are reading From The Mixed-up Files of Mrs. Basil E. Frankweiler by E.L. Konigsburg as an example of a story using New York as its setting (mainly in the Metropolitan Museum of Art). Students were encouraged to write, using New York City as a setting, share their writing-in-progress and obtain guided feedback focusing on 5 elements, namely:Title and Opening; Plot/Story line/ Theme; Character Presentations; Setting/description of the location of the events and Illustrations. I have asked each student to comment on what she/he accomplished in this course to incorporate in my evaluation report.

Criteria	Comments
Productivity as a Writer	Michael has been productive as a writer, mainly working with another student in the writing of a complex story.
Participant as a Collaborator - in writing and/or - in responding to others' writing	Michael has been collaborating on a story about a stolen diary. Collaboration is a very difficult process, but Michael seems to have developed effective negotiating strategies.
General Contribution to Effectiveness of the Writers' Workshop	When Michael is focusing on his writing, he is a positive influence on the members of the Writers' Workshop.
Development as a Writer	Michael is learning to be responsible for his work. As he becomes more focused, I believe he will continue to develop as a writer.
General Comment:	Michael has wonderful ideas for his story. As he develops the ability to be a serious student for lengthier time periods, he will be more productive as a writer which is crucial for writing to develop. I value Michael's modelling of good collaborative efforts.
Student Comment:	

____
Parent/Guardian Signature

Figure 12.1.   Michael's report card.

There were two simultaneous agendas which the teachers addressed, namely the academic/curricular content and the social development of the students. The importance of students becoming responsible for their actions and achievements was verbalized and supported. Students needed to understand themselves and shape their evolving identities as an essential element in this context. Teachers organized class activities which sponsored collaborative work, offering adolescents opportunities to learn to work with and from many different models, multiple diverse settings for engaging with others to accomplish specific activities.

Students experimented with multiple identities (social butterfly, wall flower, bully, brain, team player) and reflected on these stances in the process of creating their unique identities In this context, they also had different responsibilities, seeking counsel from more mature or experienced peers to further their own agendas while guiding younger, less sophisticated peers.

Researcher Stance

As a visitor and a newcomer to this setting, I sought to fit in with the existing organization. I was not invited as a rabble rouser or provocateur; rather I sought to be a participant in their community. For me, this meant accepting the departmentalized, segmented flow of the day. We met three times each week and the frequency, length, and placement of the time was nonnegotiable. Also nonnegotiable was the assignment to this workshop—I did not know or select any of the students and the students did not know or select me. Nor could students choose to be in the same writers' workshop as a friend. (I critiqued some of these institutional traditions in another context [Brause, 1992].)

While the students never explicitly commented on the untraditional nature of the scheduling, my participation in this setting caused me considerable angst. However, I recognized that if I wanted to discover what made the school experience special, I had to play by their rules and not make any assumptions that my experiences and learning had persuaded me of an alternative perspective! Establishing this stance enabled me to become an insider in the community, setting the stage to enhance my understanding of the dynamics involved. I needed to remind myself that I was there to learn the elements of the setting that contributed to a healthy environment for learning. I was now an insider, responsible for enforcing the rules and traditions.

My previous assignments in middle school were all grade-based and tracked. For example, I taught English to classes of "gifted seventh graders" and at other times during the day I taught "reading to eighth graders" needing intensive language and literacy "remediation."

My current assignment placed me in a room with students across Grades 5 to 8 in the same class. The students at Center Place were not tracked. Student academic achievement was not marked as successful or weak. Rather, their assignment to this writers' workshop and all other subjects was value free. Every term every student was assigned to a writers' workshop each time to a new leader. Students who attended after-school creative writing workshops were integrated with reluctant writers.

Snapshot of Writers' Workshop

Schools recognize the importance of writing as a tool in documenting and developing increasingly complex understandings as well as a vehicle for students to voice their ideas and contribute to the community dialog. As an initial assignment, I asked my group of students to write about themselves. I expected some resistance but to my amazement, I found none. My specification of a topic for this first writing was a compromise for me, unarticulated to the students. I responded to two competing agendas: my belief that good writing only results from the writer's passion for communicating the message to the audience, and my desire to know students' performance and interests. I did not ask students for their input. I did not use any standardized questionnaire.

The students turned in their texts at the end of the first class. These texts reflected a broad range of interest and achievement. Some were

Figure 12.2.   Michael's text.

brief (2-3 sentence texts), perfunctorily completed to fulfill my request. All provided evidence of the students' writing fluency with some clearly more engaged in the activity than others. I was relieved that I could consider them all writers since each submitted a text at the end of class, written in easily deciphered handwriting and evidencing knowledge of topic relevance (see Figures 12.2 and 12.3). As far as I could tell, they were fluent writers. On the other hand, these pieces lacked any semblance of passion from the author. Since my request (implicit command) came out of the blue, which initiated the writing, students saw no authentic purpose for their writing beyond response to a school-based command.

Writers' Workshop is guided by several, sometimes conflicting theories. Some settings establish a systematic sequence of 7 steps (or 5 or 9) which guide a text from initial draft to final publication (Graves, 1983; Harwayne & Calkins, 1987). In the latter context, a specific genre (e.g., memoir) may be required while in the former, free choice reigns. One seeks to promote writing while the other seeks to deliver a specific curriculum. In

Figure 12.3.   Aaron's text.

the ideal world, writers would congregate to both draft text and collaborate with self-selected peers in polishing the text in preparation for it to "go public." The initial source for creating the text emanates from the writer, seeking to communicate a heart-felt message to an imagined or real audience. But in the school context, the schedule identified a specific time period for writing—regardless of the participants' desire to communicate on any particular issue. In some settings, Writers' Workshop is a collaborative setting for writers to refine and develop their craft, drawing on the authentic writing that the students/writers are crafting.

As writers' workshop leader, I recognized the need to create a context that nurtured particularly reluctant students while enabling those who seemed relatively independent and confident as learners to proceed as they wished. I needed to build a community among these students, one which only existed on the one hand for the 40-minutes they were in the same room. On the other hand, the students knew each others' faces and perhaps more—from their joint activities, from their periodic passes through the halls, and from other classes during previous trimesters. They were not truly unknown to each other although I was a total stranger to them at the beginning. Their common assignment to the same classroom and "subject" created a peer group for interaction and instruction and potentially trusted respondents to their texts.

With students representing a wide range of achievements and a wide age range, I believed my role took on new dimensions. Instead of thinking about "the curriculum," I focused more on individual student interests and strengths. With the belief that these students were more different from each other than similar, I sought to create a situation where there would be little whole-group instruction. I created teams and small groups for sharing evolving text and targeted instruction when I noticed similarities in themes (animals) or techniques (dialog). After a time, the students shared their work-in-progress with self-selected readers and this seemed to generate useful comments regarding suggested directions as well as responding to specific questions from the partners.

I individualized instruction by encouraging students to work independently and then visited with them systematically through the week. Students independently sought feedback or the opportunity to give spoken voice to their written words. They selected their allies and enthusiastically shared these texts, some incredulous that they were responsible for the texts they were mouthing! They viewed themselves as authors, it seemed, an awesome realization for themselves and for me. Some expected me to evaluate these texts, but I intentionally marginalized myself, believing they needed to reflect and take ownership for these evolving texts. Some (including myself at times) considered this an abdication of my responsibilities.

This same tension remained throughout my experience at the school, albeit, receding in my consciousness as I addressed moment-to-moment responsibilities. I found myself providing little direct instruction and allowed the students' individual writing to dominate my attention. I neglected the implicit "writers' workshop curriculum" and focused on individual personalities and creations. As the term evolved, I vacillated between providing specific support in promoting student effectiveness in writing on the one hand, and freeing students to write without interruption from me. Although I knew they needed a purpose for writing beyond the fact that they were enrolled in the writers' workshop, I was mindful that this was "school" which implies an external accountability. Some were independently motivated while others depended on other students' suggestions or topics, sometimes blatantly adopting/copying the same story as peers, some passively resisting engagement in writing while using all the language which accompanies a writers' workshop mindset (e.g., brainstorming, revising). Some used the opportunity to advertise their acquisition of worldly goods, seeking to achieve higher status with this possession (Lensmire, 2000).

Students mainly wrote because I asked them to and that was their assignment for that particular time of day. There was one notable exception. Andrew (pseudonym) commented at the end of the trimester that although he had finished several chapters, he would continue his story independently. Some students teamed to work with a buddy creating one story with the more experienced writer recording the combined ideas. Some stories were animal lost-and-found stories. Some were focused on romance lost and found. One student established a desire to use curse words in her writing (clearly a test of my rule that "curse words" which were not sanctioned in school, would only be acceptable if the text they were creating, established a context where that language was appropriate). We had a discussion about word choice and authentic dialog and effective writing for a particular audience. The resulting writing was continued evidence of their writing fluency, particularly in a setting requiring this production (Whelan, 2008). I can, however, make a case (weak admittedly) that completion of any text may enhance their self-esteem, although not their understanding of their language proficiencies (see Figures 12.4 and 12.5). I visited with students and inquired about their progress and responded to specific questions. Infrequently I shared my writing which I accomplished during the class (in the spirit of "modeling"—at least the display of writing if not the complex writing process). There was little beyond fluency in writing which I supported or valued. This is due in part to my limited expectations as well as my response to the fragmented and artificial context in which we worked. It was only with some

Afraid to talk
by Jon ███████

Constipated thoughts
try to break through
the censored mind
closing down my opinion
in a claustrophobic jail
cell
     enclosed
raging thoughts
   dim
hum de dum turned cynic
is worse than depressed
is it that bad?

Trying to shit out the excrements
that lie in my mind
it builds up
dissolves to
liquid
     take some pepto
shove back those
constipated thoughts.

People who don't eat
have to
let waste leave .....

Figure 12.4.   Jon's text.

distance that I could reflect on this situation and try to understand it from the stances of my middle school colleagues and my students.

At the end of the term, I created an anthology of their writing, requesting each submit at least one text for inclusion. Their texts were word processed and distributed to each student in the class in preparation for the "Reading" which we held at our last session. On receiving the Anthology, each quickly found the text he or she submitted and read it through quickly—seemingly to ascertain their texts were accurately presented, uncensored. There was great enthusiasm in the room—almost as much as at a Barnes & Noble reading. Each student had time at the author's microphone, reading part or all of the text included in the Anthology. One student refused, noting a desire to keep her ideas private and was upset that her piece was included at all. The final session was a celebration – with most seeming to evidence joy and pride at their achievement.

In addition to the anthology and the reading, there were report cards which were collaboratively created evaluation/report card statements (see

Ms. Blueberry
by 
Eureka

Once upon a time there lived an old lady named Ms. Blueberry. She loved to make things with blueberries. Children called her Ms. Rose and so did some adults. They called her Ms. Rose because she was always so kind to everyone. She was once married to a stunning man named John. When he died, she was very sad. He left her by herself and lonesome. She's gotten over it, but she was still lonely once in a while. She had a dog named Milo and a cat named Carmel. With them around, she was never too lonely.

The telephone rang and Ms. Blueberry picked up the phone and said, "Hello."
"Hello, Ms. Blueberry. It's Mrs. Clinksdale," said Mrs. Clinksdale, her next door neighbor.
Ms. Blueberry nodded.

"We are having a birthday party for Katey and we were wondering if maybe, you can come, because Katey would really love for you to be there."

"Of course, I'll be there," said Ms. Blueberry with a high pitched, powerful voice. Just tell me when and I'll be there."

"Good. The party is on Saturday, the twelfth. It begins at 11:30," said Mrs. Clinksdale. "Goodbye for now. See you there, at the party."
"Yes, you will," said Ms. Blueberry.

Ms. Blueberry soon got up and went to the toy shop a block away and bought Katey a cute little Barbie doll called Pretty Miss Sparkle. When she got home, she wrapped it in "Happy Birthday" wrapping paper and stuck a pretty little red bow with glitter and sparkles on it. After she made dinner and she, and her dog and cat all ate. They all went to bed.

Figure 12.5.   Eureka's text.

Figure 12.1). My statement with a general overview of the nature of the writers' workshop with specific notation of the accomplishments of the designated writer was followed by a statement by the writer elaborating on an issue I addressed or taking a different angle on the experience. Both texts were presented to the parents for their review and response. Generally students noted progress in creating written texts. While my statements addressed issues of academic and social development, the students tended to focus on the academic element.

What I did not share with parents or the students was the fact that there was little evidence that they thought about their writing between workshop sessions. In the main, the texts were simple and predictable. I believed this was true in part because of the institutionally imposed scheduling of writing, rather than the use of writing as a personally felt desire to communicate ideas on a particular topic to a particular audience. I believed that good writing results from an internal drive to give voice to ideas. In contrast, they took pen or pencil in hand (no computers for these kids!) and wrote! Parents were informed of the supportive context in which their child was placed, a reassuring statement when collaboratively created by the student and the teacher.

In the context of Writers' Workshop writing was singularly viewed as a preparation for public sharing, a limited view of writing in an educational context. Particularly with 20/20 hindsight, I recognized missed opportunities to talk about and exemplify, personally and with the students, the preponderance of writing we do as a way of learning. It is with this continued reflection I offer further focused considerations for the curriculum writ large in the writers' workshop.

THE ACADEMIC CURRICULUM AND MORE

While the term "curriculum" typically refers to an academic discipline, my experiences in the Writers' Workshop setting emphasizes the multi-dimensionality of this concept. Three major elements contribute to the realized curriculum, namely:

- Evolution of written texts,
- School/institutional organization, and
- Individual moral, ethical, and socially responsible development.

Each of these elements (tacitly or explicitly) influenced the decisions I made. Although an academic focus dominated my conversations, other concerns influenced my plans and actions.

Writing as an academic discipline is dominated by a theoretically grounded "writing process" mindset. When this approach is translated into middle school practice, it is typically referred to as a 4- or 5- or 7-part process (Graves, 1979; Harwayne & Calkins, 1987) in which students progress over many days from step 1 (usually brainstorming) to the end which is "publication," or going public with your text. This linear process is ever-present and nonnegotiable. In the twenty-first century middle school, there is a focus on writing, either as a unit within a language arts/ English course, or separately as a writer's workshop or writing. In any case, the teacher typically assigns the focus of the students' writing. Memoir is a popular topic now, as is narrative genre. Teachers are responsible for the daily activities and the ultimate outcomes of the experience taking them from brainstorming to publication regardless of student interest or knowledge. The implicit valuing of having voice is diluted with a perfunctory completion of an assignment with an emphasis on genre study. While familiarity with diverse genres is valuable, the virtue of focusing on this knowledge seems questionable. By recognizing that writing is an idea driven, purposeful communication tool, we can adopt James Moffett's (1968) list of qualities which document student engagement in socially responsible activities to note student evolution as learners and writers:

- From implicit embedded ideas to explicitly formulated ideas;
- From addressing the small, known audience like oneself to addressing a distant, unknown, and different audience;
- From talking about present objects and actions to talking about things past and potential;
- From projecting emotion in the there and then to focusing on it in the here and now;
- From stereotyping to originality, from groupism to individualism (p. 57).

As students' responsibilities expand, they use language for socially responsible and personally meaningful purposes, expanding the numerous contexts and strategies they use to communicate important messages. Becoming sensitive to the nuances and power of language, they harness that knowledge for their advantage. Most importantly, writers' workshop leaders need to promote the students' responsibility/autonomy/empowerment as socially responsible citizens of the community drawing on writing as a tool for effective action. When we as teachers assign topics, we deny students' rights and responsibilities while encouraging ineffective "dummy runs" (Britton, 1993). When students'/writers' concerns drive the creation of the text, we discover greater attention to effectiveness of communication. Students who write in response to others' requests are fulfilling orders. When students have issues to communicate with others, they recognize their potential power in at least getting a hearing, if not influencing practice. This seems to me to be a missed opportunity in the current use of writers' workshop as a middle school subject.

School/Institutional Structures

Since all classes had multigrade participants, I was challenged to rethink my roles and my expectations while trying to utilize the advantages of these groupings. Breaking down the age/grade orientation forced me to look at the individual student performance, marginalizing the grade-level standards posted by governmental units. Looking at individual students' work enabled me to note their strengths and to create teams of students to work supporting each other's learning.

Report cards which are multivoiced are useful in documenting the diverse agendas apparent in any given classroom. While the teacher may see one element of growth—or challenge, the student may see a second one—and the parents may provide a totally different perspective. These diverse voices are important to recognize although impossible to quantify. I believe comments are more useful in guiding student—school engagement and more respectful of students, providing them with the opportunity to provide "their side" of their efforts, enabling them to see the power of their voices in this very personal setting.

Scheduling writing as a 40-minute, three times weekly activity serves institutional documentation of "covering the curriculum" but gives no evidence of real engagement. In fact the total segmentation of the day into 40-minute time capsules serves organizational, bureaucratic concerns, not student learning. While there are advantages in that students get to know more adults and students through the constant rearrangement of the schedule and they experience a broad array of ideas and learning strategies, there is probably a need for a good balance between these factors. It was not clear to me if this trimester, 40-minute subdivision was educationally effective, although I believe it is very instrumental in students' learning to get along with different people and trying on new identities for themselves through these constant "shake-ups."

Individual Growth and Development

One of the hallmarks of the middle-school years is attention to the growing responsibilities of these young adolescents socially, taking on increasing responsibility for their lives one-step at a time. This involves considering their goals, their identities, and their strengths. When students collaborate in accomplishing activities for which they are held responsible, schools promote settings wherein they learn to work with others and learn to work independently. Telling students what to write about or restricting students to one genre reduces the potential power that writing can have on students' evolution as learners. By creating cross-age groupings, we can keep the focus on individual students' learning, particularly in the middle school setting where student identities are so fragile. Middle school activities need to recognize the early adolescents' concerns and proficiencies while promoting their expanding learning strategies and interests.

REFLECTIONS

In this experience I was challenged and frustrated by competing tensions, namely:

- From my perspective, addressing my implicit curricular expectations when leading a writers' workshop in contrast with my student-centered orientation; and
- From the school's philosophical perspective, responding to the school's departmental, content-focused schedule in contrast to the social development of individual students which was implicitly at the heart of the school's philosophy.

My designation as the teacher of a writers' workshop had a profound influence on my activities in this context. While there was no established curriculum referred to, I made assumptions that propelled my daily planning, a real tension when thinking about being "ready" for the students. Seeking to make our first 40-minute meeting meaningful and to allay some of my nervousness (yes even after all these years!), I created some plans and activities in advance of meeting with the students. This simultaneously established my authority and the focus of our discussions while placing students in the role of followers.

This hierarchical arrangement and dependent relationship was alien to my personal philosophy, yet, in the crush of time, I adopted these strategies. Probably these compromises were also in the mind of the director in the design of the program. This class was part of a total school in which students were assigned to specific activities with the knowledge that evaluation of their work would be communicated to their parents. I chose to fit in as best I could with this process, particularly since I realized that to create a different context would have required a great deal more time [probably years!]. My organization of the first session subtly established how the group would function. Since I thought I had a clear perspective on the importance of middle school students' gradual acceptance of increasing responsibilities for learning and was working under significant time constraints, I sought to persuade these students of their potential power inherent in adopting such a stance. I sought to have students select the focus and purpose for their writing—but I knew this was a totally artificial endeavor. The students did, too. But most were experienced at going with the flow and causing little interruption to that flow. (They were proficient at the school game.)

Students selected topics and wrote. I read their work when they offered it for review and responded to both form and content. The only stated and imposed goal for the writing was to publish a group anthology at the end of our term together and this was my goal which subtly imposed on the group. (The importance of going public needs to be questioned. Not all writing is for publication. By adopting this goal, I lost sight of my real goal of development of each individual student.) Their writing time was isolated from all other activities, so the concept of using writing as a tool for learning was never relevant in this context. Nor was the purposefulness of writing outside of this setting considered. The Writer's Workshop was virtually a learning bubble floating in the air, contributing to filling the time during the day.

There is one powerful impact worthy of note. When the students' texts (curses, kissing, romance, guns, violence) were accepted, many enthusiastically and even collaboratively created texts which used typically censored topics and words. This seemed to respond to the students' sense of being in control and making independent decisions. I believed they were getting a sense of the power of language—and empowerment as writers. Several used the time to complete a story or to seek ideas for more effective communication, to attempt new genres or topics to add to their ongoing writer's notebooks. Some were taking responsibility for using their time productively and for their learning about writers' craft.

The importance of learning as a social activity became increasingly clear to me. Not only was it essential for these students to learn "the curriculum" but more importantly, they needed to recognize that they were responsible for their own learning and seeking settings which would promote that. They developed strength and voice when working collaboratively. They benefited from listening to each other, helping others learn and creating a community with a common purpose. Both the importance of this concept and its complexity became very apparent in this experience.

The importance of providing specific guidance and support for students' recognition and participation is now self-evident. I cannot expect students to be the impetus for this stance. I must initiate and support this stance and not wait for students to lead or to ask. This belief contrasts with that of Lapp and Fisher (2009) who believe the role of the teacher in these interactions is to wait for students to initiate the inquiry. Perhaps there needs to be a midway point in this continuum and not a dichotomy.

For some students, school is the only time they are separated from their families. This is the time for all students to learn to interact with peers and to initiate interactions, create plans, and address confrontations and disputes. School projects and conversations can create contexts for engagement in purposeful activities. Taking the time to establish meaningful projects seems like a useful strategy to enact an effective instructional program—an on-going and self-perpetuating activity, much like life itself. The arbitrary 40-minute segments numb the thinking and responsibility of students and teachers while the evolving community sustains student engagement.

DISCUSSION

The writers' workshop has been the focus of constant disputation as powerfully explained by Louis Menand (2009). Despite the controversies surrounding this activity from professional writers, I was grateful for the opportunity to work with the students and faculty in this setting. But I continue to wonder about educators' responsibilities for learning a particular curriculum. While the National Middle School Association (2003) has established principles about teaching and learning, the focus on subject matter seems potentially problematic as documented by David Elkind more than a quarter century ago (1981/2007) and Piaget (1926/1962) before him.

Early years in school are frequently dominated by teacher-directed activities. In this mode, students become dependent on teachers. In contrast, as children mature, they learn to accept increasing responsibility, reducing dependence on adults. School organizations may hinder the development of their identities as realized from self-determination and self-efficacy perspectives (Bandura, 2006; Gee, 2005; Pearson & Gallagher, 1983). The dual focus of social and academic development is anathema in most academic institutions. Acknowledging the emerging individual personality of each participant in the middle school years reflects an informed understanding of the reciprocity and at times, even the priority of one over the other. It requires educators to think outside the box by positioning themselves to support their students' achievements. In addition, this recognition of differences between children's and adolescents' interests and needs causes us to create different organizational structures and activities in middle school settings.

Is the departmental structure antithetical to promoting adolescent students' engagement and learning? What models are effective in simultaneously supporting adolescent students' sociocultural development and their academic achievement? What roles do effective teachers play in these models? What are the characteristics of an effective teacher in this context? How many "effective teachers" does a student need to have as part of a middle-school program? How does cross-age grouping contribute to students' evolving academic and sociocultural development?

Schools are influenced by standardized exams, curricular mandates, union contracts, teacher knowledge, and society's implicit and explicit expectations. There are pockets in our communities where some of these traditions and expectations are subjected to inquiry. The alternative school movement is one academic community which seriously contemplates some of these concerns as exemplified by the Coalition for Effective Schools started by Ted Sizer. Schooling is pervasive in our society. Middle school students are often considered the most challenging, perhaps because they are on the cusp of becoming—becoming independent learners, developing clearer identities which are distinct from their relatives, creating plans for their future (Loukas & Murphy, 2007).

The challenge prevails … If my goal for this writers' workshop experience was to build strengths, confidence, and motivation as writers and learners, I have little evidence to consider this a successful enterprise. Although there may be some evidence, my hopes were more grandiose. Perhaps the expectation, too, is in need of revision. I know intellectually that change and learning happen slowly. Results become apparent incrementally and retrospectively. Conscious reflection may contribute to the process. I guess impatience may be a quality not only of the young, but also of those who establish goals. By having a goal, we simultaneously create a potential road map and a projected timeline. While I will never have any incontrovertible evidence of any influence participation in the writers' workshop had on these participants, I am fairly confident that I did not do any harm (a physician's first goal!). I hope to do better.

REFERENCES

Bandura, A. (2006). Adolescent development from an agentive perspective. In F. Pajares & T. Urdan (Eds.), *Self-efficacy beliefs of adolescents.* Greenwich, CT: Information Age.

Brause, R.S. (1992). *Enduring schools.* New York, NY: Routledge.

Britton, J. (1993). *Language and learning* (2nd ed.). Portsmouth, NH: Boynton-Cook/Heinemann.

Clandinin, D.J., & Connelly, F. Michael. (2000). *Narrative inquiry: Experience and story in qualitative research.* San Francisco, CA: Jossey-Bass.

Cummins, J. (2009). Literacy and English-language learners. *Educational Researcher, 38*(5), 382-384.

Elkind, D. (2007). *The hurried child* (25th anniversary edition). Cambridge, MA: Perseus. (Original work published 1981)

Gee, J. P. (2005). *Discourse analysis* (2nd ed.). New York, NY: Routledge.

Graves, D. (1979). What children show us about revision. *Language Arts, 56,* 312-319.

Graves, D. (1983). *Writing: Teachers and children at work.* Exeter, NH: Heinemann Educational Books.

Harwayne, S., & Calkins, L. (1987). *The writing workshop: A world of difference.* Portsmouth, NH: Heinemann.

Kutz, E. (l997). *Language and literacy.* Portsmouth, NH: Boynton/Cook-Reed Elsevier.

Lapp, D., & Fisher, M. (2009). It's all about the book. *Journal of Adolescent and Adult Literacy, 52*(7), 556-561.

Lensmire, T. J. (2000). *Powerful writing, responsible teaching.* New York, NY: Teachers College Press.

Loukas, A., & Murphy, J. L. (2007). Middle school student perceptions of school climate. *Journal of School Psychology, 45,* 293-309.

Menand, L. (2009). Show or tell: Should creative writing be taught? *The New Yorker,* pp. 106-112.

Moffett, J. (1968). *Teaching the universe of discourse.* Boston, MA: Houghton, Mifflin.

National Middle School Association. (2003). *This we believe.* Westerville, OH: Author.

Pearson, P. D., & Gallagher, M. C. (1983). The instruction of reading comprehension. *Contemporary Educational Research, 8,* 317-344.

Piaget, J. (1962). *Language and thought of the child.* New York, NY: Harcourt. (Original work published 1926)

Whelan, J. (2008). On the margins of education, or two stories on arriving at school. *Ethnography & Education, 3*(3), 297-312.

Wilson, D. M. (2009). Developmentally appropriate practices in the age of technology. *Harvard Education Letter, 25*(3), 4-6.

CHAPTER 13

CAN A K-8 SCHOOL ADDRESS THE NEEDS OF ADOLESCENTS?

Nancy Bell Ruppert

A new K-8 school opened in Jacksonville, Florida in 2008. The principal intentionally housed middle school age students separately, arranged them on teams, and designated separate administrators for them. This case study provides descriptions and reflections of the year as 1 team implemented middle school practices to meet the social and emotional needs of their students. Through narrative inquiry of adolescents and their teachers I describe 6 activities associated with middle school research. The middle school activities are based on research by George (2008) and associated with *This We Believe* (National Middle School Association, 2003) and *Turning Points* (Jackson & Davis, 2000). As the number of K-8 schools increase in our nation, this study calls for the use of middle school activities to enhance middle school age children's experiences in K-8 schools.

Voices From the Middle: Narrative Inquiry By, For, and About the Middle Level Community
pp. 259–286

INTRODUCTION

I taught sixth grade in a low performing K-8 school. In January, I reflected on what I knew of their lives, wondering how they felt in the following circumstances:

- If nobody wished them happy birthday when they turned 13?
- If their boyfriend made them feel bad so they threw a pen at the teacher, who turned his back to write an assignment on the board?
- If people made fun of them because they were different from them or because they had buck teeth?
- If they were in a class with children who could not or chose not to control themselves, who were loud, disruptive, and disrespectful?
- If their dad just got out of prison?
- If their mom did very little to get them to school and they ended up staying up too late on school nights?
- If they just wanted their moms to say they loved their children?
- If the only way they could function was if they were high?
- If the only thing that meant anything to them was a family member who could not care for herself?
- If they were the oldest of three children in a family with no father and a grandmother who worked two jobs?

I worried that events impacted their self perceptions as middle school students. In May, I asked them to respond to the statement "Middle school students are ..." An overwhelming number of the students responded that they and their classmates were basically good kids, suggesting they adjusted to middle school. Their responses included:

- "I think sixth graders are very, very smart ... most of the sixth graders are kind, but all of us are special in our own way."
- "This is how I act in sixth grade. I like to have it my way. When I don't have it my way, then I don't do the assignments. When I like a certain assignment I will be quiet and finish the assignment. I don't work [well] together with close friends because I don't concentrate well. So I'll have to work with a friend, but not a close friend."
- "Some are disrespectful and some are disruptive, also, some are nice, quiet and do their work."
- "I act bad because that's all I am around and that is all I see and girls like that so sometimes I don't think about what I do."

- "I am good when I want to be, but when you [get] on my bad side, that [is] when things go wrong. So to all you guys [who] 'get' on my bad side, good luck to you."
- "I like to have it my way all the time."
- "Some are rude, some are sweet like me. I'm [one] of the sweet kids."
- "Kids in the sixth grade act like a typical kid, like talking about kids, acting up in class, play fighting, and other kid-related things; another behavior is talking back to teachers like they do to their parents."
- "But overall every sixth grade kid has something special inside of them."
- "I think their behavior is caused because of their environment and the people in their lives."

My team mates and I taught these children in a K-8 school. These comments suggest two sides to our children: the heart-wrenching stories we see and how they see themselves. While they were part of a K-8 school, we treated them as middle school children, implemented middle school activities, and sought ways to enhance the middle school experience in a K-8 setting.

This study reports the experiences of our team as we tried to implement middle school "best practices" (teaming, advisor-advisee, intramurals, curriculum enrichment, exploratories, and heterogeneous grouping) as described by George (2008). Our hope was to find ways to meet our students' social and emotional needs.

LITERATURE REVIEW

The National Middle School Association (NMSA) (2009), *This We Believe* (NMSA, 2003), *Turning Points 2000* (Jackson & Davis, 2000), and the National Forum to Accelerate Middle Level Education (2009) consistently describe adolescence in terms of children's social, emotional, physical, and intellectual characteristics. The early tenets of middle level education were based on findings related to curriculum and grouping arrangements that support these needs (George & Alexander, 2003). Traditionally, the proponents of the middle school concept suggested that students in sixth through eighth grades should be treated differently from younger children and older children (George & Alexander, 2003). Thus, when the middle school concept was adopted and middle schools created, teachers were asked to be not only teachers but also mentors, advocates for children (George & Lawrence, 1984). A curriculum focused on teaming, advisory, intramurals, exploratories, curriculum enhancement, and heterogeneous grouping emerged, incorporating strategies to address the intellectual, social, and emotional needs of young adolescents (George & Alexander, 2003; NMSA, 2003).

Middle Schools Versus K-8 Schools

During the past 30 years, the trend has been to consider serving middle school aged students in elementary K-8 settings (Hough, 1995; Pardini, 2002). Understanding and working with adolescents are the heart of middle level education, regardless of the context in which such education takes place. A middle school focuses specifically on the social, emotional, and intellectual needs of young adolescents, whereas a K-8 school crosses multiple age level curriculums and children's needs. Examining children's performance and comparing the effectiveness of middle schools and junior high schools to K-8 schools is not new. Early studies suggested that K-8 schools more effectively addressed children's needs than middle schools or junior high schools. Simmons, Blyth, VanCleave, and Bush (1979) examined the self-esteem of children in different configurations. Simmons and colleagues interviewed children in sixth grade and subsequently in seventh grade to compare levels of self-esteem in different school settings. The findings indicated that females who were in junior high schools had lower self-esteem than females in K-8 settings; meanwhile, no difference existed in males' self-esteem, regardless of the setting.

O'Reilly and Jarrett (1980) examined students in intermediate schools and K-8 schools. They determined that K-8 students were more involved in school activities than intermediate students. Moore (1984) discussed the overwhelmingly positive impact of K-8 schools when compared to middle schools. His study compared nine junior highs to nine K-8 schools in New York City. At all levels, from reading comprehension to self-esteem, attitudes toward school, and achievement, K-8 school students outperformed middle school and junior high school students. As middle schools became more prevalent in the 1970s and 1980s, researchers suggested that middle schools needed to focus more on the social and emotional needs of adolescents. Studies emerged suggesting that what happened in schools was more important than how grades were configured.

Hough (1995) introduced the term *elemiddle* to identify K-8 schools that provided structures and practices that differed for the upper grades and celebrated similar successes as high-functioning middle schools. Pardini (2002) reviewed the impact of large school districts that moved from middle school to K-8 settings. District superintendents overwhelmingly cited academic, behavior, and attendance statistics to support their decisions to establish K-8 settings. Pardini (2002) quoted Swaim, who reminded readers that not all sixth through eighth (hereafter, 6-8) grade schools implemented middle school concepts and for this reason, research should compare K-8 schools with middle schools that implemented true middle school concepts. Hough (2005) reiterated this point, suggesting that what happens in school is more important than the configuration of grade levels. His theory, based on 15 years of research, suggests that the most successful K-8 and 6-8 schools implement middle school concepts while current research most often supports K-8 schools that implement middle school concepts. Hough further discussed the lack of empirical research comparing schools across a national arena, although he concluded that K-8 settings outperformed middle schools across the board.

Some districts moved toward K-8 settings based on federal mandates. Gewertz (2004) shared a principal's view of the transition that takes place and the difficulties in licensure and implementation of extracurricular activities when K-8 schools are initially established. She further discussed parent desires to have their children closer to home and part of a community, arguing that these were integral components of the K-8 configuration and that students performed better academically in K-8 settings. Byrnes and Ruby (2007) found that K-8 school children performed significantly better academically than middle school children based on similar demographics; however, newer K-8 schools were not as likely to perform better. In addition, Gill, Engberger, and Booker (2005) presented research on schools in Philadelphia, PA which have been part of a massive takeover plan based on No Child Left Behind legislation; the research indicated that K-8 schools were more conducive to minority achievement than magnet middle schools or 6-8 schools.

Patton (2005) described the K-8 setting as one that provides an intimate setting for students, suggesting that this setting enables teachers to better manage children. This article identified research that supported K-8 schools from the views of principals, parents, and teachers. Patton further indicated that, in her district, K-8 teachers were more likely to remain in the teaching field. Poncelet and Associates (2004) reviewed two K-8 schools in Cleveland, comparing data with children in a middle school. Their findings suggested that children were happier and showed greater gains academically in K-8 settings than in 6-8 school settings.

Arcia (2007) examined the suspension rates of K-8 and middle school students, determining that suspension rates were much higher in middle schools than in K-8 schools. Yenke's (2006) data, based on the Trends in

International Mathematics and Science Studies, suggested that students began to drop out in middle schools, citing behavior and discipline issues associated with young adolescents. Furthermore, Yenke (2006) shared the results of longitudinal studies in Milwaukee, Baltimore, and Philadelphia, all citing increased achievement and participation and fewer discipline problems in K-8 schools compared to middle schools. Yenke's (2006) article applied the same strategies as the National Forum for the Improvement of Middle Level Education, namely, involving parents and setting high expectations (two strategies that have had the greatest impact on the success of schools).

The National Forum to Accelerate Middle Grades Reform (2009) developed criteria for middle schools under the Schools to Watch program. These criteria include academic excellence (high expectations), developmental responsiveness (supports the social needs of the children), social equity (heterogeneous grouping), and organizational structure (autonomy). According to this program, the statistics of exemplary middle schools reflect the same successes as successful K-8 schools.

However, not all research supports the K-8 setting. Whitley, Lupart, and Beran's (2007) comparative study found that students in a K-8 setting did not show any significant increase in their mathematical abilities when compared to students in a middle school setting. These conclusions support Hough (2005) and Pardini's (2002) ideas that children have developmental needs as well as grade configuration needs. Viadero (2006) examined middle schools and K-8 schools in Philadelphia, finding neither academic differences nor attendance differences between the two configurations. However, Viadero found that students in a K-8 school indicated higher self-esteem than children in middle schools. Weiss and Kipnes (2006) found similar results in urban schools. Furthermore, Roosevelt's (2007) report suggests that some K-8 schools experience more violence than K-5 schools. Thus, as much of the research has stated in one way or another, "efforts to improve learning in the middle school by merely changing the form of schooling are unlikely to succeed" (p. 3).

Anfara et al. (2003) summarized the characteristics of exemplary schools for adolescents, presenting the notion of leadership as paramount to the success of middle schools. Thus, it is possible that, when middle school concepts are supported by strong leadership and offered at K-8 schools, children will be successful. Although research suggests that K-8 schools may provide a rich environment for student learning, it remains unclear whether students and teachers in a K-8 school system showed any academic, social, or emotional responses to various curriculum strategies attempted. This year-long study looked closely at each of the "middle school" activities as they were addressed in a K-8 school.

A study of administrators in Florida sparked this research. Schools in Florida focus on academic success and accountability. George (2008) surveyed Florida middle school principals and found that middle school components including teaming, advisor-advisee, intramurals, curriculum enrichment, exploratories, and heterogeneous grouping are "disappearing" from middle schools. George shares the concern of middle level administrators across the state who voice a concern that developmental appropriateness is shunned in an effort to focus solely on student academic success. Styron and Nyman (2008) surveyed middle school teachers in high and low performing middle schools and found that school climate, structures, and instructional practices were not decisive elements of high or low performing schools. Both studies call for leaders to intentionally design professional development for teachers to address the needs of young adolescents by implementing middle school exemplary practices.

Research identifies strategies that are associated with developmentally appropriate practices. Research associated with K-8 and middle schools agree that schools that foster developmentally appropriate schools aide student learning. This study examined middle school practices in a K-8 school to suggest that a K-8 setting provides unique opportunities for middle school age students to have developmentally appropriate experiences.

METHODOLOGY

Setting

I taught sixth grade math in an inner-city K-8 school in Jacksonville, Florida that was in its first year of a K-8 configuration after the school system merged three small neighborhood schools. I was at the university for eight years prior to the experience and was granted a year's leave to teach. One of the reasons I returned to the classroom was to collect data about middle school activities in a K-8 school.

With permission from the school principal, I submitted a proposal to the district for researching my experiences throughout the year. I received consent from the teachers and administrators to document our year. By immersing myself in a K-8 school, I planned to study adolescents and how they and their teachers responded to the different middle school activities in a K-8 setting. In addition, I wanted to share strategies for enhancing middle school concepts using younger grade students as part of a "community focus," which was described as an advantage of the K-8 setting (Patton, 2005; Schools to Watch, 2009).

The school was low-performing based on state test scores. In 2008, 37% of the students performed at or above standard in mathematics. The school was labeled a "turnaround school" that the district supported with resource personnel and monitored very closely. This study focused on one of the two sixth-grade teams including four teachers and 60 children.

On our team, two teachers were new to teaching; the other teacher and I had 30 years of teaching experience in public schools. We each taught four classes of students. One class was designed specifically for students who were at least two grade levels below in reading, as required by the district. The other three classes were grouped heterogeneously. Students rotated as a class among us. We used Fridays as curriculum enrichment, a modified version of advisory activities, and students explored different types of jobs associated with a Microsociety. Every 9 weeks, our students rotated through exploratories including technology, art, music, and Spanish, and we implemented intramurals occasionally.

This new two-story, K-8 school housed more than 1,100 students. The sixth graders were the oldest students in the school. The plan was to move the sixth graders up as the oldest students over a 3-year period until they reached the eighth grade. One fourth of the sixth grade students had individual education plans (IEPs), and more than 95% of the children in the school were on free or reduced lunch.

The fifth and sixth grade classrooms were on the second story. Although the fifth graders were upstairs, they followed the elementary schedule, including morning meetings, Everyday Math, rotating electives throughout the week, and library time. Fifth graders participated in two-person teams. Younger students (K-4) had minimal interaction with older children, who were sometimes perceived as louder and more disruptive than the younger children. Although the younger grades had different exploratories and physical education each day, the sixth grade children were on an A-day/B-day schedule in which they alternated physical education and one of four electives (Spanish, technology, art, and music) every 9 weeks.

Sixth grade students had a separate administration (assistant principal, guidance counselor, administrative assistant, and two special education teachers who pulled students out of classes during math or reading). A safety resource officer worked with the sixth graders and served the entire school. A literacy coach and math coach worked with the lower and upper grades. This new school was equipped with computer labs, Macintosh computers in every classroom, document readers, microphones, and overhead computerized screens.

Data Collection

Narrative inquiry uses stories to describe experiences (Clandinin, Pushor, & Orr, 2007). Over the 2008-2009 school year I chose to look for stories associated with middle school curriculum, as described by George

(2008). The activities I used to generate the narratives included teaming, advisory activities, intramurals, curriculum enrichment, exploratories, and heterogeneous grouping.

Two elements of narrative inquiry are field notes and reflections (Clandinin & Connelly, 2000). Throughout the year I kept a journal of how teachers and their students responded to the activities. I interviewed team members about the activities we engaged in and asked them to share student responses to each of the activities. I recorded teachers' thoughts and students' responses. Team meetings were recorded and in my journal I reflected on how we used the concept of teaming to meet the needs of our students. Advisory activities took place in the science classroom on Fridays. The science teacher reflected on the value of the experiences and shared students' responses. As a team we attempted to implement intramurals; our reflections were recorded. Fridays were devoted to curriculum enrichment and teachers shared their successes and the challenges they faced. A schoolwide focus on creating businesses was implemented. Students and teachers responded to the impact of this type of exploratory. Heterogeneous grouping took place in three of our four classes allowing us to compare and contrast the values of each. I kept a journal of reflections and teacher responses throughout the entire school year.

Ethics

In an effort to protect the anonymity of teachers and students, I do not use real names to identify the participants. This research was participatory, meaning that I relied on my teammates to share information and discuss ideas with me. When I considered leaving out a sensitive area of the research, my colleagues assured me that what took place in our school needed to be told. In the words of Clandinin and Connelly (2000),

> As we composed our research texts we needed to be thoughtful of our research participants as our first audience and, indeed, our most important audience, for it is to them that we owe our care to compose a text that does not rupture life stories that sustain them. But as researchers, we also owe our care and responsibility to a larger audience, to the conversation of a scholarly discourse, and our research texts need also to speak of how we lived and told our stories within the particular field of inquiry. (pp. 173-174)

Analysis of the Data

Over the course of the year, I had field notes of teachers' reflections, students' responses, and my own thoughts of how we implemented and evaluated the six activities associated with exemplary middle schools. I separated the responses that pertained to each of the six activities and presented an overview of research related to each, what we did, how teachers responded to the activities, and how students reacted. Bogdan and Biklen (2007) describe this method of looking for patterns and descriptions to describe phenomena. In an effort to establish "the facts" as described by Clandinin and Connelly (2000), I invited my colleagues to serve as a "response community" (p. 182). I shared the findings and encouraged them to question, correct, or dispute any of the stories reported. Throughout the research, my intent was to tell the story of how our team responded to middle school practices.

FINDINGS

Our goal as a team was to get to know our students well, support them, set high expectations, and serve their needs. Based on George's (2008) descriptions of exemplary middle schools, I gathered data on how our team addressed each of the activities identified as exemplary and our students responded to the activities/experiences associated with them. The descriptions discussed herein are based on interviews and reflections as recorded in journal entries.

Teaming

Teaming is at the heart of the middle school movement; teams of teachers are essential to the success of middle school children (Lounsbury, 1991). Hough (1995) and Yenke (2006) view middle school children as needing teachers/leaders that care about them and work with them to develop socially and emotionally, which in turn enhances their academic performance. This aspect of our K-8 school was intentional and gave us common planning and autonomy to develop activities and events within each team.

Our team came together from very different backgrounds. At the beginning of the year, we learned about one another and talked about our strengths. One teacher had taught for 15 years in the inner-city setting; one teacher had been a forensics major and was an alternative licensed teacher, one had been a police officer, and I had been a classroom teacher and university professor. We each brought different strengths to the team.

One of the first exercises we did was to share who we were and what strengths we brought to the team. One of our first meetings included the following responses to the questions "who are you" and "what do you bring to the team":

- "Until 2 weeks ago I was a police officer on this side of town. I bring an understanding of adolescent behaviors to our team."
- "I taught at this school last year. I am very aware of the behaviors of the children and the environments they live in."
- "I worked for a year as a coteacher in an alternative certification program. I am very comfortable having children work in groups."

During the year, when a teacher was not feeling well, we pitched in to help. "If you can get a doctor's appointment, we can split up our students at the end of the day." When children were having "middle school moments," we passed them to one another for a time out or cool down. "Can you let Sonia sit in your room for a little while? She is having a conflict with Tammy." Later on in the year, team members shared the following sentiments: "This has been one of the hardest jobs I have had," and "I don't know what I would have done without the team's support."

We put together a reward system during the first few weeks. According to one teacher, "it worked very well to begin to get our students to settle down." One of our team teachers used rewards throughout the year. My students came in with their weekly prizes, often showing off what they got. As the teacher shared, "It works for me." Throughout the year we used consistent rewards and rituals and moved children around to balance personalities within our teams.

We talked about our students constantly. For example, at the beginning of one school day, one teacher shared, "Has anyone noticed a difference in Arnold? I called his mom yesterday. She says they can't afford to pay for his medication. I am concerned that his behavior is affecting his grades." We talked about this child and compared the behaviors we saw. The student's homeroom teacher kept in contact with the parent via email, and we moved the student to a different class to give the child more flexibility in the learning environment.

We talked with students and let each other know what was going on. For example, a teacher shared the following conversation she had with Celeste.

"These kids are so mean," Celeste shrieks as she storms in my classroom, throws her book bag down, and covers her face.

"Do you want to talk about it?" the teacher asks?

"No."

"Do you want to go to see the guidance counselor?"

"No."

"Do you want to go to the back of the classroom and chill?" Celeste gets up with her book bag and drags herself to the back of the class. Before class is over, she returns to participate.

In this example, another student said Celeste made a comment about another student, which was not true. We found that giving students an opportunity to cool down most often helped them move back into the class.

At the end of the year, one teammate stated, "I learned how to relax and not take things they did personally. I found that different students responded to different feedback."

Our students also learned that we worked to help them get along with their classmates. For example, one student came in and said to me, "I can't work with Thomas. Is there any way I can move to another class?" We talked about this as a team and made the decision to move him from the classroom he was in. Once he was moved, he showed more effort—not as much as we had hoped, but he clearly felt safer. During the course of the year we moved several other children who asked to be moved. Thus, the team communicated and collaborated to support teachers and children.

Advisor-Advisee

In *Turning Points 2000*, the opportunity to develop relationships and be known is one of the characteristics of an advisory program (Jackson & Davis, 2000). The advisor-advisee relationship looks at ways to help students develop socially and emotionally (George & Lawrence, 1984). We saw a need to advocate for our children because of comments such as:

- "Bald head … we're just kidding with her." [The girl, whose hair is very thin, puts her head down on her desk.]
- "Last time I was in a fight, they arrested me," says one of my smartest students. "Oh yeah, she fought over a piece of cake."
- "I've watched children gang up on another child and kick him, make up a song and dance to make fun of a child, and make comments about how dirty a child is," shared one teacher.
- "Teeth," he mocks.
- "Big ears," he retaliates.
- "Fatso," is heard as one child walks by another.

It was apparent to us that our children needed opportunities to learn how to get along with one another.

In our individual rooms, we focused on concerns we shared as a team. We found that our children's relationships interfered with their learning. Erwin (2004) suggested creating a classroom in which students learn to live in a community. Erwin (2004) and Powell (2005) pointed out the importance of planning experiences that intentionally address the needs of children to belong.

We conducted advisory activities on Fridays during the first nine weeks. One team member was trained in Covey's (2004) 7 *Habits of Highly Effective People*. She used the time to teach the 7 *Habits* curriculum to our students. The following are some of the excerpts from her reflections.

- "I was surprised that the students were willing to share their goals and ideas."
- "They responded to one another and we were able to use the language of 7 *Habits* in our regular classroom…. My kids liked the videos that accompany the lessons. I am very excited to have this series to use with my students."

Students looked forward to Fridays when they got to participate in the 7 *Habits* training. We were directed to resume an academic focus on Fridays at the end of the fall semester. Therefore, we did not continue the focus on 7 *Habit*s. One student asked, "Why don't we do Fun Fridays anymore? We liked the change of pace on Fridays."

Service learning is an advisory activity that allows students to develop social responsibility (Jackson & Davis, 2000; Scales, Blyth, Berkas, & Kielsmeier, 2000). We decided to conduct service projects for the school. Children brainstormed ideas and came up with: (1) helping the media specialists, (2) working with lower grade teachers, and (3) cleaning the school. The media specialist welcomed help with shelving and straightening books. The students read to younger children and worked with them at centers. The custodial staff provided cleaning supplies and we supervised the cleaners.

The students decided which project they wanted to participate in and went to their respective placements on Tuesdays and Thursdays in April. When a guest walked into our room one day and asked where everyone was, the cleaner told her, 'We are doing our service project. Our group is cleaning the school so it looks nice.' Meanwhile, in their journals, students shared the following responses to the service projects:

- "I like working with young children. They are very sweet."
- "This is so much fun," shared one of the library workers."
- "I love working with Ms. Kim downstairs," shared a teacher assistant."

The children were given 30 minutes to participate in the service project. Most of them returned on time and were able to settle right into class.

Students took their responsibilities very seriously and loved giving something back to the school. On Tuesdays and Thursdays, they came to class and immediately asked, "Are we going to do our service project today?"

Intramurals

Lee, Burgeson, Fulton, and Spain (2007) compiled a national survey to determine how schools set up physical education programs including health, physical education, intramurals, and interscholastic programs. In this study, the authors found that sports programs improved students' emotional health and helped to reduce risky behavior. Furthermore, Degon and Alterio (2009) found that the regular physical activity had a positive impact on "academic achievement, increased concentration, and improved math, reading and writing scores" (p. 3).

Our team found similar results. The children looked forward to playing and had a more positive attitude when they participated in physical activities.

- "We just want to play," said one of my brightest students when he came into class the day before a holiday.
- "When are we going to do that [Greek Games] again?" asked a student. "I liked that discus throw even though I wasn't any good at it."
- "Can we go outside and play?"
- "Are we going to walk today? I like it when we walk," one student says while shaking the pedometer to increase the number of steps that were registered on the tool.
- "Occasionally, we go to the playground. We hang out on the monkey bars and socialize."

During the second 9 weeks we, as a team, tried to organize Wednesday intramurals between the two sixth grade teams. The boys loved playing basketball against one another. Several of the girls wanted to play basketball, but there were not enough people for a team. Unfortunately, we did not feel successful in organizing intramurals for our students. In October, one teacher commented, "Students were willing to play pick-up games, jump rope, and walk around the track, but the opportunity to compete against one another didn't happen."

In March, the social studies teachers from both teams put together "Greek Games" as part of a unit on ancient Greece. We used grant money to purchase prizes and refreshments for the students, and the math classes made wreaths and medallions for the winners. The games took place on a Thursday morning from 9 to 11:30, and the students participated enthusiastically.

- "I can't get over how well the students played together," one of the teachers commented.
- "I thought it was awesome (Greek Games) and gave students who do not normally excel in the classroom a chance to receive recognition and be leaders," shared another teacher.
- The students shared, "Can we do this again?"
- "That was the most fun I have had this year."

In reflecting on the positive aspects of conducting the games, the general consensus from the faculty was:

"Everything went great until the tug-of-war. We had planned on having the girls go first and the boys go second. Unfortunately some of the boys jumped in line at the end of the girls' line and began to tug, at which point boys on the other team jumped on their end. The children began pulling and screaming at the same time. We managed to break up the tug-of-war event and got the children to return to the bleachers for the track races. Other than that, it went great," shared the social studies teacher.

The name of every student who placed first, second, or third in any event was put into a basket. We drew names from the basket and presented students with prizes including balls, jump ropes, signed hats, and footballs. After that we went outside to play with the equipment.

A third structured event was a fitness project. In April, we implemented an NFL "What Moves You?" fitness and goal setting grant. The physical education teacher integrated health and fitness as part of the curriculum. In math, students estimated and calculated the number of steps and miles walked over time using pedometers. They estimated their footsteps and wrote math brochures about fitness. Students had to check their homework and complete the "warm-up" for the day before they went outside. Students were anxious to walk for 15 minutes: "Hurry everybody so we can go outside and walk the field."

We worked with the pedometers for 2 weeks before spring break. There were no discipline problems. Students had to put together a brochure or a skit to share how they exercise, how it relates to math, and give suggestions for other middle school students. One student wrote:

These are a couple of ways that fitness can relate to math: swimming, jumping rope and running. [Under the section on Jumping Rope:] Ice cream, ice cream, cherry on the top, how many boyfriends do you go 1,2,3 … In jump roping you can use math by counting how many jumps you make, or by

> counting how fast your pulse gets as you jump. [On the swimming panel:] In swimming you can count how many laps you count of the pool or how many seconds you can hold your breath under water. [On the running panel:] In running you can use math by counting how many laps you run or count how many steps you take.

Another student's brochure included the number of steps she walked (1,623 steps, or .53 miles) in 15 minutes. She then calculated how many steps/miles she would walk in an hour. She reflected in her math journal that, "projects allow us to think about math differently than just doing a homework assignment from the book." Another student wrote the following in his brochure, which was separated into three sections.

> [Types of Exercise:] In the world there are many type [sic] of ways to get moving. Such as playing football, soccer, basketball, swimming or even walking is fine. Just make sure to try to exercise 30 minute every day. Also too [sic] try to eat healthy. And eat less potato chips and drink less soda. [Inspiration:] But sometimes there are some who think exercising is hard. Like pull-ups they are too and then people get discourage [sic]. Well not all exercise is hard. So like I said before exercising doesn't have to be workout. It could be anything like walking or sport. So get up and start moving. [What moves You:] Now what moves you? If you play 30 minute [sic] every day that adds up to 3 hour and 30 minutes of saving energy every week!!! How great is that, you play and save energy at the same time? So stay active and eat healthy.

The students took this assignment seriously. Their passion for exercise underscored the view that children are aware of the benefits of exercise.

As our students were too young to participate in team sports (team sports do not begin until seventh grade in our district), four teachers (three fifth and one sixth) donated their time to create a boys and a girls fifth–sixth grade basketball team. This project was expensive, and getting money for each of the children to play was a challenge. However, those who played on the teams were very excited. For example, one girl asked, "We have a game this Friday; will you come watch us play?"

A teammate and I went to see the team play. They scored four points before the end of the game. We commented about the value of playing organized sports where children learn to play as a team, support one another, and follow directions. It was fun to see two students score a basket and how excited everyone on the team was.

Furthermore, we watched the band play at a parent night and during a pep rally and cheered their efforts. "Did you see me?" was a common question the next morning. The teachers commented, "We were very proud to see you all because we know how hard you work. Was it fun?" Beaming, the students answered yes. These students had not participated in extracurricular activities; as such, their skill levels were very "new." However, this did not bother them. When asked if they had fun, all of them said, "Yes." The value of exercise and nutrition, intramurals, extracurricular activities, and opportunities to work together in a sporting atmosphere gave our students productive, social outlets and allowed us to develop better relationships with them.

Curriculum Enrichment

"I don't think these children have ever done so many projects or experiments," shared one of the teachers, "They really like being able to create things." Mastropieri et al. (2006) compared the impact of direct instruction to hands-on, peer-tutoring activities, scenarios, and other inquiry activities designed to enhance the curriculum. Thirteen classes were randomly assigned to one of the two approaches to teaching the content. While the results indicate that all students learned, those who participated in the enrichment approach enjoyed working with their peers and preferred this approach to learning.

Our students loved demonstrating their learning. One teacher shared, "I have students all over the halls tracing one another to describe the systems of the body. They were very engaged in the project. I found that they were able to relate their knowledge on their tests as well." Other examples of students' excitement about learning included:

- "May I get on the computer to work on my podcast?"
- "Can we go to the computer lab?"
- "Can we play those games again?" [regarding a Factor Game and a version of Connect Four that involved a grid board and two-color disks]
- "This is the best project we have done this whole year," one student shared when students were conducting classroom surveys to illustrate measures of central tendency.
- "We liked drawing our bodies. Look at mine," a student said after her teammate finished her drawing.
- "Can I recite my monologue to you?"
- "We have put our skit together. Will you read it?"

"Fun Fridays," as previously discussed, focused on curriculum enrichment. Students participated in activities that reinforced basic skills and curriculum addressed by the school. Our goal was to create something different from the daily schedule that engaged our students in applying their knowledge and allowed them to practice their basic skills. The social studies teacher focused on civic lessons and the science teacher conducted Covey's (2004) 7 *Habits of Highly Effective People* activities. In math and language arts, students used process skills of "making connections, problem solving, creating representations, and communicating ideas" (Zemelman, Daniels, & Hyde, 2005, p. 115) to illustrate their learning. Students' comments included:

- "I like Fun Fridays. It is nice to do something different."
- "I have my notebook organized for math, language arts, Covey (2004), and Microsociety."
- "Today I worked on 12 and 18."
- "Something I learned … I learned 12. I read the problem around and around again and answered it. I got it right."
- "I am the bird in our social studies play, Caw! Caw! Caw!"
- "We played a comprehension game in language arts; it was lots of fun."
- "I like Fun Fridays. The teachers are nicer."

In the civic lessons, students discussed different types of governments.

- "After participating in the dictator activity, I don't think I want that kind of government for our school. It wasn't fun having to bow down to the king every time I got within 15 feet of him."
- "Some of the things I am good at is listening to other people. Sixth graders are generally very nice and they do respect one another."

The teachers' views of Fun Fridays were mixed.

- "I feel like I should be teaching my curriculum. By mixing up Friday, I get behind on the learning schedule."
- "I am not comfortable planning something that isn't in the book. What should I do for an hour with students?"

Enrichment was part of regular classes. Students engaged in projects in math and experiments in science. The students shared their thoughts on projects and experiments.

- "We like doing projects. It is a different way to think about our work."
- "By doing projects we are using the information we learn in class."

- "It is a different way to do homework."

We had a student who was a very low reader; yet he helped the kindergarten children with their reading. This type of experience appeared to increase his self-confidence.

At the end of the year, we talked about the possibility of doing more integrated projects and interdisciplinary units next year. In the first year, it was difficult for new teachers to think about working on combining their standards. Although we were able to begin to experiment with interdisciplinary design, our hope was to become more intentional with regard to the use of specific language arts strategies and to reinforce math skills in science and social studies. Teachers' comments included:

- "I want to do more interdisciplinary teaching next year."
- "Now that I know the curriculum, I want to do more projects next year. The students really respond to hands-on learning."

Exploratories

In the early years of the middle school movement, the term *exploratory* focused on four specific areas: unified arts (music, art, band, physical education, foreign language), independent learning (where students chose a topic and were only guided by the teacher), academic inquiry (minicourses that students could take), and special interest activities (whereby teachers engaged students in explorations within the standards that they were teaching) (George & Lawrence, 1984). Our students had mixed feelings about the unified arts. They rotated every 9 weeks among music, technology, art, and Spanish. Each class lasted for nine weeks and alternated with physical education; thus, one week students had their exploratory 3 days a week while the next week they had it 2 days a week. Their comments included:

- "I don't want to go to art today. Can I stay in your classroom?"
- "I love going to the computer lab and creating designs."

Independent learning took place when students participated in Microsociety, a program in which children engaged in running a community complete with government, businesses, and "micro" money. Students maintained hallways, set up businesses, and sold products. Two days a week, students ran businesses. They were paid in "Micromoney" and, on specific days, spent their money on such things as "nail salon," "games," or "photography booth." On our team, students participated in banking, hair design, sports camp, law, and games.

Students looked forward to these activities; they were very proud of their jobs and talked about their successes: "When are we going to our businesses?" and "May I leave now? I have to go to my business early." One student stated, "I am going to be a hairdresser one day and this has helped me think about running a business." The same student showed leadership skills in the classroom. She was described by one of her teachers as follows, "Because she had built a relationship as a business owner, she was able to develop positive interactions with adults and classmates. Her classmates voted her most likely to run a business at the end of the year."

At the end of the year, students were asked to reflect on their business experiences.

- "I love spending money. My favorite thing to do was to get my nails done."
- "We just like hanging out with our business partners."
- "I work in the bank. It was lots of fun. We count money and help people open accounts."

Meanwhile, one teacher shared that "there was an overwhelming majority of students who loved going to the businesses. I was surprised." Another teacher shared, "we lost 2 hours of instruction time every week. I am concerned that our students aren't getting what they need academically."

At the end of the year, the sixth graders learned that they were not going to be able to participate in the businesses next year as the district was moving toward a different type of exploratory model for middle school students. They were very disappointed. One student asked, "What do you mean we can't have businesses?" The guidance counselor tried to explain that, as middle school students, there were other requirements that they were going to have to fulfill. "That's not fair," was one student's reply.

Overall, our students had the opportunity to participate regularly in unified arts and independent activities on our team. Both of these types of exploratories were supported by the administration.

Heterogeneous Grouping

The final activity identified by George (2008) as one of the elements of an exemplary middle school was heterogeneous grouping. Powell (2005) indicated that grouping in middle school is one of the most controversial topics. Heterogeneous grouping in the middle school is based on the notion that children are at very different levels intellectually and develop at different rates throughout their middle school years (Jackson & Davis, 2000). We used heterogeneous and homogeneous grouping. Our lowest readers were grouped together as they were part of a 90-minute reading program that was scripted. Because our students rotated as a whole class, these 20 children were together all year. The other three classes were heterogeneously grouped; more often, we moved students around due to their behavior.

We attempted grouping our students by gender on several occasions. The girls were more open to it than the boys.

- "I don't like being in a class of all guys. I miss the girls," said one boy.
- "I don't miss the guys at all," retorted a girl on her way out of another class.

Some of the girls liked the single gender classrooms but for the most part the majority of the students wanted to have mixed gender classes. One student stated, "There is too much drama when there are just girls in the classroom." The teachers also had mixed reviews of working with single gender classes. "I like the idea of working with just girls; but the boys seem to be more of a [behavior] problem when they are together without the girls," one teacher said.

Because children moved as a whole class, behavior problems existed. Comments included:

- "I love seeing my fourth period come to my classroom. The first two periods are a handful," one team member said.
- "I dread my third period. There are two students who are constant behavior problems," another team member said.

In our efforts to balance our classes behaviorally, we combined our most difficult students into one class. In December, we put together our first group of 12 students who were behavior problems.

- "Do we have to be here?" asked one child.
- "Can I move to a different class?" asked another.
- "Why do we have to stay in the same class?"

By February, eight of the students had been moved back into a regular classroom, and we added two different children to the group. All the students were placed back in "the regular" class by the end of April. Ultimately, students did not like being in our version of "in-team suspension." However, the value of this approach was that the majority of our students were not having their learning disrupted and over time most of the students adjusted their behavior. "Erin became very helpful of her classmates and began encouraging Alyssa and LaToya who struggled academically." We reflected that counseling sessions would have benefited these students.

We had a handful of students who excelled in math. The math coach worked with them for a month in January. They were taught during our scheduled Silent Reading Time. Their comments included:

- "Algebra is a lot easier than the math we are doing!"
- "Can we go to her class everyday?"
- "When are we going back?"
- "We like working with Dr. B."

These comments spoke to the desire of our brighter students to be challenged. The math coach reflected that her goal was to instill in these young people an "I can" attitude about taking math and furthermore attending college. The students who participated in this homogeneous setting were inspired and challenged by the opportunity. I saw a difference in the children as well; they worked well with students in the regular classroom while being challenged outside the regular classroom.

Final Reflections

In May we sat down as a team and reflected on the year. "I think we made a difference in our students' lives." "I don't know what I would have done without the support of our team." We talked about being more integrated and intentional about bringing math and language arts skills into all areas of the curriculum. "I would like to do more with measurement in the science class." "Now that I know the curriculum I want to integrate more reading strategies in my lessons." We talked about finding more ways to give the students movement opportunities and opportunities to serve the younger children in our school. "I think we need to plan more intentional activities if we have Wednesdays as early release days next year."

We agreed that the team concept strengthened our resolve as teachers and gave us opportunities to collaborate and care for one another and for our students. We shared that our students needed more opportunities to develop their social and emotional development and suggested that we needed to work more closely with our guidance counselors. We recognized that our students needed to move and interact with one another and that planned intramurals would benefit them. Along with teaming we felt that our strengths were in developing curriculum enrichment. Our hope was to find more ways to engage in curriculum opportunities together. Finally, we thought flexible scheduling would allow students to be grouped by ability for some experiences and grouped heterogeneously for other activities.

We no longer heard negative comments from students that were part of the beginning of the school year. We agreed that our students were learning how to live in community and we projected that their test scores would improve over time. As we began to look forward, our hope was that our students had developed a sense of belonging and trust. We looked forward to following the development of this team and the progress of our students in the years to come.

DISCUSSION AND CONCLUSION

George (2008) discussed the demise of middle school components in Florida. He shared that teaming, advisor-advisee, intramurals, curriculum enrichment, exploratories, and heterogeneous grouping activities were disappearing from middle schools. As K-8 schools emerge, it is my hope that we as middle level educators can support districts in implementing middle school activities. Our team was able to implement each of the six activities in a K-8 setting and the responses of teachers and students indicated that children developed socially and emotionally in each setting.

In his report, George (2008) called for more professional development to teach the value of these activities. In this study, teaming, curriculum enhancement, and exploratory activities were intentional. Teachers agreed that they were valuable experiences for helping our students develop socially and emotionally. I call for conversations with middle level educators to develop programs in K-8 schools that allow middle school age students to fully embrace a curriculum that includes George's (2008) activities and teaches K-8 teachers how to work together to develop responsible, productive adolescents. Based on this research I see ways to implement each of the activities in a K-8 setting.

Teaming

Teaming remains at the heart of the middle school movement (Lounsbury, 1991) and is "the signature component of high-performing schools" (NMSA, 2003, p. 29). In a K-8 setting, a team of teachers provides middle school age students with a group of adults who are subject area specialists, who are willing to work together to meet the social and emotional needs while providing enrichment and flexible grouping to meet the intellectual needs. The benefit of a K-8 school is that on the periphery of the team are multiple teachers who have supported the young people since they were children. The team of teachers ensures that young people have a nest of support while remaining in a familiar setting.

Advisor-Advisee

Working as a team, teachers and students can plan activities and leadership training for adolescents to enhance their social and emotional development (George & Lawrence, 1984). "Advocacy is not a singular event or a regularly scheduled time; it is an attitude of caring that translates into action when adults are responsive to the needs of each and every young adolescent in their charge" (NMSA, 2003, p. 16). In a K-8 setting, middle school age students are surrounded by teachers who have watched them grow up. They can be responsible for serving younger children, leading the school, and organizing community events because they have relationships with former teachers. The K-8 setting has the potential to be a place that provides students with a transition between elementary and high school with the middle school age students participating in different curriculum experiences that help them develop life skills. A school-wide Sustained Silent Reading can include older students reading to younger students. Service projects that are led by middle school age students can include adopting younger grade students, teaching middle school age students' responsibility and leadership.

Intramurals

A schoolwide focus on health and fitness in a K-8 school provides middle school age students with opportunities to engage in additional physical activities (Lee et al., 2007). School wide efforts must focus on health, wellness, and safety (NMSA, 2003). Middle school age students can promote wellness with younger students by being their buddies. When younger children learn how to be good sports, they can team up with older students to learn how to play and compete. After-school programs in a K-8 setting can include comprehensive intramural programs for middle school age students, allowing them to develop physically and interact socially with their peers.

Curriculum Enrichment

In exemplary middle level schools, curriculum is "relevant, challenging, integrative, and exploratory, from both the student's as well as the teacher's perspective" (NMSA, 2003). In a K-8 setting, the benefit of having a comprehensive media center ensures that resources span higher and lower levels of print materials. K-8 schools may have more resources that teachers and children can tap into. Middle school age students can present programs and presentations to younger students. A focus on specific interdisciplinary activities, hosted by various grade levels, engages the K-8 community with knowledge and support.

Exploratories

Middle school age students need multiple opportunities to explore (George & Lawrence, 1984). According to NMSA (2003), "exploration … most directly and fully reflects the nature and needs of young adolescents" (p. 23). Focusing on a schoolwide business model involved upper grade students leading younger students. This project allowed students to participate in running a business and working with one another. Younger grades benefited from having full time unified arts teachers who were part of the middle school curriculum.

Teams of teachers can explore ways to integrate exploration within content areas by focusing on common skills and themes. After school activities can include special topics that address students' process skills and interests. A comprehensive exploratory program can increase students' interactions with younger students in a K-8 school while increasing students' responsibility and knowledge.

Heterogeneous Grouping

With the use of technology and project based learning, students of different levels work well together in a heterogeneous setting. "Varying forms of group work are used, depending on the purpose, with students at different times clustered at random by ability, by interest, or by other criteria, always with the goal of increasing student engagement and learning" (NMSA, 2003, p. 25). Flexible scheduling allows for heterogeneous and homogeneous grouping. In a K-8 setting, younger students and older students can work with younger children to enhance their skills abilities.

Final Comments

I propose that middle school children can benefit from a K-8 setting if the activities that are planned include middle school practices. I had students who wanted to say hello to their previous year's teacher, who had younger siblings in the school, who were ready to be leaders, and who were navigating adolescent issues associated with risky behavior. As team members, we were able to communicate and collaborate together to assist our students socially and emotionally. Middle school activities in a K-8 school enhance the community of learning while focusing on the social and emotional needs of young adolescents. Middle school age students can be used as role models and serve the school while enhancing their own learning and potential. The key to success lies in leadership.

We know that leaders who have a vision for supporting middle school components impact school effectiveness (George, 2008; Hough, 2005; Myers & Robertson, 2007). Our leaders supported teaming and exploratories. However, if we look at the Schools to Watch (2009), Jackson and Davis (2000), and NMSA (2003, 2009), the literature and the research support an intentional grounding in all middle school components for schools to be successful. Furthermore, middle school curriculum and strategies must be comprehensive and intentional, designed to help teachers, administrators, and students succeed. Middle school advocates can and should develop middle school activities in K-8 schools.

REFERENCES

Anfara, V., Andrews, P., Hough, D., Mertens, S., Mizelle, N., & White, G. (2003). *Research and resources in support of this we believe*. Westerville, OH: National Middle School Association.

Arcia, E. (2007). A comparison of elementary/k-8 and middle schools' suspension rates. *Urban Education, 42*(5), 456-469.

Bogdan, R., & Biklen, S. (2007). *Qualitative research for education: An introduction to theory and methods*. Upper Saddle River, NJ: Allyn & Bacon.

Byrnes, V., & Ruby, A. (2007). Comparing achievement between k-8 and middle schools: A large-scale empirical study. *American Journal of Education, 114*(1), 101-135.

Clandinin, D., & Connelly, F. (2000). *Narrative inquiry: Experience and story in qualitative research*. San Francisco, CA: Jossey-Bass.

Clandinin, D. J., Pushor, D., & Orr, A. (2007). Navigating sites for narrative inquiry. *Journal of Teacher Education, 58*(1), 21-35.

Covey, S. (2004). *7 Habits of highly effective people*. New York, NY: Free Press.

Degon, P., & Alterio, M. (2009). *Action for healthy kids healthy kids learn better* [Handouts]. Retrieved from http://www.johnstalkerinstitute.org/wellness_symposium _handouts/vcavallaro_pdegon.pdf

Erwin, J. (2004). *The classroom of choice: Giving students what they need and getting what you want*. Alexandria, VA: Association of Supervision and Curriculum Development.

George, P. (2008). *Special report: Status of programs in Florida middle schools*. Gainesville, FL: The University of Florida and the Florida League of Middle Schools.

George, P., & Alexander, W. (2003). *The exemplary middle school*. Belmont, CA: Wadsworth/Thomson Learning.

George, P., & Lawrence, G. (1984). *Handbook for middle school teaching*. Glenview, IL: Scott Foresman.

Gewertz, G. (2004, May 19). City districts embracing k-8 schools. *Education Week, 23*(37), 20-23.

Gill, B., Engberger, J., & Booker, K. (2005). *Working report: Assessing the performance of public schools in Pittsburg*. Retrieved from Rand Organization website: http://www.rand.org/pubs/working_papers/WR315-1/

Hough, D. (1995). The elemiddle school: A model for middle grades reform. *Principal, 74*(3), 6-9.

Hough, D. (2005). The rise of the "elemiddle" school: Not every k-8 school truly applies best middle-level practices and deserves the designation. *The School Administrator, 62*(3), 10-14.

Jackson, A., & Davis, G. (2000). *Turning points 2000: Educating adolescents in the 21st century*. New York, NY: Teachers College Press.

Lee, S., Burgeson, C., Fulton, J., & Spain, C. (2007). Physical education and physical activity: Results from the school health policies and programs study 2006. *Journal of School Health, 77*(8), 435-463.

Lounsbury, J. (1991). *As I see it*. Columbus, OH: National Middle School Association.

Mastropieri, M., Scruggs, T., Norland, J., Berkeley, S., McDuffie, K., Tornquist, E., & Connors, N. (2006). Differentiated curriculum enhancement in inclusive middle school science: Effects on classroom and high-stakes tests. *Journal of Special Education, 40*(3), 130-137.

Moore, D. (1984). *Impact of school grade-organization patterns on seventh and eighth grade students in K-8 and junior high schools*. Paper presented at the annual meeting of the England Educational Research Organization, Rockport, ME. Retrieved from ERIC database. (ED245346)

Myers, N., & Robertson, S. (2007). Power in school connectedness. *School Planning and Management, 46*(1), 11.

National Forum to Accelerate Middle Grades Reform. (2009). *The forum's mission*. Retrieved from http://www.mgforum.org/Home/tabid/36/Default.aspx

National Middle School Association. (2003). *This we believe: Successful schools for young adolescents*. Westerville, OH: Author.

National Middle School Association. (2009). *The success in the middle act: HR 3006*. Retrieved from http://www.nmsa.org/Advocacy/MessagesfromNMSA/SuccessintheMiddleAct/tabid/1482/Default.aspx

O'Reilly, R., & Jarrett, J. (1980). Student involvement and the intermediate school. *Alberta Journal of Educational Research, 26*(1), 227-240.

Pardini, P. (2002). Revival of the k-8 school. *School Administrator, 59*(3), 6-12.

Patton, C. (2005). The k-8 bunch. *District Administration*, *41*(2), 44-51.

Poncelet, P., & Associates, M. (2004). Restructuring schools in Cleveland for the social, emotional, and intellectual development of early adolescents. *Journal of Education for Students Placed at Risk*, *9*(2), 81-96.

Powell, S. (2005). *Introduction to middle school*. Upper Saddle River, NJ: Prentice Hall.

Roosevelt, M. (2007, June 13). New k-8 schools in Pittsburgh see discipline problems, exits. *Education Week*, *26*(41), 6.

Scales, P., Blyth, D., Berkas, T., & Kielsmeier, J. (2000). The effects of service-learning on middle school students' social responsibility and academic success. *Journal of Early Adolescence*, *20*(3), 332-359.

Schools to Watch. (2009). *Our criteria*. Retrieved from http://www.schoolsto-watch.org/OurCriteria/tabid/118/Default.aspx

Simmons, G., Blyth, D., VanCleave, E., & Bush, D. (1979). The impact of junior high and puberty on self-esteem. *American Sociological Review*, *44*(6), 948-967.

Styron, R., & Nyman, T. (2008). Key characteristics of middle school performance. *Research in Middle Level Education*, *31*(5), 1-17. Retrieved from RMLE Online Research in Education website: http://www.nmsa.org/Publications/RMLEOnline/tabid/426/Default.aspx

Viadero, D. (2006, March 1). K-8 structure gives no academic boost, analysis finds. *Education Week*, *25*(25), 5-7.

Whitley, J., Lupart, J., & Beran, T. (2007). Differences in achievement between adolescents who remain in a k-8 school and those who transition to a junior high school. *Canadian Journal of Education*, *30*(3), 649-669.

Weiss, C., & Kipnes, L. (2006). Reexamining middle school effects: A comparison of middle grades students in middle schools and k-8 schools. *American Journal of Education*, *112*(2), 239-272.

Yenke, C. (2006). Mayhem in the middle school: Why we should shift. *Educational Leadership*, *63*(7), 20-25.

Zemelman, S., Daniels, H., & Hyde, A. (2005). *Best practices*. Portsmouth, NH: Heinemann.

CHAPTER 14

"SIT TIGHT"

The Uneasy Alliance Between Freedom and Control in the Middle School Classroom

Ruth Vinz

This chapter describes how 4 English language arts middle school teachers use *reconstructing narratives* to examine their classroom interactions and instructional practices. The teachers set out to understand how, or if, their practices align with the school's stated values of collaborative, project-based, and student-centered learning. By writing narratives about their classrooms, they discovered inherent contradictions and competing intentions that define their work. Their examination highlights the incongruence between teachers' intentions, practices, and the school's stated commitments; it also exposes the teaching dilemmas that underlie their continued investigations. The teachers and the researcher produced provisional knowledge that emphasizes the uneasy alliance between the perceived need to control students and the desire to create spaces of freedom in which students can take some control of their own learning. This chapter demonstrates an attempt to use narrative inquiry to conduct research *with* rather than *on* teachers.

Voices From the Middle: Narrative Inquiry By, For, and About the Middle Level Community
pp. 287–314

OPENING THE STORY

From my subway stop in Manhattan, it takes just over an hour to the station nearest Thurgood Middle School in the South Bronx. All is quiet here at 7:15 A.M. By afternoon, students rush out the school doors, happy to have a few daylight hours before homework and sleep. One subway car after another picks up and releases the swelling crowds to the accompaniment of a hydraulic hiss. This neighborhood is notorious for street corner drug trades by mid-afternoon. But mornings, it is silent and hopeful with the start of a new day. Kitchen lights glow, and I can almost hear the clink of dishes. A dog barks. Dark windows in one apartment—people still sleeping, I think. A starling flits from one branch to another. The middle schoolers I'll see in less than an hour are showering, fighting for the bathroom, looking in the mirror, or putting in a second earring. Somewhere a mother is braiding her daughter's hair.

From the alley near the school, Denise Langer, the sixth-grade English language arts (ELA) teacher emerges, a book bag in hand. "Come on," she says as she points down the street. "We have time for a café con leche." This morning I come to the school to be what Denise calls "an extra pair of eyes and ears." The ELA teachers and I met three times in the past 2 weeks to examine their teaching practices. They are particularly interested in the effect of their teaching on their 350-plus middle school students. The ELA teaching team, Florence Mentor (fifth grade); Denise Langer (sixth grade); Rashid Boyd (seventh grade); and Daniel Sanchez (eighth grade), expressed frustration with their students' seeming inability to participate in inquiry and project-based learning and collaborative projects. These teachers are trying to figure out why the students appear to prefer skills and drills teaching. The teachers asked me to join them in collaborative inquiry in an effort to understand their interactions with students and to identify the reasons for students' resistance.

We agree to take a narrative approach to our inquiry. The idea of narrative knowing draws from several disciplines, including psychology (Bruner, 1986, 1990; Polkinghorne, 1988), anthropology (Bateson, 1994), and literary theory (Coles, 1989; Nussbaum, 1990). The application of narrative to the study of teaching is still an emerging and evolving area of inquiry that encourages teachers to tell and reflect on their stories of teaching (Barone, 2000; Clandinin, Pushor, & Orr, 2007). Narrative inquiry in education focuses on the storied nature of teaching and learning and emphasizes the ways in which teachers and students make sense of and interpret events, behaviors, and outcomes. The emphasis is on "lived experience—that is, in lives and how they are lived" (Clandinin & Connelly, 2000, p. xxii). Further:

Narrative inquiry, the study of experience as story, then, is first and foremost a way of thinking about experience. Narrative inquiry as a methodology entails a view of the phenomenon. To use narrative inquiry methodology is to adopt a particular narrative view of experience as phenomena under study. (Connelly & Clandinin, 2006, p. 477)

Interpretation of and reflection on stories takes a central place in this way of thinking about narrative inquiry.

RECONSTRUCTING NARRATIVES OF CLASSROOM EXPERIENCES

According to Ely, Vinz, Downing, and Anzul (1997) and Vinz (1996, 1997), narrative inquiry places emphasis on the *telling of* the story as well as *how* it is told. I consider the *act of narrativizing* an essential way of understanding or making meaning of experience. As Nussbaum (1990) explains, "certain truths about human life can only be fittingly and accurately stated in the language and forms characteristic of the narrative artist" (p. 5). In keeping with this belief, I recommend to the Thurgood teachers that we use *reconstructing narratives* as our primary method of inquiry, writing narratives as a portal to representing and understanding experience.

I volunteer to spend several weeks observing in their classrooms and producing narrative accounts of each visit. The four ELA teachers commit themselves to write their own narratives for the same classes I observe. That is, we each write a narrative that presents our version of the class events. We agree to write in present or present progressive tense in order to live "in the moment." I use the term *reconstructing narratives* to emphasize temporality in the (re)storying process where past, present, and future unite in refractive prisms, each intensifying and casting light on the others. The ways in which we each construct our narratives is an important link to the ways we construct, order, and understand our lives. When creating narratives *as if* they were occurring in the moment, the narrative capacity to reason and to search out paradoxes is heightened. The idea of reconstructing, then, is intended to suspend the events of past, present, and future in a dynamic interaction of an imagined present "in motion."

PAUSING TO PROVIDE CONTEXT AND SETTING

The English education program, in which I am a professor, began a partnership with Thurgood Middle School in 2007 when we placed a student teacher with Daniel Sanchez, a graduate of our program (the names of the school and teachers are pseudonyms). Daniel was the first to recommend the formation of an ELA inquiry team to understand why "students resist putting themselves out there and taking some risks in expressing what they are learning. They are self-conscious at this age, but there is something more."

Denise adds, "They don't want to speak out and have conversations that reveal anything about what they are thinking."

Rashid counters, "Not that they won't say anything; it's just they don't want to participate in discussions or in group collaborations."

The fourth teacher, Florence, offers this critique, "The relatively few students participating seem less passive and conforming. Sometimes they are actually the most difficult ones to control." For me, despite or perhaps because of their immediate critique of the students, I recognize the importance of focusing on the complexities of what is going on so that student resistance does not become the normative explanation for the difficulties of implementing goals established by the school's administration and faculty.

Thurgood Middle School was created in 2006 following the break-up of a comprehensive K-8. Thurgood is a middle school (Grades 5-8) and shares the building with two other middle schools. The combined population of the three schools is approximately 900 students. Thurgood is housed on the first floor of a three-story building. The students attending the other two schools walk through Thurgood's hallways on their way to the staircases that lead to their classrooms on the second and third floors. The security dilemma this poses intensifies the sense of vigilance and watchfulness at Thurgood. The students, staff, and faculty are always "on edge."

When Thurgood Middle School opened, its faculty supported a project-based and collaborative learning curriculum and made a commitment to focus their professional development agenda on learning the requisite practices. Thurgood Middle School's mission statement promises to "create, promote, and sustain a school community where collective responsibility and action result in holistic learning and each student will make contributions to school knowledge and culture." The ELA teachers were charged with developing curricula that relied on group research projects, a writing workshop model, and an independent reading program.

Although Florence, Denise, Rashid, and Daniel agree in principle with these emphases, they struggle with the day-to-day implementation. In our first meeting, they ask the following questions. How might we better support students' development of key habits that will enhance their abilities to work on collaborative projects and inquiry-based learning? What are the causes of students' resistance to ways of teaching that foster collaborative projects? How can I reconcile my own beliefs and strengths as a teacher with the schoolwide goals? After this initial meeting, I begin my classroom observations. What follows are my narratives.

STEPPING INTO THE MIDDLE OF CLASSROOM LIFE

Denise Langer: "I Feel Like a Stranger in an Otherwise Familiar Place"

Denise and I take a final gulp of the steaming coffee and head for the school. "I was going to offer you a little preview to my attempt at literature circles today. Would you sit at the far table with Edgar and that group?" Denise's voice trails off.

"It's okay, Denise. You don't have to talk about this now unless you want. We will have time after …"

Daniel meets us on the steps of the school. "¿Qué pasa?"

Denise turns to see if anyone is within earshot. "I'm really tired of my first period. It's so hard … they just aren't interested and get out of hand. What a way to start the day, and I just don't understand them. It's just like I'm a stranger to them and they don't care what I'm thinking or asking or saying. I feel like a stranger in an otherwise familiar place."

Daniel nods and pulls Denise against his neck. "So you two are conspiring how to adolescent-proof that group?" We open the huge steel door and it bangs closed behind us. The halls in front of us emerge out of darkness, empty and cold.

By 8:10 we settle into Denise's classroom. Every move sounds hollow and echoes across the desks placed neatly in quads. The bulletin board has poster portraits of Walter Dean Myers, Sharon Creech, and Lois Duncan. Index cards, written by students, make recommendations to other students about why they might want to read a book by one of these authors. A classroom set of Myers' (1988) *Scorpions* tops the bookcases. A stack of journals partially obscures the view of an abandoned basketball court. The gate is chained. The students are not allowed to use the area since several fights broke out among adolescents from the three schools who share this building. I look at the cracking concrete, the deteriorating nets, the emptiness and wonder how different it would look and sound right now if kids had access before school. I miss the adolescent vibe and energy and bantering. I take a minute to listen to the silence and then fill the court with my own version of the sounds, movements, and smells of adolescents.

"I worked until after midnight last night and still didn't get all the planning and papers done." Denise is in her second year of teaching, and she says when she turns out the lights and settles the blankets over her, she sometimes hears herself wondering if she chose the right calling. Her word, "calling." Her sixth graders, who are rumored to be the "worst group we've ever had here" by the veteran faculty, begin to fill the room.

Keisha drags through the door with a loud sigh. "Miss…Miss…what we doin' today?"

"Shhh," Miss Langer motions toward the desks. "I'm in conversation. Can't you see that? Keep quiet and wait your turn."

Jamal is right behind Keisha. "Miss, we got time to finish readin'?" Keisha turns away with an adolescent's scornful "whatever" look and punches at Jamal's arm.

"Keep your hands to yourself, Keisha. Don't start something. Please get your journals and sit down." By now, another dozen voices fill the room and a couple of boys stroll through the room, hands on hips, drawn to the scent of girls.

"*Now,*" Miss Langer commands. "Everyone should be in a desk with your journal open. I'll only say this prompt once so you need to listen up." Her gaze sweeps the room. "Hat off, Mr. Gillian. You know." Guillermo has Janice in an arm lock. Miss Langer walks by and points at each desk. "Enough Mr. Branch. Janice needs to open her journal. *Now.*" Giggles grace the room. Miss Langer's footsteps resound as she goes to the front of the room. "Get yourselves under control. First, a free write." These adolescents fidget, wriggle, and, reluctantly open journals and scramble for pens. "Well, I see Felicia is ready." Miss Langer points toward a small girl in the corner. Felicia's head goes down. Miss Langer doesn't seem to notice her embarrassment. "Let me remind you that today you must give me the topic for your project and who you decided to work with."

Samuel interjects, "I got no one to work with. Can I do it myself?"

"Not now, Samuel. Hold that thought. We will journal first. Look at me," Miss Langer says. "All eyes up here. I'm waiting." After the free write, students move to their literature circles.

"You each have the same roles as yesterday, so let's have the discussion leader start you off. Be sure you have your charts out and you are ready to make notes."

If you are in the room with me now, you see the red-headed girl in the back quad trying to get control of the other three in her group. The boy with a comb locked in his dreads pokes his index finger in the air and sketches a triangle into the ceiling. Tessie's red curls bob up and down as she pleads with Leonard to open the book lying on the desk in front of him. He sighs and opens to some random page, then, closes his eyes and puts his head down on the desk. Tessie manages her group like the teachers she has learned from.

"Why do you think Phoebe and Sal become friends?" No takers. "Well, do you think Sal wants to see her mother?" Silence. "Why do you think Sal's mom left?" Edgar still has not opened his book, but he does respond. "Because Sal's always askin' questions, just like *you*!" Giggles from the group. Leonard's head bobs back up and he says, "Who's Sal? I haven't read that yet." Tessie's group is reading Sharon Creech's (1994) *Walk Two Moons*. Lara, the fourth member of the group, delivers a gift. "I think that as the grandparents tell stories along the way, Sal gets to learn about her mother and she doesn't know what to feel right now."

Tessie arches her back and suggests to Lara that she write that on their chart paper. Edgar slumps and turns to see where Miss Langer is. Edgar is preparing for a slow collision with Miss Langer. He rips one strip of paper after another into a pile and ignores the ensuing conversation. Denise is working the room, answering questions, entreating those who aren't participating—"focus on the job at hand," "look at that page again," "keep your eyes on your group," "get your chart and pen," "shhh," "quiet," "can you prove what you said?" "help out," "keep your hands to yourself"— each is a fragment of a larger mosaic, adding image to image, word to word in a never-ending squabble for control and focus. Miss Langer advances down the central aisle. Edgar rips the strips faster and into smaller pieces. Tessie and Lara and the boy with the comb in his hair keep listing details of what they've learned. Edgar drops one small square on the floor and Miss Langer's eyes lock on him. "Come on, Edgar," Denise moves toward him. With a sweep of his hand, the paper strips fall like confetti to the floor. In a steady, determined voice, Denise commands, "Pick up that mess. Now!" All eyes are on Denise and Edgar. There will be no more discussion of books in the remaining few minutes of class.

If you walk the halls with me as I leave Denise's room, you hear Miss Rogers in Room 103 on the right listing directions for tonight's assignment. In Room 105, Mr. Burnett's students have packed up their books and are drumming fingers, waiting for the bell that will signal their movement to the next class. Miss Gottlieb's math class is checking a last problem. Florence Mentor is asking for volunteers to read from their journals. At this moment, you see order and quiet. You hear your own breathing.

The bell rings and the halls erupt with voices, laughter, motion, and excitement. I hear Devon and Samuel talking as they race down the hall, antsy to be on the move. Samuel swipes at Devon's head. Samuel gets right into his face. They are laughing. The security guard is on top of them. "Easy, boys, easy." The school discourages touching. The boys back off and look at each other. They fidget. I move a little to the right as they race through Florence's door.

One girl whirls around and gives me an open-mouth grin. "I'm Ande. I was just in Miss Langer's class with you." She has dark brown hair springing in loose curls. Her friend joins her by nuzzling against Ande's arm. No guard appears. "What'd you think of our class? Edgar's out of control, right?" I tell her I think each group has chosen a very interesting book to read and I want to know her choice. "*Holes*," she responds, "I'm reading *Holes* (Sachar, 2000). That Edgar. He's there to entertain us." The girls slide into a room next to where I am headed.

Florence Mentor: "There's the Pressure of Never Enough Time"

The classroom door bangs open and Florence Mentor greets the two boys coming in with me. "Good morning, boys." She eyes the clock. "Time's a wasting." She gestures for me to come in.

"Can I go to the bathroom?" It's Leticia asking.

"A few minutes, please," says Miss Mentor. "I want to get class started first."

Principal Burris walks into the room. "Can I borrow José for a few minutes?" José lifts his head from his desk.

Miss Mentor sighs. "I hate to let him go. He needs to be here. I'm just trying to get everyone on task."

Mr. Burris nods, "He's the only one who saw that confrontation with the kids from the third floor. I need to talk with him. I'm just hoping he kept his hands and mouth to himself on this one. I don't want trouble from that group. They're out of control! I'll get José back soon." He beckons to José to follow him.

Miss Mentor can't pinpoint the anxiety she feels, punctuated sometimes with a feeling of frenzy. "There is the pressure of never enough time. I can't possibly teach everything the students need to learn." In an earlier conversation she queried: "How do I make choices? How do I streamline the learning? The collaborative and inquiry learning just isn't time efficient. Then, I think, shame on you!" Florence is in her third year of teaching. She lists all the impediments to keeping students on the task of learning: students pulled from class, others taking their sweet time to focus and get started, collaborative work that takes more time to control students than to help them with their work. Everything eats up the time. Every time Florence looks at the clock the hands move at breathtaking speed.

Miss Mentor asks students to begin each class with a free write which helps "settle them into their desks and gives me a minute to get focused. It saves time in the end, I think." Henry, twelve years old, is already writing in his journal as I sit at the desk next to him. He is writing about and sketching snakes. He imagines himself walking through a garden, through the gnarls and snags of bramble and the rocky ledges, just walking while the snakes slumber. Henry is mentally far from the classroom as he writes. He is also thinking about the basketball game after school, wondering if he can make just one basket—for Leticia. He thinks of her smile. As he walks on the ledge through his words, he is determined to push on until the snake appears. He wants to describe the remote shimmer and the feeling of the quickening heart. He winces at Miss Mentor's voice.

"One more minute. Hurry now. End those sentences. We have work to do." Henry is startled back into the classroom. He didn't quite make it to the encounter with the snake. He goes back to make a steep ascent into the rocks, gets caught in a thicket, and trips. "Henry. What did I just say? Close the notebook. Let's move on."

Moving on requires the students to abandon whatever they were writing to join their research teams. "Let's get into your research teams. I want you to start today with a share out of what you learned about your topic last night. Hurry. Let's not waste time. Get into your groups. Eyes on each other now."

Miss Mentor walks down the aisle as students drag their desks into smaller configurations. When she passes one group, she closes Henry's journal, points to Sam to get out his materials, and pats Sarah on the shoulder. She settles each group with her presence. She scans the room. Groups have formed; most students have their research notebook open on their desks. Henry pulls his journal out again. After all, his research and free writes have become one and the same.

"Now, spend the next 20 minutes sharing what you've learned. Be sure everyone gets equal time. Have someone monitor the time. Okay? You all ready?" Miss Mentor sees José come back in. Her mouth tightens. "José put a move on. Take your seat. We're ready to share."

"What are we supposed to write down?" Lucille asks.

Miss Mentor lowers her head. "Just ask questions of each other. See if you can help each other think about what to research next or what questions to ask. Just help each other out. Write down anything that will help you remember what to research tonight."

"But what if I don't have any questions?" Luke's question triggers four other hands to reach toward the ceiling.

"Enough for now; time's wasting. Just give each other some help and we'll check on progress in about 15 minutes. Hurry now. Let's get started." Miss Mentor takes a deep breath. "Please, decide who will start in each group and get going. The clock is ticking."

By the time everyone shares there are 10 minutes of class time left. "Let's review what you should do tonight. Take the questions from your group and try to find answers. Tomorrow we'll have some time to begin writing a rough draft. So keep researching tonight. "Was your group helpful to you?" Fidgets and small movements. "Give me an example of a question someone asked that will help you research tonight." James looks down. Sarah eyes the door.

"Help me here. What's a good example of help from your group?"

I can usually predict who will finally speak first, but this time I am caught off guard. It is Henry. "Leticia asked me why some snakes are poisonous and others aren't. She wondered if some had other ways of defending themselves. I'll look for that tonight."

Miss Mentor looks relieved. "Great example, Henry. Good question, Leticia. You see? That's how good groups work together."

Now, the infamous bell. Students burst out of the room. The security guards interrupt the usual banter in the halls with their "move along quietly" gestures. Lockers line the wall but are chained shut. Teachers stand outside their classroom doors, smiling, engaging in small talk, moving students along. All this is done in a friendly and quiet manner. "Keep a lid on the hall movements and be sure it's only our kids," Principal Burris says. The halls empty. Students are at their desks and the teachers take a collective sigh. Everything is under control again.

Rashid Boyd: "You Know, the Out-of-Control Dream"

For Rashid Boyd, a first-year teacher of seventh grade, almost any movement becomes out-of-control. He dreams about this. "You know, the out-of-control dream." He's learned the hard way. One day last week when I was getting to know his classes, a group of girls in his fourth period attempted to pass Darren's journal to another girl. "Don't touch me," Mary shrieks as he grabs for it. Darren holds his arm right above her head. He might bring it down flat on top of her head or swing it ever so slightly to the left and hit her mouth. He might lower his arm and shrug his shoulders. Mr. Boyd grabs his arm; Darren jerks away. "Don't touch me!"

"Don't push me," I hear Mr. Boyd say. The group breaks up and students head back to their desks. Mr. Boyd and Darren stand their ground. "In your seat or out the door." Darren looks left, then right. The door slams behind him.

Today, Mr. Boyd begins class with a question: "Do you think Willie Bodega's dream is realistic?" Students are reading *Bodega Dreams* by Ernesto Quinonez (2000). Mr. Boyd tried to establish literature circles early in the school year but thought that he might have better luck "keeping all the students focused on one thing that is of high interest to them. I'm just not skilled enough yet to have all those balls in the air at once. It's hard to plan and to keep the kids in line and doing what they've been asked to do. I'll work gradually toward that."

Mr. Boyd asks again. "Help me here. Look up here. All eyes on my pencil. I'll ask once more. Are Willie Bodega's dreams realistic?"

If we hold this scene still a moment, here's what you will notice: All eyes are on Mr. Boyd but no one is answering his question. It is noon. After-lunch lethargy fogs the room. There is a knock at the door. "Excuse me, Mr. Boyd. Can I see Stephanie?" The students are chatting again.

Mr. Boyd restates the question again after Stephanie leaves. "Again, are Willie Bodega's dreams realistic? We aren't going anywhere, so answer up."

Finally, Jillian blurts out, "He stepped out of his family tradition and made money. If it's drug money, does it matter? That doesn't change the dream. He's the Robin Hood and has a good purpose."

From two separate parts of the room we hear groans and comments: "That don't make it right!" "He's fixing up Harlem. We need him in the Bronx!" Laughter. "We take some of that, too," Miguel blurts out. "Bodega gets rid of that loser Fischman whose takin' all the loot." "Yeah, but de woman gets in the way. Vera, Vera and there goes Bodega forgettin." "His head in his pants." They are on a roll. Gesturing. Laughing. Pointing at crotches. Lucille stands up and wiggles her bum.

"Okay, enough," says Mr. Boyd. "Let's cool this down. You're getting out of the story and my question."

"Mister, mister. Uh, Sir. He fall on his little love knees to Vera and loses everything." Hands shoot up and the side banter starts. Comments come from everywhere and sexual energy fills the room. Some think Bodega loses the dream for the girl; others think he was really just a druggie; others see him as the Robin Hood. All seem to agree that he failed. I wonder where Mr. Boyd will take this roiling mass of opinion and energy.

"Shhh … shhh … shhh. No side conversations. Knees forward and facing me. My question: Was the dream realistic? You aren't answering that. Slow it down. Take a breath. Miguel, eyes here. Stop talking to each other now. Let's settle in. Let's take a few minutes and you can write down your response to the question."

Terence is agitated. "I had something else to say. Why can't we say more?"

"Put it in the parking lot," Mr. Boyd tells him. "Write about it. Okay, next ten minutes. Just write. No talking. I mean it. Settle down."

As I write about this moment, I remember something else: The question doesn't lead to any particular understanding or resolution by the end of class. Students have lost interest in Bodega's story and dream. They've written, shared out in some haphazard manner. Now, their notebooks and pencils are packed up. Some fidget; others send hand signals to each other; Simon reads a book; Michael plays a computer game, hiding his hand-held device under his desk. Mr. Boyd surveys the room. "Good job, today. Good work. Finish Bodega tonight and we'll continue discussion tomorrow. Okay, don't forget." Tap. Tap. Tap. His finger points to the assignment on the board. Everyone is waiting for the bell.

Daniel Sanchez: "I Really Love Them Out of Their Desks and on Their Feet"

"Hi," I call as I walk into Room 109. Books line the window ledge; the desks are pushed back to make room for an impromptu stage. A canvas backdrop covers one sidewall. Brush strokes of tempera have turned the blank canvas into a small town—a doorway to the courtyard, a town square of green and benches and monuments, and small storefronts. A high fence. A few townspeople are sketched in. On the adjacent whiteboard turned billboard, the name of the play, *The Mockingbird Monologues*, lettered carefully in red. Yellow bursts of tempera almost look like they are blinking. A courtroom scene fills the upper right corner; in the left lower corner, a girl swings in moonlight. A hush pervades the room. Daniel steps out of the closet. His arms are overflowing with props. "Can't wait for you to see these guys. They are really into this."

Daniel is in his fifth year of teaching. He learned about the *Mockingbird Monologues* from one of the student teachers in our program, who learned from an instructor who created the project 15 years ago. The purpose of the *Monologues* is to introduce these adolescent readers to the characters' experiences and motivations. As Daniel notes, "Atticus Finch says in the novel that you really can't know another person's point of view until you climb into his skin and walk around." The project takes various iterations throughout classrooms across the country now, and, Daniel, who claims to be "a sponge for good ideas," worked with his student teacher to develop the project last year. This year, he is honing and refining this into a project that combines literature and history. "There is so much hope in this," he says. "I really love them out of their desks and on their feet."

The students begin to arrive. First Jeffrey, then Rosa followed by Timmy. They begin grabbing props. "Careful now," Mr. Sanchez cautions. "Settle down. Don't get wild with those. Start organizing yourself for the performances." Each student has studied one of the nearly 30 characters in the book and has written an original monologue on some aspect of that character's life. These monologues take into account what students conjecture from both explicit and implicit information in the novel. In addition, the students spent two weeks researching historical details, beliefs, race relations, and the history of Alabama in the 1930s.

The research complete, the monologues written, experimentation with voices, tone, and gestures practiced, the setting painted, and the rehearsals over—now, the performance fills a two-hour block with other classes invited to watch. The room is a hive of excitement. Costumes come out of the closet. A small group of students has the stage makeup kits and begins working on actors' faces. Banter starts in one corner as two boys grab for the same hat. "Put a lid on it," Mr. Sanchez warns. "Let's go. Keep moving. We need to get started in five minutes. Keep your focus."

The room transforms. Suddenly Nathan Radley and Calpurnia stand talking in the corner. Atticus calls to Braxton Underwood to help him with his tie. Helen Robinson asks Mr. Sanchez if she can rehearse a few lines with Scout. "Not enough time, now. We are on a tight schedule. Everyone now, eyes on me. Settle down. I'm the star now. Eyes right here. Stop whatever you're doing." He waits, hand in the air. Each student raises a hand and, finally, even the stragglers join in. The room is silent. "Okay. Listen up. Miss Jensen's class is on the way. Take your places. Freeze frame. Don't move until they are seated and then we'll begin."

As if for one last break in the tension, Jeffrey punches Rosa's arm and leads her to the middle of the classroom. "Let me begin by saying Rosa's got to be in the middle because she starts first." The classroom door opens and other adolescents spill in. "Shhh," "quiet," "take a seat" are the teacher's commands.

Mr. Sanchez takes control. "Thanks for visiting us today. This is a play. You know how to behave when you are in an audience. Let the play begin."

The overhead lights dim and four floodlights go on. Rosa, speaking as Helen, stands in the middle of the backdrop and begins talking about loss and death. Damon, as Boo Radley, is next. His squared, set jaw, muscular neck, and stubby fingers suggest the tension within this character. It is as if a version of Boo emanates from this adolescent. I hold my breath. For a moment I think he might fly out of his skin and leap or run beyond the walls of superstition and mean-spiritedness that contained him for so long. Damon is a 13-year-old eighth grader and usually wears a hoodie and jeans. Here, now, in this moment, he is Boo Radley and the classroom erupts with applause as he exits center stage.

The play ends with a curtain call as the characters from Lee's *To Kill a Mockingbird* (1960) recede into the background and eighth graders, shedding costumes and wiping off face paint, reappear. Props disappear into the closets. Costumes are stuffed into backpacks. The bell rings. Students revel in the energy of the moment.

Later I pass Daniel in the hall. "I can't sustain this kind of thing all the time. I just can't keep up this level of energy and work. I'm exhausted," he says.

INTERSECTING NARRATIVES:
THE TEACHERS' VERSIONS OF EVENTS

There are alternative readings to my narratives. The teachers' versions exist as another perspective on the class sessions I described. The five of us exchanged narratives and read them. Principal Burris set aside a block of two and a half hours on Friday afternoons for departmental meetings. We used this time to discuss our first narrative renderings. We all agreed to write our narratives in *third person*. For the teachers, this was a way to relive their classroom experience by standing back as observers. We all titled our narratives to illustrate some meaning discovered through the writing. Excerpts from both the teachers' narrative reconstructions and their discussion of the narratives follow.

Excerpts From Denise's Narrative:
Learning From Experience

We begin our discussion by focusing on Denise's classroom. Daniel points out that my version and Denise's have some "intersecting points." Denise responds by suggesting that the two narratives together "heighten the sense of where to focus attention." Florence adds that "we each engage differently and bring our partial understandings to the classroom but the overlapping themes and ideas stand out when two versions are read side by side." Denise begins her narrative with a description of her students:

> As they come through the door, Denise sees small bundles of adolescent energy just waiting for an opportunity to explode. Keisha bolts through the door with the same question she asks every day. Keisha surely knows how the day will start. It's the same every day. Denise has built a routine and is frustrated that students cannot seem to settle into it. It's just attention Keisha wants. The tag team questions from Keisha and Jamal are just about enough to drive Denise from the room screaming. Denise thinks if she just had this better organized and the students were self-motivated they wouldn't need to ask these questions. She is disappointed by the realization that she is a crutch and not a facilitator for her students' learning. Denise turns to Ruth, Denise feels a bit embarrassed by her own request."

In the section that follows, Denise describes her confrontation with Edgar.

> "So what will he do now?" Denise notices that Edgar is tearing up small bits of paper. She continues her conversation with Laura. Laura asks for clarifi-

cation on what she needs to do to catch up from the two days she was absent. Denise can't concentrate now. She watches Edgar but nods at Laura. She can't remember what happened two days ago in class. Not now. Her focus is on Edgar. "Ask Jena for the assignments; she is in your circle." Denise feels the energy seep out of her. These literature circles aren't working out, she is thinking. The students are going through the motions and taking on their roles but they aren't really engaged with the other students or what they are reading. Mel raises his hand. Denise moves his way. "What are we supposed to be doing?" he asks. Denise is focused on Edgar. "What is he planning?" drums through her head as she realizes she hasn't answered Mel's question.

Denise walks toward Edgar. She reaches for him before he sprinkles all that paper on the floor. Just as she reaches for Edgar's hand, he sends the confetti scattering. Everyone is laughing. Denise feels that this is just another example that she doesn't have the control, and, frankly, right now doesn't want it.

As the five of us discuss the two narratives of Denise's class, we notice that Denise focuses on her thoughts and feelings of uncertainty. Her title, "Learning from Experience" underlines her determination to take action and set some goals as a result of what she was learning. Denise indicates that in writing the narrative she recognizes her inability to focus on individual students and on the class at the same time. What she notices from her reading of my narrative is all the ways she uses words to keep control of the students. She reflects on this need for control during our discussion:

I'm giving commands more than I'm teaching the kids how to do what I'm asking them to do. The kids would be more self reliant if they know how to work together, how to begin journal entries, how to start a discussion. I just tell them to do these things. I'm not modeling for them. My narrative reminds me how much of the time I am focused on myself and not on the students. I'm concentrating on how the students aren't meeting my expectations.

Denise proposes a plan of action. We discuss ways for her to fine-tune the journal writing routine that starts each class period if she intends to keep the journal as the daily starting point. "I've been *telling* students and not *showing* them." Her colleagues suggest ways to share her journal with the students, how students might share excerpts from their writing with the class, and how she might incorporate their homework into the journal writing. Denise has the last word about her plans.

I am not sure what to do to start the class, but I know I can't keep doing what I'm doing. I'm *policing* the kids, not *involving* them. I've learned that by really looking into my classroom. She laughs, of course, I also learned that I can't have direct confrontations with students. The Edgar moment is so embarrassing. I learned from that experience that you don't take the bait when it is dangling out there.

Excerpts From Florence's Narrative: "Focusing on the Adolescents"

As the five of us focus attention on the two narratives of Florence's class, our talk turns to how both narratives reveal the tenacity of the ticking clock that shapes and controls instruction for Florence. As Denise points out, "As I read the descriptions of what Florence does and says, I'm reminded how the school and how I as a teacher measure the passage of time. Think of all the phrases—a waste of time, time on task, and wait time—to name a few." From the first sentence of her narrative, Florence evokes her awareness of time:

> Florence feels the pressure of not enough time to keep the research teams moving forward but she also senses the sham of time she has created. The journal writing at the beginning of class is often a waste of time. Florence uses it as a way to "buy" herself a few minutes to get the students settled and to get her refocused from what seems the constant movement from one class to the next. She wishes she found more value in it. Mostly she monitors students. She hears herself saying, "Just try another sentence or two. There must be something you want to write about. Just three focused minutes of your time." Florence gets everyone settled when Mr. Burris interrupts the quiet. He wants to talk with José and it makes Florence think that José will be even further behind than he already is.
>
> Florence asks the students to get into their teams. At least four students object and want to work alone. Robert whispers to her that his group doesn't like his idea and is making fun of him. Florence squeezes his shoulders and suggests that he just try one more time. "Just try and I'll keep my eye on Erick. I know he is a tease. I'll watch. Just try. Let's go. No more wasting time." Walter's hand is fluttering toward the ceiling. Florence knows he'll ask to go to the bathroom. It's his way of getting 10 minutes free time. Florence ignores him and stops to talk with Nadia. Nadia can't think of questions for her project on ballerinas. Walter's hand is still waving and now he has added his, "Miss, Miss, Miss … it's im-*por*-tant. now, please." Florence cannot concentrate enough to help Nadia. "What about asking what the age range is for a professional ballerina? Or, how many hours do ballerinas practice each day?" Nadia seems satisfied and Florence closes in on Walter.
>
> "Give me one question on your research project and you get a bathroom pass." Walter goes limp. His jaw goes slack.
>
> "I can't think of one, Miss. You tell me. What's a question about astronauts? Give me one hint." By now Florence realizes there are only ten minutes left of class. Let me just check in to see if they accomplished *anything*,

she is thinking. She wonders what they have learned today. They aren't asking questions. They really aren't interested in working together.

"Let's review homework for tonight. Take the questions from your group
and try to find answers. Think about the questions from your group. Give
me an example of a good question." Florence waits and *no one* answers.
Please, let's hear a question. Florence is surprised that Henry volunteers.
She realizes she didn't know what he was researching until now. And, he
seems genuinely interested. She promises herself to check in with him
tomorrow.

As we discuss the two narratives of Florence's class, Rashid asks her to
talk about why she thinks that she never has enough time. Rashid laughs
when he says, "Sometimes I want time to pass more quickly and here you
are trying to slow it down."
Florence responds:

As I was writing my narrative, I realized how much I am controlled by my
feelings that there just isn't enough time. I'm starting to think how these little blocks of time don't give the students sustained time. When I read what
Ruth wrote, it seems I'm carving the day into tiny pieces and the students
just have to come along and wax and wane any interest or energy to meet
my next directive. Here was Henry who had put some of these little pieces
together, and I just didn't notice how he was working.

As the discussion continues, Florence points out that she feels guilty when
she realizes that she isn't really noticing students and isn't developing
relationships with them.

I can see that I haven't really been thinking of them. I haven't worked to
build relationships with them. I don't laugh much at their humor and
antics. I wanted to teach middle school students because I love their energy
and now I am trying to resist their energy.

This was a "eureka" moment for these young teachers. They spent
another 20 minutes talking about how much they focus on their own need
to maintain control and forget that these adolescents are filled with curiosity, desires, and knowledge that are not always nurtured in the classroom. Florence certainly made a promise to be more vigilant.

I will keep the Henry factor in mind here. I want relationships with these
students. I want to know what they are thinking and what interests them. I
didn't realize that I sometimes forgot they were in the room with me and the
clock!

Excerpts From Rashid's Narrative:
Creating an Environment Conducive to Learning

The introspective work continues as we turn to Rashid's narratives. He begins our discussion by reminding us that "It is hard to take it all in. I slip immediately into my out of control feelings!" His narrative provides evidence of this focus. He writes:

Rashid is living his out of control dream again!!! He begins by asking students what seems like a simple question: Is Willie Bodega's dream realistic? Rashid has decided that whole class instruction may be best for now. Rashid realizes that even with the whole group novel, attention is fractured. He plays the words fractured and fragmented off his tongue. The question about Willie hangs in the room. Rashid has the students' eyes on him. He uses the "eyes on my pencil" and "eyes on me" and the "knees forward" that he learned from a veteran teacher. But, what he wasn't taught or didn't learn was how to get these young students' minds focused.

The knock at the door is a relief from the silence for a moment. Stephanie slips out of the room and Rashid tries to get the students back before they start side conversations. "What about Willie?" he asks again. Jillian answers. She thinks Willie is a Robin Hood and that sets all the students chattering. And with one student shouting out over others, the whole conversation suddenly turns from who Willie is to what he does for Vera and then the sexual connotations start. Rashid is working hard to gain control. "Okay. Help me here. Cool down." He knows they have left the question behind. Rashid wonders how to get back on track. What's a way to get their energy? By now the students are in side conversations. Even though most are talking about the book, they seem out of control. How can Rashid harness this energy and keep the conversation going? He starts thinking: What if I move them quickly into groups and create a character map of Willie? What if I ask them to write a letter from Willie to Vera? Would that just stay sexual since they are thinking that way now? What if I ask them to divide into groups and write a character sketch on Willie?

Rashid is just not sure where to move next and the students are getting further away from the question. Rashid has ideas swirling in his mind for what to do next, but nothing seems right. He takes the easy way out and the students know it. "Write about what you are thinking," he says. The students settle but their ideas wilt away as well. Rashid has lost them, but he is relieved that the wave of energy has receded.

The group explores Rashid's need to be in control. Daniel says that Rashid seems to want clear limits on how students respond and act. Daniel asks, "How can you keep control and yet be open enough for students' interests to have priority? Rashid responds by noting that both narratives show that he works moment by moment and has not created an environment for learning. "I always feel this dread that I don't know what to say next or where to take the discussion or to get it back on track."

The discussion then moves to Rashid's practice of having students write in their journals when the discussion gets heated. Rashid admits he could not think of an alternative. All of us empathized with Rashid's feelings of having a classroom out of control. We listed a series of options. Rashid nods and admits that most are better than having students write in their journals. "I need to reconsider what is acceptable talk and learn how to keep that moving forward rather than thwarting it and trying to keep everything in check." Florence reminds him that she would have valued his students' energy and interest. As we end this part of our discussion, Rashid names some tentative next steps.

> I'm not certain where to start but I need to create a whole environment in the class that gives students room to explore ideas, to move around the classroom, and to feel invested in the learning. I'm not clear where to start. The minute I get nervous, I have the kids pull out their journals. A journal isn't a classroom. I need to start big and go small. Starting points? I'm not sure how to make an open environment. I'm always putting the control breaks on them and I really need to free them up to work through ideas. In some ways our discussions of Florence's and Denise's narratives have helped me see that I'm putting myself first and forgetting that I'm working with young adolescents who have great ideas and energy. I need an environment conducive to their learning. That may be an environment that isn't comfortable for me at first, but I'm willing to work on this.

Excerpts From Daniel's Narrative:
Are We the Collective I Imagined?

We shift our attention to the narratives of Daniel's classroom. He begins the discussion by suggesting that Rashid's issues about creating an environment are the same ones with which he struggles. "I think we set our expectations high. It is easy to say we want collaboration and inquiry work, but it isn't easy to sustain such work." Daniel's narrative opens with his concerns about expectations:

> Daniel is thinking that once you set the bar high for something like this, it is easy for the students to expect this all the time. He watches Ramona stumble over her beginning lines. His throat knots and he is hoping that she will gain back the confidence that is oozing from her. Daniel whispers one line to her. It is enough. She has it back. Daniel is thinking now that it was a good idea to have copies of the monologues to prompt them. He also wonders whether or not students are learning important skills? Daniel catalogues this in his head while Josie is performing: they wrote monologues,

they rehearsed and became better at speaking and performing for a group, and they wrote up a monologue and had the experience of editing it. Students certainly know more about at least one character in the book, and, if they are listening, they are learning about others. When Rustin begins her Scout monologue, Daniel realizes that the students aren't really collaborating. He realizes he is still doing most of the planning and work. He struggles with this idea and as the play comes to an end he realizes the students are performing monologues—they are small satellites, each working independently in a performance that creates a whole. Daniel is confused. What does collaboration mean? As the lights come on and the classroom reappears, Daniel is left wondering. How will he work from this moment to build on and strengthen a sense of community that will support students' learning?

Daniel notices that my portrayal still has him very much in charge of classroom movements and talk. "I was surprised because I just felt everything was flowing. I don't even remember saying anything." Denise notices in both narratives that Daniel's students know what they are supposed to do. Florence expresses her envy for their ability to have control of themselves. "I really need to prepare the kids to monitor themselves and set some of their own goals."

Rashid agrees. "This does give me some hope that kids are capable. I know I have things to learn to help them work in different ways." The discussion ends with Daniel expressing his appreciation that everyone thought the monologues engaged the students.

I realize that this was still my assignment and I was the director, giving little assignments that led to the performance. The students weren't designing and building this project. It was still an assignment. I'm not sure how, but I need to work on how it becomes more theirs and how they might collaborate more.

UNRAVELING THE NARRATIVES

These first narratives, of 12 class scenarios that were eventually written, provide a starting point from which to begin unraveling the threads of meaning. The teachers' initial research questions were reviewed at the end of our first meeting.

Reviewing the Teachers' Initial Questions

The first question: *How might we better support students' development of key habits that will enhance their abilities to work on collaborative projects and inquiry-based learning?* When we pose the question, Denise reiterates a point made in our discussion. "In every one of our narratives there are examples of us directing students to do certain things. I tell them to write, to get into groups, to read, and to ask questions. I realize in this entire class period I don't show them examples of good journal entries or ask them where they get ideas for journal topics. I don't create a fishbowl to show them how to talk in groups, and I don't model good questioning. There is no modeling. Just giving commands. I've just fallen into that pattern." The teachers agree that the narratives help them see that they are more often teaching by *telling* rather than *showing*. Rashid elaborates on this realization by presenting a challenge to the group. "If we work consciously to model how to work in groups it might be a first step to answering this question about how to support students' development." *To support* does not mean the same thing as *to command*. Modeling ways of working and strategies for learning are important first steps in supporting students. More direction and guidance needs to accompany group work.

All four of the teachers agree to rethink the purpose and use of journal writing in their classrooms. Daniel suggests that they work together to rethink the use of the journal. "It seems that we are often using it to manage time, manage adolescent energy, as a filler, or to give us a minute as class starts to compose ourselves. We need to think how the journal is an instructional tool to help students with inquiry." They conclude this part of the discussion with the goal of further articulating the use of journals in their classrooms.

The second question is: *What are the causes of students' resistance to ways of teaching that foster collaborative projects?* After their discussion of the narratives, the teachers rewrite this question. First, they realize that they are not actually teaching in ways that would foster collaboration or project-based work. Their revised question is: *How do we help students learn the skills necessary to work on collaborative projects?* Revising the question demonstrates an important example of their learning. All of the teachers express a desire to incorporate the skills and strategies for collaboration and for project-based work into their curriculum maps. "Getting this written into our curriculum maps will help us develop a scope and sequence for teaching collaboration," Rashid says to the group. His comment echoes an earlier one by Florence. "I must admit I don't really know how to teach collaboration. If we could articulate some steps in teaching collaboration, it would really help me know what to teach."

The third question: *How can I reconcile my own beliefs and strengths as a teacher with the school-wide goals?* All four teachers value the school's goals but express concerns about *how* to promote them in any sustained way. Daniel elucidates this point. "One of the things I notice is that I'm very fragmented. I cannot sustain an approach for long. I believe in collaboration, but I don't know how to teach students to really collaborate." The teachers realize they need to work out their responses to this over time as they elaborate on their beliefs in practice. Rashid suggests a plan to "take one belief at a time, name it, and see if we can name how it is part of what the school is actually doing and if we can see it in classroom practices." As ELA teachers, they value discussions of literature where students are invested in and can monitor their own learning. They hope to foster students' interest in researching their world. Florence emphasizes that "Since we are ELA teachers we have the advantage of a fairly open curriculum where we can emphasize research and use the literature to set up research studies." Moreover, they realize the need to mobilize these young adolescent learners' energy and curiosity in support of their self-sponsored learning.

Navigating the Distance Between Intention and Action

Many of the issues and themes raised in our narratives and discussion resonate with reports and research that examine the education of young adolescents in middle schools (Anfara et al., 2003; National Association of Secondary School Principals, 2006). The literature on middle school reform presents a reasonably consistent list of characteristics—small learning communities, developmentally appropriate learning environments, teachers who value working with this age group, schools with a shared vision, and interdisciplinary, collaborative, and active learning (NMSA, 2003). The four teachers at Thurgood struggle to enact the characteristics and values espoused and with which they are in agreement. We must question why this is the case.

Denise, Florence, Rashid, and Daniel are all within the early years of their teaching careers. They range from a teacher in his first year to a veteran in his fifth year. These young teachers constitute the entire English language arts department in this small school and do not have regular contact with veteran teachers in their subject area. They work in a high needs school in its early years of establishing its middle school identity. The approach to professional development at the school is to offer two and three session themed workshops provided by outside organizations that sell packages of materials on assessment, differentiation, and backwards design. Three of the four teachers are teaching fellows. They began teaching after a 6-week teacher preparation program. In some ways these conditions, taken together, may create a "perfect storm," a confluence of circumstances that lead to their frustrations with their abilities and with the perceived students' attitudes toward learning. These teachers understand that they will need ongoing professional development experiences to enhance and support them as they continue to learn about teaching.

I am reminded of Capelluti and Stokes' (1991) reflection. "Although there is considerable knowledge about the characteristics and interests of early adolescents, this information has not at all times been reflected in what and how we teach these students" (p. iii). Denise, Florence, and Daniel are intelligent, compassionate, and committed teachers who struggle to implement instructional practices that will empower students to take responsibility for their own learning. They simply do not know how. The literature on middle school emphasizes that teachers should design hands-on experiences but each of these teachers indicated that they have not seen examples of that enacted in classrooms (Bohnenburger & Terry, 2002). Daniel said, "the Mockingbird experience may be the closest I have come or ever seen to active learning." Florence yearns "for a vision of engagement. Frankly, I don't know what it looks like." Denise struggles with an image of "what authentic problem solving might look like when we are studying literature." As Rashid notes, "My past experiences in school don't give me images of how to teach in this new way so I'm struggling for concrete examples and images of deep engagement." These teachers remind us that teaching in the middle school requires a convergence of deep content knowledge, an understanding of integrative curriculum (Beane, 1997), a vision of active and student-centered learning (Bishop & Pflaum 2005), and the knowledge of young adolescent development (Manning, 2002). The quality of teacher preparation programs and ongoing professional development experiences has been linked to teacher effectiveness and student learning (Guskey, 2003; Pate & Thompson 2003). Responsive professional development experiences might help alleviate a perfect storm that has the potential to prevent teachers and schools from achieving their vision of a responsive middle school philosophy.

Responsive Professional Development Practices

Perhaps the writing of multiple narratives of class periods is not the most efficient way to conduct professional development. Perhaps it is too time intensive, circuitous, and does not yield direct or transportable answers. However, we did engage in thoughtful examination of belief, teaching intentions, and enactments of teaching. The formation of our inquiry team was an experiment in trying to narrow the gap between the teachers' current instructional practices and the principles of practice espoused in the middle level literature. The team approach to professional development provided opportunities for these four teachers to collaborate as active learners in their own development and understanding. In some ways our work was an attempt to parallel what the teachers were hoping to achieve with their students. Through the narratives, we moved inside each of the four classrooms. The teachers studied each others' instructional practices. They discussed the routines, the language used to talk to students, and the underlying tensions that were barriers to their hard work of learning to teach and continuously rethinking their teaching. The contradictory message of keeping students "in control" and wanting them to create and monitor their learning were much at odds. Through the narratives we began to see the mixed messages given to students through contradictory or conflicting intentions, actions and language.

The practices of literacy that the ELA teachers want to encourage are structurally and symbolically tied to collaboration, individual and group choice, and learning that is discovered rather than named. The desired literacy is a *means* through which students learn in real and significant ways. These teachers do want to take on the responsibility of awakening adolescents' curiosity, awe, and desire to learn. They know this cannot be business as usual and these teachers are "in progress." They accept the challenges of the work ahead. Along with the narrative reconstructions, we began to study the middle school movement for what all the studies and insights offered by others might contribute to our ongoing search. The group was not interested in reading about how to form literature circles, how to establish reading clubs, how to create peer response groups, how to structure project-based inquiry. The consensus was that it would be better to concentrate on adolescent development and learning and on reflective thinking, problem-solving, developing social action skills, and organizing for learning (group processes, group dynamics, and negotiations).

Rashid, Florence, Denise, and Daniel were relieved to read articles about the history of the middle school movement (Beane, 1990; Van Hoose, Strahan, & L'Esperance, 2001; Wiles & Bondi, 2001). The middle school movement from the 1980s has recognized the need for structures in schools that more fully meet the developmental needs of young adolescents (Capelluti & Stokes, 1991; Manning, 1993). Developing challenging curricula remains an area of concern. Critiques of the lack of depth and rigor in middle school curricula often represent learning as "a mile wide and an inch deep." Attempts to develop advisory programs, involve parents, institute team teaching, or create flexible scheduling have not always led to a more fully articulated and complementary program of curricula and instruction (Brown & Saltman, 2005). As we have seen with Thurgood Middle School, teachers everywhere still struggle with making informed decisions that have the desired results.

Good teaching is a crucial component of progress, and we need to keep struggling to find venues for teachers to tell their stories of teaching and to work through the maze of contingencies and contexts that will take them beyond mere technique to a more complete understanding of their theories of teacher and student identities. If Thurgood teachers or any middle school teachers who struggle to enact their principles in practice, want to move beyond a more subject-centered curriculum created for students to a curriculum that is created by and organized by students, the preparatory work is labor-intensive and calls on teachers to reflect on and rethink much of what they have taken as givens about teaching.

As a group, we read Powell's and Van Zandt Allen's (2001) thoughtful comparison of approaches to curriculum, noting the differences in traditional, interdisciplinary, and integrative curriculum that inform the middle school milieu. Since noting the language that the teachers used to "keep students in control," we began reading about the ways in which student learning is influenced not only by instructional routines set by teachers but also the language used to guide learning in the classroom (Nystrand, 2006; Wilkinson & Silliman, 2000). Simply put, our inquiry group continues to read, write, question, practice, and try to enact into our practices what we are learning.

It seems unreasonable to claim that Denise, Florence, Rashid, and Daniel (or any teachers for that matter) have solved the problems of their teaching or eliminated the contradictions of purpose and intention because they have written narratives, discussed these with their colleagues, taken action by rethinking practices, or studied the literature on middle school reform. That said, there are recognitions they have and strategies they have learned to confront their teaching dilemmas. They possess habits of mind to inquire into their teaching. They think differently about their teaching and recognize more precisely the effects of their practices on student behavior and learning.

CONCLUDING THOUGHTS

One purpose of this chapter is to encourage researchers to experiment with ways of using narrative inquiry to conduct research *with* rather than *on* teachers. It is my intention that this chapter demonstrates our attempts to work as an inquiry group, but it is still my telling of the story. I control the narrative of the larger story of the school, the teachers, and our work together. The teachers' conversations and narratives are incorporated in the conventional ways of quoting fragments of their conversations and excerpting from their narratives. Of course, there are other ways of writing this text, and I would encourage researchers who study teacher learning and knowledge to experiment with forms that allow for serious representation of the teachers' voices. We need to find multiple formats, forms, and forums.

I have argued that narrative is a space for learning—both in the writing and in the reflections on the writing. Multiple versions of a story offer an invitation to the researcher, the teachers, and the reader to think more self-consciously and reflectively about potential meaning and the nature of provisional knowledge. The narratives perform as sites of doubt as well as confirmation. To that end, narrative inquiry may have the potential to be one of the best avenues to meaningful professional development. The narrative is a passageway to the *what ifs*, captured as it is in a network of language, intention, and possibility. Perhaps this is the point. Professional development is not effective when it relies on the "should have," the "must do," and "best practice" versions of teaching. It is in the moments of discovery that Denise, Florence, Rashid, and Daniel learned about themselves as teachers and create narratives of their future teaching selves.

REFERENCES

Anfara, V. A., Jr., Andrews, P. G., Hough, D. L., Mertens, S. B., Mizelle, N. B., & White, G. P. (2003). *Research and resources in support of This We Believe.* Westerville, OH: National Middle School Association.

Barone, T. (2000). *Aesthetics, politics, and educational inquiry: Essays and examples.* New York, NY: Peter Lang.

Bateson, M. C. (1994). *Peripheral visions: Learning along the way.* New York, NY: HarperCollins.

Beane, J. A. (1990). *Affect in the curriculum: Toward democracy, dignity, and diversity.* New York, NY: Teachers College Press.

Beane, J. A. (1997). *Curriculum integration: Designing the core of democratic education.* New York, NY: Teachers College Press.

Bishop, P., & Pflaum, S. (2005). *Reaching and teaching middle school learners: Asking students to show us what works.* Thousand Oaks, CA: Corwin Press.

Bohnenburger, J. E., & Terry, A. W. (2002). Community problem solving works for middle level students. *Middle School Journal 34*(1), 5-12.

Brown, E. R., & Saltman, K. J. (Eds.). (2005). *The critical middle school reader.* New York, NY: Routledge.

Bruner, J. (1986). *Actual minds, possible worlds.* Cambridge, MA: Harvard University Press.

Bruner, J. (1990). *Acts of meaning.* Cambridge, MA: Harvard University Press.

Capelluti, J., & Stokes, D. (1991). *Middle level education programs, policies, and practices.* Reston, VA: National Association of Secondary School Principals.

Clandinin, D. J., & Connelly, F. M. (2000). *Narrative inquiry: Experience and story in qualitative research.* San Francisco, CA: Jossey-Bass.

Clandinin, D., Pushor, D., & Orr, A. (2007). Navigating sites for narrative inquiry. *Journal of Teacher Education, 58*(1), 21-35.

Coles, R. (1989). *The call of stories: Teaching and the moral imagination.* Boston, MA: Houghton Mifflin.

Connelly, F. M., & Clandinin, D. J. (2006). Narrative inquiry. In J. L. Green, G. Camilli, & P. Elmore (Eds.), *Handbook of complementary methods in education research* (3rd ed., pp. 477-487). Mahwah, NJ: Erlbaum.

Creech, S. (1994). *Walk two moons.* New York, NY: HarperCollins.

Ely, M., Vinz, R., Downing, M., & Anzul, M. (1997). *Writing qualitative research: Living by words.* Philadelphia, PA: Falmer Press.

Gusky, T. R. (2003). What makes professional development effective? *Phi Delta Kappan, 84*(10), 748-750.

Lee, H. (1960). *To kill a mockingbird.* Philadelphia, PA: Lippincott.

Manning, M. L. (1993). *Developmentally appropriate middle level schools.* Wheaton, MD: Association of Childhood Education International.

Manning, M. L. (2002). *Developmentally appropriate middle level schools* (2nd ed.). Olney, MD: Association for Childhood Education International.

Myers, W. D. (1988). *Scorpions.* New York, NY: Harper Collins.

National Association of Secondary School Principals. (2006). *Breaking ranks II: Strategies for leading high school reform.* Reston, VA: Author.

National Middle School Association. (2003). *This we believe: Successful schools for young adolescents.* Westerville, OH: Author.

Nussbaum, M. (1990). *Love's knowledge.* Oxford, England: Oxford University Press.

Nystrand, M. (2006). Research on the role of classroom discourse as it affects reading comprehension. *Research in the Teaching of English, 40*(4), 392-412.

Pate, P. E., & Thompson, K. F. (2003). Effective professional development: What is it? In P. G. Andrews & V. Anfara, Jr. (Eds.), *Leaders for a movement: Professional preparation and development of middle level teachers and administrators* (pp. 123-143). Greenwich, CT: Information Age.

Polkinghorne, D. E. (1988). *Narrative knowing and the human sciences.* Albany, NY: State University of New York Press.

Powell, R., & Van Zandt Allen, L. (2001). The middle school curriculum. In V. Anfara, Jr. (Ed.), *The handbook of research in middle level education* (pp. 107-124), Greenwich, CT: Information Age.

Quinoncz, E. (2000). *Bodega dreams.* New York, NY: Knopf Doubleday.

Sachar, L. (2000). *Holes.* New York: Random House.

Van Hoose, J., Strahan, D., & L'Esperance, M. (2001). *Promoting harmony: Young adolescent development and school practices.* Westerville, OH: National Middle School Association.

Vinz, R. (1996). *Composing a teaching life: Inquiry into the teaching of literature.* Portsmouth, NH: Heinemann, Boynton/Cook.

Vinz, R. (1997). You can't tame a polecate by caging it. In J. Trimmer (Ed.), *Narration as inquiry* (pp. 127-141). Portsmouth, NH: Heinemann, Boynton/Cook.

Wiles, J., & Bondi, J. (2001). *The new American middle school: Educating preadolescents in an era of change* (3rd ed.). Upper Saddle River, NJ: Pearson Prentice Hall.

Wilkinson, E. R., & Silliman, L. C. (2000). Classroom language and literacy learning. In M. Kamil, P. D. Pearson, & R. Barr (Eds.), *Handbook of reading research* (Vol. 3, pp. 337-360). Mahwah, NJ: Erlbaum.

CHAPTER 15

PARENT INVOLVEMENT AND STUDENT SUCCESS

Black and White in the Middle

Kathleen F. Malu

This chapter explores the call for parent involvement in middle level education and the meanings it holds for the author, a self-identified White mother who is a former classroom teacher and researcher with a Black son. Framing this narrative within the parent involvement literature the narrative begins when the mother and son participate in the school interview, a requirement for admissions to this public alternative school located in New York City. As the narrative unfolds, the author's struggles with her roles of parent, researcher, and teacher become evident. Reframing the narrative in terms of race and gender, the author begins a deeper reflection on her experiences and the multiple meanings they may hold.

The Crossroads School is a public New York City middle school, located on the Upper West Side of Manhattan in a culturally diverse neighborhood. Identified as an alternative school, Crossroads was founded on the principles of the Coalition of Essential Schools (Sizer, 1992), *Turning Points* (Carnegie Council on Adolescent Development, 1989), and the progressive education movement (Dewey, 1916/1963).

Voices From the Middle: Narrative Inquiry By, For, and About the Middle Level Community
pp. 315–338

315

This school uses recognized middle school practices including advisory groups, block scheduling, interdisciplinary classes with a hands-on thematic curriculum, authentic assessments, family conferences and narrative report cards, and heterogeneous, interage grouping. Crossroads reports that it is a caring, nurturing school that focuses on the community and issues of justice (Delpit, 1995; Fine, 1996; Jervis, 1996).

An experienced middle school teacher, Ann established Crossroads and serves as the school director and part-time teacher. She leads a seven-member faculty and has one school secretary. Including Ann, there are four female and one male faculty members who identify themselves as White; one male faculty member is African American; one female teacher is Puerto Rican and the school secretary is Dominican.

Ann prides herself on the rich mosaic of cultures represented at the school. Of the 136 students in Grades 6-8, 50% are Latino/Hispanic (predominantly from the Dominican Republic), 30% Black, and 20% White, with families from high, middle, and low socioeconomic levels. Three students have fathers from Africa (Sudan, Kenya, and Zaire/Congo) and White mothers. There is a small percentage of middle schoolers who have special education needs and others require English as a second language support.

Judging from this information, Crossroads seems to be a school that knows how to work supportively and effectively with parents and their middle aged children with diverse backgrounds.

PARENT INVOLVEMENT AND STUDENT SUCCESS

"Parents must get involved with their children's school!" Teachers and teachers' unions, school administrators, parent-teacher associations, the U.S. Congress, President Obama, and Dr. Bill Cosby call for such action. Typically parents "get involved" by monitoring homework, serving as chaperones on class field trips, and raising funds through bake sales and other sponsored activities. Parents supervise lunchrooms, read to students in their classrooms, help in classroom publishing centers, and volunteer in school offices and libraries.

Research findings are contradictory regarding the role that parent involvement plays in middle school students' academic success. Parent involvement is typically defined as parental engagement in their students' education. Parents become involved, in part, because they consider helping their children develop and succeed academically and socially to be part of their responsibility (Mo & Singh, 2008). Mo and Singh (2008) examined parent involvement at the middle level in terms of parent and child conversations about grades, homework, and future aspirations and parent assistance on children's school projects. Mo and Singh (2008) found that children who received such involvement from their parents and children who were engaged with school had higher rates of academic success. Mo and Singh (2008) suggest that schools encourage continued parental involvement by communicating with parents regarding school activities and curriculum, informing parents of their children's emotional and social development, and encouraging their help with "educational decisions" regarding their children (Mo & Singh, 2008).

Hoover-Dempsey and Sandler (1997) and Epstein, Simon, and Salinas (1997) found that adolescents whose parents were involved with their children's teachers and schools were more successful in school than children whose parents were not involved. Van Voorhis (2003) found that when middle level parents monitored their middle school children's homework and grades, their children's academic performance improved. Researchers designed (Epstein, Salinas, & Van Voorhis, 2001; Epstein & Van Voorhis, 2001) and tested (Sheldon & Epstein, 2005) various homework assignments. They determined that assignments that engaged parents and children were the most effective in improving student performance (Sheldon & Epstein, 2005). Henderson and Berla (1996) and Kellaghan, Sloane, Alvarez, and Bloom (1993) found that when parents were engaged and involved in their middle aged students' lives and schools, students experienced school success.

In contrast, a meta-analysis of research on parental involvement and student school performance (Patall, Cooper, & Robinson, 2008) found that parental help with homework improved children's performance for elementary and high school students. At the middle level parental help with homework did not increase academic performance. Patall et al. (2008) caution that parents who try to help their young adolescents with homework may experience conflict. At a time when young adolescents try to gain independence and seek a growing level of autonomy, parental help with homework may no longer be the most appropriate way for parents to support their children (Patall et al., 2008). It may be more developmentally appropriate for parents to modify their efforts by trying to support their children's search for autonomy (Patall et al., 2008).

In a study about maternal involvement and children's school performance, Pomerantz and Eaton (2001) examined the school performance of children between the ages of 10-12 and the types of support their mothers offered. Pomerantz and Eaton (2001) found that for children who performed poorly in school their mothers offered "intrusive" support. For mothers who worried about their children's continued poor performance and offered intrusive support, their children continued to perform poorly. Mothers then increased this intrusive support. Findings suggest that mothers' support of low achieving children may eventually result in improved grade performance but this performance may be no better than that of children whose mothers did not offer intrusive support.

Of further note, there is scant research that explores parental involvement in families of color, including those with diverse cultural, linguistic, and socioeconomic backgrounds (Jeynes, 2007). Few studies exist that examine the influence of individual family backgrounds or explore family and school involvement for biracial students and their families (Root, 2001; Williams, 2009). The need for studies that explore the complexities of parental involvement, particularly for biracial families, is critical and urgent.

What support can Crossroads provide to families from diverse backgrounds given this confusion in the research? What is the Crossroads approach to encouraging parental involvement for biracial parents and families when no research exists? The purpose of this chapter is to explore these questions through the narrative about my experiences as the White mother of a Black son in middle school.

DESIGN OF THIS NARRATIVE INQUIRY

The narrative that follows tells my experiences as a mother during the 2 years my son attended Crossroads. The lens through which I tell this story is influenced by my background. Specifically, at the time of this narrative I viewed myself as a middle class, White American woman. Within two years of meeting, I married a Black man from Congo (formerly Zaire). Five years later, he and I worked in Rwanda where I gave birth to our son, Joe. Within days of Joe's first birthday, his father, Joe, and I returned to the States, settling in New York City to raise him and continue our careers. In my attempt to manage the length of this narrative, I do not include the voice of Joe's father.

Elsewhere I have discussed names and the impact the use of real names and pseudonyms may have on a reader's understanding of and interpretation of qualitative research reports (Malu, Feola, & Brause, 2001). In this narrative, I use the real names of all individuals and Crossroads because they are part of the rich, thick description (Geertz, 1973) called for in qualitative research. Additionally, Fine et al. (1994) and Fine (1996) used real names in research reports about Crossroads. In this narrative, I attended to ethical matters in two ways. There has been a significant lapse of time between the events in this story and my telling of them here. Although Crossroads continues as a public middle school, all of the individuals in this narrative are no longer there. My son and I discussed this story on numerous occasions throughout the years and since he was in middle school more than a decade ago. After each discussion he gave me permission to share these experiences publically. I am grateful to him for his courage and willingness to let me share this story, which, in part, is his.

I designed this narrative research project because I wanted to understand the nature of Joe's learning in school. It was part of an ongoing project I began at his birth, collecting, storing, sorting through, and analyzing a wide variety of data over the years.

For this specific project, I originally created the narrative during Joe's ninth grade year and added to it when he was in 10th grade. I used two large data sources. One source was the data that I generated and school correspondence I saved while Joe was at Crossroads. I kept a personal-professional journal, field notes, school communications including announcements, school letters and calendars, parent-teacher meeting notes, research team meeting notes, and draft articles. The second source was data from my son. I kept and examined his report cards which were narratives written by all his teachers twice a year, my notes from our family conferences, Joe's ethnographic research notes and report, and the school work that he showed me. I gathered these data in my son's seventh grade year, the summer leading into eighth grade, his eighth grade year, and the following summer. Data for the epilogue came from my journal and Joe's completed 10th grade English homework assignment.

To write this narrative, I first placed and examined the data in chronological order, combining the first and second data sources, laying them out on a timeline, occasionally placing some pieces on top of each other as appropriate. The use of time as the organizing theme helped me understand the sequence of the narrative as it played out when Joe attended Crossroads. Using a holistic stance and discourse and text analysis, I created story elements based on recurring patterns I found in the data (Coulthard, 1985; Riessman, 1993). Additionally, I examined and reexamined the data and constantly compared it across the patterns to tentatively identify these elements. Concern for isolated patterns of data and how these patterns related to the whole was another part of this analysis (Brause, 1991; Erickson, 1986). I redefined isolated patterns as I linked more data and I used data reduction and verification to ensure the veracity of the story (Brause, 1991). The notion of trustworthiness, an essential element of narrative methodology, was assured by this systematic analysis of the data (Moss, 2004). The meaning of the larger story was of greater significance than the sum of the parts, in keeping with the design of discourse analysis (Coulthard, 1985).

As I shaped the narrative, I shared my work with Joe, engaging him in member checking, asking for his recollections and reflections about the events that occurred. I integrated his thoughts as he revealed them to me. To ensure that I accurately portrayed the perceptions of his teachers and the other individuals in this narrative I reviewed countless times the videotapes that were recorded of the research event (Fine et al, 1994). Crossroads and the Bruner Foundation published the teacher narratives (Fine, 1996) the year after Joe left Crossroads and I used these to check events and confirm teacher stories with my journal entries and field notes. This publication (Fine, 1996), a result of the Crossroads participatory evaluation research project, held much of the information and narratives I used to confirm my portrayal of the school philosophy and teacher stories.

After this analysis and narrative creation, I set the narrative aside for several years, returning to it only recently. With this perspective of time, experience, and further reflection, I revisited the narrative and this time I identified themes that I saw emerging from it. I recognize that my analysis of this narrative is open to interpretation and acknowledge the limited nature of this analysis (Connelly & Clandinin, 1990). In preparation for this chapter, I submitted the manuscript of this narrative to members of this volume's editorial review board, selecting their names randomly after writing them all on slips of paper and drawing them from a hat. Each reviewer presented me with extensive comments and all urged a tighter focus by exploring no more than two themes in the discussion. I am grateful for their feedback and suggestions.

This narrative about my parental involvement at my son's middle school is a very complex, complicated, and, at times, personally difficult narrative for me to tell. Given the scant research on biracial students and parental involvement (Root, 2001; Williams, 2009), I purposefully share this narrative to prompt further inquiry. Readers will note additional themes in this narrative. Unfortunately, space does not allow for an exploration of these here. Readers may consider my use of the terms race, ethnicity, Black, African American, African and American to be haphazard. I have chosen to reflect the inconsistent use of these terms within the public discourse and my telling of this narrative as the White mother with a Black son whose father is Congolese.

THE NARRATIVE

My narrative begins as I complete my doctoral work in language, literacy, and learning. With more than 15 years of experience as a teacher of French and English as a second language at the K-12 and college levels, I decide I want to be a teacher educator and researcher. My son, Joe, is nearing the end of his sixth grade year at a New York City public K-6 school.

Joe is African and American. He recognizes that his identify is complex and linked to his father and me. Sometimes the rich mosaic of cultures in New York gives him different identities. The most frequent are the young, urban Black/African American basketball player and Hispanic/Latino baseball player. Joe also encounters teens who have identities quite different from his. There are the typical middle school "nerdish" computer experts, the serious "nose in the book" intellectuals, and those "who like to watch ball players." Joe enthusiastically navigates *The Last Shot* (Frey, 1995) culture of the inner city basketball player and, along with his friends, he dreams of becoming a professional ball player. He is a baseball player too and moves easily with his Hispanic team mates whose parents frequently assume Joe speaks Spanish.

It's a bright spring day in Joe's sixth grade year and we must find a middle school for him to attend because his school has no middle school. This is the day we visit Crossroads for our admissions interview.

My belief that I must be an involved parent if I want to help Joe succeed is evident from this first visit. My desire to place Joe in a culturally diverse school is on my mind. As Joe and I climb the stairs to the fifth floor of the Crossroads School, I remind myself that I want a middle school that will help Joe succeed as a learner and give him opportunities to celebrate his cultural background. I want him to engage in hands-on activities and not be confined to an established textbook-based curriculum. I want him to go to a middle school where he has opportunities to explore his interests, grow as a reader, writer and thinker, and pursue his love of sports. I want a school where my wish to be involved will be welcomed.

On the fifth floor and out of breathe, I catch up with Joe who waits impatiently for me. We follow the signs to the office, a large room with two teacher desks and a Xerox machine at one end and two long work tables at the other.

"Welcome to Crossroads. I'm Ana, the secretary and I guess you're here for the admissions interview with Ann. Have a seat. She'll be here shortly." Ana points to one of the long tables. For the next several minutes, I listen carefully as Ana answers the phone, chats with students, alternating between Spanish and English. She must be Dominican, I think. Finally a short, perky, gray-haired woman enters the office, and Ana says to her, "The Malu family is here for their interview." Despite it being a New York City public school, Crossroads is an alternative school and is permitted to create its own admissions process. A family interview is requirement for every family seeking their child's admission to the school.

"Wonderful," Ann says, extending a hand as she comes to the table. "I'm the director of Crossroads. Sorry to keep you waiting. Let's get started."

During this admissions interview Ann asks Joe to share the piece of sixth grade schoolwork she asked him to bring.

"I brought my cartography project," he says, handing her the document.

"Why did you want to show this to me?"

"Because I think I did a good job on it and I like maps. Here's something about the history of map making and some of the different kinds of maps," Joe says as he pages through the project with Ann. "I have the letter I sent to this famous cartographer at the National Geographic Society and here's his answer." Joe settles back in his chair and waits for Ann's reply.

"So, you like maps. What an unusual topic! I love your work and how creative it is," Ann says as I watch Joe begin to smile. This might be the right place for him, I think.

I become more certain of this when I hear Ann's answer to my question, "Do you have any rules about children wearing baseball caps in school?" Ann seems surprised and then answers, "No, we believe that teen-ages need to show their self-expression and one way they can do this is through their clothing. We don't have any rules prohibiting baseball caps." Satisfied and comfortable with her answer, I think about the rule at Joe's elementary school "No baseball caps." Designed to help children learn baseball cap etiquette, the policy seems to me to be more about "following rules" rather than etiquette. Joe and I have fruitless arguments about following rules for rules sake.

Later in the evening I write in my journal, "I feel comfortable with Ann. Besides letting Joe go to Crossroads, I can imagine myself working for her, teaching in her school. Crossroads appeals to me not just as 'Joe's mom' but also as 'a teacher.' Crossroads will be a good place for Joe." With these thoughts, I encourage Joe to complete his application for Crossroads.

A few weeks later, Joe receives an invitation to attend Crossroads and he eagerly says, "Yes."

For seventh grade, Ann assigns Joe to her advisory group and gives him and our family the attention and support I expect to receive from this alternative public school. Joe's seventh grade year goes well. He thrives in the "law and justice class," enjoying the mock trial experience the most. He easily assumes a lawyerly stance, writing in his brief:

> May it please the court and the opposing council, Cindy Finch is not guilty. She had work to do after school in the area of the incident.

Social justice becomes one of Joe's favorite themes and this mock trial experience helps him to identify this passion.

Ann's role as Joe's advisor means that I can speak with her not just about Joe but also about school issues. Ann always reassures me that she hears my concerns and tries to address them. When I mention that there is very little geography work in the humanities class, Ann talks about creating a geography unit. I eagerly encourage this idea, reminding her of Joe's passion for maps. Because I feel Ann's open to my suggestions, I reciprocate by offering to involve myself with the school however I can despite Joe's plea that I not.

When Ann invites me to join the Parent Steering Committee to help lead the Parent-Teacher Association, I join. When Ann learns that I am an ESL teacher, completing my doctorate, we spend just as many conversations talking about Joe's work as we do talking about Ann's concerns for the school's Hispanic adolescents. It is one of these conversations that prompts Ann to invite me to conduct a small research study at Crossroads. She schedules me to share my findings at a staff development day, just one week after I successfully defend my dissertation.

On the day of my presentation, I nervously join the teachers. It's the end of Joe's seventh grade year and I suddenly realize that in 1 week, some of these teachers will assign him grades. I am confused about my role. As Joe's mom, I am involved and engaged at the school. As a novice researcher I want to report my findings as accurately and clearly as possible. What happens, I wonder, if the teachers become troubled by the findings I'm about to report?

Looking around the room, I see Joe's English and Humanities teacher, his math teacher, his science teacher, Ann, Ana, and the Spanish teacher.

I begin, "As you probably know, Ann asked me to conduct a small research study about the academic performance of some of the students at Crossroads."

I look around the room and see puzzled faces and then one teacher says, "No, we didn't know you did this. Ann didn't tell us."

Ann replies, "I'm sorry. I thought I told you about this. I guess I forgot to tell all of you. That's my fault. I'm sorry," she adds as I hear a few grumbles.

I continue, "Ann selected four students for me to interview who speak Spanish and English. She wanted me to try and understand why their academic performance is so low. First I'll tell you what they told me and then I'll tell you what the research says about second language learners. The four girls told me that they didn't think they did well academically because their teachers didn't like that they spoke Spanish in school, even when they used it only outside of class. The girls said they were angry and confused because they thought this school was supposed to be a place that valued differences."

As I say these words, I stare at Joe's teachers, watching as they shift nervously in their chairs and whisper to each other. Quickly I bury my head in my report papers. I can't face them. I see that my comments unsettle them. My mind flips from researcher to mother. I hope that Joe won't suffer any consequences because of what I report, I think.

Within a few minutes, someone says, "Of course, all the students should use English at school. I don't care if they are talking to Ana. They should all speak English, all the time."

"Why? There's no law that says they can't speak Spanish," responds the Spanish teacher.

"May I interrupt?" I ask. "Let me tell you about the research on learning a second language and my experiences as an ESL teacher."

"Excuse me. Maybe what you have to tell us is important but our discussion is very important, too. It's about the culture of the school and we need to talk about this first. Now, as I was saying, …" continues the Spanish teacher.

As the teachers, Ann, and Ana talk, I feel their anger and hostility. I listen to them, recalling the many faculty meetings I attended that were just as fiery.

As a parent, I am overwhelmed. My image of Crossroads as a supportive, nurturing middle school shatters. My desire to actively participate as a parent, sharing my professional expertise and skills evaporates. I try to weather the experience as best I can, vowing never again to reveal my professional self in a school Joe attends.

That night, in my journal I repeat nagging questions, "What happened to my image of Crossroads as a supportive, nurturing middle school? How can I actively participate as a parent at Joe's school?" Then, slowly a new question forms, revealed to me by the teachers' reactions to the student comments. "Are the students right in thinking that the school philosophy and practice don't match?" I find no answers.

I worry that the teachers' reactions to my research may somehow influence their evaluation of Joe's work. Fortunately this is not the case and Joe is promoted to eighth grade. Meanwhile, my professional life and search for a research position deadends. By August, I resign myself to another year of college adjunct teaching, wondering how I can gain more experience as a researcher.

One day in late August, Ann calls. "I created an Inquiry Team at Crossroads and I would like you to join us. We're going to research issues at Crossroads. Michelle Fine and two of her graduate students will lead the team and I've invited two teachers, the basketball coach, and Ana to join us. A small foundation will give us modest stipends. Would you be interested in joining us?"

While my mind struggles to keep my vow of not becoming involved, this invitation is too good to dismiss and I hear myself say, "Yes! This will give me a chance to gain more research experience with a nationally recognized researcher and support the school and Joe by continuing my involvement there." Only in my journal do I reveal my confusion. "Can I trust Ann? Where will my loyalties lie if I find problems again? Should I even try to help the school, given my experience last June? Can I help Joe and my career too? Is this fair to Joe? I guess only time will tell."

In September at the first Inquiry Team meeting, I learn that the team also includes 12 eighth graders. Each was selected by Ann and they will take a newly created urban ethnography class. Michelle Fine's two graduate students will teach the class and help the teens conduct their own urban ethnography studies about Crossroads. The syllabus states:

> This course will introduce students to some aspects of qualitative research. This includes understanding why and how people do this work ... and students will explore social issues of concern at the school.

Without consulting Joe, I ask for him to be included in the class. I tell Ann that I am sure he can follow up on his seventh grade interest in law and social justice. Joe's name is added to the class list.

"Just please don't tell Joe I asked for him to be included in this class," I say to Ann and the Inquiry Team. "I don't want him to think I'm meddling in his schoolwork."

"No, of course not. We won't tell him," everyone assures me.

If I did not agree to be on this team, I think, I would not have been able to give Joe this opportunity. So, I rationalize, it's a good thing I did not keep my vow from last summer. Look at these tremendous opportunities Joe and I have!

A few days later, Joe and his friends leave the school building for lunch, a sanctioned school policy. After lunch they stop at a video store where Joe gets robbed. His new, shiny gold chain is torn from his neck.

That evening after he tells me his story, I say to him, "You know I've told you not to wear those gold chains."

"Mom, I should be able to wear whatever I want. I shouldn't have to worry about getting robbed. If I want to wear a gold chain I should be able to."

"But you're just asking for trouble," I reply. "If you have to wear it then hide it when you leave school."

"No, I'm not going to. Besides, what do you expect, mom? This kind of stuff happens to kids like me all the time!" He replies as he leaves the room.

Over the next few weeks, I agonize about Joe, wondering, worrying, and writing about how safe he is. This is one of the first times that Joe does not seem to listen to me. He dismisses my appeal to logic and self-protection. His "what-do-you-expect-mom" leaves me feeling like an outsider. Not only am I the mom who "doesn't know what to expect" but I am also ignorant about "happens-to-kids-like-me-all-the-time." What happens all the time? Who does this happen to all the time? I hear it happens to young Black men in Harlem. It can't happen to my child. Not my Black son, can it? I wonder. Is Joe a young adolescent, arguing and standing up to his mother or is there more here? I can tolerate his unwillingness to remove his baseball cap but I can't tolerate his unwillingness to hide his gold chain. Why must he wear a gold chain? I know this is a fashion statement among urban Black teens. But why does Joe have to follow along with the crowd?

I fill my journal with questions and conflicts about adolescents and race. In my mind I hear over and over, "It's happening to me, mom. It happens all the time to kids like me. Get used to it. Get over it."

As the year progresses Joe engages in school, particularly with the school basketball team, and I watch as he continues to explore the identity of a young, urban, Black/African American ball player. He often says, "Mom, face it! I'm Black! Forget college! I'm going directly to the pros!" More often than not these days, our conversations revolve around basketball, coaching styles and sneakers. He wants me to see *Hoops* and *Blue Chips*, two movies about basketball.

As we sit in the theatre Joe whispers, "See that coach, mom. See the way he yells at his team. That's the way Coach at Crossroads yells at us. Real loud. Listen! Watch mom. That's just the way Coach is."

"Really?" is all I can think to say.

"Yeah, I like that 'hot temper' of the *Blue Chips* coach because he gets real angry! As angry as Coach at Crossroads and … anger in sports is O.K."

"Maybe," I respond. "But you also know that school isn't just about playing basketball, right? You want to get an education so you can do something with your life," I say.

"Come on, mom. I'm not going to college to study. I'm going to play basketball."

"Well, you can go to college to learn something and play basketball," I encourage without much enthusiasm.

While I struggle to stay connected to Joe, I continue my work on the school Inquiry Team, attending meeting after meeting. Gradually I learn more about Ann, Ana, Michelle Fine, the two graduate students, and the two teachers, Cathy and Carole. I am most intrigued with Coach and I wonder about his influence on Joe.

One day as I wait for a team meeting, Ann asks me to type up a letter for her, not an unusual request. It's one that I comfortably fulfill on various occasions while I wait for a meeting or to speak to a teacher. On this occasion, however, she has me type up a letter of recommendation for coach. As I type I learn more about this man who seems to have such a strong influence on Joe. A tall, athletic, dark-skinned African American, he was active in the Civil Rights movement. As a coach at Crossroads, Ann notes that he is vocal and adamant about his beliefs, stating his opinions without any hesitation. As I finish the letter, I have respect and a bit of fear for this man. I continue wondering about his influence over Joe.

At the beginning of February, Michelle tells us that the entire Inquiry Team, the grown-ups and the students in the urban ethnography class, will present our research at a prestigious research conference in Philadelphia (Fine et al. 1994). In the final weeks before the conference everyone works feverishly to finalize their reports.

Meanwhile, I check in with Joe about the urban ethnography class and his report. He tells me that even though the students were asked to research questions about life at Crossroads only three of them did that. His is one of these three reports but he does not reveal his topic to me.

It is a cold, spring day and our school bus arrives on time at the University of Pennsylvania. Students and grown-ups file out and into the conference building. We find our presentation room and settle into our positions. The young teens present first. I and the other grown-up team members sit in the audience.

Eagerly I wait for Joe. When it is his turn, he announces the title of his research report: Being Wrongly Accused. His study answers the question: Why are the school's basketball players always implicated whenever there are disturbances at the school? After he looks at the audience, he reads his report:

> The [research] project which I chose was on whether or not kids in my school get treated fairly or get wrongly accused of things, or does the staff choose out certain kids and give these kids more breathing room than others. Early this year, I began noticing that I was getting wrongly accused of things and as the year went on more and more things happened. Why? My own explanation was that I was … a male who plays basketball. Males in our school seem to be given the cold shoulder, especially Black and Hispanic ones …

As I listen to and watch my son read his report I marvel at his idealism. How wonderful that he could research a topic like this! How brave! I wonder how much of what he says is true. Can it be true? Not at Crossroads, I think. This is a nurturing school with ideals. This is a school that uses all the best middle school practices. The school is small so all the teachers know all the students. The school has advisories so no child is left out. This cannot be true, can it? Suddenly I am conscious of my Whiteness. Then, I hear Joe continue:

> The one thing that came up when I was interviewing the [boys] who … got accused of things unfairly was that they hardly ever got an apology … and the teachers I interviewed … all said it's not their job to apologize.

More questions spin in my head. What does he mean that the teachers don't apologize when they have been unfair? Of course they would apologize, wouldn't they? Joe cannot really mean to set this up as a race issue, can he? But, I consider further. The 5 White teachers include the English and Humanities teachers, the math teacher, the science teacher, and Ann. Coach, Ana, and the Spanish teacher are people of color. What's going on here, I wonder. Joe continues:

> our math teacher was talking about the thefts that had been going on in the school … and he said that he basically knew who [committed the thefts] and that he was just going to accuse [those boys] and when [a girl in the class] said, "That's not right, you don't have any proof." He says, "This is not a court of law."
>
> But the main thing that I ran into was that part about those boys … I interviewed some girls and they said, "Well, mostly boys do that kind of stuff. Girls … don't talk in class; they don't fool around."
>
> From doing this research I learned that there is more to my school than one might think. This is supposed to be a school where kids are supposed to be heard. But, when it comes down to the important issues, the kids are told to be quiet.

As Joe closes his notebook, I join the audience in applause. I am amazed at Joe's courage, I think. These findings may potentially infuriate some teachers at the school. He has fulfilled and surpassed the research class expectations, but, I wonder, will there be a backlash? He questions school, saying basically that it does not practice what it preaches. I fear for him now, I think, as the students and parents change seats. The grown-ups become the presenters; the students sit in the audience.

None of the grown-ups share findings that challenge and threaten the school like Joe's did. Even mine are mild. Guided by Michelle and Ann, I report the experiences of eight bilingual parents during the family conferences. I announce that most of the parents were pleased with their family conference experience. A few complained but I do not focus on them.

When our session ends, the entire team is subdued. I see exhaustion in our eyes, probably from the long day and the tension that comes from "being on stage" We file back onto the bus for a quiet return trip to New York City.

Within weeks of this presentation and only a few months before graduation, Joe begins to give me one word, or grunts, for his answers to my questions. "How's school going?" "What's up with your friends?" I notice a troubling pattern: Joe develops a "hot temper." He tells me, "Coach says I have to watch my 'hot temper.'" This hot temper is not something that anyone at the school brings to my attention.

As far as I can tell there is no fallout from Joe's report. I am the only one disturbed when he shows me his final assignment from the ethnography class. It is a piece of paper with a few paragraphs that Joe wrote in response to the question: "What have you learned in this urban ethnography class?" Joe's handwritten response is interrupted by a teacher's writing in red pen (presented in brackets and italics below):

> I am a professional researcher [*in training*] ... my name is Joe and I was put into this research class because [*my mother asked for me to be put in this class*] I'm me. This class was fun for me and I got a lot out of it. I like trying to chang [sic] things so I chose this research project so I could bring justice to kids in our school.

I am shocked! The teachers of this class broke the confidence I asked them to keep. I requested they not reveal to Joe that I asked for him to be placed into the class—but they did! I am struck by what I see as their "put downs" of Joe. They remind him that he's "in training." They disregard his pride-filled "because I'm me." In my journal I write, "I'm afraid that my involvement overshadows Joe's very being at the school. I wish I had concrete evidence of this. I guess my feelings are just not enough proof," I conclude.

One afternoon in May, Joe comes home from school and tells me, "I'm in trouble. I got into a fight." He refuses to speak further. Even though I was at Crossroads all day, I did not see or hear about the incident. Joe's advisor, Ana, calls me that evening.

She tells me, "Joe and another boy exchanged words and then, suddenly, they had each other in head locks on the gym floor. The school has a rule prohibiting students from fighting physically. The punishment for breaking this rule, however, was never clearly established. We're having a faculty meeting tomorrow to decide how to proceed. Meanwhile Joe may not come to school until you hear back from me." As I hang up I realize I have lots of questions that Ana did not answer.

The next evening Ana reports that Joe is suspended. I hear about the faculty meeting from one of Joe's sympathetic teachers, "You know we never suspended a child before. It was a very contentious meeting and most of the faculty didn't want to suspend him. But one member challenged us by saying, 'So, Joe can be our test case. Are we going to use the suspension on Joe for this kind of behavior, or not?'"

I am angry, isolated, and confused. I wonder why Joe is suspended when the faculty knew how involved and committed I was to helping him succeed. I am surprised that no one saw any signs that this fight was "brewing" or that Joe was developing a hot temper except for Coach. What was Coach's responsibility for averting or prompting this incident?

On the other hand, Joe had begun to keep his feelings hidden from me. It was impossible to know what he thought or felt. Three weeks later on a Monday in June I contact Ana and Ann, "I think something's bothering Joe but he refuses to talk with me about it. Can you keep an eye on him?

Two days later, Ana returns my call, "I talked to Joe and he told me he didn't have any problems."

The next day, Ann calls, "I spoke to Joe. He seems fine. I don't think you have anything to worry about."

On Friday Joe comes home early and reports to me, "I'm suspended again."

"What happened? Why didn't the school call me?"

"They told me to leave school. We were at music practice for graduation."

"Music? You never had music at Crossroads. Is this a new thing?"

"It's only for graduation," he mumbles.

"Okay So, what happened?"

"I got tired of the practice and I asked the teacher why we were practicing music anyway. We never had music at the school. I said these songs were a joke and they didn't make sense for our graduation ceremony. She said I talked back to her and was disrespectful and told me to leave. So, I came home."

"Okay. So, let me get this right. You were questioning why you were learning to sing songs for graduation when you never had music at the school?"

"Yeah," he answers.

"Well, you know you shouldn't talk back to anyone. That's not a nice thing to do. But I can understand your question. It makes sense to me." In my journal that night I write:

What's going on at Crossroads? They say one thing and do something else? I'm so disappointed. I'm so angry. Joe seems to always find inconsistencies in their preaching and practice. His question makes sense. Why sing when there's been no music curriculum? He challenged the activity but the teacher heard him challenge her. How much of Joe's work in the ethnography class—learning to question—is reflected here. Who's trying to help Joe make meaning out of all of this? My job is to help Joe succeed in school ... What can I do now?

The next day I tell Joe, "You must lay low, be quiet, be good for a few more days until you graduate. Please. Can you do this?" Joe does and he graduates.

Because of these incidents, my days as a middle school mother end with doubts about my involvement at the school. Most fragile for me is "the parent" role. In my journal I note, "Raising a teenager is hard work. Harder still is working with a school that seems to betray my trust, asks for my involvement and leaves me isolated, changes from welcoming me as a parent and professional to presuming they are the sole authority. Most overwhelming!"

As if in epilogue to this story, Joe's 10th grade teacher assigns the class to write an autobiographical piece about five areas of his life. One area Joe writes about is his middle school experience and coach:

> I had only one teacher who stood by my side and that was my basketball coach. He was big and looked scary ... after tryouts, the coach pulled me aside and said that not only was I on the team but that I would play a big role on the team. It surprised me ... but with that confidence I was able to play much better.

Joe continues:

> My eighth grade year started with me and my friends getting robbed ... this kind of bad start was a bad omen for the entire school year. I was suspended from school twice for reasons which are not even clear to me today. Actually, I liked these because they gave me a day off from school.

The irony is not lost on me. Joe enjoyed the suspensions because he did not have to go to school. Did he learn that breaking rules may lead to rewards?

REVISITING PARENTAL INVOLVEMENT AND STUDENT SUCCESS, BIRACIALLY

Based on this narrative, I question the idea of parent involvement and the specific connections there are between parent involvement and teen success at the middle level. I question the usefulness of examining parental involvement and student success without giving equal attention to race/ethnicity, gender, and identity. In this section, I revisit the themes of parental involvement and student success and layer them with race/ethnicity, gender and identity as they appear to me at this moment of writing and reflecting.

I wonder about the national call for more parent involvement. Is this a call to become genuinely involved? Or, is it a call to serve? If it is a call to serve, then who do parents serve when they get involved with their children's education as intimately as I did? What types of parent service are schools explicitly and implicitly willing to accept? Is there a price to be paid for parent service? What is that price and who pays it?

As a parent who wanted to be involved in the education of my son, I wonder whom I served by getting involved in my son's school. How much did I serve my professional self-interests and how much did I serve Joe's best interests? When Ann invited me to research the Hispanic girls' learning, my findings created conflict within the faculty and revealed that Ann might have been an ineffective communicator, "I'm sorry. I thought I told you about this. I guess I forgot to tell all of you." I am conflicted about sharing my research and the repercussions I worry it may have on Joe, given that I report on and question his teachers' actions. I am conflicted as I sit in the audience and listen to Joe reveal that his school does not listen to all voices. I am proud of his courage and fearful that there may be repercussions. I present my research on bilingual parent conferences, toning down the problems they share with me. I am mindful of the faculty's reactions to my previous research and seek to avoid conflict again.

I am hopeful that my involvement helps teachers give Joe "just a little bit more" support, encouragement, and attention. When I was a teacher, I remember how helpful it was to know my students' parents, call on them, and have their support for the work I did with their children. I expect Joe's teachers will do the same for us. This appears to be the case in Joe's seventh grade year. In eighth grade, the "blanket of extra attention and support" I hoped for is removed. Joe's suspensions are proof. Are Joe's actions wrong? Of course they are. Are the consequences appropriate? No. Do I expect my involvement to immunize Joe? Honestly, yes. Should it? Of course not. Perhaps as Pomerantz and Eaton (2001) report, it is my worry and concern that precipitate Joe's actions that lead to his suspensions.

Patall et al.'s (2008)'s suggestion that parental involvement at the middle level may need to match the developmental needs of young adolescents may be significant. As Joe aged through his two years at Crossroads, perhaps I needed to modify the way in which I was involved. If Joe was seeking independence and autonomy as a young adolescent, was my ongoing presence at Crossroads helpful? Was it a factor in the fight and his response about the music at graduation?

Did my involvement improve and enhance Joe's learning? What did he learn from my involvement? What did I learn from my involvement? Parent involvement in schools and the influence and impact this involvement may have in adolescent success needs further exploration. More middle level parents must share their narratives.

White mothers and their Black sons may need different kinds of care, nurturing, guidance, and support from teachers and advisors than do mothers and sons who have one ethnic identity (Brown & Leaman, 2007;

Root, 2001; Twine, 2004; Williams, 2009). Support may need to specifically consider issues of identity, gender, and ethnicity. White mothers with Black sons may represent a microcosm of Black and White issues at play in the United States. This theme is the hardest for me to explore, in part, because it is deeply personal.

My experiences as a White girl in a mixed gendered school with no ethnic diversity and then a small, all girls high school (with only 2 African American students and 4 Hispanic students per grade) help me relate to the literature on the struggles of girls in school (Barbieri, 1995; Gilligan, 1982) and offer me little understanding of ethnic diversity and no understanding of boys' experiences in school. My teaching experiences up to my son's middle school years reinforced my expectation that most girls were "good" and a few boys were "trouble." My personal experiences living in an interracial marriage gave me numerous complex experiences, too vast and complex to report here. My life in this relationship offers me insight here and gives me a lens to look at this … this informs my reflections and struggles.

As the mother of a son, I was at a loss to understand Joe and what he needed through his middle years. Crossroads' focus on helping girls by offering a Girls Talk class and boys by offering them basketball reinforced my ignorance (boys need to learn to behave, girls don't) and prompted feelings of isolation (I'm the only mother whose son was suspended), confusion (how could they suspend him when I've been so involved? I was at the school when the incident happened so why didn't anyone tell me immediately?), and shame (I'm a teacher and I have a son who doesn't know how to behave in school?). I was unable to understand clearly my son's school experiences.

It is only today that I can more deeply reflect on and ponder the possible meanings in this narrative. Joe's "no problems, mom" is a remark that typifies the boy code (Pollack, 1993). Pollack describes this code as a mask of masculinity that our society uses to enshroud our boys. This mask encourages boys to hide their feelings and assume an "All's fine" response—or silence—to questions. Left in place, this mask may camouflage feelings of pain and anger that may later result in acts of violence, withdrawal, and drug and alcohol abuse.

Kindlon and Thompson (2000) and Pollack (1993) suggest that individuals who care about boys need to help release boys from this stereotypical image of the "tough guy." Breaking the code of silence is one way to help release boys. Boys' "tough guy" stance may, in fact, be a cry for help. Teaching boys emotional literacy (Pollack, 1993) may give them the tools they need to free themselves from the mask of masculinity. When boys can begin expressing their emotions and identifying them with language, they may begin to examine their feelings and responses in ways that can be productive in their personal, psychic growth.

Reflecting on the Crossroads narrative, I see that part of Joe's struggle was with another one of the stereotypical masks: Black, handsome, tough, competitive sports player. He was tall and strong for his age. He appeared to be more physically and intellectually mature than most of his peers. Because of this he excelled at sports and this excellence was encouraged by his coaches—in and outside of school. This broad cultural sports image was difficult to combat. What did Joe's teachers and coach need to do to help him? Is there a place in middle level teacher preparation for an understanding of the psychological issues that boys deal with? Is there a place in teacher preparation to learn ways to break down the boy codes and create safe spaces for boys' emotional literacy to develop and flourish?

This was my struggle as well—I, too, saw Joe as an excellent sports player. If I could replay this experience, what might I try that would have helped Joe more consciously balance his expressed love of sports and encourage him to identify academic areas of interest? I encouraged Ann to create the geography unit but that did not materialize. I used to think, "Joe was a boy in a man's body." His appearance, even to me, deceived me into believing at moments that he was "mature" and could not possibly be acting like a middle school teenager! These thoughts came to me particularly during the suspension experiences. From an education point of view, Joe's fighting needed to be stopped. In the first suspension Joe physically fought a classmate. In the second suspension Joe intellectually fought a teacher. He needed to experience the consequences of his actions. By suspending Joe, he did not experience consequences that matched his action. He was punished with a "day away from school," learning that he "liked" suspensions?

In my response to Joe, I perpetuated the boy code mask of silence. This mask of silence, I reminded him, would allow him to graduate. Individuals, particularly boys, can use silence as a protective shield against pain. If I had been able to help Joe talk through and express his emotions, might he have been able to assume a different stance when he felt his "hot temper" surfacing? From the school point of view, might a Boys Talk class have been just as useful for the boys as the Girls Talk class was for the girls? How can parents and teachers at the middle level help boys develop emotional vocabulary and ways to identify and talk about their feelings? Boys with high activity levels need places where they can safely be as active as they need to. Can we create such safe places in schools for them?

Inseparable from gender is the theme of ethnicity in this narrative. Recently, while reading the citation to follow, I gained courage to explore more deeply my White mother-ness. My consciousness regarding the theme of Black sons and White mothers was raised and problematized:

> I think sometimes that had I known [my mother] would not survive her illness, I might have written a different book—less a meditation on the absent parent [my father], more a celebration of the one [my mother] who was the single constant in my life. (Obama, p. xii, 2004)

Obama's suggestion that his mother was an always steady and constant presence in his life helped me wonder about my relationship with Joe. Obama does not highlight race in this citation. I do. This prompts further questions. I wonder what influence my Whiteness played on Joe's experiences of Blackness at Crossroads? Did his teachers instinctively expect him to behave well because his mother was White? I wonder what influence Joe's Blackness played on my experiences at Crossroads?

When Joe became disruptive did they suspend him, unconsciously selecting the most extreme and untested punishment, "Joe can be our test case" because he was Black? Or because he was biracial, "we've never suspended anyone before"? Did his teachers hold higher expectations for Joe because of me?

Calls for further research on home and family, the schooling issues of biracial students and their parents (Brown & Leaman, 2007; Chiong, 1998; Jeynes, 2007; Root, 2001; Udry, 2003; Williams, 2009) must be addressed.

Adolescence is a critical time in ethnic identity development (Brown & Leaman, 2007). It is extremely important that middle level teachers, leaders, and parents understand the role that ethnic identity development needs to play in teaching and learning at this level. Equally important is the need for teachers to effectively collaborate with parents in supporting, guiding, educating, and nurturing their teenagers in ways that will help them be successful—in the middle—and for years to come.

CONCLUSION

In this chapter I tell my story as a White mother with a Black son, an African and American son who attends a middle school that uses recognized middle school best practices. Framing this narrative through the theoretical lens of parent involvement and student success and then layering it with themes of ethnicity/race, identity, and gender, I reveal the complexity and complications that result from my efforts of involvement. As a mother, teacher, and researcher I continue to reflect on this story and what it means to me and may mean to others. At this moment of conclusion, I urge my readers to ponder with me the deep meaning of parental involvement for all families, those with one ethnic identity and those with multiple identities. When we call for parental involvement in our children's schools, what is it, exactly, that we want and hope for from parents and students? What can parents and students hope for from teachers and schools? What are the hopes of each of these individuals? Turning to the future, what will be the narratives of parent involvement and student success?

ACKNOWLEDGMENT

I wish to thank the following individuals, listed in alphabetical order—except for Joe—for their thoughtful questions, comments, and support on earlier drafts. Joe Malu, Rita S. Brause, Helen Churko, Jeong-Hee Kim, Marie Grace Mutino, Anne Ogg, and Kate Shackford.

REFERENCES

Barbieri, M. (1995). *Sounds from the heart: Learning to listen to girls*. Portsmouth, NH: Heinemann.

Brause, R. S. (1991). Hypothesis generating studies in your classroom. In R. S. Brause & J. S. Mayher (Eds.), *Search and research: What the inquiring teacher needs to know* (pp. 181-206). London, England: Falmer Press.

Brown, D. F., & Leaman, H. L. (2007). Recognizing and responding to young adolescents' ethnic identity development. In S. B. Mertens, V. A. Anfara, Jr., & M. M. Caskey (Eds.), *The young adolescent and the middle school* (pp. 219-236). Charlotte, NC: Information Age.

Carnegie Council on Adolescent Development. (1989). *Turning points: Preparing American youth for the 21st century.* New York, NY; Carnegie Corporation of New York.

Chiong, J. A. (1998). *Racial categorization of multiracial children in schools*. Westport, CT: Bergin & Garvey.

Connelly, M. F., & Clandinin, D. J. (1990). Stories of experience and narrative inquiry. *Educational Researcher, 19*(5), 1-14.

Coulthard, M. (1985). *An introduction to discourse analysis: New edition*. New York, NY: Longman.

Delpit, L. (1995). *Other people's children: Cultural conflict in the classroom*. New York, NY: The New Press.

Dewey, J. (1963). *Experience and Education*. New York, NY: Collier Books (Original work published in 1916)

Epstein, J. L., Salinas, K. C., & Van Voorhis, F. L., (2001). *Manual for teachers involve parents in schoolwork (TIPS) language arts, science/health, and math interac-*

tive homework in the middle grades. (Grades 6, 7, & 8). Baltimore, MD: Center on School, Family, and Community Partnerships, Johns Hopkins University.

Epstein, J. L, Simon, B. S., & Salinas, K. C. (1997, September). Involving parents in homework in the middle grades. *Research Bulletin, 18*.

Epstein, J. L., & Van Voorhis, F. L. (2001). More than minutes: Teachers' roles in designing homework. *Educational Psychologist, 36*(3), 181-194.

Erickson, F. (1986). Qualitative methods in research on teaching. In M. C. Wittrock (Ed.), *Handbook of research on teaching* (pp. 119-161). New York, NY: Macmillan.

Fine, M. (Ed.). (1996). *Talking across boundaries: Participatory evaluation research in an urban middle school*. New York, NY: Bruner Foundation.

Fine, M., Weiner, A., Bell, C., Calderwood, P., Chanlatte, A., Foresta, C., et al. (1994, February). *Creating communities of inquiry in middle school*. Panel presentation at the 15th annual Ethnography in Education Research Forum at the University of Pennsylvania, Philadelphia, PA.

Frey, D. (1995). *The last shot: City streets, basketball dreams*. New York, NY: Simon & Schuster.

Geertz, C. (1973). *The interpretation of culture: Selected essays*. New York, NY: Basic Books.

Gilligan, C. (1982). *In a different voice: Psychological theory and women's development*. Cambridge, MA: Harvard University Press.

Henderson, A. T., & Berla, N. (1996). *A new generation of evidence: The family is critical to student achievement*. Washington, DC: Center for Law and Education.

Hoover-Dempsey, K. V., & Sandler, H. M. (1997). Why do parents become involved in their children's education? *Review of Educational Research, 67*, 3-42.

Jervis, K. (1996). "How come there are no brothers on that list?": Hearing the hard questions all children ask. *Harvard Educational Review, 66* (3), 546-576.

Jeynes, W. H. (2007). The relationship between parent involvement and urban secondary school academic achievement: A meta-analysis. *Urban Education, 42*(1), 82-110. doi: 10.1177/0042085906293818

Kellaghan, T., Sloane, K., Alvarez, B., & Bloom, B. S. (1993). *The home environment and school learning: Promoting parental involvement in the education of children*. San Francisco, CA: Jossey-Bass.

Kindlon, D., & Thompson, M. (2000). *Raising cain: Protecting the emotional life of boys*. New York, NY: Ballantine Books.

Malu, K., Feola, D., & Brause, R. S. (2001, June). *Theoretical and practical concerns in naming research study participants: A collaborative conversation*. Collaborative enterprise presented at the 13th annual conference on Ethnographic and Qualitative Research in Education, State University of New York at Albany.

Mo, Y., & Singh, K. (2008). Parents' relationships and involvement: Effects on students' school engagement and performance. *Research in Middle Level Education Online, 31*(10), 1-11.

Moss, G. (2004). Provisions of trustworthiness in critical narrative research: Bridging intersubjectivity and fidelity. *The Qualitative Report, 9*(2), 359-374.

Patall, E., Cooper, H., & Robinson, J. C. (2008). Parent involvement in homework: A research synthesis. *Review of Educational Research, 78*(4), 1039-1101.

Pollack, W. (1998). *Real boys: Rescuing our sons from the myths of boyhood.* New York, NY: Henry Holt.

Pomerantz, E. M., & Eaton, M. M. (2001). Maternal intrusive support in the academic context: Transactional socialization processes. *Developmental Psychology, 37*(2), 174-186. doi: 10.1037/0012-1649.37.2.174

Riessman, C. K. (1993). *Narrative analysis.* Newbury Park, CA: Sage Publications.

Root, M. M. P. (Ed.). (2001). Parents, children, and race. In M. M. P. Root , *Love's revolution: Interracial marriage* (pp. 136-163). Philadelphia, PA: Temple University Press.

Sheldon S. B., & Epstein, J. L. (2005). School programs of family and community involvement to support children's reading and literacy development. In J. Flood & P. Anders (Eds.), *Literacy development of students in urban schools: Research and policy* (pp. 107-138). Newark, DE: International Reading Association.

Sizer, T. (1992). *Horace's school: Redesigning the American high school.* Boston, MA: Houghton Mifflin.

Twine, F. W. (2004). White Antiracism in multiracial families. In M. Fine, L. Weis, L. P. Pruitt, & A. Burns (Eds.), *Off White: Readings on power, privilege, and resistance* (pp. 395-410). New York, NY: Routledge.

Udry, R., Li, R. M., & Hendrickson-Smith, J. (2003). Health and behavior risks of adolescents with mixed-race identity. *American Journal of Public Health, 93*(11), 1865-1870.

Van Voorhis, F. L. (2003). Interactive homework in middle school: Effects on family involvement and students' science achievement. *Journal of Educational Research, 96*(9), 323-339.

Williams, R. F. (2009). Black-white biracial students in American schools: A review of the literature. *Review of Educational Research, 79*(2), 776-804. doi: 10.3102/0034654309331561

CHAPTER 16

LOCATING AN AUTHORIAL VOICE

Engaging a School Reform Debate Through the Roles of a Mother, Teacher, Community Member, and University Professor

Cynthia C. Reyes

In the following narrative, the author examines a community process in action where school board members, teachers, community members, and administrators reviewed the middle level multiage house system in her children's school vis-à-vis a reconfiguration committee. As the committee moved to recommend organizational changes to the multiage house, Grades 5-8, the author struggled to reconcile the multiple roles that she played, including the role of parent, community member, former classroom teacher, and university professor as she followed the reconfiguration process. Using the feminist methodological perspective of the insider/outsider, the author analyzes her multiple roles. These roles had positive and negative effects on her determination to support the current middle school program.

Voices From the Middle: Narrative Inquiry By, For, and About the Middle Level Community
pp. 339–357
Copyright © 2010 by Information Age Publishing

ADVOCATING FOR WESTBRIDGE MIDDLE SCHOOL

Dear Westbridge School Board and Westbridge Middle School Administration:

It's fair to say that I already had a bias when we chose to move to Westbridge Community, because I've always wanted my children to attend a progressive school system during their middle school years. In the past, I've either taught in, or had my children attend, a variety of public and private schools that had the traditional junior high focus. After these experiences, I've come to embrace the multiage houses at Westbridge Middle School for the following reasons: I like a school structure that allows teachers to team or to work collaboratively on curriculum, to share information about students, or to problem solve, a kiva or advisory that allows students a forum for discussing their concerns or to celebrate their work, and, most of all, I like the opportunity for younger and older students to interact.

This is how I started the letter I sent, as a concerned parent and community member, to express my support for my children's middle school program. I sent this letter because our middle school was in jeopardy. A small group of parents and community members were unhappy with the multiage grade structure. Calling themselves the *reconfiguration committee*, the group called for whole school reform, which primarily targeted a change to the multiage middle school house (team) system (Grades 5-8), which had been in existence for more than 15 years. I had participated in social protests and rallies before to support ideals that I believed in, but I never experienced an issue that created more distrust or incited more passion around schooling than this effort at middle school reform.

In the following narrative, I describe a community process where school board members, teachers, community members, and administrators reviewed the middle level multiage team system in our school vis-à-vis the reconfiguration committee and the effect that this process had on its community members, parents, and teachers. I write, using the metaphor of wearing multiple hats, for the roles that I assumed as a parent, community member, former classroom teacher, and university professor. In the methodology section, I describe narrative inquiry as the method that I used. I highlight the feminist methodological perspective of the insider/outsider to analyze these roles, which positively and negatively influenced my determination to continue supporting the existing middle school program.

THE MOVE TO WESTBRIDGE

My family and I moved 5 years earlier to Westbridge, a quiet community in Vermont. I joined the faculty in the Middle Level Teacher Education Program at the University of Vermont in the position of middle and secondary literacy educator. Westbridge Middle School, my new colleagues told me, was a fine, progressive school. The teacher education program regularly placed interns there because of the unique multiage curriculum and teaming practices. Having come from a single grades experience as a student and a teacher, I was curious about the middle school concept and the multiage house structure.

We first visited the school in July with my two children who were in elementary and middle school. As we drove up to the entrance, we passed the town library on our left, a quaint, white two-floor building with garden and patio in back. I later came to appreciate it as a safe, cozy environment for children where working parents, such as myself, could leave our older children after school and feel confident that they would be fine. The children engaged in a variety of library-initiated activities, such as completing homework in the homework center, searching for information on the computers, or participating in book or social clubs. The proximity of the library to the school created a town-community connection. When we entered the school on that hot, muggy July day, no one greeted us except the darkly lit hallways and the smell of wet carpet. We found our way to the central office and there the principal and administrative assistant welcomed us warmly and took our children's school transfer papers. The custodial workers were busy running their industrial-sized vacuum cleaners in the classrooms and hallways. The principal invited us to walk around and visit the classrooms, referring to them as *houses*. We picked up our feet gingerly around the vacuum cords and hoses as we made our way into the different classrooms.

PHILOSOPHY OF WESTBRIDGE MIDDLE SCHOOL HOUSE

We turned on the light in the first classroom and I was surprised to find not one classroom but four that were separated by four wall partitions. I remembered that the principal referred to this large space as a *house*. Each of the four houses had a name and this one was called *Skybound*. Without the pulse of student and teacher energy and clutter of books and school items, we immediately sensed the quiet, still air. We noticed the *kiva* area that dominated the center of the house, the four levels of low stairs that wrapped around the kiva for people to sit on. This led down to the center stage at the bottom with the whiteboard in front. The word *kiva* has its origin in Pueblo Indian culture and it represents a large chamber used for religious or other important ceremonies. In this setting, the kiva was the place where the team came together for special announcements or public acknowledgement. Chairs were stacked up like minitowers along the sides of the room, and three or four long tables stood in the middle of each area. Without any human presence in such a large space, it felt lonely.

I learned more about the *house* philosophy during curriculum night at the beginning of the school year. The principal shared the school goals in a PowerPoint overview. These four goals were to (1) create a balanced sense of school and house, (2) increase student learning especially for those students on individualized educational plans (IEPs) and with low socioeconomic status, (3) increase equity across the houses, and (4) manage social and academic peer interactions across grades. This language, I felt, resonated with the sentiment of the National Middle School Association's (NMSA) *This We Believe* (NMSA, 2003). The principal's PowerPoint included excerpts from "This We Believe" in her descriptions of the characteristics of children ages 10-15 and the kinds of structured environments the school needed to create for this age group. As my children went through the Westbridge Middle School, I experienced the following NMSA-endorsed characteristics of my children's house: a positive, safe learning climate for all of the students, parental involvement, teaming, and advisory.

These goals reflected my daughter's experiences in the school. As an eighth grader, my daughter mentored the in-coming fifth graders and she experienced the pride of being the older and wiser student. She remembered her fear when she entered the house as a fifth grader and how she was in awe of the older students. She also identified closely with her house and she felt her teachers worked together to foster her learning.

PARENT AND COMMUNITY PERCEPTION OF TEAMING

At a Westbridge school board meeting during my daughter's eighth-grade year, a small group of parents and community members raised the question of inequity between houses. This group of teachers, a guidance counselor, and community members, were organized and goal driven. This group had strong voices and believed that the house system was flawed and inequitable. They felt strongly that, as taxpayers for the school in their community, they should have input into how the house system was practiced.

Through the local school board meetings and editorials in the local newspaper the group raised social and academic concerns that they attributed to teaming. Their litany of concerns included questioning the imposition of a poor teaching style on a student for 4 years. They were concerned that the system exposed children to the same four teachers from Grades 5 through 8 and perpetuated a significant lack of consistency in quality education across the five houses. They argued a 4-year house commitment limited exposure to age- and gender-matched peers. Furthermore, they asserted the house system was highly repetitive and competed for mutual resources, supplies, and expertise. They strongly objected to the close interactions between the fifth graders and eighth graders whom they argued were developmentally, socially, and emotionally different.

Some of the concerns were imbued with rhetoric; for example, one community member wrote in an editorial, "The house system amplifies the effects of imperfections in the education of our children four-fold." Yet the growing concerns of this small group of vocal parents materialized into authentic questions about education. The questions that they raised during the school board meetings reflected a general lack of awareness that families, old and new to the system, had about the goals of middle grade houses. Their questions indicated their misperceptions about middle level organization. For example, they asked, "Why are we forced into this four-year house system? Is there some economic benefit? What is the 'educational philosophy' of the Upper Houses? Does the school have an 'educational philosophy?' Why is there such inconsistency in academic quality between all houses? How can the school ignore 78% of parents who want children of the same grade housed together at one site? Can't the community take a look at the numbers to see whether it would work? Why is there such enormous inconsistency in upper house curriculum?"

The small group coalesced into a "reconfiguration group" whose platform was to challenge the status quo. This reconfiguration group scheduled a community forum where they presented a PowerPoint that focused on specific concerns about the current house configuration. They emphasized that in the current system teachers had to be skilled in addressing developmental and academic needs of a large age range. They felt the house system did not offer children diverse teaching styles and approaches to learning. The group expressed concern that students and families identified strongly with their houses to the detriment of the whole school. And they felt that house assignments created undue stress in families of in-coming fifth graders.

In response to this meeting and repeated calls for change, the school administrators decided to develop a committee to which they invited teachers, community members, students, administrators, and education experts. Then they hired an individual who did not live in the community to facilitate the committee meetings. The goal of this committee was to look at potential teaming configurations. At the beginning of the process, a few community members encouraged me to volunteer and join the committee to review the middle house structure. I felt that those community members believed that I would listen to viewpoints fairly, and that my views would balance out the current call for changing the structure. Since

I could not attend all the meetings, I volunteered as ad hoc committee member and the newly appointed facilitator contacted me about meeting to address any questions she and the committee had pertaining to education and middle level organization.

THE DILEMMA OF THE OUTSIDER WITHIN AND FINDING ONE'S VOICE

As Deborah Britzman (in Connelly & Clandinin, 1990) explained:

> Voice is meaning that resides in the individual to participate in a community.... The struggle of the voice begins when a person attempts to communicate meaning to someone else.... Finding the words, speaking for oneself, feeling heard by others are all a part of this process. (p. 4)

Most would agree with Brtizman's notion of voice as it relates to the dynamic of people negotiating ideas. But what happens when an individual comes to the process with different experiences? In this case, I wore multiple hats: parent of children in the house system; community member who voted and paid taxes in the school district; and university professor in a middle level teacher education program teaching graduate students who are completing their yearlong internships at the school.

To understand the multiple roles that I brought to the reconfiguration process, I employed narrative inquiry as a methodology. Connelly and Clandinin (1990) describe the central focus of narrative inquiry as evident "when it is grasped that people are both living their stories in an ongoing experiential text and telling their stories as they reflect upon life and explain themselves to others" (p. 4). In addition, I found it useful to draw upon the feminist methodological perspective of the insider/outsider that non-traditional (ethnic, racial, or gendered) researchers experience in the field regarding subjectivity and power relations. This perspective is also similar to autoethnography or reflexive ethnography, an "autobiographical genre of writing and research that displays multiple layers of consciousness, connecting the personal to the cultural" (Denzin & Lincoln, 2000, p. 739). According to Connelly and Clandinin (1990), narrative inquiry data can be in the form of field notes, journal records, autobiographical writing, letter writing, and unstructured interviews. In the twelve-month period that the reconfiguration process occurred, I collected the monthly meeting notes from the reconfiguration committee meetings, observations of my meetings with the facilitator, teachers, and administrators, newspaper articles on the process, editorial pages, school documents, and reflection notes on my observations. I used these data to construct a narrative chronology of the reconfiguration process. Analyzing this chronology, I highlighted my own experiences in this narrative to understand my positioning in the various socially constructed settings and the self-other interactions in which I engaged. The personal narrative, which is usually in first person reporting, invites alternative interpretations and readings of the story (Bochner & Ellis, 2003). In writing this narrative, I share how I locate my own voice in this process.

Feminism has contributed to validating reflexive ethnography (Behar, 1996; Personal Narratives Group, 1989) by authorizing voices that have not traditionally been privileged in social science research, such as women of color and postcolonial perspectives (Behar, 1993; Collins, 1991; Henry, 2003, 2007; Kondo, 1986; Narayan, 1993; Rosaldo, 1989; Sherif, 2001). Feminist theory has substantially informed ethnographic methodology on the influence that subjectivity can have on research relationships and the power dynamics of such relationships (Tedlock, 1995). For example, a body of feminist research focuses on subjectivity and the insider/outsider dilemma with the question: How does one account for one's identity in and out of the field? As one who considered herself a middle class, Southeast Asian American who identified more with her upbringing in the U.S. Midwest, I was conscious of the outsider identity that I brought to this small, New England university town where I lived for only five years.

Collins' work on Black women, particularly academic women, who refer to themselves as the *outsiders within* (1991), describes how they reconcile their cultural experiences with the discourses and social practices of the sociological paradigm in which they work. She suggests that the insider group maintains similar worldviews while the other group, the practitioners, is involved in the becoming of insiders. Non-traditional researchers assert the White, middle-class researcher who "inhabits positions of power" (Henry, 2007, p. 71) and researchers who themselves are ethnic, racial, or gendered may experience power relations in certain contexts differently. As a first generation South Asian researcher, Henry (2007) reflected on her experiences of being an insider and outsider doing her fieldwork in India, where she exerted her Western view in some settings and in others where her participants assumed that she would behave according to cultural expectation. She discovered that achieving agency with her participants was different in the contexts that she inhabited and that she had to bargain differently with them from one context to the next (Henry, 2007).

When reflecting on how our identities move from one setting to another, it is useful to think of the identity as a socially constructed self (Holland, Lachicotte Jr., Skinner, & Cain, 1998). As researchers, each new setting is filled with powerful, often dominant, discourses that we need to negotiate. This framework helps to describe the power relations that exist. According to social constructivists, we associate subject positions to one another and make claims about who we are to one another, including the nature of our relationships.

The complexity that exists for some ethnic and minority researchers with the outsider within approach also resonates with Collins' earlier work of using this approach to construct creative tension within each setting that she worked in (1991). She said:

> The approach suggested by the experiences of outsiders within is one where intellectuals learn to trust their own personal and cultural biographies as significant sources of knowledge ... experienced reality is used as a valid source of knowledge for critiquing sociological facts and theories, while sociological thought offers new ways of seeing that experienced reality. (1991, pp. 53-54).

In the following section, I describe the hats I possessed as I experienced the school process. Together, they provided a layer of complexity and a unique way of looking at the reconfiguration process. A strong bias for one of those perspectives resulted in what I eventually perceived as the loss of my voice at the negotiating table.

THE PARENT/COMMUNITY MEMBER HAT

As the parent, I realized from this reconfiguration issue the frustration that parents/family members can have when they lack information they need to make educational decisions for their child. Even more frustrating for parents is their lack of educational discourse for communicating with teachers and administrators, insights on young adolescent development, and general understanding of educational concepts.

At social gatherings in my neighborhood, where most families are active in the town council or school system, predictably the conversation turns to concerns about a school policy or teaching practice. As parents, we worry incessantly about whether our children are creating and maintaining friendships in school, enjoying what they learn, and meeting academic challenges with success. Parental concerns include the desire to understand the school and how it works. This is made easier when there is a mutual understanding between home and school about parental involvement. There are various models that specifically suggest the components of good communication between home and school (Epstein & Salinas, 2004). In the literature on home and schooling, better reporting and communication efforts between school and home can enhance parent understanding of the school mission (Brough, 1997).

At times, my neighbors ask me to clarify a concept or to share insight about education and usually they are grateful for the information, but sometimes they still meet my information with a skepticism based on what they themselves experienced in school. The questioning does not surprise me. And the questioning often helps to clarify complex ideas about teaching and learning. But if parents do not understand the underlying rationale for pedagogy or the language that describes a school practice, they will always return to what they themselves experienced in school.

THE UNIVERSITY PROFESSOR HAT

As a university professor I support a certain professional orientation regarding middle level teacher education preparation. It is a belief based on a commitment to student identity and voice, constructivist teaching, student centered education, and teaming. In our program, we model how middle level organization goes hand in hand with constructivist teaching. In constructivist classrooms, the teacher is one source of information for learning and not the entire source; the curriculum encourages thoughtful question-asking and discussion; students, not the teacher, drive the lessons; and students engage with experiences that question previous ideas of existing knowledge (Brooks & Brooks, 1993, p. 25).

In our education classes we model best practices whether it is in curriculum, organization, or literacy. We ask our pre-service teachers to explore student voice, a central tenet of the middle level concept. In our various classes, we ask them to construct and to reflect on their young adolescent autobiographies, to create videos of their literacy development as young adolescents, and to view curriculum through young adolescent lens.

THE TEACHER HAT

As a former classroom teacher I sympathized with the teachers during the reconfiguration process. In a chance meeting at school, one of the teacher leaders involved in our middle level program confided in me that teachers were experiencing a declining climate of trust because of the committee work. Many teachers felt that the community and parents no longer supported their work. Some had even begun to question a practice and curriculum they had felt so strongly about for the last few years. Instead of feeling motivated to critically reflect on their practice, they felt discouraged.

The teacher leader explained that most teachers felt like they did not have a united voice in this process. The administrators had not been forthcoming about the committee's progress or goals nor had they planned any meeting with the teachers to discuss their concerns. This contrasted with one of the markers of a good middle level program: the level of empowerment and collaboration that teachers experience (Seed, 2006) Administrators tend to empower their teachers more when they initiate some of the following practices, including developing teacher governance that allows teachers to have voice, assisting with staffing and teaming, or supporting their block scheduling so they can meet (Seed, 2006). In a time when high-stakes testing creates a climate of heightened accountability, schools and administrators must consider how to keep teachers energized. The literature addresses the ways that schools can use teacher skills and expertise in creative ways rather than assign them to uninspired and prescriptive curriculums (Lambert, 2003; Reeves, 2004).

According to the teacher leader, some of the Westbridge teachers felt the teacher representatives on the reconfiguration committee were not sharing all of the information that they learned and were unable to address any of their colleagues' questions. Teachers felt the overall, uneasy climate brought about an increase in negative student behavior and unrest. On impulse, I asked the teacher leader if it would help if I talked to the teachers and listened to their concerns as a representative of the university program. She said she would ask the teachers and let me know. The teachers knew me as one of the university instructors and they always welcomed me when I made occasional visits into their classrooms at my graduate student's request to observe a literacy lesson.

I immediately consulted the reconfiguration committee facilitator and shared my idea of meeting with the teachers. Wouldn't it be reasonable, I asked, for me to hear them out especially since the facilitator could not do it for fear of compromising her leadership on the committee? Someone ought to meet with the teachers, I thought, especially since committee discussions were now focusing on potential changes to the current middle level configuration. I asked whether the teachers were being apprised of these possible changes and whether the administration would agree to them. I was concerned about the effect these changes would have for curriculum. I remembered how the district curriculum coordinator and I agreed on this point that curriculum change could not occur without administrator and teacher consent. It raised a serious question for me: Could a community, most of whose members were non-teachers, non-experts in the field of education, potentially change a school curriculum?

When the reconfiguration facilitator explored a similar question with the administrators she found out that, indeed, the school was going to give the community an opportunity to influence the current middle level configuration. While a change to configuration would not directly impact curriculum, it would change the teachers who teamed and planned together.

Change may not always be negative. However, given the speed with which this process was happening, this response made me reflect on who had the right to influence school curriculum. I believed in empowering all constituencies when addressing education, but was the community going too far and was the administration negligent in enabling community members to change curriculum? I wondered how much power each constituent group should have in shaping education for our children. Ultimately, who should be qualified to change it?

Similar questions go to the heart of what everyone cares most about education. After meeting with the teachers, the administrators, and attending the community forum, I recognized there was no one group for whom this reconfiguration change mattered more; everyone had equal investment in the school.

I decided to meet with the teachers after the teacher leader informed me that she received favorable responses from many about the proposed meeting. I was prepared to go, when the facilitator called me with a grave concern. A committee member wanted to know if I was representing the reconfiguration committee, and, if so, why had I not notified the committee of my plan. I was no longer perceived as an impartial observer. My action might compromise the process and furthermore it showed my bias toward the teacher perspective and the current middle level configuration. Even though I had separated my role as ad hoc member from that of university professor, the separation from my teacher hat was not enough. The facilitator was concerned about the process, especially at this juncture where she really needed community trust. I reassured her that I would act on my own and that I would ask the teacher leader to convey this message in an email that very day. While it left me unsettled, we ended our conversation with the mutual agreement that she would no longer consult me on the education piece. To continue doing so would jeopardize the confidence that she had already achieved with the committee and community. Although I was aware of the steps that I was taking in my decision to meet with the teachers, I felt naïve. In the back of my mind, my researcher stance told me that I should have created more distance between the teachers and me but my teacher role identity took hold. Paulo Freire's words on self-actualization and the use of education to shape society (Freire, 1970) came to mind and rejuvenated my instincts as a teacher. I no longer felt that I could be effective as the parent or community member. In that instance, my teacher hat made me sympathetic to teachers' concerns about not having voice during this process.

MULTIPLE HATS

I began to rethink my researcher stance and my inability to be objective. In an effort to seek agency as teacher, parent, or university instructor, I wanted to claim the experience and knowledge that I possessed with each role and I wanted to investigate further the dynamic and tension that was created when I engaged each one. For example, I noted in the parent section how my expertise in teacher education was not always called upon. I did not feel that I was the expert in those settings because parents still met my research-based evidence with skepticism. I wondered whether my identity as the university expert was in question in this particular setting because I was not perceived as fitting the part or because I represented different ideas and notions of school reform. As Henry (2007) noted about the importance of agency in the field, "If one's identity is always in question (either insider or outsider of the field), it is difficult for one to operationalize the capital associated with dominant and hegemonic identities" (2007, p. 78).

In the teacher settings, the teachers were familiar with my identity because they often saw me in the school not only as a parent but also as the university instructor of some of their student teachers. Some had had conversations with me about literacy practice and so from these exchanges my authority and legitimacy with the content grew. In their eyes, I represented a qualified expert and therefore a legitimate listener to the present school conflict. The concerned group of teachers saw themselves as disempowered in the process. In the following section, I continue the narrative, revealing the complexity of the multiple hats I wore during my meetings with the teachers and the administrators.

WHAT TEACHERS SAID

Of the 125 teachers in the school, 25 attended this meeting. There were others who wanted to attend but had other obligations. In the teacher gathering, it was clear that most people did not know why I was there. A few were my children's former teachers and they seemed happy to see me but they wondered what I could do for them. I began the meeting by explaining what brought me there and what I thought I could do. As soon as I suggested that I would type up their comments after our meeting and meet with the administrators to share their concerns, I sensed an onslaught of predictable skepticism. If they were not being listened to now, they wondered, what good would it do for me to share their concerns? Despite their worry, I stressed the importance of getting something down on paper and having me present it to the principals and speaking on their behalf as a community resident, teacher, and university representative. With their input, I suggested, the administrators could more effectively address their concerns about the reconfiguration process every step of the way.

The small group was vociferous. Their concerns were unified and specific. On a positive note, they appreciated the three teacher representatives who were on the reconfiguration committee and attended the bimonthly meetings. They acknowledged that one of the principals was new and was trying to work with teachers through this difficult process. One of the teacher representatives felt that parents on the committee supported the teachers. She also thought that the committee would produce recommendations that most of the teachers could support.

The most pressing concern for these teachers was their lack of voice, even with the teacher representation. Teachers wanted a significant role in shaping the configuration process. They wanted their expertise and knowledge to influence those recommendations. They wanted the community to understand that there was a symbiotic relationship between the configuration and curriculum, and that teachers needed time to prepare for any curriculum change.

They were also concerned that the reconfiguration process did not acknowledge the original mission and vision statements related to the current house system. They asked, "What happened to the criteria that we valued in the past? Where is it evident in the current process?" This omission distressed them because the mission drove their beliefs about teaching in this particular middle level structure and it represented continuity for their program. Changes put into effect at the beginning of the school year due to low student enrollment exacerbated the lack of trust. As a result, teachers reported that they felt disoriented and so did the families and students. One house was dismantled, students were shuffled into other houses, and teachers were placed into other teams. Teachers expected to make these changes work. But with the looming threat to reconfigure the houses the teachers were leery. "How can we gauge whether something is working or not if we are expected to constantly change or adapt our instruction? How is the change process being honored?" one asked in frustration.

WHAT THE ADMINISTRATORS SAID

After my meeting with the teachers, I met with the three principals. As I walked into the room, the assistant principal and building principal were already at the table. We were waiting for one more. Everyone was reserved and serious. I sensed trepidation in the air and assumed that, like the teachers, they did not know what to expect from me. How was I going to be able to articulate the teacher's message? I was not yet sure what that message would be. Initially, I thought I would give them the notes that came from the teacher meeting and share and discuss them. But then, what? Where would this information go? In a folder, and then into a file cabinet, my most pessimistic voice told me. When everyone was present, they read my notes and began to comment on some of the teachers' perspectives. One of the principals remarked on the comment that teachers needed their community to hear them. She said that as concerning as it was, she felt that parents and the community would only perceive that as whining.

I reminded the administrators that there was another side to this perspective, which was the overall scrutiny of teachers nationwide. Most teachers recognize the need to allow student voice in their classrooms. Teachers need to know that they, too, have voice in the educational arena. One of the principals added that sometimes parents perceived teachers as having too much power. The argument followed that the school belonged to the community and not to the teachers. Isn't everyone accountable to the school, I asked? Another mentioned how most of the information on my sheet focused mainly on the past, while her intention was to focus on the here and now. The school had to move forward. One of the principals who worked in the community the longest supported this view, adding that it was only in the last two years that he noticed an increase in parents complaining about the house configuration. They loved their home in Westbridge, but they hated their school. At the same time, he acknowledged that there would always be parents who were dissatisfied with school. I realized then how ill prepared I was to respond to such comments. My goal was merely to bring some public pressure on the administration to hear teachers' voices during this process. Instead, what greeted me was their continuing struggle to be accountable to the Westbridge community.

THE COMMUNITY FORUM: COMING TOGETHER

A month after I met with the administrators and the teachers, the committee sponsored a community forum to present the final reconfiguration options that they identified based on their research. Since my meeting with the teachers the reconfiguration committee facilitator began meeting with them on a regular basis. She met with them in a closed meeting right before the community forum to share the final options.

The community forum took place in the school cafeteria. When I walked in, people were already sitting down at the tables that faced a

PowerPoint presentation. The facilitator provided a brief overview of the history of the committee and then explained the committee's reconfiguration options. Five were focused on Grades 5-8. She reviewed the options, asking for parents to hold their questions until later in the forum. At the end of the PowerPoint presentation, people would have a chance to go to one of the easel boards set up around the cafeteria, each representing a reconfiguration plan, and ask questions about the option in which they were most interested. School board members and one of the principals were also present to respond to questions.

As the audience gazed at the PowerPoint slides and the reconfiguration sheet in their hands, I noted the discomfort: a wrinkle of an eyebrow, eyes gazing from one neighbor to the next, and closer scrutiny of the sheets and slides. My first reaction to the reconfiguration plans was the amount of time and energy that the committee took to work through all of the details on the separate diagrams. I heard some of the adults at my table murmur about the specificity in the visuals. The next thing I noticed was confusion as people flipped to the page with the chart symbols, so that they could interpret the diagrams. The most commonly used symbols were the ones used for "middle grades house," "transition," "multiage," and "single grade."

Of the middle grades reconfiguration options, I made the following observations. They offered looping or multiage options mostly for fifth with sixth and seventh with eighth, and single grades options at the fifth and eighth grade levels. The current 5-8 configuration was offered as an option. Before the parents walked to the different easel boards, the facilitator asked us to consider the criteria that the committee had developed on the last sheet to evaluate the reconfiguration options. Any of the committee's twelve criteria could have come from *This We Believe* (NMSA, 2003). The list included the following: fosters a strong sense of community and rich relationships over time, develops continuity of family/teacher/student relationships, fosters an academic rigor and achievement, fosters opportunities for student leadership, mentoring, and role modeling, considers the social and emotional developmental needs of every student age group, and maintains the philosophy and best practice of middle school, as supported by current research. In that vein, I walked over to the easel that represented the current configuration and, as a community member, I asked the scribe to list all of those criteria under the "positive" side in support of that option. I noticed that other adults had already listed what they deemed positive and that list seemed longer than the "negative" side.

I also noticed that others had mixed feelings about the option but they needed more clarity on the number of new detailed offerings before choosing the best solution. A few still wanted to see the single grade span and others still questioned the equity differences between each house.

The forum that evening reaffirmed for me that changing the configuration would not be the key to solving these issues. As I reflected on the concerns of the various constituencies, I realized that we all named fundamental issues that a reconfiguration change could not resolve alone. Perhaps these were the issues that had to be addressed rather than the configuration piece. I also questioned whether my perspective as the ad hoc reconfiguration committee member alone would have led me to that conclusion. Instead, I believe the loss of my voice helped me understand that I was biased from the very beginning. I discuss these reflections in the final section.

REFLECTIONS

"Is it possible to put the brakes on this process? When will the administration, committee, and community at large recognize the low teacher morale?" This teacher quotation captures how I felt about my role as ad hoc member in the configuration process. It came from my inability to find a place where I could voice my feelings about the process. Everyone, including the facilitator, committee members, administrators, teachers, and me created this process as we went along. Teacher morale was already sinking. I felt the administrators should have provided an informal question and answer session for teachers after each committee meeting.

Naively, I thought that by disrupting the process we could slow down what was happening and the different constituencies—teachers, parents, administrators, students—would recognize that their need to be heard was the same, but some did not share that view. For example, while the teachers were happy to have a listener, they did not feel it would change the current environment. While I met with the administrators, they were not sure what to do with my information nor did they believe it would gain community sympathy. In the end, the facilitator explained that some committee members felt I had a bias and therefore they could not consult my educational expertise any longer. I lost my voice on the reconfiguration committee, but I realize the voice I wanted was the one that advocated for the existing middle level configuration.

Using the feminist methodological perspective of the insider/outsider to examine my multiple hats helped me to understand the complexity and range of the different discourses. The perspectives of administrators, teachers, parents, students, and community members all contributed to the configuration process. Existing within the groups were additional layers of complexity since there were even multiple voices and perspectives within each group. No one group was static or spoke with one unified voice.

As I engaged with each group my identity as an *insider* in that group became questionable as the perception of my claim to be an insider changed. My identity as expert in the reconfiguration committee and the parent community were called into question. As a result, my ability and authority to negotiate in both groups became minimal. In contrast, the teacher community acknowledged my experience and skills with the school and its classrooms. It valued my role as a listener and an advocate. However, I was unable to transfer that same identity to the setting with the administrators. While they listened attentively and may even have sympathized with the teachers, whose voices I tried to represent, larger power dynamics were at play as the more powerful voices from the parents, community, and editorial letters from the community's newspaper influenced the administrators' abilities to hear the teacher concerns. Although the initial question to change the school configuration was easy to ask, the layers of power relations mediated the discussions between and among the groups.

Given the notions of identity, agency, and power relations I described earlier, it is ironic and illuminating that as the reconfiguration process continues in my community, the final decision has been delayed and the issue of equity, as the committee described it, stands out for me as critical. From my viewpoint, we missed an opportunity to address this topic of equity. Most parents did not understand the rationale for using teaming and its developmental benefits for this age group. We skimmed over it and immediately went to the structural piece that some argued would address equity issues. On one occasion, I reviewed the meeting notes on equity that the facilitator shared with me. The committee questioned the equity across houses with regard to the issues of curriculum, parental participation, placement process, and learning expectations.

In reality, these equity issues relate to people's perceptions of the different houses. People could not help but compare them, from which house had a stronger team to which house had more technology resources, to which team offered more enrichment activities. These differences related to the kinds of social and community practices that occurred in each house. Ultimately, there was a compelling need to normalize practices and experiences across houses because that was what we found most familiar. We could relate to this based upon our own school experiences.

At the same time, such biases are complex, and a fundamental view on one end makes it difficult to understand the views of others. Whatever socio-cultural knowledge and experience we bring into our home or work communities often necessitates negotiating and renegotiating practices from one setting to the next, even as we seek agency and authority with the hats that we wear. In recalling Collins' (1991) synthesis of the outsider within the sociological paradigm, she suggests three scenarios for the outsider within. Some outsiders within resolve the tension that their new status brings by acclimating to the new setting and adopting all of its social practices without question. Others decide to continue their status on the outside, deciding not to become a member of the community. Both, she recommends, create a loss of creative diversity to the community. The third sphere that she suggests is one that fosters creative tension by "encouraging and institutionalizing outsider within ways of seeing" (p. 53).

With this narrative I intended to make my bias more explicit, which, in turn, forced me to look more critically at others' viewpoints. My teacher hat disrupted the reconfiguration process for me, enabling me to make sense of the competing needs, from the concerned parents and students to the reconfiguration committee and administrators. It was during the teacher meeting that I felt most agency, by listening to the teachers' stories and later conveying these stories to the administrators. This narrative suggests that we accept these places of tension as the norm, similar to what Collins (1991) suggests above, as spaces where difficult yet rich conversations need to occur in order to recognize and engage the multiple voices.

REFERENCES

Behar, R. (1993). *Translated woman: Crossing the border with Esperanza's story.* Boston, MA: Beacon Press.

Behar, R. (1996). *The vulnerable observer: Anthropology that breaks your heart.* Boston, MA: Beacon Press

Bochner, A. P., & Ellis, C. (2003). An introduction to the arts and narrative research: Art as inquiry. *Qualitative Inquiry, 9*(4), 506-514.

Brooks, J., & Brooks, M. (1993). *In search of understanding: The case for constructivist classrooms.* Alexandria, VA: Association for Supervision and Curriculum Association.

Brough, J. (1997). Home-school partnerships: A critical link. In J. Irvin (Ed.), *What current research says to the middle level practitioner* (pp. 265-274). Columbus, OH: National Middle School Association.

Collins, P. H. (1991). Learning from the outsider within: The sociological significance of Black feminist thought. In M. Fonow & J. Cook (Eds.) *Beyond methodology: Feminist scholarship as lived research* (pp. 35-59). Bloomington, IN: Indiana University Press.

Connolly, F., & Clandinin, D. (1990). Stories of experience and narrative experience. *Educational Researcher, 19* (5), 2-14.

Denzin, N., & Lincoln, Y. (2000). (Eds.) *Handbook of qualitative research* (2nd ed.). Thousand Oaks, CA: Sage.

Epstein, J., & Salinas, K. (2004). Partnering with families and communities. *Educational Leadership, 61*(4), 12-18.

Freire, P. (1970). *Pedagogy of the oppressed.* New York, NY: Continuum.

Henry, M. (2003). "Where are you really from?" Representation, identity and power in the fieldwork experiences of a South Asian diasporic." *Qualitative Research, 3*(2), 229-242.

Henry, M. (2007). If the shoe fits: Authenticity, authority and agency feminist diasporic research. *Women's Studies International Forum, 30,* 70-80.

Holland, D., Lachicotte, Jr., W., Skinner, D., & Cain, C. (1998). *Identity and agency in cultural worlds.* Cambridge, MA: Harvard University Press.

Kondo, D. (1986). Dissolution and reconstitution of self: Implications for anthropological epistemology, *Cultural Anthropology, 1*(2), 74-88.

Lambert, L. (2003). *Leadership capacity for lasting school improvement.* Alexandria, VA: Association for Supervision and Curriculum Development.

National Middle School Association. (2003). *This we believe: Successful schools for young adolescents.* Westerville, OH: National Middle School Association.

Narayan, K. (1993). How native is a "native" anthropologist? *American Anthropologist, 95*(3), 671-686.

Personal Narratives Group. (1989). *Interpreting women's lives: Feminist theory and personal narratives.* Bloomington, IN: Indiana University Press.

Reeves, D. (2004). *Accountability for learning: How teachers and school leaders can take charge.* Alexandria, VA: Association for Supervision and Curriculum Development.

Rosaldo, R. (1989). *Culture and truth: The remaking of social analysis.* Boston, MA: Beacon Press.

Seed, A. (2006). Making empowerment and collaboration part of the lives of highly qualified team teachers. *Middle School Journal, 37*(5), 40-44.

Sherif, B. (2001). The ambiguity of boundaries in the fieldwork experience: Establishing rapport and negotiating insider/outsider status. *Qualitative Inquiry, 7*(4), 436-447.

Tedlock, B. (1995). From participant observation to the observation of participation: The emergence of narrative ethnography. *Journal of Anthropological Research, 47*(1), 69-94.

CHAPTER 17

THE FAMILY LEARNING INSTITUTE

Committed to Improving the Reading Skills of Middle Level Learners

Denise L. McLurkin

The Family Learning Institute (FLI) is a nonprofit organization in Ann Arbor, Michigan that was cofounded in 1999 by Doris Sperling. The primary goal of the FLI is to improve the reading skills of students in upper elementary and middle school grades who are at least 2 years behind with their reading development and who have limited financial resources. Through the lens of narrative inquiry, I tell Doris's story of her experiences from conceptualizing, creating, and maintaining the FLI, to the decision to purposely focus on the academic and social/emotional needs of middle level learners who are behind with their reading development. I end with advice Doris has for individuals or groups interested in starting a program such as the FLI in their community.

Voices From the Middle: Narrative Inquiry By, For, and About the Middle Level Community
pp. 359–379

"We can't give up on these kids. They matter too."

—Doris Sperling (Cofounder of the Family Learning Institute)

INTRODUCTION

As children reach early adolescence and progress through the school system, the need to think, listen, read, write, and speak critically, and comprehend, synthesize, evaluate, and critique information from multiple genres, perspectives, and texts (Alvermann, 2001; Biancarosa & Snow, 2006; Moore, Bean, Birdyshaw, & Rycik, 1999) becomes paramount. Unfortunately, not all students are prepared to handle the literacy demands presented to them. Even with the plethora of literacy research, techniques, materials, and prevention programs, some middle level learners may need intensive efforts in order to improve their reading skills.

There are approximately eight million children and young adults between fourth and twelfth grade who struggle with reading (Biancarosa & Snow, 2006). The task of improving the reading skills of these students is more daunting when we consider that the needs and challenges facing middle level struggling readers vary enormously. There are middle level learners who struggle with word recognition, comprehension, and fluency (Adams, 1990; Chall, 1996; LaBerge & Samuels, 1974; Stanovich, 1986). Additionally, there are middle level learners who can read words accurately and fluently, yet who do not use strategies to help them facilitate comprehension (Palincsar & Brown, 1984). Biancarosa and Snow (2006) note that while literacy educators have an array of tools to use with each type of struggling reader, there is not an overall strategy for directing and coordinating these remedial tools to maximize the learning opportunities for middle level struggling readers. Thus, more research is desperately needed in this area.

On January 8, 2002, President Bush signed the No Child Left Behind (NCLB) Act of 2001 (2002). This act laid out the ambitious goal that all American students should reach proficiency in reading/language arts and math in twelve years. The basic principles of the NCLB Act included increased accountability, greater choice for parents and students, more flexibility for states and districts with the use of federal educational funds, and a focus on scientifically research-based emergent and early literacy instruction (No Child Left Behind of 2001, 2002). Unfortunately, with most of the program money in the NCLB Act targeted for the early grades (Conley & Hinchman, 2004), little was made available for middle level learners, and in particular, middle level struggling readers. Many researchers vehemently argued for the need to focus attention and resources on the literacy needs of middle level learners (Alvermann,

2001; Biancarosa & Snow, 2006; Moje, Young, Readence, & Moore, 2000; Moore et al., 1999; National Council of Teachers of English (NCTE) Commission on Reading, 2004; Vacca, 1998; Vacca & Padak, 1990). Tragically, the federal government has yet to acknowledge or adequately fund these critical areas of need.

Notwithstanding the lack of financial assistance and other support, in many communities after-school community-based volunteer tutorial programs were created and supported by community members with the noble goal of assisting students who need additional help with their reading skill development. In his State of the Union address in 2002, former President Bush called on Americans to volunteer at least 2 years of their time serving others. According to Grossman and Furano (2002), over 90 million Americans contribute over 20 billion hours of service to others as volunteers. Doris Sperling and other community members in Ann Arbor, Michigan, who helped to create the Family Learning Institute (FLI), heeded that call and volunteer their time, money, and effort to improving the reading skills of upper elementary and middle level learners who are at least two years below their grade level in their reading development.

With so many children and young Americans suffering with poor reading skills (Biancarosa & Snow, 2006), it is imperative that this critical educational area is examined as there may be dire consequences if not. Although poor reading skills do not directly cause students to drop out of high school, become involved in criminal activity, or become incarcerated, juveniles who have poorer reading skills are more likely to become incarcerated or drop out of high school than their proficient reading peers (Drakeford, 2003; Ensminger & Slusarcick, 1992; Suh & Suh, 2007). Since efforts are being made by community members like Doris Sperling to ameliorate these unfortunate statistics, more research is needed. In particular, we need to find out more about the conceptualization of such a program, how the program is maintained, how it is funded, the type of manpower needed to continue such a program, and the lessons she learned during her more than 10 year journey.

METHODOLOGY

For this inquiry about the FLI and its creator, Doris Sperling, I utilized narrative inquiry (Clandinin & Connelly, 2000) because it allows Doris, in her own words, to tell her story—what her thinking was prior to starting the FLI, why she is so committed to working with older students with weak reading skills, and what she learned about the whole process of creating and maintaining an organization such as the FLI. I utilized and audiotaped two, 1-hour, semistructured interviews. Following each interview, the tapes were transcribed. I also utilized field-notes from three unstructured interviews with Doris. Lastly, I utilized notes from my research journals of my work at the FLI, which spanned over 5 years, in order to create this narrative. When all of the data were collected, I read and reread the transcripts, fieldnotes, and journal entries. The transcripts, fieldnotes, and journal entries were categorized and coded around the guiding research topics: the conceptualization of the FLI, Doris's motivation for helping older students, and what she learned over the years. After the data were categorized based on the guiding topic, the data were arranged and rearranged until Doris's story was told. Finally, in order to ensure validity, Doris Sperling was asked to read the narrative inquiry.

The Setting

The FLI, a nonprofit organization in Ann Arbor, Michigan, was created in 1999 with the primary goal of improving the reading skills of upper elementary and middle school students with limited financial resources and a 2-year delay in their reading development. The services provided by the FLI are free for those families that qualify for free or reduced school lunches based on the federal guidelines. Typically, there are approximately 100 students who receive tutoring at the FLI annually.

The FLI relies on volunteer community members to provide the tutoring services to the students. Since most of the volunteer tutors do not have teaching backgrounds, training is provided to them on several occasions throughout the academic year. The tutors, referred to as reading coaches, receive a New Reading Coach orientation and training workshops titled Phonics and Vocabulary Instruction I and II; Comprehension and Fluency Instruction I and II; Attitude, Effort, and Attention Span; Cultural Diversity; Writing Instruction, and Instruction for English Language Learners. These workshops usually take place on Saturday afternoons and are conducted by the consultants, paid teacher consultants who are former teachers. They work individually during the times that tutoring takes place throughout the week to provide support and give advice to the reading coaches.

Tutoring takes place on Mondays, Tuesdays, Wednesdays, and Thursdays during two separate sessions on each day (3:30-5:30 and 6:00-8:00). The first session (3:30-5:30) is typically reserved for the students in middle school, and the second session (6:00-8:00) is typically reserved for the elementary grade students. According to Doris, "Actually, the elementary students used to come at 4:00 and the middle school students came at 6:00. But we found out that the middle school students actually get out earlier than the elementary grade students, so it just works out better this way." Additionally, Doris says that a big change took place when the first tutoring time was switched from 4:00 to 3:30. "We did this because not only did the teacher consultants need a break to get ready for the next session, but we found that it gave them an opportunity to talk with parents, reading coaches, students, and "just to get caught up."

The 2-hour instructional block for tutees includes a 50-minute one-on-one tutoring session in a separate room with a volunteer reading coach, during which time phonics, comprehension, and/or vocabulary development are taught. The tutees also spend 45-minutes to an hour writing, and a teacher consultant works with the tutees as they create original pieces that they take through the writing process. For all steps of this process, the tutees have access to computers. One aspect of the tutoring program that has changed is the 30-minute discussion group. During a discussion group, four tutees and a discussion leader, typically an undergraduate student from the local university, come together to discuss a chapter of a book, an article out of a magazine, or a current event. The focus on the discussion group is to develop the tutees' oral language skills. According to Doris, "The discussion groups, although very important in the development of their critical thinking skills have been so hard to staff. We would get college students, but during midterms and finals or breaks, they wouldn't show up. So we had to change things quickly, so the discussion time collapsed into the writing time. So now they get more time to improve their writing skills." Additionally, the tutees also receive a snack at the FLI before their tutoring session begins.

Approximately every 6 months (fall and spring), each child who receives tutoring at the FLI is assessed with the Qualitative Reading Inventory-III (Leslie & Caldwell, 2001) on their word recognition, fluency (rate and prosody), and comprehension (explicit and implicit) skills. After the assessment the students take a test. The specialist writes a report that outlines the tutee's reading strengths and needs. The teacher consultants are then responsible for discussing the QRI results with the reading coaches. The information gathered from the QRI-III assessment is used for instructional purposes (i.e., lesson planning). It is also used to show individual progress and the progress of the entire tutee population at the FLI.

Doris's Story

In 2000 I met Doris Sperling, an energetic, retired elementary school teacher who just began the FLI. She intended to focus on improving the reading skills of upper elementary and middle school students who were at least 2 years behind with their reading development. Over lunch, Doris told me her background, and vision of the FLI. During that lunch date, Doris said:

> I retired in '94 after over 40 years in education. I was an art teacher for 17 years, and then I went back to school and got my elementary certification and taught fourth and fifth grade for 15 years. Then, I worked in the research office with Ann Arbor public schools for about 6 years. During that time, that's when people were just beginning to focus on teacher accountability. We had some classes that if the teachers were great, the kids did well, and if the teachers were not so great, the kids did not do well. But, there was nothing in place to hold teachers accountable. So, I worked in that office to help create measures to assess teacher accountability.

Following that introduction and light chitchat, Doris perused my resume. At the time I was a doctoral student at the University of Michigan and trained to use the Qualitative Reading Inventory-II (QRI-II) (Leslie & Caldwell, 1995). Not one to mince words, she asked me if I would be the Assessment Specialist. She wanted me to test each student with the QRI-II, write a report of my findings, and report them to each reading coach. She then candidly stated, "Now, we don't have a lot of money right now, but I will see to it that you get some money for all of your hard work as soon as I can." That was not the part of our conversation that moved me. I vividly remember becoming excited because she had palpable enthusiasm and compassion about her vision. She had been in "the trenches" and knew what the reality was for students who were behind with their reading development. She saw too many otherwise bright and articulate youngsters, who just gave up on themselves, their educations, and ultimately, their futures because of their poor reading skills.

Following lunch, Doris and I walked a short distance to a store front with large windows and a sign that read Family Learning Institute. What was most striking were the rooms reserved for the one-on-one tutoring sessions. According to Doris, she tutored prior to the creation of the FLI, and these experiences impacted her thinking about what older children who experienced academic failure possibly needed to begin to improve their reading skills. "I used to tutor kids in a school library. This was just horrible for the kids because they were so self-conscious. They were embarrassed to be working on their reading skills, so that made it even worse to be out in the open like that. Plus, the noise was hard to deal with." Remembering those experiences, when it came time to find a place for the tutoring, Doris knew exactly what she was looking for. With pride, Doris later recounted:

As soon as I saw the space that we eventually got, I thought that this was perfect. The greatest strength of the program is the one-on-one tutoring in private rooms. All of the things that say, "You're different. You're not as smart. You need extra help," doesn't happen here. Everyone who comes here is in a similar situation. But even then, when they do their actual reading work, they have privacy. No intimidation. They don't have to be worried about who's seeing them. Two big open spaces, one for the office and the other for writing, and small rooms on the side. It gives the kids their privacy so that they won't be embarrassed.

Even before we finished lunch, I was on board and a proud member of the FLI.

When asked how the FLI came into being, Doris recounted that she and Lefiest Galimore, a community services professional, frequently attended meetings where the focus was on narrowing the achievement gap of African American students in Ann Arbor public schools. As a matter of fact, they attended meetings with the Community Academic Success Team (CAST) for 3 years before Lefiest, in a meeting at Doris's house asked, "Oh, why don't we just do it ourselves?" Following the meeting at her house, Doris had time to think about what she wanted and needed to do. According to Doris, "Being able to read is so important to people's lives. I can't imagine where I would be if I couldn't read." After thinking about it some more, Doris goes on to state, "There is research out there that says that the planning of future prisons is based on 4th graders' reading scores. That is just tragic, but it is a reality that we have to deal with. And if they are building prisons, that just shows you what people think not being able to read can do to your life." For Doris, the decision to create an organization to help older children improve their reading skills was simple. She continues, "After that meeting, I had the rest of that evening and I said, 'Why not?' So I called Lefiest the next morning and I said we should do it."

Following that initial conversation, Doris and Lefiest met regularly to conceptualize their ideas for a program to help older children improve their reading skills. She tells me:

I would go to Lefiest's office and we would talk about it. He had good organizational background and he knew all about focus groups. So one of the things we did, we had four or five focus groups. To find out if it would be good for us to start a business or a company or a non-profit that would teach reading to children. Part of the data that we collected showed that it was the low-income kids who were the lowest with their ability to read. So that's the group that we focused on. And we had one group of teachers, Ann Arbor school teachers, that were very anxious for us to do this. Everybody thought that it was fabulous. The reception we got was wonderful. So after the focus groups we started planning. That's more when I came in. With the curriculum. It took about a year to really get the program up and running.

Finally, after about a year of planning, securing funds and resources, and finding the "perfect place," the doors of the FLI opened with seven students. "We incorporated with the state of Michigan in 1999," Doris states with pride.

It is clear that Doris truly believes in all children having a fair chance at a bright future. She sees the primary avenue to a brighter future is through education. That's one of the main reasons why she and the members of the planning committee were adamant that the organization that was created focused on the literacy needs of upper elementary and middle school learners. Doris states, "We can't give up on these kids. They matter too." Doris continues:

> I think that in schools, the focus on teaching reading is in kindergarten through second grade. Especially first grade. So, we thought that we should focus on older children because what happens to them? If they can't read, they'll do poorly in school, and then continue to feel like failures. In those grades, the children are being asked to read for information, so if we go back to the basics and work on stuff like phonics and spelling, maybe those children will learn how to read so that they could be successful in school.

When talking with Doris, I felt that she truly believes that all children and people matter and she is committed to making sure that they have every chance available to improve or enhance their lives. One of her greatest concerns is what she refers to as "the failure syndrome." Doris states:

The greatest challenge that we've had are children who feel like failures. I call this the failure syndrome. They have struggled with reading and then avoid it at all costs. Even if they have to misbehave or act silly in class to avoid reading. But that doesn't help them at all. The main issue is that they feel like they will never succeed in reading. So, why bother? But, I really believe that they've always had the capacity to learn to read. It just takes time and going back to the basics to help them learn how to read.

Several key points that Doris constantly talks about is the need to build up the students' self-esteems, be honest with them, empower them to take control of their destinies, and help them to begin to believe that they can one day become proficient readers. She says:

> I work really hard at helping them believe that they can become readers. That is hard because most of our kids have that failure syndrome I talked about earlier. They have just been beaten down so much that they don't believe that they'll ever learn how to read. But, I then tell them that in life

and in learning, there are roadblocks and that they will get frustrated, but that you have to be able to travel that road with confidence in order to continue to grow. So, I tell the kids, "When you are ready to move on, let me know." I've even heard kids say, "Oh, I'm at a roadblock." They now understand that this is normal, but that they have the control to change things. That's so important to me. That the kids feel empowered. That's why I am always telling them, "You're the boss here." If things aren't going well, I encourage them to tell me if things aren't going well. I encourage them to tell their reading coaches if they are going too fast or if they understand it. They don't need to be bored because the reading coach is staying on a topic or concept they already know. But they have to feel that they have control over their lives in order to be more assertive with their needs. I tell them that they need to tell their teachers too. If they don't understand something. Otherwise, they will continue to struggle in silence. I also encourage our coaches to look for successes and to fuss over those successes. Many of our students have had so much failure in their lives that they are just in shambles. So, we need to help build them back up. So, I tell them to make a big deal about even the smallest success. It's a success, so it should be recognized.

In one case, Doris beams with pride as she talks about Tony (pseudonym). According to Doris, "Tony is now a 22-year-old funny and loveable young man. When we first got him, he had been in Special Ed and never learned to read. As a matter of fact, he didn't even know any of his letter sounds and he was in the sixth grade." I too remember Tony. He was one of the first tutees that I tested at the FLI. I remember as if it were yesterday all of the avoidant behaviors he exhibited prior to the actual test—he wanted to know about my hair, clothes, family, college, car, and hobbies. Finally, we started testing, and sadly, he couldn't even read the preprimer passage.

Because Tony was such a charming and talkative student, Doris found out a lot of information about him. As Doris states, "I would ask him all of the time what he did in class and he would tell me that he would daydream all day. He truly didn't believe that he would ever learn how to read and his teacher also told him that. So, his self-esteem was pretty low when he came to the Institute." Tony received tutoring at the FLI until the end of eighth grade. He worked hard every week, had a mother who was on him to make sure that he did his reading at home, and became more proactive with his learning. Doris continues, "We didn't just improve his reading. We taught him how to read.… He told me that he is reading for pleasure now. He comes from a mixed family—his mother is African American and his dad is white, so he likes to read books about others who come from mixed families too."

Tony finished high school and is paying for singing lessons at a local college. Summing up her experience with Tony, Doris says, "I asked him,

'What would you have done if you wouldn't have ever come to the Institute?' He always tells me, 'You are all miracle workers.' He thinks that we are miracle workers. But he's another case where he always had the capacity to learn how to read, he just needed to believe that he could, and be given another chance to work on his reading skills."

But, even in difficult situations, as Doris tells it, there are things that can be done to help preserve a tutee's dignity, and "get the job done." In one example, Doris tells of students who read well below their grade level and who need to read books written at their level that may be of little to no interest to them or embarrassing to carry around. She says:

> Now, we do have some kids who are in the sixth grade who are still reading at a first grade level and some fifth graders who read at second grade levels. So we do have books geared towards younger kids in our library. I know that it's embarrassing for the kids to have to read those types of books, but really, that's where they are with their reading levels. So, in order to not embarrass them, I put their books in brown paper bags so no one can see them. That's so important that the kids don't become embarrassed about having to read those books.

Doris was adamant that a rosy picture was not painted of creating an organization such as the FLI or tutoring students in upper elementary and middle school grades who are behind with their reading skills. Doris says, "It's just plain hard. But the rewards are priceless." When asked what advice she would give others who want to create a program in their community like the FLI, she quickly states with a giggle, "Find others who share your dream and vision. That's important. It's too much to do on your own." After a few minutes, Doris continues, "Next, get teachers on board. You will need the leadership and expertise of teachers to help you with curriculum and instructional issues. Also, get retired teachers to volunteer to tutor. Some retired teachers retire and they retire [laughter]. But they are really valuable resources and when they work with our kids, great things happen. So, getting the word out to those retired teachers would be great."

According to Doris, funding (both startup and maintenance) is a very important issue to consider when creating a program such as the FLI. "It's so hard," she says. Fortunately, Doris was not shy about asking for money from friends, family members, or whomever else she thought would be able to donate to a worthy cause. Doris states, "I knew, fortunately, so many people who I sent letters to. Or I would see them. Then we got businesses to help support us." The staff of the FLI hosted lunches and talked about the program and gave prospective donors a tour of the FLI. When asked about grant writing, Doris sighs before saying, "We all wrote grants. It's not working so much now because of the economy. The city of Ann Arbor and Washtenaw County gave us grant money." After a few minutes, Doris came back to this issue. "Actually, even before the economy turned bad, we always had trouble finding big grants for the age range that we work with. More money goes to younger kids. It just doesn't seem fair."

If volunteer community members without teaching experience are going to be the primary tutors or reading coaches, training and supporting reading coaches are major aspects of a program that should be seriously considered and well thought out. According to Doris, "This is always a struggle. To stay in contact with the tutors. We call and check on them and check on their binders. But it's still hard." At the FLI, teacher consultants are the ones whose primary responsibility is to educate and support the reading coaches. The teacher consultants are the ones who provide the training workshops for the reading coaches, sit down with reading coaches and set goals for the tutees, plan lessons, and are present on the days that tutoring takes place to offer suggestions, advice, and feedback.

In some cases, reading coaches struggled with their tutees' academic needs, behavioral problems, and emotional needs. As Doris highlights:

> Sometimes they have trouble with behavior. Or their student is just not learning. Some coaches feel self-conscious about saying that I'm having trouble with my kid. A typical one is when a child comes in and they say that they hate reading. I mean, what does a nonprofessional do with that? So they need help with that. Or the children who are masters at distracting. Having distracting or avoiding behaviors.

According to Doris, an individual in this case needs extra support from a teacher consultant. Doris says, "I think it varies with the teacher consultants how much support they give the reading coaches." So for some reading coaches, "They may have a teacher consultant who is attentive to their needs and understands that they do not have a teaching background and others who have a teacher consultant who may not provide as much support." One suggestion Doris gives is, "hiring a curriculum person who can hire teacher consultants who make sure that they keep in contact with the reading coaches."

Developing working relationships with the local school district and schools is also important to consider when developing a program such as the FLI. Doris says, "Well it's never been good enough. I'm going to tell you honestly." In Ann Arbor public schools, Doris says, "The assistant superintendent for elementary schools has always thought we've done an excellent job. As a matter of fact, she sends out letters to teachers encouraging them to send students to the Institute. She'll do all of that." Additionally, Doris and a fellow reading coach go around to the various schools to recruit students. "We talk with the teachers to get the teachers excited about referring their students to the program." Unfortunately, Doris is still not as pleased with the relationship or lack of a relationship the FLI has with specific teachers. "I understand that teachers are busy, but we have a great program that can help their students improve their reading skills. I wish they would refer the students or at least let their parents know about our program." With a sigh, Doris continues, "Plus, we need to develop better relationships with the classroom teachers because they have information that we need at the Institute about their students' reading abilities." When asked how to improve these relationships, Doris states, "We need a strong administrator, who will be a strong advocate with principals, who will be a strong advocate with teachers who will see that they go through the process of sending kids to organizations like ours."

Consideration regarding prospective student enrollment in the FLI is important. Doris states that she's an advocate of enrollment on a rolling basis. "So, if the child, their family members, or even their teachers think that they would benefit by coming to the Institute, then they could start tutoring as soon as we had the completed application and they had gone through the orientation." In the past, they tried a once-per-semester enrollment period. Doris tells me:

> Although that was easier—we could get the families in as a group and do one orientation. But it didn't allow us the time to really get to know the families and the children individually. I like giving the orientation to a single family instead of a group because they can ask their questions and I can too. When they are in a large group, some don't feel comfortable asking questions. Also, this is a big issue for me. That means that more time is wasted if the child has to wait until the next open enrollment period. That could be several months depending on the time the child and their parent comes in. This is serious and is critical. So, that's why I like the rolling enrollment better.

Although Doris is still committed to the FLI not being an organization that simply helps students with their homework, she understands that students have homework and may be concerned about not being able to complete their homework because they are at tutoring for 2 hours per week. Doris suggests "try to notify the teachers that the child is going to the Institute and that they may need to have less homework on the days that they have tutoring." In most cases, Doris finds that teachers are amendable to this. Doris states, when the student's reading skills have improved enough, "They bring in their textbooks and do work with their reading coaches. They use the books to help them to continue to improve their reading skills. Like reading textbooks and informational texts and improving their critical thinking skills. They need help with those too." Doris is committed to the students improving their reading skills so that they can become independent readers and thinkers. So, "as far as them doing homework every time they come in for tutoring, no."

Another key area that Doris focuses on is how to involve parents in the tutoring process. According to Doris, this is one of the areas that has been "evolving since the beginning and we're still working on better ways to improve parental involvement at the Institute." When I was the assessment specialist, there was a parent empowerment specialist. She was a social worker who was responsible for keeping in contact with parents and answering any questions they may have had. "That didn't work out because of budget," Doris says, "now we get interns from the School of Social Work at the University of Michigan. They help us." In the past, many parents waited in the parking lot and their child would leave the FLI without the reading coach or the teacher consultant ever seeing them. So, another way that they tried to get the parents more involved and to give the teacher consultants and reading coaches an opportunity to at least speak with the parents on a weekly basis is by "making the parents come into the institute to sign their children in. Then, when they leave, they can't just stay in the car and wait for their child to come out. They have to come in and sign their children out. So that way, if the reading coach or one of the teacher consultants has questions or wants to ask them about their child's home reading log or whatever, they can do so then. I've heard that it is really successful."

Assessment is a key issue that needs to be thought out prior to opening a program such as the FLI. It is the primary way to collect data on the tutees' progress, and can be used for lesson planning, training, and securing funding through grants. "We use the Qualitative Reading Inventory, the QRI. That test gives us lots of information," Doris tells me. "It tells us their word recognition levels, fluency, and reading comprehension. I am really happy because it even tells us about implicit comprehension." At the FLI, they have an assessment specialist who is trained to administer the QRI-III tests to each tutee. The test usually takes approximately 30 to 45 minutes depending on the reading skills of the tutee being tested. He or she is then responsible for typing a report that discusses the reading strengths and needs of each tutee. This report is given to the teacher consultants, who then discuss the results with the reading coach and plan instructional goals for the tutee based on those results.

When thinking about the type of facility that a community should look for, Doris reiterates, "Get the kids away from school. So, find a place where the kid can work with a reading coach in a private place. It can even be a church basement. They could get those big dividers to give the kids some privacy. The noise would probably still be an issue, but at least they would have some privacy." After a slight pause, Doris adds, "Then, I thought that we could use the Sunday school classrooms that are in many churches. They wouldn't be used during the times that we would need them so that may be perfect too."

When asked what would be the most important thing to keep in mind, Doris thought for a minute and said, "Know that this is an evolving process. We have been doing this for 10 years and we've learned a lot. We've tried some things that have been great and others that haven't been great. But we keep trying to improve because what we are doing is so important."

REFLECTION

I remember the frustration, confusion and anger that I felt. I was a fifth grade teacher, and I had several students who struggled with reading. There was Margaret, Paul, and Greg (pseudonyms). I will never forget their names or their faces. I sought help from my fifth grade team members who also had students who read below a fifth grade level. Sadly, we found that there was no financial support available for us to attend professional development workshops or purchase materials to improve our fifth graders reading skills. Most of the funding for literacy instruction was earmarked for primary grades and resources that were more appropriate for our students' reading levels were securely held and used by the primary grade teachers. They did not feel "comfortable" with us borrowing them.

Although a bit bruised but not deterred, I decided to see what resources were available in the community to help our students. What I found was disappointing. If their parents or guardians could afford several hundred dollars per month, our students could receive tutoring from several for-profit tutoring centers or they could order phonics programs that they would have to do at home. There were after-school programs geared primarily for homework help and enrichment activities, but not the improvement of reading or literacy skills. All of these disappointments made me wonder—What is available to middle level learners who are behind with their reading development, yet who do not qualify for special education or resource services, and whose families do not have the money to pay for private tutoring?

When I was told that several of my students 'struggled with reading', I initially did not consider the impact that it had on my ability to teach them, or the lack of resources that were unavailable to me and them. As far as my ability to teach them, I wondered:

- How do I improve a student's reading skills without the appropriate training or materials and resources?
- How would I teach them the concepts in math, science, and social studies if they could not read the expensive textbooks that the administration required that I use?

- Do I read the books to them? Get them books on tape? Do I have another student buddy read with them?
- What impact does their inability to read well have on their self-esteem and self-concept?
- Is it fair to grade them on homework that requires sufficient grade level reading skills?
- What if their parent or guardian has a difficult time with reading as well? Is it fair to put them in a possibly embarrassing situation of telling their child that they cannot read well or at all?

In reflecting on Doris's narrative, I understand her compassion and fully empathize with her drive. We can not give up on these children. They matter too. They have a legal and moral right to an education. I remember as a classroom teacher not having the answers to the questions above, nor knowing where to go to find the appropriate answers. This is what led me to the University of Michigan to pursue a master's in literacy education and a doctorate in the literacy, language, and cultures program. There, I had time to read, study, analyze, ponder, and question.

- Who is ethically, legally and financially responsible to ensure that middle level learners who are behind with their reading development receive the best education possible? The federal government? The school districts? The community? The parents?
- Are classroom teachers responsible for students' learning during non-school hours? Thus, how involved should a teacher be with a program such as the FLI if their parent or guardian decides to enroll them in such a program?
- Are community volunteers who do not have teaching experiences, although genuine and caring, even with the best support, the best 'teachers' for middle level learners who are behind with their reading skills?
- With the focus on preventing reading difficulties for so many decades, when will there be recognition and support that intervention is also necessary in order to ensure that *all of our students* get the education that they legally have a right to?

DISCUSSION

In today's society, the need for literacy skills is crucial. Middle level learners are asked to think, read, and write critically, and comprehend, synthesize, evaluate, and critique information from multiple genres, perspectives, and texts (Alvermann, 2001; Biancarosa & Snow, 2006; Chall, 1996; Moore et al., 1999; National Council of Teachers of English Commission on Reading, 2004). Unfortunately, not all middle level learners are prepared to handle adequately the literacy demands presented to them. In response, after-school, community-based reading tutorial programs are available for such students. My review of the literature regarding after-school reading tutorial programs highlights the components of successful programs for primary-grade students (Juel, 1996; Wasik, 1998), and programs that improved the word recognition skills of primary grade students (Baker, Gersten, & Keating, 2000; Fitzgerald, 2001; Heins et al., 1999; Invernizzi, Juel, & Rosemary, 1996; Juel, 1996; Morris, Shaw, & Perney, 1990; Vadasy et al., 1997; Wasik, 1998). In the several studies on middle level learners who were tutored that resulted in improved reading skills (Harmon, Keehn, & Kenney, 2004; Houge, Geier, & Peyton, 2008; Ivey, 1999; Lee & Neal, 1993; Morris, Ervin, & Conrad, 1996), instruction is provided by highly trained teaching professionals who had knowledge of the reading process, the academic and social needs of middle level learners, and they understood the importance of instruction that was geared towards students' reading level, interests, and strengths.

With regard to the quality of the tutoring services provided, Topping (1998) argues, "Tutoring methods should be structured to maximise [sic] the potential advantages and minimise [sic] the potential disadvantages of volunteer tutors. Quantity and quality of tutoring should be carefully balanced" (p. 48). Topping (1998) states that "Training, support, and monitoring should focus on methods designed specifically for tutoring, with durability and fail-safe mechanisms built in" (p. 48). Elbaum, Vaughn, Hughes, and Moody (2000) also suggest that schools could provide the much-needed extra assistance for struggling readers if they provide one-on-one tutoring with trained tutors who work closely with a qualified reading specialist or teacher. Elbaum et al. (2000) suggest that the instruction provided to struggling readers should be a supplement to classroom instruction by a certified teacher, not a substitute for it. In addition, Elbaum et al. (2000) stress that their findings do not in any way suggest that tutors with little or no formal training can equal the instruction delivered by highly skilled professionals under "circumstances other than those of a well-designed and well-monitored intervention in a circumscribed domain" (p. 616). Thus, given the literacy needs of middle level learners, in particular middle level struggling readers, I question whether the tutees at the FLI who work on word recognition skill development and/or who have a learning disability will ever get to a proficient level in their literacy development with only 120 additional minutes per week of tutoring by volunteer community members who are not as highly trained as the teachers cited in Morris et al. (1996) and Lee and Neal (1993).

Furthermore, in closely examining the NCLB Act, little attention is paid to the individuals providing the instruction to students. For instance, the guidelines for paraprofessionals under the NCLB Act require they have at least 2 years of college-level study, have an associate's degree or higher, and demonstrate their knowledge of and their ability to assist the classroom teacher, with reading and writing instruction (No Child Left Behind Act of 2001, 2002). However, my inquiry suggests that there are individuals with less training and knowledge of reading methodology who are expected to *teach* children how to read. These findings are quite alarming considering that the literature shows that qualified, knowledgeable, and trained tutors who are well supported and have adequate resources are keys to reaching the goal of improving the reading skills of middle level tutees (Harmon, Keehn, & Kenney, 2004; Houge, Geier, & Peyton, 2008; Ivey, 1999; Lee & Neal, 1993; Morris et al., 1996).

Although this discussion appears to be negative, it is not intended to be. There have been many successes at the FLI with reading coaches who did not have teaching backgrounds and worked with tutees who had weak reading skills. However, the majority of those cases were with tutees who had grade-level word recognition skills, did not have a learning disability, and needed to improve their comprehension skills (McLurkin, 2006). For the tutees who had learning disabilities and/or who were behind with their word recognition, fluency, and comprehension skills and were tutored by community volunteers without teaching backgrounds, their fates were not as positive. Thus, I firmly believe there is definitely a place and a need for after-school community-based volunteer reading tutorial programs for students who have weak reading skills. I also firmly believe that more research is desperately needed to ascertain what is the best learning environment and instruction for all of our students. Otherwise, our neediest students, and ultimately our society, will continue to suffer in the long-run.

LESSONS LEARNED

When tutees come to the FLI, they are told that they will improve their reading skills. When reading coaches come to volunteer their time tutoring a tutee, they believe that they are going to help a youngster improve their reading skills. To provide the best situation possible for all parties to continue to grow and feel good about themselves, I offer several suggestions. Tutees should not be placed with a reading coach until the initial assessment is completed. That way, the tutee's reading needs, strengths, and interests may be taken into account when pairing them with their reading coach. This may give an organization more time to solicit information from the tutee's classroom teacher so that a more complete picture of the tutee is presented. Doris suggests that a curriculum person be hired who can hire teacher consultants who must keep in contact with the reading coaches. It is apparent that the role of the teacher consultant is very important to the success of the program at the FLI. Only individuals who are highly qualified and willing to do the work should be considered for such positions.

Third, we should heed the advice given by Doris. Extra effort needs to be made to recruit retired teachers who have the teaching experience and expertise to work with the neediest children. That way, following the initial assessment, when reading coaches and tutees are paired together, the dyads can be paired based on the reading needs and strengths of the tutees and the educational and employment backgrounds of the reading coaches. Tutees who have severe difficulties will be paired with the most qualified reading coaches, and the tutees who do not require as much support can be paired with individuals who, although they do not have teaching experience, are trained and well support by a teacher consultant.

CONCLUSION

The main thrust of the NCLB Act of 2001 is to provide federal funding to support research and instruction targeted at the primary grades. The main problem with this is that there are children who do not achieve proficiency with their reading development during their primary grade education. While there is literature that supports the pairing of the neediest middle level learners with expert reading specialists (Ivey, 1999; Lee & Neal, 1993; Morris et al., 1996), the literature also shows that there are children whose reading skills can be remediated with the services provided by trained and well supported volunteer reading tutors with no teaching experience (Cohen, Kulik, & Kulik, 1982; Hock, Pulvers, Deshler, & Schumaker, 2001; Juel, 1996; Shanahan, 1998; Wasik, 1998; Wasik & Slavin, 1993). However, for some of the reading coaches that Doris discussed, tutoring a middle level struggling reader was extremely difficult for them. More research is needed to investigate the nature of middle level struggling reader learning when volunteer reading tutors are used. Moreover, the literature on after-school reading tutorial programs also shows that staffing, materials, training, and support are critical to the success of these types of programs, yet all of these cost money, and sadly, the federal government has yet to adequately respond to these calls.

REFERENCES

Adams, M. J. (1990). *Beginning to read: Thinking and learning about print*. Cambridge, MA: MIT Press.

Alvermann, D. (2001). *Effective literacy instruction for adolescents*. Executive Summary and Paper Commissioned by the National Reading Conference. Chicago, IL: National Reading Conference.

Baker, S., Gersten, R., & Keating, T. (2000). When less may be more: A 2-year longitudinal evaluation of a volunteer tutoring program requiring minimal training. *Reading Research Quarterly, 35*(4), 494-519.

Biancarosa, C., & Snow, C. E. (2006). *Reading next-A vision for action and research in middle and high school literacy: A report to Carnegie Corporation of New York* (2nd ed.). Washington, DC: Alliance for Excellent Education.

Chall, J. S. (1996). *Stages of reading development* (2nd ed.). Fort Worth, TX: Harcourt Brace College.

Clandinin, D. J., & Connelly, F. M. (2000). *Narrative inquiry: Experience and story in qualitative research*. San Francisco, CA: Jossey-Bass.

Cohen, P., Kulik, J. A., & Kulik, C. C. (1982). Educational outcomes of tutoring: A meta-analysis of findings. *American Educational Research Journal, 19*, 237-248.

Conley, M. W., & Hinchman, K. A. (2004). No child left behind: What it means for U.S. adolescents and what we can do about it. *Journal of Adolescent & Adult Literacy, 48*(1), 42-50.

Drakeford, W. (2002). The impact of an intensive program to increase the literacy skills of youth confined to juvenile corrections. *Journal of Correctional Education, 53*(4), 139-144.

Elbaum, B., Vaughn, S., Hughes, M. T., & Moody, S. W. (2000). How effective are one-to-one tutoring programs in reading for elementary students at risk for reading failure? A meta-analysis of the intervention research. *Journal of Educational Psychology, 92*(4), 605-619.

Ensminger, M. E., & Slusarcick, A. L. (1992). Paths to high school graduation or dropout: A longitudinal study of a first-grade cohort. *Sociology of Education, 65*, 95-113.

Fitzgerald, J. (2001). Can minimally trained college student volunteers help young at-risk children to read better? *Reading Research Quarterly, 36*(1), 28-46.

Grossman, J. B. & Furano, K. (2002). *Making the most of volunteers*. Philadelphia, PA: Public/Private Ventures. (ERIC Document Reproduction Service No. ED 472117)

Harmon, J. M., Keehn, S., & Kenney, M. S. (2004). Tutoring struggling adolescent readers: A program investigation. *Reading Research and Instruction, 44*(2), 46-74.

Heins, E. D., Perry, A., Piechura-Couture, K., Roberts, D., Collins, R., & Lynch, M. (1999). Stetson reads: An after-school tutorial program for at-risk students. *Reading Improvement, 36*(3), 116-121.

Hock, M. F., Pulvers, K. A., Deshler, D. D., & Schumaker, J. B. (2001). The effects of an afterschool tutoring program on the academic performance of at-risk and students with learning disabilities. *Remedial and Special Education, 22*(3), 16-23.

Houge, T. T., Geier, C., & Peyton, D. (2008). Targeting adolescents' literacy skills using one-to-one instruction with research-based practices. *The Journal of Adolescent and Adult Literacy, 51*(8), 640-650.

Invernizzi, M., Juel, C., & Rosemary, C. A. (1996). A community volunteer tutorial that works. *The Reading Teacher, 50*(4), 304-311.

Ivey, G. (1999). Reflections pm teaching struggling middle school readers. *Journal of Adolescent & Adult Literacy, 42*(5), 372-381.

Juel, C. (1996). What makes literacy tutoring effective? *Reading Research Quarterly, 31*(3), 268-289.

LaBerge, D., & Samuels, S. J. (1974). Toward a theory of automatic information processing in reading. *Cognitive Psychology, 6,* 293-323.

Lee, N. G., & Neal, J. C. (1992/1993). Reading rescue: Intervention for a student "at promise." *Journal of Reading, 36*(4), 276-282.

Leslie, L., & Caldwell, J. (1995). *Qualitative reading inventory-II.* New York: Longman.

Leslie, L., & Caldwell, J. (2001). *Qualitative reading inventory-III.* New York, NY: Longman.

McLurkin, D. L. (2006). *An analysis of the expectations, training, and perceived support of the volunteers at an after-school community-based tutorial program.* Unpublished doctoral dissertation, University of Michigan, Ann Arbor, MI.

Moje, E., Young, J., Readence, J., & Moore, D. (2000). Reinventing adolescent literacy for new times: Perennial and millennial issues. *Journal of Adolescent and Adult Literacy, 43*(5), 400-410.

Moore, D. W., Bean, T. W., Birdyshaw, D., & Rycik, J. A. (1999). *Adolescent literacy: A position statement for the commission on adolescent literacy of the International Reading Association.* Newark, DE: International Reading Association.

Morris, D., Ervin, C., & Conrad, K. (1996). A case study of middle school reading disability. *The Reading Teacher, 49*(5), 368-377.

Morris, D., Shaw, B., & Perney, J. (1990). Helping low readers in grades 2 and 3: An after-school volunteer tutoring program. *The Elementary School Journal, 91*(2), 132-150.

National Council of Teachers of English Commission on Reading. (2004). *A call to action: What we know about adolescent literacy and ways to support teachers in meeting students' needs.* Retrieved from http://www.ncte.org/about/over/positions/category/read/118622.htm

No Child Left Behind Act of 2001, 20 U.S.C. § 6301 (2002).

Palinscar, A. S., & Brown, A. L. (1984). Reciprocal teaching of comprehension-fostering and comprehension monitoring activities. *Cognition and Instruction, 1*(2), 117-175.

Shanahan, T. (1998). On the effectiveness and limitations of tutoring in reading. *Review of Research in Education, 23,* 217-234.

Stanovich, K. E. (1986). Matthew effects in reading: Some consequences of individual differences in the acquisition of literacy. *Reading Research Quarterly, 21,* 360-407.

Suh, S., & Suh, S. (2007). Risk factors and levels of risk for high school dropouts. *Professional School Counseling, 10*(3), 297-306.

Topping, K. (1998). Effective tutoring in America Reads: A reply to Wasik. *The Reading Teacher, 52*(1), 42-50.

Vacca, R. T. (1998). Let's not marginalize adolescent literacy. *Journal of Adolescent & Adult Literacy, 41*(8), 604-609.

Vacca, R. T., & Padak, N. D. (1990). Who's at risk in reading? *Journal of Reading, 33*(7), 86-88.

Vadasy, P. F., Jenkins, J. R., Antil, L. R., Wayne, S. K., & O'Connor, R. (1997). The effectiveness of one-to-one tutoring by community tutors for at-risk beginning readers. *Learning Disabilities Quarterly, 20*, 126-139.

Wasik, B. (1998). Using volunteers as reading tutors: Guidelines for successful practices. *The Reading Teacher, 51*(7), 562-570.

Wasik, B., & Slavin, R. E. (1993). Preventing early reading failure with one-to-one tutoring: A review of five programs. *Reading Research Quarterly, 28*, 178-200.

CHAPTER 18

RECOMMENDATIONS AND RESOURCES FOR NARRATIVE INQUIRY AND RESEARCH

Kathleen F. Malu

The middle level community continues its efforts to change and improve practice. Narrative inquiry is a useful approach to gain insights and explore the complexities in these settings. To help those who may be new to the field of narrative inquiry and those who may wish to update their knowledge and skills, this chapter reviews outstanding narrative research, offers recommendations, and lists a collection of useful resources.

Taking the lead from Caskey (2005) who highlighted useful information regarding action research in a previous volume in this *series*, this chapter offers readers who may be new to narrative inquiry, a set of similar resources. The chapter begins with a rationale for conducting narrative inquiry, followed by outstanding examples of narrative inquiry reports at the middle level. Next, is a list of books and journals that focus on narrative inquiry. The chapter ends with electronic sites to explore. These lists are not extensive. They are presented as potential jumping off points for entrance into the world of narrative inquiry.

Voices From the Middle: Narrative Inquiry By, For, and About the Middle Level Community
pp. 381–388

RATIONALE FOR USING NARRATIVE INQUIRY

Why engage in narrative inquiry? Simply put, unlike other research methods, particularly quantitative methods, narrative inquiry enables the researcher and the researched to collaborate and become one in the story telling. This process of collaboration allows the story told to develop rich complexity and nuance that cannot be revealed in other types of research designs. In the creation of the narrative, the writers seek to frame the themes of their stories within theories and research, thereby connecting the narrative to broader discourse communities with the aim to expand and deepen our knowledge.

Narrative inquiry is a useful tool for researchers. It lets researchers, who employ narrative tools, explore and discover underlying themes and complexities that may be hidden when quantitative research methodologies are used. The goal of narrative inquiry is to reveal the multiple layers of an experience, storying it into a narrative that captures the essence of the lived experience for readers and researchers alike.

Narrative inquiry may be equally useful for teachers and those who may "shy away from" the notion of engaging in research. The realization that we are all storytellers may help to facilitate entry into this process of telling a story, particularly for individuals who might otherwise not consider conducting "research." Novices to narrative inquiry may begin by identifying a question or puzzle they wish to explore. By recording events in a notebook, conducting interviews, observing and writing up field notes, and then crafting the story as it emerges from these data, teachers and novices may begin engaging in narrative inquiry. As the story emerges, so, too, do the themes that the story represents. The construction of the story engages writers in the process of writing to learn. The story becomes a story-in-the-making as the writers learn, deeply, the themes and meanings that their story holds for them and the data they collected. For references regarding the rationale for using narrative inquiry and learning the process of engaging in this type of inquiry see below. Examples of outstanding narrative inquires follow.

OUTSTANDING EXAMPLES OF NARRATIVE INQUIRY

This volume in the series of *The Handbook of Research in Middle Level Education* holds stellar examples of narrative inquiry. The volume begins with Kim's overview of narrative inquiry, including a definition of the term and a discussion of the components of narrative inquiry. She explains the important role that narrative inquiry must play in light of the No Child Left Behind Act of 2001 (2002) and NCLB's promotion of "scientifically based research." She highlights the reasons why narrative inquirers are essential to continuing research in the field of middle level education. Kim concludes her chapter with a discussion of the notion that it is our human responsibility to listen to the voices in the middle.

Chapters that reveal the multiple layers of adolescents and their identities help to show why narratives are essential to complete a full research agenda at the middle level. Yoon frames her narratives within the theories of identity, positioning, and English language learners. This frame reveals the struggles her participants have as they move back and forth between the mainstream and ELL classrooms. These students move from positions of power to powerlessness and Yoon questions the impact this may have on ELLs' identity development and learning. She urges mainstream teachers to support ELLs by offering them classrooms that encourage and nurture their growth. Coulter uses the theories of bullying and cultural identity to position her narrative about the experiences of immigrant girls in a suburban middle school. While her research is not intended to critique the bullying program in place at the school where her participants attend, this inquiry highlights the complexities of a bullying prevention program and the subtle and overt ways this program was "coopted" into the culture of bullying at this school. Coulter's call for more research in the areas of bullying and bullies, victims, and bystanders is critically supported by her narratives. Piazza examines adolescent identity, specifically as it relates to literacy for African American males. As her participants talk about their notions of masculinity, race and "being cool" during reading assessments, Piazza gradually examines and begins to explore her own positionality in the research. Her narrative reveals the role that inquiry can play in prompting self-reflection for white female researchers. Rhodes uses the story of Izzy (Voigt, 2005) to prompt discussions with six adolescents, framing her study within the theories of reading, specifically Rosenblatt's (1978) notion that readers transact with text to make meaning. As she changes the contexts of their discussions from individual, to single gender, and finally to a mixed gendered group, the participants reveal different understandings of the text. Rhodes highlights questions for further research that focus on the contexts for reading in the middle. Schaefer's narrative of Sandy's reading and writing development is located within the work of Roney (2001) and the notions of effective middle school teachers. Schaefer uses a story of her own literacy development and one from a previous professional experience to reveal the complexity of her narrative about Sandy. This narrative of Sandy's development parallels Schaefer's professional development and reveals a scene in which Schaefer identifies the deep empathy she discovers she has for Sandy's intense struggles with learning to read.

There are chapters that present outstanding reports that focus on the stories of middle level educators. Turner positions his report within the politics of the No Child Left Behind Act of 2001 (2002). He tells the stories of three preservice teachers who must learn to teach in this era of high stakes accountability. Through these narratives readers hear the voices of these teachers who prepare to enter the moral and ethical teaching dilemma of how much time to spend on teaching using middle level practices and how much time to spend on test preparation. Turner finds that his participants may continue to challenge and question the role that high stakes tests should play in the education of middle level students. Dana, Delane, and George present the narratives of teachers at the opposite end of the spectrum from Turner's. Dana, Delane, and George tell the stories of veteran teachers who long for a return to the Camelot era of middle level education when teachers worked more than the required hours, teamed with enthusiasm, and focused on the needs of their young students. Using the metaphor of a jigsaw puzzle, these researchers reveal their participants' experiences before and after the era of high stakes tests and the questions this new era raises for these experienced teachers. Their findings include a call for middle level teachers to become researchers and political advocates. They urge researchers to contribute to ways of balancing the calls for accountability with the need for developmentally appropriate middle level teaching practices. Bahr and Pendergast frame their narratives within the middle years teacher preparation program in Australia. Reporting the narratives of four teachers who entered teaching in the middle through different avenues, this study frames an important concern for all those engaged in the middle. In whose hands lies the future of middle level reforms? Do middle level teachers and leaders have the power to continue pushing the middle level reform agenda? Matteson et al. report their experiences as middle school teachers and the influence their experiences played in their pursuit of doctoral degrees. Evidence from their narratives suggests that their experiences as a team of teachers in a middle school played an important role in their desires to continue learning and growing. Framed with their voices of individuals pursuing doctoral degrees, this study finds that more middle school teachers need encouragement to seek advanced degrees so they can enter higher education and help to train the next generation of middle school teachers. Smith narrates the experiences of a middle level literacy coach. Given the lack of research in middle level coaching, Smith highlights a critical need for further research in this area, given the difficult and confusing experiences of the coach whose narrative he tells.

The final sequence of chapters are narrated by researchers who place themselves in middle level contexts and reveal their complex, complicated experiences. Brause returns to a middle school as a writers' workshop teacher and hopes to understand the reasons why her selected school is considered by many to be a successful middle school. Through her experiences and deep reflections she discovers contradictions and conflicts between school philosophy and her own actions and struggles as a teacher. Framing her narrative within writers' workshop theory, she calls for further research and reflection on ways that middle level practice can promote the individual development, self-efficacy, responsibility, independence, and autonomy of middle level learners. Positioning her narrative in the literature and theory of K-8 schools and middle level best practices, Ruppert returns to a middle school classroom as a mathematics teacher to examine the possibility of using middle level practices in this setting. Using middle level student narratives and comments, Ruppert finds that middle school practices can and should be used in K-8 settings. She calls for middle level advocates to support this notion. Vinz uses narrative inquiry as a form of professional development to help 4 middle level teachers examine their teaching practice. Vinz offers these teachers her narratives of her visits to their classrooms. They, in turn, create narratives of the same visit. When the two narratives are placed side-by-side and read by Vinz and the participants, these narratives help the teachers examine and question their teaching practice. Vinz notes that such narrative work will help to construct research that is conducted with, rather than on, middle level teachers.

Malu's narrative is framed within the theory of and public calls for parent involvement in their children's schools. Her involvement as a parent becomes complicated when the director of her son's middle school asks her to participate not only as a parent but also as a researcher and former classroom teacher. Her findings suggest the tensions inherent in parent involvement and the struggles of parents to help and protect their children. On a deeper level this narrative is the story of a white mother with a black son. Malu begins to tentatively explore these notions within the theories of race and gender. Her narrative with this frame of race and gender is an unfinished and evolving story. Reyes reports an equally complex story of parent involvement. Framing her narrative within the feminist methodology of insider/outsider, Reyes tells her story of community involvement when the parents and community members of her children's middle school seek to reconfigure it in more traditional ways. Reyes finds that the multiple roles that she plays during this process, those of parent, former classroom teacher, university professor, community member help to shape her understanding and interpretations of the events in this story. She asks that tensions in such settings be accepted and explored so multiple voices can be heard. McLurkin's narrative of a retired teacher with more than 40 years of experience places this volume within the broader public community. Doris's story of her creation and implementation of the Family Learning Institute to help struggling adolescent readers is powerful and informative. McLurkin frames this story in the principles of adolescent literacy and No Child Left Behind (2002). She calls for further research to understand the struggling reader and the role that volunteer tutors may play in reading improvement.

These examples of outstanding narrative research help to highlight the important role that narrative inquiry can play in our understanding of the complexities at the middle level. These narratives reveal areas for further research and make suggestions for actions the middle level community can take on the issues these narratives reveal.

RESOURCES

The following lists are presented as starting points for readers to further explore and begin to engage in narrative inquiry. These lists are not comprehensive. They are designed to encourage further exploration of this important research methodology. Note that narrative inquiry, as a qualitative research design, may overlap other research methodologies including action research, case study, hypothesis generation, and ethnography to mention a few. The creation of narratives is an important step in the process of developing a narrative research report.

Selected Books on Methodology

Clandinin, D. J. (Ed.). (2007). *Handbook of narrative inquiry: Mapping a methodology*. Thousand Oaks, CA: Sage.

Goodson, I. (Ed.). (1992). *Studying teachers' lives*. New York, NY: Teachers College Press.

Riessman, C. K. (2008). *Narrative methods for the human sciences*. Thousand Oaks, CA: Sage.

Webster, L., & Mertova, P. (2007). *Using narrative inquiry as a research method: An* introduction to using critical event narrative analysis in research on learning and *teaching*. New York, NY: Routledge.

Selected Examples of Narrative Inquiry Books

Andrews, M. (2007). *Shaping history: Narratives of political change*. New York, NY: Cambridge University Press

Casey, K. (1993). *I answer with my life: Life histories of women teachers working for social change*. New York, NY: Routledge.

Clandinin, D. J., Huber, J., Huber, M., Murray-Orr, A., Murphy, S., Pearce, M., Steeves, P. (2006). *Composing diverse identities: Narrative inquiries into the Interwoven Lives of Children and Teachers*.   New York, NY: Routledge Falmer.

Michie, Gregory. (2005). *See you when we get there: Teaching for change in urban schools.* New York, NY: Teachers College Press.

Paley, V. (1989). *White teacher.* Cambridge, MA: Harvard University Press.

Paley, V. (1995). *Kwanzaa and me: A teacher's story.* Cambridge, MA: Harvard University Press.

Selected Journal Articles

Barone, T. (2007). A return to the gold standard? Questioning the future of narrative construction as educational research. *Qualitative Inquiry, 13*(2), 1-17.

Connelly, F. M., & Clandinin, D. J. (1990). Stories of experience and narrative inquiry. *Educational Researcher, 19*(4), 2-14.

Coulter, C., Michael, C., & Poynor, L. (2007). Storytelling as pedagogy: An unexpected outcome of narrative inquiry. *Curriculum Inquiry, 37*(2), 103-122.

Gordon, E., McKibbin, K., Vasudevan, L., & Vinz, R. (2007). Writing out of the unexpected: Narrative inquiry and the weight of small moments. *English Education, 39*(4), 326-351.

Schaafsma, D., Pagnucci, G. S., Wallace, R. M., & Stock, P. L. (2007). Composing storied ground: Four generations of narrative inquiry. *English Education, 39*(4), 282-305.

Schaafsma, D., & Vinz, R. (2007). Composing narratives for inquiry. *English Education, 39*(4), 277-281.

Websites and Professional Organizations

The websites and professional organizations listed below support narrative inquiry.

Center for Narrative Inquiry: http://www.geocities.com/Athens/Delphi/9759/main02.html

Center for Narrative Research: http://www.uel.ac.uk/cnr/newsletter.htm

Middle Level Education Research Special Interest Group of the American Educational Research Association: http://www.rmle.pdx.edu/

Narrative and Research Special Interest Group of the American Educational Research Association: http://www.narrativesig.cahs.colostate.edu/

National Council of Teachers of English: http://www.ncte.org

REFERENCES

Caskey, M. (Ed.). (2005). Recommendations and resources for action research. In *Making a difference: Action research in middle level education* (pp. 285-298). Greenwich, CT: Information Age.

No Child Left Behind Act of 2001 (H.R.1), Title II. Public Law 107-110 (2002). Retrieved from http://www.ed.gov/policy/elsec/leg/esea02/index.html

Roney, K. (2001). The effective middle school teacher: Inwardly integrated, outwardly connected. In V. A. Anfara, Jr. (Ed), *The handbook of research in middle level education* (pp. 73-105). Greenwich, CT: Information Age.

Rosenblatt, L. (1978/1994).*The reader, the text, the poem: The transactional theory of the literacy work*. Carbondale, IL: Southern Illinois University Press.

Voigt, C. (2005). *Izzy, Willy-Nilly*. New York, NY: Simon & Schuster.

ABOUT THE AUTHORS

Nan Bahr is a professor of education and an assistant dean, Teaching & Learning, Faculty of Education, Queensland University of Technology, Australia. She has oversight of the teaching quality in the faculty, and the readiness of graduates for the profession as beginner teachers or as leaders. She researches middle years of schooling, the nature of adolescence, resilience, and learning development. She has received several national and institutional awards for excellence in teaching and program design, and has published widely.

Rita S. Brause is a professor of education and coordinator of the advanced language and literacy education programs at Fordham University Graduate School of Education Division of Curriculum and Teaching in New York City. She has authored numerous books and journal articles.

Cathy Coulter is an associate professor of education at University of Alaska, Anchorage. Her research interests include the public school experiences of English learners and narrative research as a methodology. Recent publications include articles in *Educational Researcher*, *Curriculum Inquiry*, and *Bilingual Research Journal* and a book entitled *Teaching Immigrant Students and English Learners in Secondary Schools*.

Cheryl J. Craig, PhD, is a professor in the Department of Curriculum and Instruction, College of Education, University of Houston, where she coordinates the Teaching and Teacher Education program area. Craig is a regular contributor to such journals as *Teaching and Teacher Education*, *Teachers College Record*, and *American Educational Research Journal*.

Nancy Fichtman Dana is professor of education and director of the Center for School Improvement at the University of Florida. Under her direction, the center promotes and supports practitioner inquiry, or action research, as a core mechanism for school improvement. One part of the center's work targets middle school education. Dr. Dana has authored or coauthored five books and published numerous articles in professional journals focused on teacher professional development, teacher research, and related topics.

Darby Claire Delane is a clinical assistant professor at the University of Florida. She served as a general and special educator in middle school for 10 years and has her National Board Certification in social studies for early adolescents. She currently coordinates the Professional Development Community Program at the University of Florida, designed to foster unique teaching and learning partnerships between the university and local public schools. She also coaches and teaches teachers across the state of Florida through the Teacher Leadership and School Improvement Program.

Richard M. Fletcher taught at the middle school level for 6 years before becoming an administrator in the Copperas Cove Independent School District, in Copperas Cove, Texas. He is a student at the University of Mary Hardin Baylor where he is pursuing an EdD in education administration. He and his wife Alice, a special education teacher, have two children. His interests include special education, underserved student populations, and preservice teacher education.

Doris I. Garrett, a middle school teacher for 5 years, is currently the Base Realignment and Closure (BRAC) Liaison for the Region 12 Education Service Center in Waco, Texas. As the BRAC liaison she provides training, support, and resources for multiple stakeholders within school districts that educate children of military personnel. She has completed her coursework for a Doctor of Management from Webster University and is working on her dissertation. Doris is a military spouse with three children.

Paul George has been studying middle level education for 40 years. He is a NMSA Lounsbury Award winner, a frequent contributor to the *Middle School Journal*, since its inaugural issue, a presenter at every NMSA annual conference for nearly 4 decades, and distinguished professor of education, *emeritus*, at the University of Florida.

Jeong-Hee Kim is an assistant professor in the College of Education at Kansas State University. Her scholarship centers on narrative theorizing and curriculum theory, particularly exploring students' school experiences and teacher agency and praxis. She received two awards from AERA, Outstanding Narrative Research Article Award (2007) and Outstanding Narrative Theory Article Award (2009). She currently serves as a coguest editor for the *Journal of Educational Research* for the special issue on narrative inquiry.

Kathleen F. Malu is an associate professor of literacy and language in the Department of Secondary and Middle School Education at William Paterson University of New Jersey. She teaches anthropology in education at the undergraduate level and numerous graduate courses including literacy, writing, and research in the Graduate Reading Program. She designed several graduate level online courses which she teaches. With more than 20 years experience at the K-12 level including many years in the middle, she has taught in a wide range of schools including a high school in Congo and at the United Nations International School in New York City. Additionally she served as a curriculum developer for the Ministry of Education in Kigali Rwanda and recently a Fulbright scholar, conducting research and preparing teachers at the Kigali Institute of Education. Middle level education, narrative inquiry, literacy, memoir writing, and international education are her research interests. Her publications include chapters in previous volumes of *The Handbook* series and articles in NCTE journals.

Shirley M. Matteson is an assistant professor of middle level education at Texas Tech University in Lubbock, Texas. She teaches undergraduate and graduate level mathematics education courses. She is a National Board Certified Teacher in early adolescence/mathematics. Her research interests include middle school student understanding of mathematical representations, technology in the mathematics classroom, and the integration of mathematics and science concepts. She worked for 27 years in public schools, primarily at the middle school level.

Denise L. McLurkin is an assistant professor in the Childhood Education Program at the City College of New York, City University of New York. She is a former classroom teacher and supervisor of student teachers. She holds a BA in psychology from the University of California, Irvine, a MS in counseling psychology from California Baptist University, a MA in literacy education and a doctorate in educational studies in the Literacy, Language and Cultures Program from the University of Michigan.

Donna Pendergast, associate professor, is head of School of Education and Professional Studies at Griffith University, Australia. She has served as program director in pre- and in-service middle schooling teacher education programs for a decade and has conducted many national research projects investigating literacy and numeracy, lifelong learning, resilience, and productive pedagogies in the middle years. She has published widely and is highly sought after as a consultant, school auditor, and speaker on issues related to middle schooling.

Susan V. Piazza is an assistant professor of literacy studies at Western Michigan University. She serves as director of the Dorothy J. McGinnis Reading Center and Clinic in the College of Education and Human Development where she works with graduate students to provide literacy outreach services in the surrounding community. Her research, teaching, and professional development activities focus on literacy achievement as it relates to equity, culturally relevant pedagogy, and learners traditionally marginalized in school settings. She has published in *The Reading Teacher, English Journal, Reading Today, Reading Writing Quarterly,* and is currently supporting local school reform efforts.

Stefinee Pinnegar is a graduate of the University of Arizona and a teacher educator at Brigham Young University. Her research interests focus on teacher thinking, teacher development, and self-study. In terms of self-study, she is interested in the methodology of self-study and in improvement of her practice as a teacher educator. In examining the development of teacher thinking, she has particular interest in the development of practical memory for teaching and the use of narrative inquiry in such research.

Cynthia C. Reyes is an associate professor in the Middle Level Education Program at the University of Vermont where she teaches literacy education. Her research includes the role of identity in literacy, digital literacy, diversity, and educational foundations. Currently, her work focuses on the use of digital story for teaching narrative to young adolescent English language learners. She also serves on the leadership team for the National Writing Project in Vermont.

Carole S. Rhodes is professor and literacy education program director at Queens College of the City University of New York. She received her PhD from New York University, Steinhardt School of Education. She has written and edited four books and dozens of articles which have been published in professional journals. Carole is a frequent presenter at national and international professional conferences where she also serves as chair of several committees. Her areas of specialization are literacy, technology, middle school, and school reform. She has received multiple awards for innovative teaching.

Nancy Bell Ruppert is an associate professor of middle level education at the University of North Carolina at Asheville. She is in her 30th year as a middle grades educator. Nancy taught sixth–ninth grade math and science for 14 years and has been at the college level for 14 years. Her chapter is a reflection of a year's leave from the university in which she returned to the classroom to teach sixth graders in a K-8 school.

Mary Beth Schaefer, EdD, is an assistant professor in the Department of Curriculum and Instruction at St. John's University in Queens, New York. She completed her doctorate at the University of Pennsylvania in Reading/Writing/Literacy. She taught English and reading to middle school students in New York and Texas and helped launch the Early College High School in New York. Her research interests include school-college partnerships, adolescent literacy, and career development in secondary schools.

Antony T. Smith is an assistant professor of education at the University of Washington, Bothell, where he teaches courses in teacher education, research methods, and literacy instruction. A former classroom teacher, his current research interests include classroom-based reading assessments, narrative inquiry, effective models of professional development, and adolescent literacy.

Tamera Tidwell teaches fifth grade mathematics at Arlon Seay Elementary School in Spring Branch, Texas. A veteran educator with 25 years of experience, she previously taught in California and North Carolina. She is currently working on her EdD in curriculum and teaching from Northcentral University. Tamera and her husband have two children.

Steven L. Turner is an assistant professor of middle childhood education in the Department of Teaching, Learning and Curriculum Studies at Kent State University. His research is focused on the learning sciences (how people learn) and investigating how high-stakes tests influence middle level curriculum, instruction, and learning. His work has appeared in *Middle School Journal*, *Teachers College Record*, and *American Secondary Education*.

Ruth Vinz is professor in English education and holds the Enid and Lester Morse Endowed Chair of Teacher Education at Teachers College, Columbia University. She is the author of 13 books and numerous articles on teaching writing and literature. Her book, *Composing a Teaching Life*, received the CEE Richard Meade Award for Outstanding Research in English Education. Her current interests include inquiry into teachers' narratives as examples of living educational theories, the development of narrative inquiry methodologies, and adolescent literacies.

Bogum Yoon, PhD, is an associate professor in the School of Education at the State University of New York at Binghamton. She has worked in the field of literacy as a teacher educator in South Korea and the United States. Her research interests include teacher education and adolescent English language learners, critical literacy, cultural and social identity, and multicultural education. Her most recent articles were published in *American Educational Research Journal*, *The Reading Teacher*, and *The New Educator*.

84382835R00226

Made in the USA
Columbia, SC
18 December 2017